The Birth of Theory

The Birth of Theory

ANDREW COLE

The University of Chicago Press
Chicago and London

Andrew Cole teaches in the Department of English at Princeton University. He is the author of *Literature and Heresy in the Age of Chaucer* and coeditor of *The Legitimacy of the Middle Ages: On the Unwritten History of Theory*.

The University of Chicago Press, Chicago 60637
The University of Chicago Press, Ltd., London
© 2014 by The University of Chicago
All rights reserved. Published 2014.
Printed in the United States of America

23 22 21 20 19 18 17 16 15 14   1 2 3 4 5

ISBN-13: 978-0-226-13539-7 (cloth)
ISBN-13: 978-0-226-13542-7 (paper)
ISBN-13: 978-0-226-13556-4 (e-book)

DOI: 10.7208/chicago/9780226135564.001.0001

Library of Congress Cataloging-in-Publication Data

Cole, Andrew, 1968– author.
    The birth of theory / Andrew Cole.
        pages ; cm
    Includes bibliographical references and index.
    ISBN 978-0-226-13539-7 (cloth : alkaline paper)—ISBN 978-0-226-13542-7
(paperback : alkaline paper)—ISBN 978-0-226-13556-4 (e-book)   1. Hegel, Georg
Wilhelm Friedrich, 1770–1831—Influence. 2. Dialectic—History. 3. Theory
(Philosophy)   I. Title.
    B2949.D5C635 2014
    121—dc23

                                                        2013037618

♾ This paper meets the requirements of ANSI/NISO Z39.48-1992
(Permanence of Paper).

for Cathy

Centuries and centuries of idealism have not failed to influence reality.
JORGE LUIS BORGES

The philosopher wishes to preserve a number of fixed values;
he is frightened by the bohemian's dialectical reversals.
JEAN HYPPOLITE

Alter ideas and you alter the world.
FORTUNE COOKIE, Szechwan House, Hamilton, NJ

Contents

Preface
Very like a Whale

Whales aren't just for syllogisms—nor are they only for bestiaries. Just ask Melville, who delighted in the thought of the whale and saw the leviathan as something more than a mammal, more than a vertebrate, and nothing short of a marvel, noting its perception to be far keener than the one-eyed pisciform surface depicted in so much traditional art.

Melville tells a bloody tale of whale harvest in his great novel, but along the way he pauses to revere the whale. At one moment, he goes so far as to think like a whale and invites us to think along with him. So let's try. Imagine rejigging your head so that your eyes are located at your ears, like the whale's eyes, on each side of its head. In this case, says Melville, "you would have two backs, so to speak; but at the same time, also, two fronts (side fronts): for what is it that makes the front of a man—what indeed, but his eyes."[1] So it goes with the whale, which "must see one distinct picture on this side, and another distinct picture on that side; while all between must be profound darkness and nothingness to him." And herein lies "a curious and most puzzling" problem, easier to describe than perform, because no human has the mental capacity to process at once *two distinct pictures* shining at each eyeball: "It is quite impossible for him, attentively, and completely, to examine any two things . . . at one and the same instant of time. . . . But if you now come to separate these two objects, and surround each by a circle of profound darkness; then, in order to see one of them, in such a manner as to bring your mind to bear on it, the other will be utterly excluded from your contemporary consciousness." Profound darkness and nothingness overcome you, and you cannot think. For to see two things at once is possible only on two conditions: you would either have to be a whale yourself, or be gifted with a cetacean mind and a leviathan imagination:

> How is it, then, with the whale? True, both his eyes, in themselves, must si-
> multaneously act; but is his brain so much more comprehensive, combining,
> and subtle than man's, that he can at the same moment of time attentively
> examine two distinct prospects, one on one side of him, and the other in an
> exactly opposite direction? If he can, then is it as marvellous a thing in him, as
> if a man were able simultaneously to go through the demonstrations of two
> distinct problems in Euclid. Nor, strictly investigated, is there any incongruity
> in this comparison.

The thrill of thinking, the pleasure of thought, comes in this moment of "combining . . . two distinct prospects" across the great expanse, overcoming nothingness in turn.

Hegel, had he the chance, would have called the whale "dialectic."[2] It is not hard to see why. For dialectic, like the whale, regards two distinct pictures, two different ideas, and combines them into a single thought. But from what depths did this whale-like thought process emerge in Hegel? The origins of dialectical thinking have long been mysterious. Hegel didn't invent this dialectic, as he knew perfectly well. He realized that the roots of his dialectical thinking traced back *not* to antiquity, when the old discipline of dialectic began, but to that age once deemed a darkness itself, the Middle Ages. It was in the Middle Ages that dialectic took on a specific logical form—the dialectic of identity and difference—designed to solve problems that never worried the ancients, such as the problem of nothingness as an absolute negativity. Hegel recuperates the dialectic of identity and difference, and, in so doing, he largely erases the marks of his debt to the Middle Ages—which is why the link between Hegel and medieval dialectic has never been satisfactorily discussed in the philosophical and theoretical traditions he begot.

In this book, I demonstrate how Hegel's dialectic emerged from the philosophical practices of medieval thinkers, mapping as precisely as possible the lineaments of Hegel's debt and the implications of acknowledging that debt (chaps. 1 and 2). Hegel's adoption of this distinctly medieval dialectic was an intellectual risk in the extreme, especially for a young man convinced that he deserved the Berlin chair in philosophy but confined by the academic system to catch-as-catch-can gymnasia teaching. The choice of dialectic placed Hegel in opposition to Kant and countless other philosophers who had viciously mocked dialectic as an outmoded scholastic discipline, a holdover from the dogmatism of the Middle Ages. Hegel recognized that Kant and company didn't fully understand the dialectic they rejected; they failed to see its capaciousness, the philosophical potential of the categories of identity and difference. Even Hegel himself couldn't have foreseen the transformative effects of his choice—that the daring extension of the medieval discipline of dialectic into modernity would ultimately lead to what in the twentieth and twenty-first centuries is called "theory."

Hegel responsible for "theory"? Today "theory" generally names the kind of critical thinking applied *against* figures like Hegel, while any mention of "Hegel" in a conversation about "theory" implies the Frankfurt School and "critical theory," where Hegel fares only marginally better. Granted, Theodor Adorno and Herbert Marcuse—to take two leading figures—turn to Hegel in an effort to develop a Marxist critique of culture only notionally present in Marx, offering aesthetic theories that do not double as economic laws. While both find Hegel useful, they clearly indicate that Hegel's dialectic stands for ideology: Marcuse's observation that the "very structure of capitalism is a dialectical one" is repeated in Adorno's claim that "mass culture has finally rewritten the whole of Hegel's *Phenomenology of Spirit.*"[3] The dialectic is the problem, not the solution: as Adorno proclaims in *Negative Dialectics*, "dialectics is the ontology of the wrong state of things."[4] Hegel is valuable for modeling *avant la lettre* the "positive infinity" or closed system of late capital—which means that theory must instead embrace the openness and *potentia* of negative dialectics.[5] For Adorno it is a desideratum, as he says in *Minima Moralia*, to work "in opposition to Hegel's practice and yet in accordance with his thought."[6] This Adornian idea of threading the Hegelian needle—working in oppositional accordance with the dialectic—exemplifies the way in which "theory" has placed Hegel's works behind a mediating concept called "Hegelianism": a sort of translucent scrim that reveals the general outline of Hegel's thought but obscures its details and complexities. Under the rubric of "theory," it becomes impossible to think of Hegel himself in any clear or straightforward way.

The aim of this book is to get behind that mediating scrim in order to think about Hegel's work directly, unencumbered by the weight of Hegelianisms and energized by his daring appropriation of the dialectic of identity and difference. It is also to indicate something specific by the word "theory." By "theory" I mean, above all, the move away from philosophy *within* philosophy itself. Even as Hegel retained Kant's idea of philosophy, he completely broke it apart from within, placing inside the modern academic discipline a figure, a form of thought, that is decidedly medieval and indelibly *linguistic*: dialectic. Hegel discovered and developed his dialectic, working over Kant more thoroughly than those commentators who view Hegel as a Kant 2.0, or for that matter a Schelling++, are willing to admit. In a move central to the philosophical project he imagined for himself, Hegel rejected Kant's view of the Subject, deep within which lies the logical a priori categories that sort and present experience (as "representation"). No amount of history, no contingency of situations, can alter Kant's transcendental subject, always hardwired to present experience by dint of the categories. Yet Hegel yanked out the wires and crossed them (or, as Brecht would have it, he set the Kantian concepts down to dinner to let them fight it out). He extirpated the a priori "forms of experience," as Kant called them, and animated them within narratives whose exposition—whether in the service of phenomenology, logic, history, aesthetics, religion, or indeed philosophy—involves concepts confronting one another dialectically, one relating to the other and taking on the features of its opposite. Hegel's pithy statement that "it is in language that we are conceptually productive" bespeaks the drift of his thought, his move from philosophical foundations to theoretical constructs, from Kantian idealism to dialectics.[7] In so many words, theory is the move from Kant to Hegel.

Quite simply, then, Hegel's turn away from philosophy in the name of philosophy accords with the persuasive definition of "theory" offered by Fredric Jameson: "Theory begins to supplant philosophy (and other disciplines as well) at the moment it is realized that thought is linguistic or material and that concepts cannot exist independently of their linguistic expression."[8] Jameson's definition refers to deconstruction and Althusser, not to Hegel, yet I believe it is important and enabling.[9] It allows us to think of Hegel as a *theorist* who made possible the insights that "all truths are at best momentary, situational, and marked by a history in the process of change and transformation," that "concepts are not autonomous but rather relational," and that the "philosophical problem" is, "namely, that of representation, and its dilemmas, its dialectic, its failures, and its impossibility."[10] The focus of Jameson's definition of theory on linguistic expression also asks traditional Hegelians to rethink what is a fundamentalist stance about dialectical thinking—in other words, to embrace the notion that while dialectical thinking in its modern guise originated in Hegel, it has developed and changed in a very productive way over the past two centuries. I am not referring to Hegel's influence, though I will discuss his direct effect on later thought several times in the pages that follow. Rather, I am pointing to the many examples of lowercase theorizing—the deconstructing of binaries and paradigms, the tracking of identities in difference, the exposition of "intersectional" identity, the critique of ideology, normativity, representation, and institutions—that owe their fundamental structure to Hegel's definition of the dialectic. The widespread use of "dialectical" in the academic and public press alike attests to this very basic notion of "theory" as a kind of critical thinking in opposition to a postulated unity or grand philosophical system, but it also obscures the larger point I will make here about the history of philosophy and theory. I argue in this book that whatever theoretical debt is owed to Marx for these common, so-called dialectical procedures is illusory—illusory, in the first instance, because Marx himself mystifies Hegel where Hegel himself appears most Marxist. Theory, as we have known it and practiced it for a century or more, finds its origin in Hegel—and Hegel himself finds his theory, his dialectic, in the Middle Ages.

By "theory," then, I intend to point to Hegel's own, very sharp dialectical *critiques* of contemporary life whose bite can be felt once some basic facts about Hegel have been grasped. For to speak of his appropriation of "medieval dialectic" requires that we always remember, always acknowledge, something quite obvious about his own historical context. Plainly stated, the late eighteenth-century German world into which Hegel was born was fundamentally still a medieval world, structured by feudalism and by the relationship between peasants and lords. Hegel, moreover, witnessed events, personal and social traumas, as well as wars, that transformed the Middle Ages of his birth into modernity, such as the dissolution of the estates, of the Holy Roman Empire, and of all that goes by the name *ancien régime*. Here, however, because we are dealing with Hegel, whose own dialectical habits of mind meant that there is never a clean and easy break between past and present, we must linger not only on the new but also on the old, not only on the emergent but also the residual, not only the modern but also the medieval.[11] Insofar as much of my own thinking about history is rooted in Marxism—I, like so many, came to Hegel first through Marx—it helps to observe a basic fact about contemporary modes of production that even non-Marxist historians spell out repeatedly.[12] James J. Sheehan, in his magisterial *German History, 1770–1866*, finely documents the fact that Germany remained feudal in Hegel's own lifetime (1770–1831) and beyond. In broad terms, this late feudalism is defined by its peasant/lord relations: "Freeholders and some lessors were legally free, even if the latter were often caught in a web of servile obligations because of the way they held their land. But many, and probably most, German peasants were personally subject to one or more lords; they lived in *Erbuntertänigkeit*, hereditary subjection, which limited their rights to move, marry, and do certain kinds of work."[13] Characterize how you will a given historical present; name it the nineteenth century, call it the twentieth century; celebrate as you may the arrival of this or that new idea or aesthetic: as long as there are feudal arrangements like those Sheehan describes, there is an entire institutional apparatus of expropriation, law, language, and socio-symbolic practice that puts you, or someone, effectively in the Middle Ages. Even if Arno J. Mayer frames this historical matter differently and more broadly by distinguishing between "the old and the new capitalisms" in Europe—between, in other words, agriculture production and industrial production—he shows that the newer model of finance and monopoly capitalism was "in its first rather than its highest or last phase" as late as 1914: "Not only the growth of industrial capitalism but also the contraction of 'premodern' economic sectors proceeded very gradually."[14]

Hegel lived in this earlier time. He was born in the Protestant estates of Württemberg, a feudal kingdom "that had survived into the modern world."[15] His mother taught him Latin at home, grooming him to become a theologian someday, just as young men had been trained to do for centuries. As a boy making his way to the Stuttgarter Gymnasium Illustre, whose curriculum was a mix of medieval and Enlightenment training, Hegel looked upon a town everywhere shaped by the old guild system. Later in life, among the German universities he could have attended—these were, apart from Berlin, all "semi-feudal corporations" with "inherited medieval privileges" and were perceived to be "mere relics of an outmoded scholasticism"—Hegel chose the seminary in Tübingen, where he donned a long black monkish coat, the appropriate garb for a medieval city and university. Of course, you could say that Hegel abandoned these medieval habits once Napoleon came to town and the feudal privileges of these estates were dissolved, including of course those of Württemberg. But you'd only be partly right. By that time, it is true, Hegel counted himself among the revolutionaries. Despite the modernity of his aspirations, however, he found himself, time and time again, enmeshed in the old, medieval social arrangements. Right from seminary in Tübingen, for example, he gained employment in an aristocratic household as a private tutor or *Hofmeister*, more or less a domestic—another very old social station. Yet during his downtime he read "works of English modernity" in the household library and translated an "anti-Bernese pamphlet attacking the quasi-feudal system," upon which that same household depended. Eventually, of course, he acquired positions teaching philosophy; and as he went from post to post, eyeing all along the Berlin chair in philosophy, he endured more of the same, a world in which modern ideals were perpetually confronted by medieval realities. He arrived to take up his job in Nuremberg to find a fundamentally medieval academic institution run by guilds, in which the absence of toilets was the icing on the cake. In Heidelberg, whose beautiful ruined castle overlooked the town—you can catch a stunning view of it on the Philosophenweg—and whose university dated from the early fourteenth century, Hegel participated in a medieval network of exchange, accepting supplementary payments for his work the old-fashioned way: "in kind."

I could go on. But this is enough to sum up one of my main points in this book—namely, as soon as Hegel's historical present is taken as a frame of reference for his philosophy, then that philosophy itself can be properly recognized as a trenchant critique of contemporary conditions, rather than only a mysticism that withdraws from them, as Marx says. To be clear, mine is not a task in historicizing Hegel so much as paying attention to the words he writes on the page, the terms and problems he takes up in his philosophy and which point to his historical present. As I show in chapter 3, for example, his master/slave dialectic is an extended reflection on precisely the kinds of feudal expropriation still practiced in the German states; his description of an *Herr* and *Knecht* in a dialectical struggle is the key, hidden in plain sight, to unlocking the meanings in that most famous passage from the *Phenomenology of Spirit*.

It is a cliché, however a helpful one, to observe that dialectical thinking attends to the "residual" and the "emergent"—these are Raymond Williams's terms—but the more exact, the more capacious, version of this point is to say that Hegel thinks at the temporal conjunction of the medieval and the modern.[16] For every example you could name in which Hegel excitedly used modern ideas to decimate any persistent medieval *residua* (the so-called "Württemberg Debate" of 1815–18 in which he critiqued the belatedness of that state comes to mind); for every outburst of initial enthusiasm for the French Revolution you can cite, you can also discover Hegel writing in a more realistic vein, understanding the practical need to admit that the present was a mishmash of medieval and modern and that social analysis must proceed from this fact if it is to have any chance of shaping a future.[17]

Look no further than his *Philosophy of Right* (1820), in which Hegel argued "for the continued legal recognition of the estates and some of the corporate structures of the ancien régime."[18] He knew that abolishing these medieval institutions was impractical and unrealistic, if for no other reason than the German states had been there and done that (see Napoleon). For that view, he got grief from all sides, and then some. But he continued on in this vein. Very late in life, for example, he wrote "The English Reform Bill" (1831) and parted ways with many of his contemporaries on the question of England's modernization and its consequences. In tones now reminiscent of historical materialism, Hegel writes:

> The moment of transition from feudal tenure to property has passed by without the opportunity being taken to give the agricultural class (*Klasse*) the right to own land. . . .The power of the monarchy was too weak to oversee the

transition [from feudal tenure to landed property] already referred to; and even after the Reform Bill, parliamentary legislation will remain in the hands of that class (*Klasse*) whose interests—and in even greater measure its ingrained habits—are bound up with the existing system of property rights.[19]

Here, Hegel is speaking of the enclosure movement. He views the practices in a colonized Ireland as especially troublesome and unjust, however "legal":

> The propertylessness of the agricultural class has its origin in the laws and relationships of the old feudal system, which nevertheless, in the form in which it still survives in several states, does guarantee the peasant who is tied to the land a subsistence on the land he cultivates. But while the serfs of Ireland [die irischen Leibeigenen] do on the one hand have personal freedom [persönliche Freiheit], the landlords [die Gutsherren] have on the other hand taken such complete control of property that they have disclaimed all obligation to provide for the subsistence of the populace which tills the land they own.... They [Gutsherren] thus deprived those who were already without possessions of their homes and their inherited means of subsistence as well—all in due legal form.[20]

When Hegel cites the "personal freedom" of Irish serfs, he wants his readers to hear the irony he implies (and his use of the word "freedom" is quite close to Marx's own meaning of the term vis-à-vis day-wage labor).[21] Quite simply, for him, modernization makes feudalism look good by comparison—a point he arrives at, to be sure, out of no love for the medieval period, but which is an idea drawn up from historical circumstances that almost all of Hegel's readers fail to appreciate as they continue to hold him to be the mouthpiece for the Prussian state. It is with that accusation in mind that we might recall that even Marx and Engels faced the facts of their own historical present in their early "Demands of the Communist Party in Germany," proposing ways "to bind the interests of the conservative bourgeoisie to the Government."[22] Grudging concessions to conservatism, apologetics, *realpolitik*, what have you: if Marx and Engels get a pass for acknowledging that the world can't and won't change overnight, slogans or no slogans, then so might Hegel.

When it comes to interpreting Hegel, biography aligns with philosophy, life with work, thought with action. He held modern ideals, was ever impatient with antiquated, feudal institutions, but was thoroughly realistic about the mixed composition of the present, at once modern and medieval. That he propounded a unique version of what we now call "periodization" only confirms this assessment. One of the reasons that Hegel is such a salutary thinker to revisit now is that he had no interest in the contemporary obsession with

drawing a distinction between "premodern" and "modern." (Literary critics
are especially obsessed with this divide.) For Hegel, there is no period distinction *to problematize*, as the imperative goes, because the medieval is already
modern or, to use Hegel's own terms, "romantic."[23] Which means that the
present is always peculiarly uneven and inherently dialectical—a present exhibiting every day some new contradiction or break that may take seconds,
hours, or years to notice. Hegel offers up a theory of historical unevenness
that accommodates all scales of time, all durations from the instant to the
larger period or episteme. This idea of "historical unevenness" is echoed, of
course, in Marxism, which uses it to characterize the fits-and-starts expansion, globalization, and spatialization of capital. In other words, Hegel is presciently Marxist in his critical thinking, but not for the usual clever reasons
that emerge only in retrospect—that is, by reading Hegel through Marx and
then winnowing Hegel's proto-Marxian germ from the Hegelian chaff. Instead, the idea here is to recognize in Hegel those ideas that made Marx Marx,
and we can be open to this recognition only by bearing in mind two analogies. What the Middle Ages is to Hegel, modernity is to Marx; what feudalism
is to Hegel, capitalism is to Marx. These analogies can guide our thinking,
I believe, foremost in the refusal to follow Marx all the way in his critique
of Hegel, who takes Hegel to task for failing to criticize a capitalist mode of
production that was not even there to be seen. But the medieval and feudal
modes abounded, and Hegel never tired of critiquing them.

These analogies, likewise, inform my thinking throughout this book on
the question of "Hegel and Marx," because they enable new and surprising
links between these thinkers and their traditions. As I demonstrate in the
chapters that follow, Hegel's theory of medieval eucharistic fetishism shapes
Marx's meditation on the modern commodity (chap. 4); Hegel's reflections
on the emergence of political economy from medieval institutions constitute
a literary historicism that matches, as well as influences, anything evidenced
in the later Marxist tradition (chap. 5); Hegel's figural approach to concepts
provides for a broader sense of utopian literature as an historical and imaginative form and can, in turn, revitalize dialectical thinking by resolving one
the greatest antinomies in theory today—that between dialectics and Deleuze (chap. 6). Each chapter contributes to a cumulative argument about
the relevance of medieval dialectic to Hegel and critical theory, drawing into
dialectical theory what has always been disavowed, thanks to the usual modernizing impulses in theory, but which has always been there: the medieval
dialectic of identity/difference. In fact, the phrase "very like a whale" conveys precisely this problem of recognizing and misrecognizing what Hegel's

dialectic fundamentally, and quite straightforwardly, is. In citing these famous words from Shakespeare's *Hamlet*, I do not mean to bore anyone with
points about the variability of interpretation with quips that a cloud can take
any shape and look like anything. But it *can* be said that Hegel's dialectic,
having endured some two centuries of criticism, seems like a shape-shifting
cloud itself, changing in meaning from book to book, article to article, comment to comment, purpose to purpose. It's all the more crucial at this point,
then, to pause, step back, and behold the obviousness of the whole thing
and state it in equally plain terms. Clouds look like clouds because they *are*
clouds. And Hegel's dialectic, with identity/difference operating as its central
mechanism, resembles nothing more than what in the Middle Ages Plotinus
and others called "dialectic," which operated with identity/difference at *its*
center. Hegel's dialectic resembles that dialectic because it *is* that dialectic.
Granted, every student of medieval philosophy (then as now) knows that
there are many kinds of dialectic in the Middle Ages involving high scholastic *summae*, university *quodlibets* and *quaestiones*, commentaries on Aristotle
and Cicero, sophistic treatises, and so forth. Hegel knew this fact, too, as he
regularly lectured on Julian of Toledo and Paschasius Radbertus, Alexander
of Hales and John Buridan, Peter Abelard and Roger Bacon, and the Arabic
commentaries on Aristotle. But as I show in this book, the medieval dialectic
of identity/difference should be the basis upon which historical and theoretical interpretation of Hegel's dialectic proceeds, because it is the one dialectic
Hegel chose to adopt for his entire system. By extension, our present-day
sense of Hegel's dialectical creativity must be qualified by acknowledging his
debt to a Middle Ages still persisting in his own time. For if we don't understand what the Middle Ages has to do with Hegel, if we don't discern what's
feudal about his age and what's philosophically medieval about his dialectic,
then we won't understand Hegel very well, let alone what makes Hegel *Hegelian*, or for that matter worth reading.

Finally, the larger narrative arc of *The Birth of Theory*, as it moves from the
dialectical terms of identity/difference in the first chapter to those of figure/
concept in the last, represents an attempt to overcome not only the arbitrary
distinctions between medieval and modern but also those between dialectical and anti-dialectical thinking. It is not news to anyone reading this book
that the divisions between Nietzsche and dialectics or Deleuze and dialectics
are either passionately maintained or simply taken for granted. Perhaps my
effort at reconciliation will appear to be an example of dialectics enacting
its own cliché, its own caricaturized tendency to subsume opposition and
erase difference. But readers know that this is indeed a real opposition in
modern theory, especially that between Deleuze and dialectics, and therefore

not an easy one to manage. While it is best to let that argument unfold over many pages, I can indicate here that what draws these two theoretical sides together, first and foremost, is the phenomenological style that both have in common, and which is *itself* a premodern dialectical invention. Only by taking on board the ideas of two renowned anti-dialectical thinkers, Nietzsche and Deleuze, can dialectics properly apprehend its own intellectual history rooted in a past whose conceptual challenges and frameworks still energize our current habits of critical thought and—one hopes—the utopian futures we wish to figure.

Athens, Georgia
June 2013

Acknowledgments

Thank you, C. D. Blanton, Aidan Wasley, Vance Smith, Michael Uebel, Maura Nolan, Bruce Holsinger, Eduardo Cadava, Fredric Jameson, Michael Hardt, Mladen Dolar, Slavoj Žižek, Zdravko Kobe, Samo Tomšič, Brit Harwood, Russ Leo, Britt Rusert, Ryan Daniel Perry, Brooke Holmes, Jack Murnighan, Keith Banner, Bill Ross, and Alan Thomas. Thanks, too, sweet Billy and Joan. I dedicate this book to you, Cathy Dailey—love of my life.

*

Chapters 3 and 4 are revised versions of essays previously printed as "What Hegel's Master/Slave Dialectic Really Means," in *Journal of Medieval and Early Modern Studies* 34, no. 3 (2004): 577–610, and "The Sacrament of the Fetish, the Miracle of the Commodity: Hegel and Marx," in *The Legitimacy of the Middle Ages: On the Unwritten History of Theory*, ed. Andrew Cole and D. Vance Smith, with an afterword by Fredric Jameson (Durham, NC: Duke University Press, 2010), 70–93.

PART ONE

Theory

If the building of a new city in a waste land is attended with difficulties, yet there is no shortage of materials; but the abundance of materials presents all the more obstacles of another kind when the task is to remodel an ancient city, solidly built, and maintained in continuous possession and occupation. Among other things one must resolve to make no use at all of much material that has hitherto been highly esteemed. But above all, the grandeur of the subject matter may be advanced as an excuse for the imperfect execution.

HEGEL

1

The Untimely Dialectic

The way the earliest single light in the evening sky, in spring,
Creates a fresh universe out of nothingness by adding itself,
The way a look or a touch reveals its unexpected magnitudes.

WALLACE STEVENS

It's easy to say that Nietzsche, not Hegel, marks the beginning of what can be called "theory" as a mode of thought distinct from philosophy. He critiques the subject as an a priori construction or Ego set over and against objects, and he vigorously questions systems of knowledge production and the value of values expressed in ethics, morality, theology, and indeed philosophy. That's the Nietzsche we all know and love, whose stance on the institutions of criticism, history, and thought resembles the best of twentieth-century minds, like Foucault or Deleuze, who modeled their work after his. But we have, thanks in part to Foucault and especially Deleuze, lost Nietzsche, especially the Nietzsche who was deeply and imaginatively dialectical without ever worrying how Hegelian he may have sounded. We have lost the Nietzsche who while philosophizing with a hammer also wielded a keen pick and horsehair brush, excavating valuable ideas from the hardened philosophical clichés that have accumulated over the centuries around him. This is the Nietzsche I care to recover in this chapter, because he models a method by which to rethink the dialectic as an intense and complicated abstraction that is deeply historical—embedded in a past that is obscured by the (then) current philosophical fashions. He lays the groundwork for our discussion in chapter 2 of the Hegelian dialectic of identity/difference whose own history has yet to be acknowledged by theorists and philosophers today.

So who is this Nietzsche? Recall that Nietzsche believed that his erudition in classical studies could enhance the discipline of philosophy. In the *Untimely Meditations*, he writes: "The learned history of the past has never been the business of a true philosopher. . . . If a professor of philosophy involves himself in such work he must at best be content to have it said of him: he is a fine classical scholar, antiquary, linguist, historian—but never: he is a philosopher. And that, as remarked, is only at best: for most of the learned work done by university philosophers seems to a classicist to be done badly."[1] For all the variety of Nietzsche's body of writing—from its Wagnerian juvenilia to its later blistering aphoristic and self-aggrandizing style—these words, I believe, describe at least one consistent theme within his work: to combine his erudition in classical studies with his fervent critique of philosophical fashion, all in the effort to make philology and historical scholarship "philosophical" in his new sense of the term.[2]

Nary a philosophical cliché escapes Nietzsche's careful attention to pollute his prose, so how could I claim, as I plan to do, that Nietzsche wishes to think deeply about dialectic—that "d" word we know (despite centuries of worry about it) to have most everything to do with Hegel, a man who himself desperately tried to work his way into academic philosophy, and who (according to almost everyone you ask) is Nietzsche's personal punching bag? At least when talking about *The Birth of Tragedy*—the text I will discuss here—Deleuze was supposed to have settled the matter of Nietzsche's Hegelianism a while ago, saying that "it is quite clear that Nietzsche wrote [this work] not as a dialectician."[3] Perhaps this claim is true from the point of view of Deleuze's own clichés about Hegel in *Nietzsche and Philosophy*. This is a brilliant work, but too often Deleuze caricaturizes the Hegelian dialectic, citing the usual canard of thesis, antithesis, and synthesis: "It is not surprising that the dialectic proceeds by opposition, development of the opposition or contradiction and solution of the contradiction."[4] If this is the sort of dialectic we're after in Nietzsche, then we will have a very hard time finding it, thus deciding with Deleuze that he so despises dialectic in *The Birth of Tragedy* as to construct an "absolute anti-dialectics" as an aggressive response to Hegel. One can extend the argument about Nietzsche's dislike of Hegel and dialectics, just in the way Nietzsche seems to do in various places. But for every time one finds a critic citing that hilarious line in *Ecce Homo* about *The Birth of Tragedy* smelling "offensively Hegelian"—as if to say that the latter is not properly "Nietzschean"—one should counter with Nietzsche's words from *Twilight of the Idols*, published in the same year as *Ecce Homo*. Here, Nietzsche expresses the need to "come back to the place that once served as my point of departure—the '*Birth of Tragedy*' was my first revaluation of all values: and now I am back on that soil where my wants, my *abilities* grow—I, the last disciple of the philosopher Dionysius, —I, the teacher of eternal return."[5] My claim in this chapter is that what makes *The Birth of Tragedy* Nietzschean is what makes it dialectical—a view that should become clear once a more sophisticated notion of dialectics is brought to bear in our interpretation than hitherto done.[6] We'll resume this conversation with Deleuze in chapter 6, asking whether—after all—Deleuzianism and dialectics can be reconciled.

Meanwhile, to acquire a sense of what it means to be Nietzschean and dialectical all at once, we must disentangle the critique of Hegel from the critique of Socratic, ancient dialectic—the two are so often confused today—and only then try to interpret *The Birth of Tragedy* anew. This disambiguation of dialectics (Hegelian, Platonic, Socratic) anticipates my effort in chapter 2, which shows how Hegel partitions his dialectic from the ancient kinds, favoring instead what I call "medieval dialectic." Here, however, I wish to make a methodological exhibit of Nietzsche, who also distinguishes between kinds of dialectic and forms of dialectical abstraction. I begin by showing how Nietzsche in his *Birth of Tragedy* explores some rather abstruse dialectical problems—what now goes by the name of "abstract determination." We recognize this phrase as Hegel's. While Hegel was not the first to ponder "abstract determination," not by a dozen centuries (as I will show here), he did label it in a way that allows us to observe this specialized process at work in Nietzsche: it is the logical and temporal step before the dialectic of real determination, determinate negation, or identity and difference. It is, in other words, the way in which difference enters into the heart of identity but lingers there as a distinction without difference. Nietzsche, I suggest, involves this kind of predialectical logic within his decidedly contemplative history of tragedy by, namely, imputing the process of abstract determination to the birth of tragedy itself—that is, to the emergence of Greek dramatic practice before Socratic dialectic appeared on the historical timeline and consequently, as the story goes, ruined tragedy.

Nietzsche, in sum, is doing things with the dialectic—chiefly, historical things. His placement of different kinds of dialectic at various moments in the history of art, drama, and philosophy is an argument about which sort of dialectical thinking is worth maintaining or reviving, such as identity/difference, and which kinds of dialectic sustain, in Nietzsche's view, the "knowledge-lusting Socratism of today."[7] What Nietzsche gives us in *The Birth of Tragedy*, then, is an "untimely dialectic," which (after his definition of untimely classical scholarship) acts "counter to our time and thereby acting on our time and, let us hope, for the benefit of a time to come."[8] What we ourselves discover, in turn, is the "untimely Nietzsche," a philosopher who can be productively grouped not only with Hegel but with Plotinus, who (as I argue in this and the next chapter) stands at the beginning of a lasting premodern dialectical tradition with abstract determination and identity/difference operating at its very center.

Predialectic as History

The content of the drama is a becoming or a passing away.
NOVALIS

Nietzsche puts the question of the origins of Greek tragedy this way: "Where in the Hellenic world did that new germ first become evidenced which later evolved into tragedy and the dramatic dithyramb?"[9] He offers two answers, the first, a rather concrete one, noting that in the "ancient world" there was a continuous "placing [of] *Homer and Archilochus* side by side on brooches and other works of art as being the progenitors and torch-bearers of Greek poetry."[10] He surmises that these "two equally and entirely original natures deserve to be considered" in something like a dramatic encounter: "Homer . . . the archetypically Apolline, naive artist, now gazes with astonishment at the passionate head of Archilochus." Nietzsche decides, however, that "this interpretation is of little help to us" and smacks of the conclusions of "recent aesthetics," which are mesmerized by distinctions between "subjective" and "objective" art, passionate and dispassionate artistry.[11]

So Nietzsche hazards a second answer even more "aesthetic" and metaphysical than the first—an answer that seeks to explain the "mysterious unity" of the "Dionysiac-Apolline genius and its work in art": "We are in a position to explain the lyric poet, on the basis of . . . aesthetic metaphysics."[12] Building on Schiller's idea that lyrical composition is inspired by a "*musical mood,*" Nietzsche suggests that the lyric poet imagines the world in a way never imagined before, representing "the primal contradiction and pain" of the inner, musical landscape. By the lyric imagination, which envisions the pain and ecstasy of this inner world, tragedy is realized, lived, and felt for the first time. Born are Dionysian (dithyrambic) hymns sung by the chorus of this dramatic form.

To embellish this already complicated point, Nietzsche writes an even more complicated passage about "the most important phenomenon in the whole of ancient lyric poetry, the combination, indeed identity [Identität], of the lyric poet with the musician."[13] This combination, for Nietzsche, produces the tragic artist, so it is no small moment in his aesthetic history. I would say it is *the* moment. Here is how he explains the identity between these two different persons, lyric poet and musician:

> In the first instance the lyric poet, a Dionysiac artist, has become entirely at one with primordial unity, with its pain and contradiction, and he produces a copy of this primordial unity as music, which has been described elsewhere, quite rightly, as a repetition of the world and a second copy of it [eine Wie-

derholung der Welt und ein zweiter Abguss derselben]; now, however, under the influence of Apolline dream, this music in turn becomes visible to him as in a symbolic dream-image. The image-less and concept-less reflection [bild- und begrifflose Wiederschein] of the original pain in music, with its release and redemption in semblance, now generates a second reflection, as a single symbolic likeness (*Gleichnis*) or *exemplum* [Exempel].[14]

To run through this one more time, by dint of paraphrase: the Dionysiac artist (not as yet a lyric poet) is identical with, "entirely at one with," the "primordial unity." First things first: unity. Then, through music, this artist offers a "repetition of the world" or a "second copy of it," of that unity. This copy soon "becomes visible," however. What was once unseen and only heard takes on form; the "image-less and concept-less reflection of the original pain in music . . . now generates a second reflection [zweite Spiegelung]," a third copy, which is here a "single symbolic likeness" that is lyric poetry. Nietzsche states the result of this process: "The Dionysiac-musical enchantment of the sleeper now pours forth sparks of imagery, as it were, lyric poems which . . . are called tragedies."[15]

So what to make of this? I suggest we not read this process as the "eternal return" of Nietzsche's later works, an idea (as I understand it) that expresses the horror of the same, shocking one to accept, nay love fate (*amor fati*). If "you do not want anything to be different," as the maxim goes, then there's no use in talking about the difference between kinds of artist, is there?[16] I also propose that we hold off on finding here only Schopenhauer's scheme of the arts or desire in the *World as Will and Representation* to move from personality to the "subject of pure knowing," that is, from difference to unity, which runs in a direction opposite to what Nietzsche describes here.[17] Rather, I believe it is right to say that Nietzsche experiments with the idea that difference arises from successive attempts to produce the same—the repeated attempts to copy identity whereby the copy itself finally emerges as a "difference" that is eventually discernible and knowable. This passage, in short, is a dialectical explanation of the production of "likeness" and ultimately difference out of "unity." As such, it partakes of the earliest, most lofty ambitions within premodern dialectic (above all) to think through seemingly insurmountable philosophical problems, such as, How do you get being from nothing? How do you get difference from identity, plurality from unity? And how do you narrate the transition from one to the other without projecting one term into the other?

Nietzsche, I suggest, patterns his narrative about the "birth" of tragedy after these long-standing dialectical questions, only here he seeks to explain the emergence of the tragic artist from the "one-ness [Ur-Eine]" of the world. We can best appreciate Nietzsche's dialectical narrative in this passage by comparing it to two examples named at the outset, Plotinus and Hegel, the former who improves the already ancient discipline of dialectic, the latter who practices dialectical philosophy in a curiously premodern fashion, as I will show later.

Yet now we leave Nietzsche for a bit to focus on Plotinus, who puts a twist on what we know as the dialectical image or, better, dialectical imaging when seeking to explain the transition from unity to plurality, from identity to difference.[18] Plotinus's explanation involves two mysterious deities or supremes, what is called the One, which is beyond being and quite close to nothing, and what is called the Intellectual Principle, which flows from the One as a cosmic consciousness and archetypal Being with a capital B. For Plotinus, the One stands for unity and identity; the Intellectual Principle, for difference and plurality, and he wants to know how the latter follows from the former, how from the One there can be many. Here's his exposition, written from the point of view of the Intellectual Principle as it rubs its eyes to behold the One for the first time:

> Thus the Intellectual-Principle, in the act of knowing the Transcendent [One], is a manifold. It knows the Transcendent [One] in very essence [sic] but, with all its effort to grasp that prior as a pure unity, it goes forth amassing successive impressions, so that, to it, the object becomes multiple: thus in its outgoing to its object it is not (fully realized) Intellectual-Principle; it is an eye that has not yet seen; in its return it is an eye possessed of multiplicity which it has itself conferred: it sought something of which it found the vague presentment within itself; it returned with something else, the manifold quality with which it has of its own act invested the simplex. If it had not possessed a previous impression of the Transcendent [One] it could never have grasped it, but this impression, originally of unity, becomes an impression of multiplicity; and the Intellectual-Principle in taking cognizance of that multiplicity knows the Transcendent [One] and so is realized as an eye possessed of its vision.[19]

For Plotinus, the Intellectual Principle attempts to realize itself by "successive impressions" of the One, here named the Transcendent. The inchoate Intellectual Principle takes a first impression of the Transcendent, but because this impression cannot be visualized—for pure unity cannot be seen or thought, lacking (as it does), determination—the Intellectual Principle returns to take a second impression, and in this accumulation of impressions, it finally "sees the One."[20] In the "amassing successive impressions," it moves from identity with the One to difference from it, from unity with the One to multiplicity:

"this impression, originally of unity, becomes an impression of multiplicity."[21] And by this, the Intellectual Principle becomes conscious.

Plotinus offers what I argue is the first example of a specific dialectical process, whereby difference emerges from the repetition of the same; in Plotinus's "eye that has not yet seen" we hear Nietzsche's formulation, centuries later, of "image-less and concept-less reflection"—a visuality that is not quite visual but through repetition resolves into images and likenesses. Indeed, when Plotinus in *Ennead* 5.1 states that the Intellectual Principle "stands as the image of the One . . . carrying onward much of its quality, in other words that there . . . [is] something in its likeness as the sun's rays tell of the sun," he uses "likeness" in a very specific way: for "likeness" itself specifies identity in difference.[22] Simply put (and as Plato knew) likeness is not the same as the same; more on this below. Suffice it to suggest that these lines of thought draw Nietzsche to the term "likeness" (*Gleichnis*) for its distinctly dialectical capacities and demand that he think about abstract determinations, differences that at first make no difference.[23]

Nothing is dialectical simply because one says so, however. Here is where Hegel comes in, dialectical as ever. He knows just what these processes of repetition and abstraction are good for. He even recognized in Plotinus the importance of "how the One came to the decision to determine itself" by means of a "pure distinction that remains at the same time identical with itself."[24] But Hegel's interest in these processes are by no means limited to his already limited discussion of Plotinus; and as chapter 2 suggests, it is not entirely clear that Hegel is willing or able in his lectures on the history of philosophy to recognize his deep methodological affinity with Plotinus, even if he sees in this late antique philosopher a "higher idealism."[25] And so we must turn to other works by Hegel for an appreciation of the dialectical richness of these processes, beginning with the *Science of Logic*, in which the section on "identity" (appropriately enough) exhibits what is now the familiar narrative pattern. There Hegel shows that when pure identity first attempts to express difference, it stalls in illusion and vanishing, terms that already evoke the oxymoronic images of the "eye that has not yet seen" (Plotinus) and "image-less and concept-less reflection" (Nietzsche). When, in other words, "simple, abstract identity"—a "pure movement of reflection"—posits an "other," that other appears "only as reflective shine, as immediate disappearing."[26] Hegel illustrates the point by exploring that law of identity well known in philosophical circles, A=A, and tarrying with its own identity until there is negativity, until A=A becomes not a law of identity (or a night in which all cows are black)[27] but rather a law of contradiction, A=not-A, or more forcefully, A=B.

Yet, as he shows, rendering the proposition, A=A, into *something other* than a law of identity is difficult:

> "A is" is a beginning that envisages a something different before it to which the "A is" would proceed; but the "A is" never gets to it.[28]

Any account of Hegel will tell you what he says again and again: that any "proposition," even this one, *moves*, and for that reason, propositions are never static and end up doing dialectical things like wending their way to their opposite.

But Hegel's point about "A=A" is more historically significant than such logical abstractions admit. What's key here is that Hegel adopts the narrative pattern we find in both Plotinus and Nietzsche, and he uses it to revamp the "laws of identity." For him, you only get the law of identity out of the *failure* to produce difference on the first try. That is, there is a going out from itself, an "*A is* . . ." that "goes back into itself" as "*A is—A*."[29] But in the failed attempt to generate a "different something," a proposition is nonetheless written, A=A, which can be understood in a very particular way, after tarrying with it. A is copied, there is repetition, and we start to look at that second A in a different way and ponder how its repetition makes it different, as, say, A_1. This repetition—and this is the other key point—is the basis for the production of difference out of identity, premised on both the failure to achieve difference on the first try and on the reproduction of the same from which difference emerges.[30] All the same, however, literally: A=A here becomes both a law of identity and a law of difference.[31] I'll return to this problem of identity and difference in a moment—the idea that the identity of one thing is bound up in its difference from another thing.

Meanwhile, let's note here that what amounts to an abecedarian fail, with A collapsing back into itself like a stunt on a diving board gone wrong but inviting intense observation (or repeated viewings on YouTube), brings us to even stranger ideas about identity, being, and thought. For Hegel, the law of identity is also the principle of being and especially what he calls "pure being," which, to conceptualize it, requires a special kind of thought, what he calls "pure thinking." Pure what? It is just this nexus of issues— identity, being, and thought—on which is based almost the entire critique of Hegel from Marx to Adorno, from Derrida to Deleuze, and beyond. It's this kind of abstraction and fantasies of a pure anything that gives idealism a bad name, but let's grant for a moment that Hegel here isn't meaning to tarnish idealism but rather advance it. Let's also admit that verbalizing this old critique of Hegel is now uninteresting and will in the long run keep us from thinking

newly historically about dialectic, the ways in which abstractions, when posited or derived by the right kind of dialectical idealist like Hegel, immediately
flip over into their opposite and point to material consequences and signifi-
cances—in this case, to the very specific history out of which the abstraction
arises and from which it can never distinguish itself. In other words, these
propositions and odd abstractions—identities producing difference first as
an abstract difference, then as a real one—admit the earliest of philosophical problems related to topics to which I have yet only alluded: the topics
of being and nothing, which so fascinated the ancients and which absorbed
Hegel's attention as yet another instance, perhaps even the greatest test case,
for dialectical method.

Hegel knows you cannot talk about being and nothing without thinking
within and, as I wish to show, against the received history of philosophy. In
his *Encyclopaedia Logic*, he states that the question of being and nothing was
asked "for the first time" by Parmenides and is "the proper starting point for
philosophy."[32] Here is Hegel's description of this "starting point":

> Being and nothing are at first only supposed to be distinguished. . . . But being
> is precisely what strictly lacks determination, and nothing is this same lack
> of determination also. So the distinction between these two [terms] is only
> meant to be such, a completely abstract distinction, one that is at the same
> time no distinction at all.[33]

And so to think of being and nothing as at all different is to think of them as
the same, as a distinction without a difference, "a completely abstract distinction." Hegel is not joking when he states that this is "really one of the hard-
est propositions that thinking dares to formulate"—the idea that being and
nothing are both the same and not the same—and he readily admits that "no
great expense of wit is needed to ridicule the proposition."[34] And yet everyone
piles on the guy for making the proposition? A lot of good disclaimers do!

Nonetheless, Hegel entertains this proposition about being and nothing
because it allows him to show that the logical categories of identity and difference operate at the very start of the dialectic and function even at the highest
level of abstraction at a moment when there is no determination, no distinction. We appreciate this point when Hegel elaborates on the aforementioned
"abstract distinction . . . that is at the same time no distinction at all":

> In all other cases of distinguishing we are always dealing also with something
> common, which embraces the things that are distinguished. . . . By contrast, in
> the case of being and nothing, distinction has no basis and, precisely because
> of this, it is no distinction, since neither determination has no basis.[35]

Yet, we still think, we still say, that being and nothing are identical and different:

> Correct as it is to affirm the unity of being and nothing, it is *equally* correct to say that *they are absolutely diverse too*—that the one is *not* what the other is. But because this distinction has here not yet determined itself, precisely because being and nothing are still the immediate—it is, as belonging to them, *what cannot be said*, what is merely *meant*.[36]

This last part seems murky, "*what cannot be said*, what is merely *meant*," but I believe Hegel here is elaborating on a similar point in his earlier *Science of Logic*, where he says that this kind of abstract determination "belongs . . . to our reflection."[37] It's what we think, what we contemplate.

How is Hegel's extreme abstraction here an argument about the history of philosophy? To begin with, the very fact that Hegel is writing about being and nothing, and using the problem to assert the relevance of abstract determination at the very start of philosophy, has implications for our understanding of the history of philosophy that (for Hegel) doubles as a history of dialectic. And it will be this history of dialectic that is germane to understanding what's dialectical about Nietzsche's *Birth of Tragedy* (and, in chap. 2, what's irretrievably historical about Hegel's dialectic). Hegel, we recall, said that Parmenides asked the question of being and nothing for the first time but he does not tell us that Parmenides had the answer. This is a crucial point, because it is quite clear that Hegel does not mean to toe the ancient, much less, Parmenidian line about being and non-being, for in Parmenides' great poem and in Plato's commentary that goes by the name, *Parmenides*, you cannot find what Hegel treasures, abstract determination, much less real determination. Echoing Parmenides' famous insight about all that Is, Hegel indicates as much: "When we consider the entire world, and say simply that everything is, and nothing further, we leave out everything determinate, and, in consequence have only absolute emptiness instead of absolute fullness."[38] Hegel is showing, though not at all stating it outright, that it was not always the case that philosophers grasped what is fundamental to any thought of abstract determination—that is, the dialectic of identity and difference, and the dialectic of abstract identity and difference.

This point has everything to do with how we think about the historicity of dialectical procedures, and so let's linger a bit more to discuss what the dialectic of identity/difference *is not* before deciding what it is (as chap. 2 does), *where* it is not before where it is. Even a brief look at Plato's *Parmenides*, the Athens to which all the roads of being and nothing lead, is instructive in this respect. To be sure, in that text, we do find some germane logical operators named "likeness" and "unlikeness," as mentioned by Socrates.[39] Socrates proposes that a single thing can be both like and unlike: "If one could point to things which are simply 'alike' and 'unlike' proving to be unlike and alike, that no doubt would be a portent, but when things which have a share in both are shown to have both characters, I see nothing strange in that."[40] Parmenides, however, states that the proper approach is not to think in terms of what is "both like and unlike" within the "visible" field, ruling out immediately how modern phenomenologists usually think of these terms in the study of appearances. Rather, Parmenides presses the question of being instead of appearances, telling Socrates to think, first, more broadly about what "is" and what "is not," and then, second, ask how likeness and unlikeness, sameness and difference tell us something new about the being (or archetype) in question.[41] My point here is not to summarize the exhilarating, even if often bewildering, litany of possible likenesses, unlikeness, and so forth—which you can at any rate find in Aristotle's brilliantly done *Topics*. It is only to say that Parmenides, and of course Plato, do not have an analogue to the categories of identity and difference, as we know them today, in their expositions on dialectic. And Socrates, for his part, is smacked down for offering a promising line of thinking on likeness and unlikeness that approaches identity/difference and is instead instructed to think otherwise. Dialectic, the ancient discipline, in other words, does not center itself on the question of identity/difference . . . not yet. One cannot speak of ancient dialectic as dialectical in the way we speak of Hegel's dialectic as dialectical. And to the extent that Plato understood "relative being"—that ontological category that describes relations of identity/difference—he does not elevate it to the first of primary forms (Being, Motion, Rest, Identity, and Difference).[42] As others have shown, Plato cannot define "relative being" without involving a so-called Platonic form in the definition.[43] Which gets us right to the point: in Plato, difference is always a Form.[44]

Without the logical operators of identity and difference, even in their most abstract form, Plato cannot conceptualize *mediation* in his statements on how one thing becomes another. Here is his take on the "transition" or change from one thing to another:

> There is no time during which a thing can be at once neither in motion nor at rest. On the other hand it does not change without making a transition. When does it make the transition, then? Not while it is at rest or while it is at motion, or while it is occupying time. Consequently, the time at which it will be when it makes the transition must be that strange thing, the instant. The word 'instant' appears to mean something such that from it a thing passes to one or other of the two conditions. There is no transition from a state of rest so

long as the thing is still at rest, nor from motion so long as it is still in motion, but this strange thing, this instant, is situated between motion and rest. . . . Accordingly, the one, since it is both at rest and is in motion, must pass from the one condition to the other—only so can it do both things—and when it passes, it makes the transition instantaneously. . . . The same holds good for its other transitions. When it passes from being in existence to ceasing to exist or from being non-existent to coming into existence, it is then between certain motions and states; it is neither existent nor non-existent.[45]

The "middle," the "instant," the "strange thing"—literally the thing out of place (ἄτοπον, atopon)[46]—is the farthest Plato could take the problem of transition without a viable notion of identity/difference. Aristotle was similarly stumped when it came to pondering this "middle" and so settled on the law of the "excluded middle," which holds that "there cannot be an intermediate between contradictories."[47] Kant, to think very far ahead, cottoned onto just this problem deep in the *Critique of Pure Reason* and solved it, and its calculus of increasingly miniscule degrees of qualitative change—not by adopting identity/difference but by replacing the instant with time and burying it as an a priori intuition where phenomenological observation is moot.[48] (Kant's solution is, among other things, an answer to both Leibniz's "law of continuity" and "Principle of the Identity of Indiscernibles.")[49] My point here is to discern what missing, conceptually, right at the very moment it would come in handy. Only a conception of identity and difference, real and abstract, could help Plato with this logical, temporal, and narrative task of transition.[50] Lacking such a conception, he simply says that a transition takes place in "no time." And when you exclude time, you exclude becoming. You exclude narrative and especially the advantages it affords in inhabiting the syntax of unfolding, even a syntax as simple as the logical, tautological form of A=A.[51]

Now, Hegel says none of this, but he practices it everywhere in his dialectic of identity/difference. To say that the dialectic of identity/difference was not fully grasped by the ancients is, I'll say it, a profound point: for tracing the emergence of this particular dialectical form, when it arose, will tell us, above all, which premodern kind of dialectic most closely approximates Hegel's. That is the task of the next chapter, where I show that the dialectic of identity/difference, as we've come to know it in Hegel, is also a dialectic discovered in the Middle Ages as a way to improve the commentary tradition on the *Parmenides* and revive, and intensify, the problem of nothing and not-being as something other than a "form" of difference, as we find in Plato. If you really want to "tarry with the negative," then you have to get medieval. After all, what precisely is Hegel saying, what is he showing us, in his famous passage from the *Phenomenology of Spirit* concerning the dialectical delectation of tarrying with the negative?

> The life of Spirit is not the life that shrinks from death and keeps itself untouched by devastation, but rather the life that endures it and maintains itself in it. It wins its truth only when, in utter dismemberment, it finds itself. It is this power, not as something positive, which closes its eyes to the negative, as when we say of something that is nothing or is false, and then, having done with it, turn away and pass on to something else; on the contrary, Spirit is this power only by looking the negative in the face, and tarrying with it. This tarrying with the negative is the magical power that converts it into being. This power is identical with what we earlier called the subject.[52]

Much can be said of this passage. Adorno, for instance, in *Negative Dialectics*, says that Hegel "waits"—not thinks, not writes, not philosophizes, not imagines—but "waits until Being and Nothingness have been equated," blurring into that third term, becoming; he goes on to say that Hegel is "following the model of the late Platonic dialogues."[53] But Adorno misses the mark in suggesting that Hegel is thinking in strictly Platonic terms, for to think of being and nothing as two immediacies in a face-to-face encounter with each other is to think in a distinctly *post-Platonic* fashion—otherwise, negativity would be nothing more than a form of difference. Examining Hegel's words in the Plotinian frame—allowing Plotinus above to serve as just one of many examples to be detailed in chapter 2—we realize that both the tarrying and the looking convert the negative into being in that uniquely phenomenological way: there is delay so as to acquire vision, to see what is at first unseeable, to undergo a formative experience (*Bildungs-Erfahrung*) that, through repetition, sharpens perception and establishes the phenomenological investigation of appearances. This is the "eye that has not yet seen." It is "image-less and concept-less reflection."

Once the eye has seen, once image and concept, figuration and thinking, are conjoined, then a properly dialectical phenomenology is underway. But even here, the very operation of the dialectic, its bare-bones formality and basic process, reminds us of the original premodern procedure. This is to say, if after the problem of being and nothing is answered and we have *becoming*, which informs all subsequent dialectical scenarios, then we quickly realize that the "solution" to that initial problem is carried forward and expressed in subsequent iterations, shapes and forms, of the dialectic itself. What, in other words, logically mediates the moment of immediacy between being and nothing works, as well and quite easily, at subsequent, more mediated, less aporetic moments. That "what" is identity/difference.

See, for instance, how Hegel talks about the emergence of self-consciousness from consciousness in the final paragraphs of the first division of the *Phenomenology of Spirit* ("A. Consciousness"):

> Accordingly, we do not need to ask the question, or even that it is a question philosophy cannot answer, the question, viz. '*How*, from this pure essence, how does difference or otherness *issue forth* from it?' For the division into two moments has already taken place, difference is excluded from the self-identical and set apart from it. What was supposed to be the *self-identical* is thus already one of these two moments instead of being the absolute essence. That the self-identical divides into two means, therefore, just as well that it supersedes itself as *already* divided, supersedes itself as an otherness.[54]

We do not need to ask the question about how difference and otherness issue forth from pure essence because the question has been asked and (as it is here) answered, not only by Hegel but by other philosophers before him like Plotinus, who asks: "From such a unity as we have declared The One to be, how does anything at all come into substantial existence, any multiplicity, dyad, number?"[55] These are, again, the big questions of premodern first philosophy. And by raising the question in the effort to suggest that we need not answer it, Hegel draws attention to premodern dialectics for which no transition is too difficult or large, which in turn makes transitions lesser than that of nothing/being a walk in the park.[56] His lectures on the history of philosophy only confirm this point.[57]

And so the seemingly *impossible* transition from negativity to positivity, from non-being to being that characterizes Plotinian dialectic is, Hegel must have known, the very *possibility* of dialectic itself as it courses over lesser transitions such as that from consciousness to self-consciousness (I call this a lesser transition, because Fichte, as Hegel surely knew, dispatched it with ease by just starting with self-consciousness as the product of the subject/object dichotomy).[58] Throughout all of Hegel's dialectical displays in his work, but especially in his *Phenomenology* and his Logics, anytime we find a discussion of indeterminate difference or abstract difference, at whatever moment of dialectical transition (or for that matter temporary stasis), he sets at the center of his dialectic a premodern formal procedure for mediating absolute difference. I will continue this story in the next chapter. For now, let's just say that Hegel thinks historically about dialectic in ways more complex than his oft-cited, oft-derided pronouncement from the *Phenomenology of Spirit* that we must "comprehend the diversity of philosophical systems as the progressive unfolding of truth"[59]—his lectures on the history of philosophy standing as the grand study of such unfolding, with the dialectic showing up any and everywhere.[60]

The Birth of Tragedy

Like Hegel, Nietzsche thinks equally deeply about the dialectic within history, the dialectic as an historical event. We now return to Nietzsche's proposition about the birth of tragedy, which partakes of the processes requiring a first try, a dialectical attempt followed by a dialectical failure, a first impression, then a second impression, the repetition of unity to produce difference. In this, he offers us a model of "abstract determination" that is lost on Plato but consistent with Plotinus and Hegel, and he does so for historiographic as much as theoretical reasons. For "abstract determination" is, in logical terms, a predialectical process that, in historical terms, corresponds to the moment before Socrates and Socratic dialectic. It corresponds to the moment of tragedy and is available only at that time. When Socrates arrives, it goes away, and we get the death of tragedy. In just this point, Nietzsche offers a history lesson about dialectic and the dialectical, making distinctions (as Hegel does, without averring as much) between what the ancient, Socratic discipline of dialectic can and cannot do, and what genuinely abstract, even mysterious dialectical processes can do. In other words: consistent with Hegel's latent critique of ancient or Platonic dialectic, Nietzsche shows that Socrates (as we have him only in Plato) cannot think dialectically, even as (ironically) he champions the discipline of dialectic.

This means, then, that as we read *The Birth of Tragedy*, we must bear in mind the distinction between *the dialectical* and *dialectic*, the former familiar to the Hegelian tradition, and the latter, the long-standing discipline. And Nietzsche's historical narrative helps us with this cognitive task. For depending on where you are in historical time—that is, on what page you happen to be in *The Birth of Tragedy*—you will find either Socratic dialectic or something else approximating, through figuration, the dialectic of identity and difference as abstract determination.

Look, for example, at how Nietzsche discusses the "duality" of Dionysios and Apollo that was sustained until the advent of Socrates *cum* the death of tragedy. He insists that in the Greek world before Socratic dialectic, there was an "enormous opposition" between these two gods—"different drives exist side by side, mostly in open conflict, stimulating and provoking one another to give birth to ever-new, more vigorous offspring in whom they perpetuate the conflict inherent in the opposition between them."[61] He echoes this sentiment later, stating that "the Dionysiac and the Apolline dominated the Hellenic world by a succession of ever-new births and by a process of reciprocal intensification," a veritable "to-ing and fro-ing."[62] Tragedy gives expression to this "to-ing and fro-ing," whereby the Dionysiac and the Apollonian "duality" becomes intertwined: the "essence of Greek tragedy" is the "expression of two interwoven artistic drives," "their mutual interaction and intensification."[63] What we have here is *the dialectical*, not dialectic. Nietzsche asks us to contemplate with him and think of these oppositions, interactions, and reciprocities in *abstract* terms because, historically speaking, there are as yet no concepts, no thoughts wedged into syllogisms, no hankering for knowledge, no hard and fast determinations, only images of "mysterious" identities and experiences of "the primordial unity, with its pain and contradiction."[64]

Now let's observe the return of tragedy, the rebirth of tragedy when in modern times Socratic dialectic finally is pushed aside. The Dionysiac impulse returns to confront the Apollonian, and both enter once more into the same kind of mutual intensification we just reviewed: "Both of these artistic drives are required to unfold their energies in strict, reciprocal proportion."[65] Particularly intriguing is Nietzsche's enthusiastic crescendo narration of the second coming of tragedy—a passage that concludes his chapters on Socratic dialectic (chaps. 14–21):

> If drama, with the help of music, spreads out all its movements and figures before us with such inwardly illuminated clarity, as if we were seeing a tissue being woven on a rising and falling loom, it also produces, taken as a whole, an effect which goes *beyond all the effects of Apolline art*. In the total effect of tragedy the Dionysiac gains the upper hand once more; it closes with a sound which could never issue from the realm of Apolline art. Thereby Apolline deception is revealed for what it is: a persistent veiling, for the duration of tragedy, of the true Dionysiac effect, an effect so powerful, however, that it finally drives the Apolline drama into a sphere where it begins to speak with the Dionysiac wisdom and where it negates itself and its Apolline visibility. Thus the difficult relationship of the Apolline and the Dionysiac in tragedy truly could be symbolized by a bond of brotherhood between the two deities: Dionysios speaks the language of Apollo, but finally it is Apollo who speaks that of Dionysios. At which point the supreme goal of tragedy, and indeed of all art, is attained.[66]

Is not Apollo's negation while speaking the language of Dionysios an intentionally distorted or, shall one say, abstract model of identity and difference? The question is worth asking, because it seems that Nietzsche is alluding to Hegel in his suggestion that we experience the "rising and falling loom" of tragedy's many "movements and figures." That is, Hegel himself states that "reason is no more than a loom intertwining warp (say, identity) and woof (say, difference)."[67] For Nietzsche, when tragedy is reborn and dialectic dies, *the dialectical* returns, along with identity and difference as abstract determinations. This vanishing dialectic, I believe, emblematizes a historical folding of pre- and post-Socratic phases and processes, but it is no less the logical complement to the allusive, illusory, and non-determinate operations of dialectic before (and after) Dialectic, the ancient discipline. This is Nietzsche's "untimely dialectic"—motile, unwelcome, critical, and historical.

Archaeologies of the Dialectic

The Birth of Tragedy, I would say, is part of a specialized dialectical tradition that is not reducible to the hokum of thesis, antithesis, and synthesis, against which Nietzsche is always said to be opposed (by Deleuze and others, including Nietzsche himself!).[68] Even more, Nietzsche shows us the way towards a new approach to the history of dialectic, the tasks of thinking historically about logical terms that seem to transcend history and seem to have always been available, there from the very beginning. In one sense yes, when talking about the dialectic; in another sense, no, when talking about dialecticians across history looking for the appropriate logical terms by which to mediate absolute difference. Nietzsche, furthermore, shows us the advantage of disassociating dialectic and *the dialectical* from its Platonic, Aristotelian, and generally classical forms, as well as all else that goes by the antique arts of dialogue and definition. By positing the dialectic outside of these strong traditions (very much today seen, reflexively, to be the traditions informing the modern examples of dialectic), he at once clears a space for a renewed dialectic that is useful for a critique of the present, crazy for the older, worn-out dialectic.[69] This is not to say that what Nietzsche does with the dialectic is Hegelian but it is to say his task is dialectical in a manner possible only in a post-Plotinian universe (and I do mean universe). The historical significance of this claim will have to wait until chapter 2.

So why does Nietzsche even bother with dialectic, predialectic, and the histories of these forms? There have to be many answers to this question. I imagine, for example, that Nietzsche would feel a lingering dissatisfaction with Marx and Engels's *German Ideology*, in which the dialectic very much remains "the matter of Hegel," in the way one speaks of the matter of Rome as a singular obsession guiding a good deal of historical inquiry in the Middle Ages—only here the historical issue of the dialectic concerns *contemporary* German thought, Hegel, and his followers. Such a confined historical view explains why the dialectic in Germany came to be synonymous with

"Hegel"—apart from Hegel's wide popularity among, to begin with, the Young Hegelians[70]—when in fact, as both Nietzsche and Hegel knew, dialectic was almost two millennia old by their time and deserves at least some historical treatment and some reflection within the histories of its unfolding. Compared to Marx, then, Nietzsche attempts to think differently historically about the dialectic, and Hegel, not surprisingly, emerges as the only figure to precede him in this effort. Nietzsche knows that a new history of the dialectic (not a new menu of slogans or aspersions) is necessary to deal with the modern limitations of and clichés about dialectic. His effort is recuperative, which is why he never speaks of Hegel in this work and why "dialectic," whenever named, is the matter of Socrates and (again) not Hegel. If he named Hegel, just once, then thinking about the dialectical in *The Birth of Tragedy* would be a non-starter.

It would seem to me, then, that a new history of the dialectic can offer a perspective on the best of dialectical critical practices and observations within Marxism, which has its own way of thinking historically about the dialectic—from Adorno declaring that "dialectics is the ontology of the wrong state of things," to Herbert Marcuse stating that "the very structure of capitalism is a dialectical one," to Fredric Jameson noting what is by now a given, that "the dialectic does not become visible historically until capitalism's emergence."[71] These all seem to me to be versions of Marx's idea that history begins when class society ends—only here, of course, dialectic persists as long as capital is around—but the question of history can be posed in broader terms, because these aforementioned historical assessments of the dialectic seem to me to have limits.

This is to say that perhaps, after Nietzsche, some new sense of the term "philosophy" might be brought to bear on these matters in an "untimely" fashion, juxtaposing premodern problems with those of the present moment, as a contribution to a philosophical Marxism. Jameson, the consummate student of dialectic, offers material with which to think through such an untimely project, given his decades-long effort at translating a variety of cultural forms, past and present, into a "positive hermeneutic" for Marxism (which in one version, by the bye, adopts the allegorical protocols of medieval exegesis; see chap. 5).[72] In his *Valences of the Dialectic*, he refers to the "metaphysical humiliation" of a grand (and presumably premodern?) dialectic that fails as a "theory of everything" and is relegated instead to a "local law of this or that corner of the universe, a set of regularities observable here or there." But this humiliation can be "taken in stride," Jameson continues, if one can "abstract a form of thinking sufficiently empty of content to persist throughout the multiple local dialectics" and "retain a recognizable and identifiable shape through a variety of materials, from the economic to the aesthetic."[73] He goes on to say that "the identification of such an empty form will no doubt have to build on Hegelian groundwork, even though it need no longer struggle with the unrewarding starting point the latter had to navigate in its initial struggles with identity and with being as such."[74] I have, in the foregoing, been concerned precisely with such a "starting point," "its initial struggles," but is it really so "unrewarding"? It may be helpful, rather, to think about this "starting point" in a different way: in relation, again, to the thought experiments Jameson proposes in *Valences of the Dialectic* and to those entertained by premodern dialecticians.

If, for example, a premodern thinker would rightly initially consider the transition from nothing to being to be impossible and unthinkable, therefore requiring dialectical techniques that encourage the dialectician to change the valences on these terms and think of nothingness as being and being as nothingness until becoming comes into view, then not a few modern critical minds may find it equally impossible to conduct the particular dialectical thought experiment Jameson proposes—a dialectical union of opposites, whereby the American superstore Wal-Mart is viewed as Utopia.[75] Jameson chooses Wal-Mart as the problematic example for dialectics precisely because it is hard to change the valences on it and conceptualize what good can come of this capitalist monstrosity which swallows up independent retailers in small communities, refuses to allow its employees to unionize, and consistently hires workers into part-time jobs so as not to provide any benefits, such as medical insurance. Yet, for Jameson, we are not to revile Wal-Mart or only moralize about it, but rather study it and contemplate its opposite, performing a utopian thought-experiment about what might replace it. By this dialectical method Jameson intends to put into motion a new kind of thinking about "possible and alternate futures," a thinking that "revives long-dormant parts of the mind, organs of political and historical and social imagination which have virtually atrophied for lack of use, muscles of praxis we have long since ceased exercising, revolutionary gestures we have long lost the habit of performing, even subliminally."[76]

It is a tantalizing suggestion to say that within the mind lie atavistic dialectical faculties, or that there are mental "muscles of praxis," an unconscious or preconscious of concepts ready to be exercised when the moment is right. Yet what is more intriguing is this rejuvenated task of tarrying with the negative, which requires the positing in advance of a truly unthinkable or inconceivable content—a content that is at the outer limits of thought and being—as one of the poles in the dialectic of Wal-Mart as monopoly *and* Wal-Mart as Utopia, a starting point for rethinking the situation so as to establish a new system. Granted, there is an intellectual risk in this activity that Marx long ago recognized in his prefaces and postfaces to *Capital*, worrying over the fine line between theoretical criticism and complicit description of conditions like a dyed-in-the-wool political economist (see chap. 5)—only here the newer dialectical enterprise, if not done right, can suddenly look "spontaneous," uncritical, or downright frustrating, at which point thinking becomes ridiculous.

But sometimes even the ridiculous must have a place, whatever it takes to estrange a situation or way of thinking. For example, as both Jameson and Slavoj Žižek suggest—each crediting the other for the idea—it is easier to conceptualize the end of the world by dint of some cataclysmic destructive natural force than it is to conceive of the end of capitalism.[77] The point is funny, but no less true. It's also interesting because a supervolcano is already an impossible thing to perceive, let alone conceive. It would extend beyond the perceptual field; so enormous as to extend beyond the curvature of the earth (and as such probably qualify as The Sublime). And so one conceptual impossibility is easier to think than another? The dialectical problem of "nothing" and "being" begins to look strangely familiar because there are now equally unlikely pairings, supervolcanos and/or socialism, Wal-Mart and/or utopia on the table for critical thinking. My point is that when the demand is to think the unthinkable, then dialectical technique has not strayed very far from the initial set of unthinkable terms within premodern dialectic and that this formal procedure was there all along—maybe not where we expect it—and may serve as a useful starting point, after all.

The Birth of Dialectic

This book, itself about starting points, requires a dialectical thought experiment of the order we have just discussed—namely, to revalue the idea of "origins" and switch its valence from the negative to the positive, from a conceptual task roundly ridiculed once theorists absorbed Foucault's critique of origins in "Nietzsche, Genealogy, and History" to a project whose aim is to open up, reorient, and rethink the history of theory and philosophy where it touches on the dialectic.[78] In any event, after so many expositions of "Ends," which now seem to have come to an end and have returned to the discipline of their emergence (ethics), the time has come for this new thought of origins, continuing the untimely thought experiment suggested by Nietzsche himself in the title to his great work, *Die Geburt der Tragödie aus dem Geiste der Musik*.

Understand that I am not on a fool's errand in thinking that "origin" will henceforth never be a dirty word in theory, and I'm loathe to use it again in this book, because I know how it sounds. But let us recall that the term itself was lyrically recuperated long before Foucault in the work of Walter Benjamin, who was obsessed with the *Ursprung* of *Trauerspiel*. In his *Origins of German Tragic Drama*, he says:

> Origin (*Ursprung*), although an entirely historical category, has, nevertheless, nothing to do with genesis (*Entstehung*). The term origin is not intended to describe the process by which the existent came into being, but rather describe that which emerges from the process of becoming and disappearance. Origin is an eddy in the stream of becoming. . . . That which is original is never revealed in the naked and manifest existence of the factual. . . . On the one hand it needs to be recognized as a process of restoration and establishment, but, on the other hand, and precisely because of this, as something imperfect and incomplete. . . . The principles of philosophical contemplation are recorded in the dialectic which is inherent in origin. This dialectic shows singularity and repetition to be conditioned by one another in all essentials.[79]

Benjamin's fluid and dynamic metaphor is rich in significance, because it identifies "origin" as "becoming" in a special way, a counter-current, an eddy swirling in reverse against the flow, emerging right where the obstructions lie. The eddy goes with the flow by turning against it. Benjamin means to say that we have a counter-origin at hand, not the usual old "genesis (*Entstehung*)" but a counter-memory that is thought against the current of opinion, against what's taken for granted, and what stands in the way, the "existence of the factual." I see nothing objectionable in this notion of origins, and it is one that inspires my proposed revision to our understanding of the origins and meanings of Hegel's dialectic. It doubly inspires this work because even Benjamin falters in his view of the dialectic, suggesting that it was always there to begin with: "Dialectic . . . is inherent in origin." He overlooks the possibility of thinking on the origin of the origin itself, the inception of the thought of "singularity and repetition" so crucial to the premodern thought experiment to generate difference out of identity, out of dialectical failures. And so we need to look again.

The Medieval Dialectic

The Notion of true dialectic is to show forth the necessary movement of pure Concepts, without thereby resolving these into nothing. . . . We certainly do not find in Plato a full consciousness that this is the nature of dialectic.

There is no good . . . in calling the Middle Ages a barbarous period.

HEGEL

"The dialectic," so often discussed within critical theory, is a product of the Middle Ages and not classical antiquity. That is my claim, which continues from the previous chapter. Hegel was the first modern philosopher to recognize the dialectic in medieval thought and bring it back to philosophical prominence—to boot, at the worst possible time, after Kant had devastatingly parodied dialectic in his "four antinomies" as just so much sham scholasticism; his is just one of countless critiques of dialectic since Descartes.[1] Hegel took an extreme intellectual risk in recuperating dialectic. But it paid off. For his recovery of dialectic, above all, opened the way to theoretical innovation: with dialectic, he made philosophy new, lastingly modern, and enduringly critical.

Yet we ourselves need a new, even if partial, history of the dialectic to appreciate Hegel's intellectual risk and dialectical insight, because the major introductions to dialectic, Hegel, Marx, and almost all of the specialized studies on Hegel, make one fundamental historical claim: that Hegel's dialectic derives from antique or classical sources combined with this or that piece of Kantian or post-Kantian philosophy. Thinkers from Gadamer and Heidegger to Adorno and Badiou hold this position.[2] So much is this the prevailing wisdom that two key resources, *A Hegel Dictionary* and *The Hegel Dictionary*, codify it without having to list the relevant authorities who support it: both define the dialectic as an expression of ancient and modern ideas—the crossing of the *via antiqua* and the *via moderna*. The problem with this predominant view is that it's an assumption built on the wholesale omission of that great middle of intellectual history, the medieval period, which, through the transmission of the relevant classical texts on dialectic and commentaries thereon, makes the crossing of the ancient and the modern possible in the first place.³ Yet rarely, if ever, do the Middle Ages factor into studies that write the history of dialectic *as* a history of modern, critical dialectical theory, *except* when the aim is to associate Hegel with a given medieval philosopher—a laudable approach in its own right that, frustratingly, amounts to shouting in a bag, because the insights gained by such a comparison are ensconced within the field of medieval studies or philosophy departments (never exactly overrun with Hegelians and Marxists).⁴

A history of the Hegelian dialectic that includes the Middle Ages needs to be written, not for the sake of advancing a specialized agenda in medieval studies about which non-medievalists may not care, but rather because the accurate understanding of Hegel depends on such an inclusive history—which in turn has implications for every field of study impacted by this philosopher's ideas, idioms, and indeed dialectic. The best way to approach this task, I believe, is to write a history of two logical terms that themselves seem, like all logical terms, to have no history, or at least a history that begins in Hegel and picks up in the twentieth-century reception of his work: identity and difference. When I refer to Hegel's dialectical insight above, I mean to describe his use of these two terms in his well-known challenge to the three laws of identity and, above all, his formulation of a new "law of contradiction": "All things are in themselves contradictory." Hegel came to that view by thinking deeply about identity/difference: "Now if the first determinations of reflection, identity, difference, and opposition, have been formulated each as a principle, all the more should the one determination into which they pass over as in their truth, namely contradiction, be grasped and enunciated as a principle: 'All things are in themselves contradictory.'"⁵ These "first determinations of reflection" that are identity, difference, and opposition are, to be sure, among Hegel's favorite logical and dialectical terms and, whether he always names them or not, they are as crucial to the function of his dialectic across all of his works as the ubiquitous terms "individual" and "universal."⁶

When Hegel used identity/difference to rethink the three laws of identity, he knew he was onto something new. Approaching ancient problems in a way that never dawned on his predecessors, Hegel influenced countless others after him, especially in the mid-twentieth century when theorists, following Alexandre Kojève's and Jean Hyppolite's expositions of Hegel, examined the dialectic of identity and difference exemplified in the so-called master/slave dialectic (see chap. 3 for examples). To be sure, an equal amount of theoretical work rejected or revised Hegel's dialectical terms—from Adorno's pairing of non-identity and difference in *Negative Dialectics*,⁷ Heidegger's ontic reorientation of identity and difference (considered separately in his two famous lectures),⁸ Derrida's early attempts to explain différance as a negativity different from the old negations of neoplatonism;[9] to Lyotard's reflections on phraseology and negation in *Le Différend*,[10] Deleuze and Guattari's multiplicity,[11] and Jameson's "difference relates."[12] These examples break apart the paired terms of identity/difference by breaking from identity itself, and all that falls under the rubric of Being and Sameness, in search of a concept or even anti-concept more powerful, more material, more multiple, than "difference." Here, identity is not first, nor One. Difference is all there is, and without identity, difference amounts to a disaggregated Many and takes on a determining force of its own in the work of—to take two other instances—Luhman and Latour.[13] This litany of modern instances, extremely incomplete, is not the only history of identity/difference available to us, however. Even so, this much is clear: the dialectic of identity and difference, including its negative and anti-dialectical supplements, are only modern, only familiar as selected high points of theory because Hegel made it possible.

How so? To answer, we must put Hegel's dialectic of identity/difference into historical perspective (again), asking where, precisely, did the dialectic of identity and difference originate; inquiring when, exactly, did philosophers start talking about dialectic as almost *exclusively* the province of these two logical categories. The answers will point us to the dialectical precedents that most matter to Hegel, and these I name *medieval dialectic*, which is (to be very clear) itself just *one* example of the *many* dialectic practices and traditions available in premodernity. But it is a strong one. As I show in the pages that follow, Hegel turned to the Middle Ages, and its prominent instances of the dialectic of identity and difference, to develop his dialectic and make history, renovating ancient philosophy after Plato and modern "critical" philosophy after Kant, with whom I conclude this chapter.

The Dialectics of Plato and Aristotle

Cards on the table: the medieval dialectic of identity and difference, I argue, begins with Plotinus, a philosopher typically hailed as the last of the antique philosophers and first of the medievals, and includes Proclus, who systematized so many of Plotinus's ideas and transmitted them to later medieval thinkers from Pseudo-Dionysius to Nicholas of Cusa. Hegel's dialectic, I hope to show by the end of this chapter, is a distinctly medieval dialectic for the way in which it, like the dialectic of these earlier thinkers, depends on the terms of identity/difference to make the dialectic itself *work*. To be clear, when I say "medieval dialectic," I do not mean to suggest that there is only one kind of disciplinary practice in the Middle Ages that goes by the name of dialectic. There are as many traditions of dialectic as there are other medieval philosophers who could be included in this chapter. For example, the late medieval English philosopher William Penbygull found roundabout ways toward a dialectical notion of identity and difference, but you have to be steeped in his modes of argument and the particulars of his thought to see it.[14] Indeed, with enough argumentative to-do or, let's say, cookie cutting, you could mold any given thinker into the right dialectical shape, in keeping with the Kierkegaardian dictum that "everything is dialectical."[15] Numerous other philosophers, in other words, could be added to my own discussion and made to conform to the narrative, from Porphyry (even his Aristotelian "tree") to Boethius's logical works,[16] Abelard's *sic et non*,[17] and Aquinas's commentary on Boethius's *De Trinitate*;[18] from John Scottus Eriugena's affirmations and negations in his *Periphyseon*,[19] to Giordano Bruno,[20] and to other thinkers who cling to dialectic as it passes in and out of favor over the years through early modernity. However helpfully such figures would embroider this chapter, they would also complicate and perhaps overcomplicate the dialectic when what's now needed is an exposition that for once risks clarity and simplification; hence, my treatment of philosophers who adopt identity/difference within dialectic in a way that we can instantly recognize.[21]

Yet before I turn to this account, some treatment of ancient dialectic is necessary, so that we can tell the difference between classical and postclassical dialectic. This task is all the more pressing because both Plato and Aristotle spoke of dialectic and both have given much thought to the terms *identity* and *difference*. Furthermore, their ideas remain front and center to most late antique and medieval discussions of dialectic, even those that oppose their methods. My aim for the moment, then, is to establish a comparative baseline, demonstrating whether either ancient philosopher places identity and difference at the center of the art of dialectic itself, and from there I present those medieval philosophers who do exactly that.

In various works Plato defines dialectic (διαλεκτική) broadly as debate,[22] the asking and answering of questions, but dialectic as the art of definition and division as a means to "determine what each thing really is" is overwhelmingly his most frequent explanation of the practice, subsuming the tactics of debate and purposes of dialogue.[23] And it is a practice that involves a keen sense of *likeness*, arranging subjects and things "kind by kind" in the broad investigation of analogies between entities; "not taking the same form for a different one or a different one for the same" is indeed "the "business of dialectic."[24] In ordinary perception, "we bring a dispersed plurality under a single form, seeing it all together—the purpose being to define so-and-so"; yet dialecticians explore the "reverse" of this process, "whereby we are enabled to divide into forms."[25] Chiefly, dialectic involves just this sort of definition and division: "First, you must know the truth about the subject. . . .; that is to say, you must be able to isolate it in definition, and having so defined it you must next understand how to divide it into kinds, until you reach the limit of division."[26] The dialectician thus seeks to partition difference and unlikeness from likeness—a division achieved by cutting up likenesses into smaller and smaller analytical units. Here is a good example:

> Then now you and I have come to an understanding not only about the name of the angler's art, but about the definition of the thing itself. One half of all art was acquisitive—half of the acquisitive art was conquest or taking by force, half of this was hunting, and half of hunting was hunting animals; half of this was hunting water animals; of this again, the under half was fishing, half of fishing was striking; a part of striking was fishing with a barb, and one half of this again, being the kind which strikes with a hook and draws the fish from below upward, is the art which we have been seeking, and which from the nature of the operation is denoted angling or drawing up [aspalienutike, anaspasthai—transliterated Greek].[27]

By these means, the dialectician divides what initially looks to be a whole into its different and opposing parts. And the division goes on and on, even beyond the limits of empirical observation, nonetheless bringing to mind the fullness and plurality of "the many," of which each single member inevitably falls under the One—some genus or form—because without the One, there would be only a collection of singularities, a disaggregated and unknowable reality.[28] Likewise, for Plato, different things themselves do not, and this is key, remain in a local or horizontal relation of mutual determination and only enter into a relation of "likeness" by dint of their participation in the Form of "likeness" itself.[29] Similarly, their difference is understood as participation in the Form of "difference."[30] In sum, individual things always relate to one other by virtue of relating vertically to the Forms.[31]

Plato, as we have already seen, is certainly aware of identity and difference as categories. In fact, he touts these terms as part of his dialectical "discovery" of the five primal forms that comprise all intelligibles and existents:[32] Being, Motion, Rest, Identity, and Difference. And as we will soon see, these last two terms are the basis upon which later thinkers would construct a dialectic of identity and difference. At most, Plato hints at the special powers of "identity" and "difference" but does not take the step to think of these two terms as distinct from the remaining three primal Forms. And, as we recall, Plato dreams up these five forms in order to validate the Parmenidean lesson about being and not-being, and the lingering question of whether "what is not" has "being."[33] He answers this question by recourse to the "science of dialectic,"[34] which thinks of "not-being" in a very special way—chiefly, in relation to the five primal forms.[35] So: when we establish that something is not identical with "existence," such as "motion," then it is, naturally, "different" from "existence" and thus can be called simply "not-existence" or, more colloquially, "what is not existence but something else, such as motion." In other words, Plato is not stating that nothingness exists, but rather that existence isn't everything and that "not-being" is said to "be" on account of the existence of what is not-existence, again, Motion or any of the other primals. Thus, " 'not-being' is a single kind . . . dispersed over the whole field of realities" and is a term designating difference among the many.[36]

Does this mean, then, that Plato suggests that identity/difference defines the relations between the five primals or even existents, as Proclus would do centuries later? It initially looks that way in his proposal that any one primal form is both identical and different, but by this Plato means that forms are identical to and different from themselves. Motion is identical to itself—Motion *is* Motion and thus participates in the form Identity—and Motion is different from itself because Motion isn't, literally, that other primal form called Identity. Here is how Plato puts this strange argument:

> Motion, then, is both the same and not the same; we must admit that without boggling at it. For when we say it is "the same" and "not the same" we are not using the expression in the same sense; we call it "the same" on account of its participation in the same with reference to itself, but we call it "not the same" because of its combination with difference, a combination that separates it off from the same (sameness) and makes it not the same but different, so that we have the right to say this time that it is "not the same."[37]

To be sure, we mustn't allow boggling to obscure the crucial point here, which we already reviewed.[38] That is, a thing or form is identical with itself, or different from itself, by virtue of its *participation* in a Form, not by dint of a differential relationship whereby identity can *only* be defined by its difference from another, lest the entire being/non-being apparatus falls apart: motion/not-motion or, say, rest/not-rest must abide by the logical principle of x/not-x inherent in the original Parmenidean insight about being/not-being. Otherwise, Plato's invention of the five primals is all for naught . . . truly. That we are far from Hegel's landscape of reciprocity as illustrated in the master/slave dialectic, whereby the identity of the master depends on his difference from the slave, could be no clearer than in Plato's formulation of this very relationship in the *Parmenides*: the identity of the master depends not on the slave but on the master's participation in the Form called "mastery."[39]

Aristotle, across his works, offers a more consistent discussion of dialectic than Plato and more overtly logical and argumentative, establishing a version of dialectic that Plotinus and other later Platonists would counter with a new dialectic of identity and difference. Indeed, his version of dialectic even runs exactly opposite to the textbook definition of Hegelian dialectic as the synthesis of opposites. Take, for instance, Aristotle's definition of dialectic in the *Topics*:

> We must say for how many and for what purposes the treatise is useful. . . .
> For the study of the philosophical sciences it is useful, because the ability to
> puzzle on both sides of a subject will make us detect more easily the truth and
> error about the several points that arise. It has a further use in relation to the
> principles used in the several sciences. . . . It is through reputable opinions
> about them that these have to be discussed, and this task belongs properly, or
> most appropriately, to dialectic; for dialectic is a process of criticism wherein
> lies the path to the principles of all inquiries.[40]

The dialectician must "puzzle on both sides of the subject." Or as Aristotle explains in the *Rhetoric*, one must be able to reason "on opposite sides of a question, not in order that we may in practice employ it in both ways (for we must not make people believe what is wrong), but in order that we may see clearly what the facts are, and that, if another man argues unfairly, we on our part may be able to confute."[41]

By way of pause: this method perhaps will seem familiar, as it appeared in various forms over the centuries. Both Cicero in his *Topica* and Boethius in his *In Ciceronis Topica* and *De topicis differentiis* established a commentary tradition on Aristotle's *Topics* that would last throughout the Middle Ages,[42] be bolstered by Albert the Great's own commentary on the *Topics*, and come to define the discipline of dialectic, as featured in the *trivium* of medieval universities (grammar, dialectic, rhetoric), informing such late works as Philipp Melanchthon's *De dialecta libri* iv (1528).[43] Some, however, tested dialectic's disciplinary distinction from rhetoric, and Rudolf Agricola's *De inventione dialectica* (1479) is a signal example of a turn from Aristotelian dialectic to rhetoric, or some complex combination thereof.[44] But such changes did not stop authors from mocking anyway the syllogistic Aristotelian enterprise of dialectic because it survived at least into the seventeenth century, a point that has been well documented.[45] If anything, it encouraged them. Very early in the turn against dialectic, François Rabelais pens this side-splitting satire in the 1530s:

> Who was befuddled and perplexed when Pantagruel was born? Gargantua
> his father, for seeing on one side his wife dead and on the other his son Pan-

tagruel born and so big and fair, he knew not what to say or do. The doubt which troubled his mind was namely this: ought he to weep out of grief for his wife or laugh out of joy for his son? He had good dialectical arguments for both sides. They choked him, for he could marshal them very well in syllogistic modes and figures but he could come to no conclusion. So he remained caught like [a mouse in pitch, or] a kite in the nets of a fowler.[46]

And well into the turn against dialectic, Descartes, who is hailed by many as the first of modern philosophers, twists the knife by writing staidly philosophically in his *Discourse on Method* (1637) about all the doubt that remains in dialectic:

> Concerning philosophy I shall say only that, seeing that it has been cultivated for many centuries by the most excellent minds that have ever lived and that, nevertheless there still is nothing in it about which there is not some dispute, and consequently nothing that is not doubtful, I was not at all so presumptuous as to hope to fare any better there than the others; and that, considering how many opinions there can be about the very same matter that are held by learned people without there ever being the possibility of more than one opinion being true, I deemed everything that was merely probable to be well-nigh false. . . . Nor have I ever observed that, through the method of disputations practiced in the schools, any truth has been discovered that had until then been unknown. For, so long as each person in the dispute aims at winning, he is more concerned with making much out of probability than with weighing the arguments on each side.[47]

So dialectic fails to achieve its own ambitions of "weighing the arguments on each side," its own goal to move from questions and doubts to answers and probabilities—probabilities never being enough for a certain someone seeking mathematical certainty in his clear and distinct ideas.[48] Authors ranging from Chrétien de Troyes to Jonathan Swift express, and mock, just this aspiration of dialectic to think both sides of a given problem.[49] And so when early modern and modern philosophers parody or insult dialectic as "drivelectic," or claim that "but for the theologians of those Universities, the Dialectic science would for many ages have been banished from the world," they (like Erasmus here) had in mind this long Aristotelian tradition.[50] Likewise, these same philosophers hung on John Buridan the tale of "Buridan's ass"—that silly but sad example in which a donkey, standing between food on one side and water on the other, dies of starvation and thirst because he can't decide which source of sustenance to consume first: both are equally appealing. Too bad for Buridan, author of that great *Summulae de dialectica*, because he never tells such a tale, but this sort of unearned aspersion gives one a sense of how intensely the dialectic of equipollence was derided.[51] Even

Kant's four antinomies, complete with their anti-medieval aspersions, are, as I show below, consistent with this reaction against the older dialectic logic in the universities. Kant adeptly argues both sides of the four proofs, and for this Hegel will name Kant's dialectic "skeptical," criticize it for the failure to achieve *genuinely* the unity of opposites, and offer in turn his own version, drawing from different medieval traditions *not* aligned with Aristotle.

Suffice it to say that the fundamentally Aristotelian method of pondering both sides of the opposition is a footnote to Plato. Aristotle, for all his differences with Plato on the matter of dialectic,[52] follows his predecessor on this point. As Plato writes in the *Sophist*:

[Educators] cross-examine a man's words, when he thinks that he is saying something and is really saying nothing, and easily convict him of inconsistencies in his opinions; these they then collect by the dialectic process, and placing them side by side, show that they contradict one another about the same things, in relation to the same things, and in the same respect. He, seeing this, is angry with himself, and grows gentle with others, and thus is entirely delivered from great prejudice and harsh notions, in a way which is most amusing to the hearer.[53]

From here, Plato enlarges the practice of dialectic. He moves from the facile problem of "saying nothing" per the stubborn Sophists (in his view) to a high philosophical discussion of non-being, deploying dialectic to ascertain the five primal forms and merging rhetoric, metaphysics, and ontology. Yet Aristotle, who claims that "Dialectic is merely critical where philosophy claims to know," makes no such leap and rather continues to refine dialectic as the art of refutation.[54] While the dialectician can think both sides of a problem at once, he typically is to choose one side and proceed deductively until he can affirm or deny the statement in question.[55] Usually, his conclusion will find "the contradictory of a given thesis" or "an aporeme," which is "a deduction that reasons dialectically to a contradiction."[56] The dialectician can also contradict a contradiction: the proposition that "one ought to do good to one's friends" meets its contrary in "one ought to do harm to one's friends," which itself should be contradicted with "one ought not to do them harm."[57] At no point do we find the synthesis of opposites, or contradiction, to be anything but problematic. In fact, the synthesis of opposites, of conjoining "both sides," is what, for Aristotle, produces perplexity, not insight: "an equality between contrary reasonings would seem to be the cause of perplexity; for it is when we reflect on both sides of a question and find everything alike to be in keeping with either course that we are perplexed which of the two we are to do."[58] Think the "befuddled and perplexed" Gargantua. (Think, too, I might add, the metaphysical wit and conceit in English poetry, as described by Samuel Johnson: "Wit, may be more rigorously and philosophically considered as a kind of *discordia concors*; a combination of dissimilar images or discovery of occult resemblances in things apparently unalike. . . . The reader . . . is seldom pleased.")[59]

Aristotle never entertains what we now recognize, thanks to Hegel, as the dialectic of "difference" and "identity," wherein identity fundamentally depends on difference.[60] Of things, Aristotle says, "if two contraries are equally liable to occur naturally in a thing, and the thing has been defined through the one, clearly it has not been defined; otherwise there will be more than one definition of the same thing."[61] Or, when speaking of a position one may hold, Aristotle says: "See, for destructive purposes, if the property rendered is a property of the affirmation; for then the same term will not be a property of the negation as well. Also, if the term rendered is a property of the negation, it will not be a property of the affirmation."[62] By such demonstrations, which account for an array of analytical and rhetorical contingencies, Aristotle offers countless ways of deploying the terms of "sameness" and "difference" to shim apart an adversary's arguments. If "argument about definitions is mostly concerned with questions of sameness and difference,"[63] the *Topics*, above all, is a veritable manual for employing these analytical and rhetorical terms, enabling one to define what a thing is,[64] and, equally, to discern where an adversary's arguments falsely associate inherently different things or definitions. Indeed, the dialectician's job is to "take hold of contraries in whatever way they may be of use both in demolishing and establishing a view";[65] it is to be alert to finer and finer shades of opposition.[66] Aptly, Aristotle repeatedly calls this practice "destructive purposes." Plato would call it eristic and advise against it.

In all of this discussion so far, we have been running along the edges of the famous three laws of thought. About the first law—the principle of non-contradiction—Plato and Aristotle are of one mind against Heraclitus's position that identity can contain difference within itself, that an entity changes because it already contains what it is to become.[67] Aristotle, of course, builds up a more logically articulated defense of the law of non-contradiction than Plato, and he has supplementary examples throughout his work to support it. In the *Topics*, he cautions readers about relatives and insists that dialecticians should ferret out false relatives, cases where one of the relatives in the pair fails to reciprocate.[68] For Aristotle, relative being is not real,[69] insofar as relatives themselves are only a matter of perspective, of naming and comparing, and finding correlatives[70]—though even in this practice he issues the reminder that "it is impossible for a thing to be its own contrary."[71] Owing to all of these, and many more, examples, there is no mistaking in Aristotle a dialectic of identity and difference, no intimations like we find in Plato, if only Plato had (like Hegel) thought about the negative more deeply.[72] It really should come as no surprise to learn that Aristotle demotes "same" and "different" from the five primals of Plato to ninth in the list of important philosophical terms![73]

Hegel, however, challenged these laws of thought.[74] He was the first to do so, too. This important common insight cannot be emphasized enough. For it admits two related points that remind us of Hegel's novelty, his risks in going against the philosophical grain, and his place in the history of philosophy. He rejects these laws of thought in order, first, to recuperate "contradiction," which "is ordinarily the first to be kept away from things" or viewed as "a blemish, . . . a defect or failure."[75] Instead, he views "contradiction" as the essential, generative principle for "anything concrete, every concept."[76] Second, in the name of "contradiction," Hegel reinstates the operations of identity/difference, viewing all identity as determinate, containing difference within itself. Hegel's familiar emphatic phrase that expresses this new "law of contradiction"—"All things are in themselves contradictory"—is, as I noted at the outset, the culmination of an insight about identity/difference itself: "Now if the first determinations of reflection, identity, difference, and opposition, have been formulated each as a principle, all the more should the one determination into which they pass over as in their truth, namely contradiction, be grasped and enunciated as a principle: 'All things are in themselves contradictory.' "[77] He does this all in the name of dialectic, a way of synthesizing opposites, a way of thinking identity in difference. Not even Heraclitus, what remains of his thought, would call (*pace* the retrospective celebration by Hegel and Engels)[78] these procedures "dialectic." To find this new kind of dialectic, a dialectic *contra* dialectic, we must turn to the post-ancient traditions of philosophy. We must enter the Middle Ages.

After Plotinus: The Dialectic of Identity and Difference

To find dialectical precedents for Hegel is, I argue, to discover where identity/difference emerges as the central terms within the discipline of dialectic and thereafter in medieval philosophy. In short, what is needed is a different history of dialectic from that typically, even if helpfully, given in the focus on the vicissitudes of Aristotle's *Topics* or *Categories* across the centuries. After all, Hegel would hardly look to this tradition to develop his own dialectic if he could proclaim that the aforementioned traditions of dialectic were philosophy only in name:

Thus in the West hardly anything was known beyond the Isagoge of Porphyry, the Latin Commentaries of Boethius on the Logical works of Aristotle, and extracts from the same by Cassiodorus—most barren compilations; there is also what is just as barren, the dissertations ascribed to Augustine *De dialectica* and *De categoriis*, which last is a paraphrase of the Aristotelian work upon the categories. These were the first make-shifts or expedients for carrying on Philosophy.[79]

These words have, I believe, gotten scholars off the trail when exploring how *other* kinds of medieval dialectic fascinate Hegel, informing his entire system that he still—despite these animadversions—calls dialectic! Those other kinds begin with Plotinus, who offers a distinct dialectical contrast to these aporetic methods, as do philosophers after him in the so-called "neoplatonic" tradition.

"Neoplatonism" is no singular thing, and the term remains an anachronism I hesitate to use but am constrained to do so for two reasons. The first is that scholars routinely refer to the neoplatonic procession and return as dialectical, though not dialectical in a Hegelian way.[80] The second is that prominent thinkers like Gadamer have taken pains to elide this philosophical tradition in the reading of Hegel. In his classic essay, "Hegel and the Dialectic of the Ancient Philosophers," Gadamer cursorily mentions neoplatonism as the "origin" of Hegelian concepts but never explores the specificity of the dialectic within that tradition.[81] Had he looked at all into what he calls "the two thousand year tradition of Neoplatonism" that comes "close to the speculative self-movement of thought as it is explicated in Hegel's dialectic," he might have seen that Hegel's interest in the problems of identity/difference, likeness/sameness points to the postclassical, medieval tradition that brings these terms to the center of dialectic itself.[82] My own contribution in this chapter is to suggest that what puts the "neo" in "neoplatonism," what makes Plotinus and others so different from Plato and Aristotle, is this discrete dialectic of identity and difference, quite evident in so many late antique and medieval examples and by no means reducible to generalizations about neoplatonic "procession" and "return," or for that matter "apophasis," itself the starting point for so much deconstructive engagement with medieval mysticism.[83] Here, I collect examples within this broader medieval dialectical tradition of identity and difference. Any one of them would suffice for an analysis of Hegel, insofar as, in philosophy today, scholars successfully pair Hegel with this or that earlier philosopher in order to describe what is distinctly, even if singularly, Thomist or Platonic about his ideas—the assumption being that a philosopher of note, as Hegel imagined himself to be even during his days lecturing to teenage boys at the

gymnasium, would have absorbed the work of his distinguished predecessors, or at least inevitably thought what has been thought before.[84] Yet my
case is broader, because the examples are wide ranging, separated by centuries. Perforce I do not argue for the influence of any one thinker and rather
only seek to evince what's been overlooked in histories of dialectical critical theory, and the obviousness and ubiquity of a premodern dialectic that
is the dialectic of identity and difference—all toward the argument (one
of several in this book) that what makes Hegel modern is his turn to the
medieval.

And so we begin with Plotinus, who, taking his cue from Plato and de-
parting from Aristotle, expands dialectic beyond rhetoric and the pondering
of "both sides" to ontology, metaphysics, and cosmology. In his tract on dialectic, Plotinus explores this expansive dialectic while rejecting efforts to narrow it, stating that "Dialectic does not consist of bare theories and rules."[85] In
answering the basic question about dialectic, "what, in sum, is it?" Plotinus
replies:[86]

> It is the Method, or Discipline, that brings with it the power of pronouncing
> the final truth upon the nature and relation of things—what each is, how it
> differs from others, what common quality all have, to what Kind each be-
> longs and in what rank each stands in its Kind and whether its Being is Real-
> Being, and how many Beings there are, and how many non-Beings to be dis-
> tinguished from Beings.[87]

Plotinus's definition, even the syntax of "what each is, how it differs from
others, what common quality all have" follows the dialectic order of All that
is: when Being is substantiated, identity and difference immediately follow,
after which the tasks of observation and description can proceed.[88] Likewise,
his emphasis on relation—specifically, "the nature and relation of things"—
corresponds precisely to a dialectic analysis of "what each is, how it differs
from others, what common quality all have." That Plotinus foregrounds relation in the analysis tells us something about his renewed version of dialectic,
whereby relation is something more than a subset category à la Aristotle,
Cicero, Boethius, and others. Above all, however, Plotinus's recommenda-
tion that dialecticians query about "how many non-Beings [are] to be distinguished from Beings" speaks volumes about a dialectic that requires identity/
difference in its abstract and determinate forms (to refer to the terminology
of the previous chapter). Why does this dialectic depend on identity/differ-
ence? Because it attempts to think across the void of non-being and being
and seeks to conceptualize the transition from the former to the latter without giving up and dismissing the problem as a "strange thing"—literally, in

Plato's words, a thing out of place (ἄτοπον or atopon)[89]—or, as in Badiou's unfriendly analysis, "the general ruin of dialectical thought."[90]

It so follows, then, that a major question asked by Plotinus in *Ennead* 5.1 (now called "The Three Initial Hypostases") is: "From such a unity as we have declared The One to be, how does anything at all come into substantial existence, any multiplicity, dyad, number?" He is indeed right to say that this is "the problem endlessly debated by the most ancient philosophers."[91] In addressing it, he has a far more difficult *theological* task than Aristotle or Anselm, because his One is intensely more Other. His God, called the "One," is not an "unmoved mover" like Aristotle's, which moves in a self-caused fashion.[92] As Plotinus admonishes readers, "we may not ascribe motion to it . . . origin from the Supreme must not be taken to imply any movement in it; that would make the Being resulting from the movement not a second principle but a third; the Movement would be the second hypostasis."[93] What's more, Plotinus's One is not an intellect: "The One has no need of minute self-handling since it has nothing to learn by an intellective act."[94] It "neither knows itself nor is known in itself."[95] To boot, it is not even a being, much less the "highest Being" one can conceive, after Anselm. For, as Plotinus states, "the First is not a thing among things"; it is "a Principle which transcends Being; this is the One."[96] It is, rather, non-being, "no member of existence, but can be the source of all"; "in order that Being may be brought about, the source must be no Being but Being's generator."[97] By disassociating the One from movement, intellect, and being, Plotinus has made all the more difficult his task of showing that the One is the origin of exactly these three things, movement, intellect, and being, which, as we will soon seen, compose the second hypostasis, the Intellectual Principle.[98] The point here, meanwhile, is that Plotinus needs to think dialectically to explain the transition from non-movement to movement, non-intellect to intellect, and, most notoriously, non-being to being, because he cannot use easy models of likeness in his explanation, in the manner of Aristotle, who, in proposing God to be an "intellect," can effortlessly argue how intellectual beings spring forth from this already intellectual deity; nor can he shift the problem of nothing and being into the Christian formulation of divine creation *ex nihilo*, whereby the highest Being, "than which nothing greater can be conceived," makes something from nothing—a very ancient Judeo-Christian insight perfected by Anselm, emphatically, as a way around the difficult philosophical problem of nothing: "Let it rather be declared, then, that nothing did not exist before the supreme Being" and that, *stricto sensu*, "not anything" else precedes God.[99]

So Plotinus is really setting up a hard problem for himself when he asks "from such a unity as we have declared The One to be, how does anything

at all come into substantial existence?"[100] Or, better, he is setting us up for a
dialectical narrative that can attend to the impossibilities of absolute difference, such as that which the divide between being and non-being presents,
and *relate* the two sides together, ultimately bringing them into a relation
of identity/difference.[101] Plotinus, for instance, explains the genesis of being
from non-being, the Intellectual Principle from the One, by conceptualizing
identity in difference. In *Ennead* 5.3 (now entitled "The Knowing Hypostases
and the Transcendent"), he goes in dialectical steps, first by positing the Intellectual Principle as a negation of the One, emerging now as "the Not-One."[102]
From here Plotinus explains that the One and the "Not-One" nonetheless
bear a relation to each other that turns on the logical (and Primal) categories
of identity/difference: "The second principle [Not-One, i.e.] shows that it is
next in order (after the all-transcendent One) by the fact that its multiplicity
is as the same time an all-embracing unity: all the variety lies in the midst of
a sameness, and identity cannot be separated from diversity since all stands
as one."[103] What Plato did not conceive in the distinction between being/not-
being, in which "not-being" is not supra-ontological and is only a mode of
difference, Plotinus finds in the opposition of one/not-one: a dialectic of iden-
tity/difference. Plotinus, in short, takes Plato's binary, being/not-being, and
reverses its terms, not-being/being, thereby placing negativity as the starting
point of dialectic itself. (In Hegelian terms, Plotinus thinks from the side
of the negative.) For the identity of the "Not-One"—again, the Intellectual-
Principle—lies in its difference from the One that is not-being, but it is not a
difference that is absolute. Indeed, it is a difference that is barely intelligible,
bordering so closely on identity itself. As we learned in *Ennead* 5.1 ("Three
Initial Hypostases"), and in our investigations in the previous chapter, these
two hypostases are proximate and immediate to each other "with nothing
intervening"; they are "without mediation."[104] That ever-persistent feature of
dialectic involving two sides now, for Plotinus, falls within a single unity, just
in the way rhetoric and dialectic themselves now become ontology.

Plotinus, in *Ennead* 5.3 ("The Knowing Hypostases and the Transcendent"), offers variations on this theme of "two sides" falling within a unity,
such as "all the variety lies in the midst of a sameness" or "variety side by side
with identity"—and in each case, he is bringing to bear the categories of iden-
tity/difference, which—Plotinus is prepared to say—give birth to the hypostases: "We have observed that anything that may spring from the One must
be different from it. Differing, it is not One, since then it would be the Source.
If unity has given place to duality, from that moment there is multiplicity;
for there is variety side by side with identity, and this imports quality and
all the rest."[105] It should begin to become clear why Plotinus prioritizes the

categories of identity/difference above all others, ranking them second only to the hypostases themselves. For these are the only categories that can help him write the narrative of transition from One to many, from non-being to being. It's the only way he can talk about beginnings.

That these terms rank so high in his philosophical system could not be clearer than in the following passage, in which he proclaims:

> Thus the Primals (the first 'Categories') are seen to be: Intellectual Principle; Existence; Difference; Identity: we must also include Motion and Rest: Motion provides for the intellectual act, Rest preserves identity as Difference gives at once a Knower and a Known, for, failing this, all is one, and silent.[106]

This is a major statement, even moment for the history of philosophy: Plotinus compresses Plato's primals, if not reduces them. Motion and rest are now last in the list of primals and serve identity/difference ("Rest preserves identity as Difference," etc.), rather than, as for Plato, the other way around. He also fuses the first two primals, "Intellectual Principle; Existence," having already demonstrated in the tract that there is a "two-sided" unity of these two, the unity of thought and being—an idea, taken from none other than Parmenides and rendered into the first avowed notion of what Hegel would call abstract determination, as I argued in chapter 1.[107] After the Intellectual Principle itself, and indeed coterminous with it, is "Difference; Identity"; Plotinus is compelled to say more about these two primals above all, as the engines of divine intellection: "The objects of intellection (the ideal content of the Divine Mind)—identical in virtue of the self-concentration of the principle which is their common ground—must still be distinct from one another; this distinction constitutes Difference."[108] While the Intellectual Principle knows things perfectly in ways humans never can, it knows them through the operations of identity/difference by which *all intellection*, including human thought, happens. Even where, as in *Ennead* 6.2, Plotinus reverses the priority of these primals and places Motion and Stability before Identity and Difference, we find that, in fact, the very operations of identity/difference define every primal, not only because Rest overlaps with Difference (as above), but insofar as identity/difference, as a process, expresses what it means to be *any* genus: "Genus demands that the common property of diverse objects involve also differences arising out of its own character, that it form species, and that it belong to the essence of the objects."[109]

Where Plotinus uses the terms of identity/difference to draw *analogies* between the divine and human domains (especially cognition), Proclus goes further, using these terms in the attempt to integrate both domains—an effort quite visible, as we will soon see, in his development of the idea of procession and return. In Proclus's immense commentary on Plato's *Parmenides*, one can trace out a variety of threads and influences across the centuries into early modernity,[110] but his contribution to dialectical thought is graspable when taken through our own intentionally narrower topic of the dialectic of identity and difference, the same and other, and like and unlike. Three passages are especially important in this respect—two involving Proclus's explanation of how God (the Demiurge) can make the created order both like and unlike him, and one detailing how it is that the created order bears likenesses and unlikenesses up and down the grades of being, a key development in the dialectic survey of creation to which Plotinus only alluded. Taking his cue from a passage in the *Cratylus* and offering the characteristic gloss that extends Plato's own point, Proclus states:

> There is, then, in the Demiurge a potency and cause able to liken to himself the things that he creates. If this is so, there is in him an idea of likeness by which he makes his creations like himself and one another. But if so, he must also provide the cause of unlikeness to himself on the part of the things created; for it is not possible for a likeness to be brought into being unless there is also a notion of unlikeness; for without this, Plato says (*Crat.* 432c), there would be two Cratyluses, Cratylus and a likeness of Cratylus. Consequently, the things brought into being are unlike him, being perceptible, instead of intelligible; and they must also possess unlikeness to one another along with their likeness. And this, furthermore, accords with the will of the "Father." For the cosmos necessarily comes to be a cosmos from things harmonized with one another, and every harmony is a conjunction of things unlike and different, a proportion which is, as it were, a likeness among the unlike.[111]

Proclus personifies both the Platonic *eidos* and the Plotinian Intellectual-Principle, rendering him a deity who thinks and creates by means of likeness and unlikeness.

Having stated that the Demiurge contains both likeness and unlikeness within itself, Proclus anticipates a question, if not objection: "If we say that that higher being is indivisible, how can it have parts that are divided so as to be unmixed and without community with each other?"[112] To answer, he offers this program statement about identity/difference:

> Consequently, we must not suppose that the Ideas are altogether unmixed and without community with one another, nor must we say, on the other hand, that each one is all of them, as has been demonstrated. How, then, and in what way are we to deal logically with this question? We must say that each of them is precisely what it is and preserves its specific nature undefiled, but also partakes of the others without confusion, not by becoming one of them, but by participating in the specific nature of that other and sharing its own

nature with it, just as we say that Identity partakes in a way of Difference without being Difference (for there is a plurality in it: not only is it different from
Unlikeness but also different from itself), and that Difference likewise partakes of Identity inasmuch as it is common to all other things and in another
way is the same as itself; Identity is not Difference, nor Difference Identity;
this has been refuted by what we said earlier; and again we say that Unlikeness
partakes of Likeness (inasmuch as all Ideas have a character in common they
are like one another), and Likeness of Unlikeness, for if Likeness, like all Ideas,
contributes something of itself to others, it is unlike them, for otherwise in so
doing it would not be the contributor, and the others partakers, and if Unlikeness contributes something of itself to others, it becomes like them, more than
that, itself and Likeness becomes like; and that Likeness is not Unlikeness, nor
Unlikeness itself Likeness. Likeness as likeness is not unlike, nor Unlikeness
as unlikeness like.[113]

All of the "Ideas" (what are commonly called Platonic "forms," in other
words) are arranged in relations of identity/difference in the mind of the Demiurge. Even the great Platonic terms of the One and the Many emerge, for
Proclus, in a relation of likeness and unlikeness—a key point to which we will
return in our interpretation of Hegel.[114]

Between these two fundamental assertions about the structure of the cosmos come Proclus's reflections on procession among the order of beings,
what links everything together:

In general, procession occurs either by way of unity, or by way of likeness, or
by way of identity—by way of unity as supercelestial henads, for there is no
identity among them, nor specific likeness, but unity only; by way of identity,
as in the indivisible substances, where that which proceeds is somehow the
same as what it came from, for being all safeguarded and held together by
eternity, they manifest identity of part to whole; and by way of likeness, as in
the beings of the intermediate and lowest levels, which, though intermediate,
are the first to welcome procession by way of likeness, whether in some cases
it be identity and difference or likeness and unlikeness that is their cause.[115]

Apart from the "supercelestial henads," which enjoy "unity only" and
uniquely partake of the One through analogy (which is a mode of difference), the entire celestial order proceeds or declines by way of identity and
difference, from the monads or "indivisible substances" all the way down to
the lowest forms of being.[116]

And so what bundles all of Proclus's ideas about identity/difference in the
disparate intellectual and sensible realms? Dialectic, of course. Proclus states
that there "is need . . . for the dialectical 'survey' (planē) in the study of these
Forms, to give us preliminary training and instruction for the comprehension

of them."[117] But this survey must start in the sensible world, to which "dialectical training" applies itself in the "survey" of "a multiplicity which goes from opposites to opposites," "the mixture of Forms in the sense objects" themselves.[118] Having studied the world of appearance, the dialectician completes the task by reflecting upward: "Like and unlike exist together at the level of sense-perception, but we want to see their interaction also in the intelligible world. This is the desire that Socrates is uttering, dismissing the mingling of visible things, and ascending to the communion of intelligibles, and Parmenides accepts this as expression the sentiments of a notable and magnanimous soul."[119]

Proclus thus authorizes his form of dialectic, at points critical of Plato (putting the "neo" in his Platonism), by linking it back to the Platonic method described in the *Republic*, where Plato states that, by the "power of dialectic," one can "rise to that which requires no assumption" and "proceed downward to the conclusion, making . . . use . . . only of pure ideas moving on through ideas to ideas and ending with ideas."[120] But more than that, Proclus (like Plotinus) sets identity/difference at the center of dialectic and shows that these two logical terms explain the relation of All, from the Demiurge on down, thereby authorizing a strain of neoplatonism that is, on the one hand, dialectical in the sense we recognize today as the interplay of identities and differences, and on the other hand phenomenological, as a study of appearances. In this way, dialectic is conceived to be both a description of beginnings, in ontological and epistemological terms, and a starting point for an analysis whose habits of thought are hoped to adequate themselves to the unfolding relations of All that is and to the divine intellect in which identity/difference operates as the greatest abstraction imaginable. In sum, in both Plotinus and Proclus we find an important moment in the history of philosophy when we can for the first time describe as "dialectical" the discipline of "dialectic"—indeed, an important event that revises Plato's *Parmenides*, in which the namesake figure is, through the art of neoplatonic back projection, rendered into a dialectician of a sort Plato himself never could have conjured up and a dialectic that he was never equipped to conceive.

Medieval Dialectical Phenomenology

So what happens, then, when this very specific kind of dialectic practice is absorbed within Christian theology? Pseudo-Dionysius and a long tradition of dialectical mysticism is what happens and—with them—a whole new set of concerns that, nonetheless, express this very particular medieval dialectic of identity and difference, but now with increasing emphasis on the study of appearances, a phenomenology in which the soul meditates on the contradictions evident in the world of things and appearances (rather than what we found in Plotinus, a cosmological phenomenology of hypostases and other divine entities regarding each other). That the soul inhabits and mediates contradictions is nothing new to philosophy, for Aristotle writes in his *Topics*: "if two contraries are equally liable to occur naturally in a thing, and the thing has been defined through the one, clearly it has not been defined. . . . For how is it any more a definition to define it through this one than through the other, seeing that both are equally liable to occur naturally in it? Such is the definition of the soul, if defined as a substance capable of receiving knowledge."[121] But Aristotle does not develop this line of thinking; indeed, even in his *On the Soul*, this idea plays a very minor role,[122] and if anything he moves the problem of contradiction to how others (mis)interpret the soul, "those who construct the soul out of . . . contraries" or who say it is a "composition of contraries."[123] This is to say, philosophy would have to wait for Pseudo-Dionysius (and those after) to develop what is commonly called "dialectical mysticism," involving meditations on both the soul and the world of appearances, rife with contradictions.[124]

The history we have so far traced of postclassical dialectical thought—a very specific practice of thinking of contradictions in a unity, all in the name of dialectic—would be no doubt amenable to a Christian theologian, Pseudo-Dionysius, who brings contradiction, opposition, and negation to the center of his contemplative system. We will follow his conscientious adoption of the prominent, now long-standing formulations within the medieval dialectic of identity and difference, along with his inclusion of much of the architecture of procession and return put in place by Plotinus and Proclus—the latter of whom he follows at almost every turn and calls as "Hierotheus," "my famous teacher."[125]

To begin with, witness his reflections in *The Divine Names*—a work in which Pseudo-Dionysius concedes that "the enlightenment of divine knowledge," though it happens in the "soul" and not the "mind," still transpires "through discursive reasoning."[126] He is, in other words, speaking about dialectic, which is the way to knowledge through the activity of reasoning. That he speaks of unity and difference, including the unity and difference of God, should therefore come as no surprise in light of the foregoing. He writes, for example: "Greatness and smallness, sameness and difference, similarity and dissimilarity, rest and motion—these all are titles applied to the Cause of everything. They are divinely named images and we should now contemplate them as far as they are concerned."[127] Pseudo-Dionysius calls some of these familiar "primals"—such as "sameness and difference," "rest and motion"—

"images" and "names," and they are just a few of the dozens he retails in this tract, showing again an awareness of the traditions of dialectic toward which his mysticism ultimately bends, and that is a tradition in which post-Platonic (medieval) thinkers experiment with Plato's primals. It so follows that he emphasizes the categories of sameness and difference, always setting them within dialectical relations, whereby (in many places) identity is constituted by difference: "He precontains all opposites in one, single, universal cause of all sameness," a "difference" that is a "unity amid many forms," "unified differentiations."[128] Simply put, "There is distinction in unity and there is unity in distinction."[129] And, not surprisingly, Pseudo-Dionysius projects these terms into scripture: "All the causes of the unions or differentiations in the divine nature as revealed by scripture were systematically discussed by me to the best of my abilities in my *Theological Representations*," a lost work that would no doubt bear great significance to this inquiry![130]

More than just the obligatory slogans of neoplatonism, these ideas stand at the center of the contemplative and conceptual practice Pseudo-Dionysius recommends to his readers, whose scriptural hermeneutics are the first step toward contemplative ascent. Within the "revealing symbols of scripture," the contemplative seeks what was once a primal, a divine image of "similarity and dissimilarity" written into scripture.[131] That is, he or she seeks "dissimilar similarities," which in turn inform one's observation of the world itself, from which like "dissimilar similarities" can be observed. As Pseudo-Dionysius states in *The Celestial Hierarchy*, "Everything . . . can be a help to contemplation; and dissimilar similarities derived from the world . . . can be applied to those beings which are both intelligible and intelligent."[132] By such contemplation, one is lifted "up through the perceptible to the conceptual," from percept to concept.[133] The mystical task is to think the entire procession of the created world, already dialectically unfolded among the grades of being (Proclus), in one enormous, almost unthinkable, paradoxical thought: "So true negations and the unlike comparisons with their last echoes offer due homage to the divine things."[134] This is, it should be clear, the sort of "true" negation that makes his a "negative theology," not exclusively a matter of apophasis requiring the repeated declarations of what cannot be said, which is all too general of an explanation of what is at stake.[135] Rather, Pseudo-Dionysius prescribes negation in order to make visible the contradictions that then must be thought through, and overcome in the contemplative ascent, only after which point language, words, and figuration fall away and conceptualization takes over.[136] He cautions, however, that the contemplative must "be careful to use the similarities as dissimilarities" and avoid collapsing these differences into identity, "to avoid one-to-one correspondence, to make appropriate adjustments as one remembers the great divide between the intelligible and the perceptible."[137]

These "dissimilar similarities" are the dialectical supplement to his theology, literally, his thesis about God as a unity of difference. As a dialectical form—form, insofar as "dissimilar similarities" can contain any content, any phenomena, any object or creature, including worms—"dissimilar similarities" do what dialectic has always aspired to do: to move from language to concept, sensible to intelligible, matter to ideal, horizontal to vertical, or the inspection of the created order to the contemplation of divine hierarchies. For Pseudo-Dionysius, the "dissimilar similarities" are thought not as some negative capability or insoluble opposition or paradox, as if *relia* was set into the oppositions that beset both the Stoic and the Skeptic in their own versions of dialectic. Rather, humans think through the "dissimilar similarities" by, to use Heidegger's term borrowed from Meister Eckhart, himself a reader of Pseudo-Dionysius, "Gelassenheit," which is a meditative receptivity to paradox itself.[138] Thought brings unity to the dissimilar similars or, if one can bear that tautology, thought is the unity in which the dissimilar similars are thought. What unifies all of these oppositions is the soul, but, as we will see below with Hegel's absolute, these contradictions never disappear and remain in place as the mystic, the phenomenological observer, ranges from difference to difference.

My reference to Heidegger here is not aleatory and means to explain that long arc of intellectual history that puts Plotinus, Proclus, Pseudo-Dionysius, Eriugena, Eckhart, Hegel, and Heidegger all within the same long tradition of dialectical thinking, be it the thinking of the hypostases or that of the mystic—yes, even Heidegger, whose most dialectical moments emerge in his work on mystical thinking. Indeed, he shows that meditative thinking ("das besinnliche Denken") is dialectical through and through; though he never names this thinking "dialectic" as such, his description is on point with the exact kind of dialectic we have been studying here: "Meditative thinking demands of us not to cling one-sidedly to a single idea, nor to run down a one-track course of ideas. Meditative thinking demands of us that we engage ourselves with what at first sight does not go together at all."[139] "One-sidedly": that long-standing dialectical epithet used to condemn non-dialectical thought (as we'll hear uttered a few more times in this book). The mystic in dialectical contemplation moves from paradox to paradox, appearance to appearance, drawing the oppositions into a reflective unity, rather than—as in the tradition of skeptic dialectic—fixing on either side of the contradiction without resolution (a method recently instanced in Slavoj Žižek's "parallax view, constantly shifting perspective between two points between which no synthesis or mediation is possible").[140] For Pseudo-Dionysius, "dissimilar similarities" is a part, then, of the long-standing medieval dialectic of identity and difference, and while we are still, needless to say, many centuries away from dialectic as a form of ideological demystification, we already have at hand in Pseudo-Dionysius the major idea in critical theory made famous by Marx's claim to adopt a dialectical critical practice that gets behind appearances. For Pseudo-Dionysius, one is "provoked to get behind the material show, to get accustomed to the idea of going beyond appearances."[141] How ripe for dialectical thinking this motif will become, as the next chapters of this book show![142]

Pseudo-Dionysius could not have had more influence on western thought all the way up through reformation writers, let alone his enormous influence in eastern philosophy and theology. But there is no greater exponent of these Pseudo-Dionysian dialectical procedures, and no better premodern antecedent to Hegel (as we will soon see), than Nicholas of Cusa, whose work will be our final stop in this partial history of medieval dialectic before arriving at Hegel's own dialectic of identity and difference. This most important of the German scholastics—second only to Eckhart, who, as a reader of Proclus and Pseudo-Dionysius, cannot be discounted—perfects these dialectical traditions.[143] He offers his amazingly abstract *Di Li Non Aliud* (On the Not-Other) in the name of all we have explored so far: the *Parmenides*, Proclus's commentary thereon, and Pseudo-Dionysius's ideas about divine otherness.[144] In fact, he aspires to draw these traditions together and supply a helpfully reductive exposition of their contributions *in toto*—"We would like to hear whether or not there occurs to you a briefer and clearer route to the points which are dealt with by the aforenamed [sic] individuals"—while simultaneously and avowedly turning away from the long Aristotelian tradition of logic he will expose to be not sufficiently dialectical in its absence of a proper theory of otherness, with consequences so serious as to rationalize the conclusion that "the Philosopher failed in first philosophy."[145] Yet Pseudo-Dionysius, according to Nicholas, "seems to have come the closest" to a concept of divine otherness, in believing "that the Creator is neither anything nameable nor any other thing whatever," and in so doing "expressed the secret of Not-other, which secret he everywhere exhibited in one way or another."[146] Nicholas here construes the purportedly most important idea of Pseudo-Dionysius to be a "secret"—that is, only latent in his work and recoverable through diligent study—because he wishes to move beyond the kind of "negative theology" that confines itself to what Pseudo-Dionysius made a veritable discipline, the talk of the "unnameable" and ineffable. Instead, Nicholas works toward a conception of the Not-other that is *definable* in language as, I argue, the outcome of dialectics. This concept, taken from Anselm's most famous sentence (see above) but not premised on the so-called ontological argument, "quite closely befigures the unnameable name of God," which "defines itself and every other thing."[147] To closely befigure the unnameable tells us that Nicholas is expanding the limits of what one can do and think in language, boosting the capacities of adequation itself, and this, of course, is the task—imaginative as much as metaphysical—of dialectics.

That Nicholas intends to emphasize the dialectics of negative theology could be no more clear than in the opening paragraphs, which focus on the most ancient and long-standing notion of dialectic as advanced by Plato— dialectic as *definition* and *contemplation*: "If with all your might you turn the acute gaze of your mind toward the Not-other, you will see with me the definition which defines itself and everything."[148] What's remarkable about Nicholas's "definition" here is that the Not-other replaces the human work of dialectic and presents itself, and its powers of definition, as the apex of dialectic itself, the summit of identity/difference, which (as I have already shown), stands for divinity, the *eidos,* and divine mind in a strong tradition of commentary on the *Parmenides,* which itself, as Nicholas is clear to say, lacks a concept of otherness.[149] In other words, Nicholas's "Not-other" collapses identity and difference into this one term; all things participate in this "Form of forms,"[150] insofar as all things are "not other" than themselves: "all these things are other than their respective opposites."[151] It is the last notion, whereby the identity of "all these things" is figured as the "other" of "their respective opposites," that enables Nicholas to think of the entire created order as the "coincidence of opposites [oppositorum coincidentia]," an idea he developed over many years as he pondered the aforementioned Platonic traditions.[152] No wonder, then, that he places this unique model of identity/ difference at the center of his system as a definition of all that is:[153]

> For Not-other is the most congruent Form (*ratio*), Standard, and Measure of the existence of all existing things, of the nonexistence of all nonexisting things, of the possibility of all possibilities, of the manner of existence of all things existing in any manner, of the motion of all moving things, of the rest of all nonmoving things, of the life of all living things, of the intelligibility of all intelligible things, and so on for all other things of this kind. I see this to be necessary, in that I see that *Not-other* defines itself and, hence, all nameable things.[154]

One can recognize the now faint presence of the Platonic primals (being, motion, rest) with the Not-other, as a simplex of identity/difference, standing prior to them, prior even to "non-existence" (as a mode of real

determination)—a move that, if we think far back in the history of this kind
of inquiry, begins with Plotinus.

To say, then, that the Not-other is prior to all, even to what used to be
the primals, and indeed to assert that this One is a *simplex* of identity/dif-
ference is to introduce, once more, ideas about abstract determination (see
chap. 1). It is, moreover, to think abstract determination in relation to the
real determination of identity in difference figured forth in the entire created
order. Nicholas, this is to say, embraces the greatest problems of dialectic, as
did those before him, in thinking about how difference is introduced into the
heart of identity. He follows a model quite close to Plotinus's, discussed in
the previous chapter, whereby repetition of the same, the iteration of identity
in the mode of A=A, produces difference, only here Nicholas adds another
term to yield, A=A=A. Of course, I am referring here to his discussion of the
three identities of the Trinity, as "Not-other and Not-other and Not-other":

> "Not-other and Not-other and Not-other"—although [this expression] is
> not at all in use—the triune Beginning is revealed most clearly, though it is
> above our apprehension and capability. For when the First Beginning—signi-
> fied through "Not-other"—defines itself: in this movement of definition Not-
> other originates from Not-other; and from Not-other and the Not-other which
> has originated, the definition concludes in Not-other. One who contemplates
> these matters will behold them more clearly than can be expressed.[155]

Where there is movement, there seems to be no movement at all; where there
is difference, no difference. Through this accretion of singulars, this replication of identity, however, come both movement and difference, and the
distinctions necessary to think of one God as triune. That is, this explanation
of the "beginning" of the Trinity centrally involves repetition of the identity
that is at once a difference, the "Not-other": "If the same thing repeated three
times is the definition of the First . . . then assuredly the First is triune. . . .
For this trinity is not other than unity, and [this] unity is not other than
trinity."[156]

Nicholas understands, effectively, "abstract determination," just as Plotinus and Hegel do, and he got to it (like Plotinus and Hegel) by thinking
on the terms of identity/difference and figuring the repetition of identity as
the way to difference. Granted, Trinitarian theology and creedal Christianity—the Athanasian Creed, to begin with—could bring Nicholas to a conception of abstract determination, the *thinking* of and believing in difference
where there is no real determination, no real difference: "ut unum Deum
in Trinitate, et Trinitatem in unitate veneremur [We worship one God in
trinity and the Trinity in unity]." But Nicholas also conceptualizes abstract

determination in general (i.e., non-Trinitarian) terms, attempting to think
this unique mode of difference in, say, his discussion of the quiddity of quantity, in which he puzzles over how a divine quiddity—divine because "quiddity . . . is the shining forth of the First Quiddity"[157]—can bear any quantity
or, for that matter, anything "other than" itself. After all, "quantity is not
something necessary to the quiddity of magnitude, as if magnitude were constituted by quantity."[158] But if the human imagination is involved, in addition
to the procedures of "mentally view[ing]" quiddity, then abstract difference
is imagined: "If magnitude is to be imagined or to appear imaginatively, then
quantity is immediately necessary."[159] And if human understanding is involved, then, abstract difference is *known*: "In the understanding magnitude
shines forth intellectually—i.e., abstractly and absolutely, before corporeal
quantity."[160] These are the procedures of dialectical contemplation, *thinking* difference within identity, quantity within quiddity, that remind one of
Plotinus's contemplation of a hypostasis, Nietzsche's contemplative history
of dialectic in *The Birth of Tragedy* (see chap. 1), and Hegel's own insight that
abstract determination "is such . . ., *for us, in our reflection,*" "belongs . . . to
our reflection."[161]

Evidently, Nicholas of Cusa is a dialectical thinker. Yet, had Ernst Cassirer his druthers, we should view him "als den ersten modernen Denker"
(*pace* Blumenberg!).[162] Edmond Vansteenberghe goes further in wondering
whether the Cusan is "un de pères de la pensée allemande" who anticipates
"Tout Hégel."[163] Erwin Metzke says: "Und doch ist niemand dem Denken des
Nicolaus von Cues so nahegekommen wie Hegel."[164] These claims may all be
true, but true for reasons that are bigger than either Nicholas or Hegel: they
both resemble each other because both draw from the larger medieval dialectical tradition of identity and difference. To be sure, this tradition shifts in
focus over the centuries, from Plotinus, who effectively moves dialectic from
rhetoric, logic, and dialogue to ontology, metaphysics, cosmology, and theology; to Proclus who systematizes dialectic of this precise sort and codifies
the centrality of identity/difference to dialectic; to Pseudo-Dionysius, who
enfolds dialectic into Christian contemplative practice, the meditation on the
contradictions in the world of appearance and the movement through these
from difference to identity to difference again; to the rest of philosophical
history up to Nicholas of Cusa, who in his tantalizingly quasi-modern way
carries on the mystical project within the enclosure of scholastic theology,
thinking his way (after all his years of reflection) to a superconcept that is the
Not-one, a conflate of identity/difference. My aim here is not to be exhaus-
tive, nor is it to be an Edward Casaubon, all promise and no goods. I intend,
rather, to identify when this dialectic of identity/difference emerged, and

for what reasons.[165] Having done that, I hope we can now begin to see what
Hegel saw in dialectic, and so clearly valued as *the* dialectic—the dialectic of
identity/difference.

Hegel's Way

Our task now is to make new sense of Hegel's dialectic—both his great interest in the categories of identity and difference and his words about the
dialectic as a problem reaching back to the Parmenides and forward to the
present.

If there is anything predictable about the *Phenomenology of Spirit*, it's not
that there is a telos to the whole work; rather, it is that Hegel believes in error
as a key component of the dialectical process. As he asks in a key passage:
"Should we not be concerned as to whether the fear of error is not just the
error itself?"[166] The answer, for Hegel, is obviously, yes. But what has now
become an epistemological cliché about the necessity of error in any process
of discovery and knowing should not screen us from viewing quite how he
frames this dialectical insight:

> To know something falsely means that knowledge is not adequate to, is not
> on equal terms with, its substance. Yet this very dissimilarity is the process
> of distinction in general, the essential moment in knowing. It is, in fact, out
> of this active distinction that its harmonious unity arises, and this identity,
> when arrived at, is truth. But it is not truth in a sense which would involve the
> rejection of the discordance, the diversity, like dross from pure metal; nor,
> again, does truth remain detached from diversity, like a finished article from
> the instrument that shapes it. Difference itself continues to be an immediate
> element within truth as such, in the form of the principle of negation.[167]

This passage—and the many others like it in Hegel—lacks punch because
most who are reading these words right now are, let's be frank, jaded by some
combination of Russian Formalism, structuralism, poststructuralism, and
postmodernism, all of which express the exact same point about the true
and the false differentially conceived. It is even a point that precedes Hegel.
But what remains important, and what will not suffer from overemphasis, is
that Hegel makes this claim *in the name of identity/difference*—dissimilarity
(*Ungleichheit*), distinguishing (*das Unterscheiden*), unity and identity (*Gleichheit*), diversity and difference (*Ungleichheit*). And he offers the claim as his
best explanation for how the dialectic *moves*, how it works, its rhythm.[168]
Even consciousness, even experience, follows the up and down, back and
forth motion of identity/difference.[169]

Granted, we quickly forget the centrality of identity/difference to Hegel as we read his prose, scratching our heads to figure out his exact meaning in any given passage. Adorno put it perfectly: "Hegel is no doubt the only one with whom at times one literally does not know, and cannot conclusively determine, what is being talked about."[170] But even in this case, we are dealing with Hegel's technique, his need to complexify (to borrow the French expression) the dialectic of identity/difference in all its variations and subtleties, if for no other reason than to narrate over the course of hundreds of pages sundry dialectical moments, step by excruciating step, without reduplication. It is in this narrative task that Hegel's vocabulary comes in handy—above all, the terms "in itself," "for itself," and "for and in itself"—which intricately describe kinds of relation, identity and differentiation among, and within, entities.[171] For example, elaborating on one of his more widely known remarks that "the spiritual alone is the actual," Hegel says, "It is essence, or that which has *being in itself*; it is that which *relates itself to itself* and is *determinate*, it is *other-being* and *being-for-itself*, and in this determinateness, or in its self, or in its self-externality, abides within itself; in other words, it is *in and for itself*."[172] And so it goes on, Hegel's penchant for describing, with his peculiar post-Kantian phraseology, all the possible modes of self- and other-relation, all the possible combinations whereby something (be it Spirit or consciousness)[173] differentiates itself within itself, relates itself to itself, and to others—or, and this next part is just as important, all the ways in which something falls back into itself and thus fails to enter into one mode of relation or another, at which point the dialectical movement comes to a halt.

But where the dialectic stops, it soon restarts. That, you can count on. Even in such cases it is not enough to speak of "error" or "failure," for a reading of Hegel demands a more precise generalization, which is what I now propose here: namely, it is often the case that the dialectical process becomes erratic, sluggish, or faltering only when his *preferred dialectic* breaks down into another kind of dialectic quite like those that build on the Aristotelian version of two sides at odds with one another, both with a legitimate claim to the truth of their position. In other words, the dialectic of identity and difference often runs into the sands and becomes, temporarily, a dialectic characterized by antinomy or equipollence, only to regain dialectical momentum when equipollence is overcome. We can observe this feature—it, too, is a narrative pattern—in three famous episodes in the *Phenomenology of Spirit* (though I hasten to say it is instanced across the entirety of this philosophical work): the passages on sense-certainty, the lord/bondsman, and the unhappy consciousness.

In his very first chapter on "Sense-Certainty," Hegel describes everyday, unreflective perception of things in the world, as they are given to the senses, as things before our very eyes: "All that [sense-certainty] says about what it knows is just that it *is*; and its truth contains nothing but the sheer *being* of the thing (Sache)."[174] Eventually, however, sense-certainty moves from immediacy to mediacy, from perceiving the sheer plurality of things to a sensing that there are differences among them, as well as differences between me and the objects I perceive:

> Among the countless differences cropping up here we find in every case that the crucial one is that, in sense-certainty, pure being at once splits up into what we have called the two "Thises," one "This" as "I", and the other "This" as object. When we reflect on this difference, we find that neither one nor the other is only *immediately* present in sense-certainty, but each is at the same time *mediated*: I have this certainty *through* something else, viz. the thing; and it, similarly, is in sense-certainty *through* something else, viz. through the "I."[175]

Hegel has just explained "difference" for the first time in the *Phenomenology* proper. As soon as "we reflect on this difference," as soon as we enter into reflective rather than spontaneous thinking about things, we discover mediation. Certainty originates not only in my mind but through "something else." Easy enough, but we are not yet at identity/difference, nor for that matter self-consciousness, even if Hegel's language of reciprocity here conveys exactly that impression, for the simple reason that the lesson about difference here is about the "I" and its sense-certainty, not about the thing. To be sure, Hegel wishes to ask questions about the thing *in* sense-certainty: "What is the *This*," after all?[176] And in so many sentences he shows that sense-certainty can only answer this question, can only define the thing, by stating what the thing is not.[177] But the trouble is that if you define any object by negation, then you discover its *indifference* to relation: that is, the object "is not in the least bit affected by its other-being."[178] It is entirely "in itself." Lest it seem that Hegel thinks that only objects can be indifferent, he turns back to the "I" to make the same point, showing how it falls back into "immediacy" and "indifference."[179]

There is a lot of back and forth here, and that is Hegel's point. He gives us a feel for a particular kind of dialectic that cannot function in ways we may expect as we cotton onto the allusions to reciprocity, or recognize the all too brief moments of mediation, the promise of intersubjectivity. His other point, as every commentary will tell you, is that all of this emphasis on the particular (the "This") generates its opposite, the "universal." Yet even in that lesson, we understand that difference comes first and makes the universal even possible, a point to which I will return below. For now, we can plainly see that in sense-certainty, there is no forward movement, only circularity; "it is always forgetting" what it learned and "starting the movement all over again."[180] It never achieves the kind of difference—or indeed the kind of identity in difference, and difference in identity—necessary to budge thinking to a new place. Thus, and not surprisingly, Hegel is comfortable winding down his analysis of sense-certainty by associating this kind of dialectic—and he calls it "dialectic" several times in this passage—with skepticism, which is, historically speaking, exactly the kind of dialectic that lacks a workable concept of identity/difference: "It is therefore astonishing when, in the face of this experience, it is asserted as universal experience and put forward, too, as . . . the outcome of Scepticism, that the reality or being of external things taken as Thises or sense-objects has absolute truth for consciousness."[181] So much for the universal. But looking back on all of what we have read in this section, we retrospectively realize that Hegel has in fact staged a skeptic dialectic encounter before naming it:

> In this relationship sense-certainty experiences the same dialectic acting upon itself as in the previous one. I, *this* 'I', see the tree and assert that 'Here' is a tree; but another 'I' sees the house and maintains that 'Here' is not a tree but a house instead. Both truths have the same authentication, viz. the immediacy of seeing, and the certainty and assurance that both have about their knowing.[182]

Hegel calls this situation "dialectic [Dialektik],"[183] because it is a taking of sides in a special way: "Both truths have the same authentication," a conclusion that sorts very well with the kind of skeptic dialectic perfected by Sextus Empiricus in his *Outlines of Pyrrhonism*, in the way both sides of a question or problem can be argued as, or authenticated as, truths.[184] That, clearly, is not the dialectic Hegel cares for, but we've gained enough from this section on sense-certainty: we've seen what sort of dialectic results when difference, mediation, and other-being do not stick around, and vanish just as quickly as they appear, dissolved either into the "in itself" or the "for itself."

Not so for the lord/bondsman dialectic. Before Hegel ever names the key players in question ("The former is the lord, the other the bondsman"),[185] he offers some program statements about what's required for self-consciousness to emerge—chiefly, reciprocity:

> Self-consciousness exists in and for itself when, and by the fact that, it exists for another. . . . Its moments, then, must on the one hand be held strictly apart, and on the other hand must in this differentiation at the same time also be taken and known as not distinct.[186]

Differentiated but not distinct, "teils in dieser Unterscheidung zugleich auch als nicht unterschieden."[187] Note Hegel's peculiar vocabulary I described above: self-consciousness has a "twofold significance [Doppelsinnigkeit]"[188] in that its identity—its moment of "in and for itself"—is at once "for another," a difference. What's more, self-consciousness epitomizes identity/difference because it recalls the very ancient problem of being and not-being to which Plotinus and those after him applied these logical terms to good effect: as Hegel puts it, self-consciousness is "aware that it at once is, and is not, another consciousness."[189] When both consciousnesses recognize one another, then they are set into a *relation*, whereby "each is for the other what the other is for it."[190] But if both separate and retreat into "lifeless, merely immediate, unopposed extremes," then "the two do not reciprocally give and receive one another back from each other consciously, but leave each other free only indifferently, like things."[191] And with the term "indifference" (*Gleichgültigkeit*),[192] we come to that non-dialectical designation Hegel uses so very often to describe relations of difference in identity that fail, absent of the desire to reciprocate.

It would seem that in cautioning against "indifference" Hegel anticipates his section on the Unhappy Consciousness, which follows immediately after the lord/bondsman dialectic and stands as an example of how the dialectic of identity/difference can "fall apart,"[193] breaking into Stoicism and Skepticism: the former renders difference into "lifeless indifference," the latter transforms difference into a "vanishing magnitude" and not a determination, not a real difference but "only the abstraction of differences."[194] No wonder, then, that when the Unhappy Consciousness finally appears as an outgrowth of Skepticism above all,[195] it cannot make heads or tails of its relation to the world, and instead resorts to jejune games, making a mockery of the categories of identity/difference:

> It keeps the poles of this its self-contradiction apart, and adopts the same attitude to it as it does in its purely negative activity in general. Point out likeness or identity to it, and it will point out unlikeness or non-identity [Wird ihm die Gleichheit aufgezeigt, so zeigt es die Ungleichheit auf]; and when it is now confronted with what it has just asserted, it turns round and points out likeness or identity. Its talk is in fact like the squabbling of self-willed children [ein Gezänke eigensinniger Jungen], one of whom says *A* if the other says *B*, and in turns says *B* if the other says *A*, and who by contradicting themselves buy for *themselves* the pleasure of continuing contradicting *one another*.[196]

Were these youngsters to use the categories of identity and difference in tandem, and as a way to generate dialectical *relation* (and not absolute difference), they would no longer be divided. They would be *related*, and the Unhappy Consciousness would be resolved. And that is Hegel's point: dialectic without the dialectical operations of identity/difference is worthless and puerile. The *Phenomenology* is rich in such moments (one of the best being §666–71).

In point of fact, you can go through the entire *Phenomenology of Spirit* in this fashion, picking out where identity/difference succeeds, dialectically, and where it falls into a non-dialectic of identity/*in*difference. In other words, my point about identity/difference is by no means local, intended to describe only the colorful or well-known passages by Hegel. Consistently throughout the *Phenomenology of Spirit* (and in the *Science of Logic*), Hegel displays these terms in their operations and—equally compelling—failures, and the sheer number of instances indicates to us that, indeed, these are Hegel's primary dialectical terms.[197] Yet many readers of Hegel have stated that he above all prefers the categories of individual/universal, and it is absolutely true that he does—the interplay between these two terms are on almost every page of the *Phenomenology of Spirit*—but he prefers them in a very specific way that points to the difference between the *content* of the dialectic and its *form* or formal operations. For Hegel, individual/universal does not name an operation of distinction making (or "determination"); rather, they point to a mode of content. These terms can be aptly described as the content of the dialectic itself in all its phases. Identity/difference are, however, as Hegel uses them, operations, processes of distinction making that frequently transform individuals into universals (as above), or universals into individuals, and for these reasons have no content on their own: they are processes of determination. As Hegel says declaratively, "Unity, difference, and relation are categories each of which is nothing in and for itself, but only in relation to its opposite, and they cannot therefore be separated from one another"—after which he goes on to show how these terms effect "the transition . . . from the form of the *one* or unit into that of *universality*."[198] Numerous passages evince the ways in which identity/difference operate as the relay between individual and universal, setting these terms in relation, and even (at one moment) defines the meaning of a universal as "what remains *identical with itself*."[199]

The entire *Phenomenology of Spirit*—the text with which I am chiefly concerned in this book—from its first chapter to its last, exhibits an overarching chiastic structure, with identity/difference appearing first and last and individual/universal emerging in between, appropriately enough, as the products of dialectical mediation. Hegel spoke of his speculative method as a circle, where the ending contains the beginning, but the repetition unfolds in reverse, like chiasmus. That is, in that first chapter on "Sense-Certainty," "difference" first teaches us, as we've already seen, to appreciate "sense-certainty *through* something else" (as above) giving rise to our knowledge of mediation, universals, and the momentary lesson that "it is in fact the universal that is the true content of sense-certainty";[200] whereas, in that final chapter on "Absolute Knowing," Hegel first turns his attention to individual/universal as reciprocal terms—"the movement of the universal through determination to individuality, as also the reverse movement from individuality to . . . the universal"[201]—before discarding them altogether and turning finally to the more ubiquitous and everlasting terms of identity/difference that, strikingly, survive even in the Absolute thanks to the "determinateness" of the Absolute itself: "For the self-knowing Spirit, just because it grasps its Concept, is the immediate identity [Gleichheit] with itself, which, in its difference [Unterschiede], is the certainty of immediacy, or sense-consciousness—the beginning from which we started."[202] Without identity/difference, then, there would be no dialectic of individual/universal or any other binary for that matter, insofar as all binaries are governed by an opposition of terms, each of whose identity is a function of that difference. Without those two terms at all, there would be no dialectic—a point that has as many historical implications as Hegelian ones.

If the *Phenomenology of Spirit* is, famously, the disposable propaedeutic to the *Science of Logic*, or to the rest of Hegel's writings for that matter, then it can be said that Hegel has worked something out here for himself to be featured in his other works: a dialectic of identity/difference that stands above all other dialectics, which includes not only the dialectic of universal/individual but the supreme dialectic of ancient philosophy, our very own starting point in thinking about Plato: the one and the many. In his *Science of Logic* Hegel construes the *quintessential* Platonic dialectic proposition involving the one and the many to be lacking in several respects:

It is an ancient proposition that *the one is many* and especially that *the many is one*. It should again be observed in this connection that, as expressed in propositions, the truth of the one and the many appears in inadequate form; such a truth is to be grasped and expressed only as a becoming, as a process, a repulsion and attraction—not as being, in the way the latter is posited in a proposition as inert unity. Earlier mention was made recalling Plato's dialectic in the *Parmenides* on the derivation of the many from the one, specifically from the proposition: the one is. It is the internal dialectic of the concept that has been expounded; it is easiest to grasp the dialectic of the proposition, *that the many is one*, as external reflection; and, inasmuch as the subject matter also, *the many*, is a mutual externality, reflection may indeed be external here. This comparison of the many with one another immediately shows that each is absolutely determined just as any other; each is a one, each a one of many; each is by excluding the others—so that they are absolutely the same; absolutely one determination is present. This is a *matter of fact*, and all that needs to be done is simply to grasp the fact. If in its stubbornness the understanding refuses to do it, it is only because it *also* has distinction in mind, and rightly so; but distinction is not left out because of that fact, as surely as the fact is no less there despite distinction. One could, as it were, reassure the understanding concerning this simple grasp of the fact of unity that distinction will also come in again.[203]

Why is it that "the truth of the one and the many appears in inadequate form" when it is "expressed in propositions"? This question gets at the root of Hegel's concern not only with ancient dialectic—the propositional content from which the very problem of the one/many is derived as "the one is"—but also with propositions themselves. Hegel here indicates that "such a truth" (of the one/many) "is to be grasped and expressed only as a becoming, as a process," not only as a proposition. If we've eaten our vegetables that is the propaedeutic *Phenomenology of Spirit*, we already know what's required of propositions if they are going to have anything to do with dialectic. That is, in that earlier text, he writes that "dialectical movement . . . has propositions for its parts or elements," but a proposition must not be the assertion of a static position and "mere content" but also a formal process, an "opposite movement," which he calls the "return of the Notion [or Concept] into itself."[204] What any given proposition *says* is less important than how it moves, goes out from itself to propose *something else*, and returns to itself having gone through its opposition: it returns modified, only to repeat the process again.[205] Thus, "this movement . . . constitutes . . . the dialectical movement of the proposition itself."[206] Applying this lesson to the *Science of Logic* in the above passage, Hegel indicates that the ancient dialectic of the one/many must appreciate that "each is absolutely determined just as any other"; only a stubborn expositor would refuse this point—a refusal, Hegel is clear to say, that itself points to the ineluctability of "distinction."

And so? The simple point is before our very eyes. *Hegel applies the dialectic of identity/difference to the ancient problem of the one/many precisely in the way medievals do.*[207] Hegel knows what's up. For him, there is no pure Plato; only a mediated Plato, mediated by centuries of medieval commentary on the *Parmenides*, commentary within which the dialectic of identity/difference was conceived.

Coda on Antinomies: What about Kant?

If it appears that this brief history of the medieval dialectic of identity and difference is a creature of Hegelian observation—that only Hegel would understand the historicity of these logical terms, only Hegel would use them in contradistinction to classical forms of dialectic or zombie forms of modern skeptic dialectic—we should give Kant, hailed at the outset of this chapter, the final say, if for no other reason than to show the proximity of these premodern dialectical problems to what can be loosely called German idealism and, more specifically, transcendental idealism. We would not, after all, want these issues to seem too much of a thing of the past. Or would we?

Kant would say yes. In his *Critique of Pure Reason*, he offers a series of dialectic examples in his four antinomies, which mimic that scholastic disputational form of arguing "pro" and "contra" on a proposition as a matter of formal training within the university. Rather brilliantly, he argues both sides, the "thesis" and the "antithesis," of propositions such as, "Does the world have a beginning in time and is limited by space?"[208] In arguing both sides, he shows that both the thesis and the antithesis of any proposition about the world, the composition of things, and the problems of freedom, necessity, and contingency can be thoroughly and persuasively argued. That very demonstration is both the point and the problem: the self-consistency and confidence of each side begins to appear troubling and shows the degree to which each position is rationalized on its own terms. While, technically speaking, Kant intends to expose the outright failure of "pure reason" to understand the difference between the matters of empiricism (or appearances), intuition (or the a priori of space and time), and pure speculation (metaphysics), his overall aim is to expose dialectic to be, to use his phrase, "merely dialectical."

What does he mean by this criticism? I believe Kant intends to show that dialectical arguments, dialectical oppositions, that proceed according to the logic of identity/difference are false ones. In other words, for Kant, the "merely dialectical" seeks to prove itself true by showing its opposite to be false; it establishes its own identity through, obviously, difference.[209] Kant goes on to show that what is lost to both sides caught in a "merely dialectical" scenario—and this point gets at the core of his effort to vitiate the dialectic of identity and difference, ensconce it within the table of categories, and demote its importance to just one of several logical functions, and instead offer his own "transcendental" alternative—is that each opposite is already a false one, an artificial difference mistaken for a real one, because each side is, from the first, talking about different orders of reality: one speaks of appearances, the other of noumena. If you are caught up in the world of appearance, you are not arguing against a supposed opponent concerned with noumena, thereby precluding any effort to construct an opposite as the negative image of your own position, and so forth.[210] Of course, Kant, as is his wont, makes order out of this disorder, stating that all four of the antinomies—again, un-beknownst to the dialecticians—evince a proof for transcendental idealism in the ways they split up reality according to noumena and phenomena.[211] By rather ingenious argumentation, then, Kant casts the dialectic behind as the empty shell of history.

But of what history? The Middle Ages? Kant opts for a distinct anti-medievalism—a "most acute criticism" indeed—to put to rest the flights of fancy notorious among the pure reasoners.[212] For him, the dialectic is a moi-ety of archaic modes, scholastic argumentation peppered with quasi-feudal ideas about honor and conflict:

> Unfortunately for speculation (but perhaps fortunately for the practical voca-tion) of humanity, reason sees itself, in the midst of its greatest expectations, so entangled in a crowd of arguments and counterarguments that it is not feasible, on account either of its honor or even its security, for reason to with-draw and look upon the quarrel with indifference, as a mere mock fight.[213]

In viewing the dialectic as a "mere mock fight" involving the noble value of honor and a militaristic sense of security, Kant is rendering the dialectic not only as philosophically irrelevant but as an antiquarian curiosity evoking knights in armor: "For the only battleground for [pure reason] would have to be sought in the field of pure theology and psychology; but this ground will bear no warrior in full armor and equipped with weapons to be feared."[214] Such anti-medievalism freely flows forth throughout the *Critique*: "Fight as they may, the shadows that they cleave apart grow back together again in an instant, like the heroes in Valhalla, to amuse themselves anew in the blood-less battles."[215]

Kant's fish to fry is not medieval philosophy, however. It is contempo-rary philosophy, especially metaphysics, that has fallen "back into the same old worm-eaten *dogmatism*."[216] In particular, though here without naming names, Kant is referring to the philosopher Christian Wolff, whose "theoreti-cal philosophy" falls rather precisely into the four "propositions" of Kant's antinomies.[217] Wolff is by no means a theological throwback to the Middle Ages—instead, he was an inveterate reasoner using mathematics as a basis for all inquiry[218]—but Kant painted him and his present-day students with the brush of anti-medievalism, in which "what rules is tedium and complete indifferentism, the mother of chaos and night in the sciences, but at the same time also the origin . . . of their incipient transformation and enlighten-ment."[219] In the preface to the second edition of the *Critique*, Kant is even more explicit in his choice of terms and target. There, he lets us know that contemporary metaphysics are a holdover from an earlier age—"it is older than all other sciences, and would remain even if all the others were swallowed up by an all-consuming barbarism";[220] it is a form of pseudo-debate (or non-dialectic), in which disagreement is the norm and mock contestations the convention: "it is so far from reaching unanimity in the assertions of its adherents that it is rather a battlefield, and indeed one that appears to be especially determined for testing one's powers in mock combat."[221] And here, the target emerges as "the famous Wolff, the greatest among all dogmatic philosophers," heralding the "dogmatic way of thinking prevalent in his age, and for this the philosophers of his as all previous times have nothing for which to reproach themselves."[222] For Kant, Wolff's methods are as old as they come; disagreement in the schools is saddled, if not by *politesse*, then by ungrounded debates that go nowhere and everywhere all at once, devolving into contradictions left and right and never making an advance toward an empirically grounded science.

Hegel would have none of this. And one can be sure it is not on account of Wolff,[223] nor, for that matter, medieval scholastic logic, which, like so many previous schools in the history of philosophy, Hegel found to misunderstand the dialectic, as his lectures on the history of philosophy make abundantly clear.[224] His main objection to Kant comes in both the *Science of Logic* and *Encyclopedia of the Philosophical Sciences*, in which Hegel shows that Kant fails to recognize the key characteristics of dialectical method: "Since each of the two opposed sides contains its other within itself and neither can be thought without the other, it follows that neither of these determinations, taken alone, has truth; this belongs to their unity. This is the true dialectical consideration of them and also the true result."[225] Kant's sham scholastic debate is anything but dialectical because, primarily, both opposed positions neglect to define themselves over and against their Other, *even if* they are talking about different domains. Hegel is quite correct in this criticism, because elsewhere in the *Critique of Pure Reason* Kant views the dialectical process as the contriving of artificial counter-hypotheses, objections for the sake of objecting that are "not steeled through any law of experience" and which themselves have no limit; as Kant says, "But you could go even further, and indeed raise new doubts, which have either not been suggested before or else have not been driven far enough."[226]

Yet Hegel's *best* objection to Kant—one that opens the door to the next chapter on the lord/bondsman dialectic—revolves around the problem of self-consciousness: "Kantian philosophy no doubt leads reality back to self-consciousness, but it can supply no reality to this essence of self-consciousness."[227] Hegel regards the transcendental subject (what he finds to be Kant's attempt to describe self-consciousness) as "completely void and

general," "completely indeterminate and abstract."[228] Kant himself, according to Hegel, "fall[s] into contradiction, what with the barbarity of the conceptions which he refutes, and the barbarity of his own conceptions which
remain behind when the others are refuted."[229] For Hegel, Kantianism is as
crude and barbarous as the scholasticism Kant himself seeks to caricature in
his barbarous antinomies: "This philosophy made an end of the metaphysic
of the understanding as an objective dogmatism, but in fact it merely transformed it into a subjective dogmatism,"[230] because "it does not know how
to obtain mastery over the individuality of self-consciousness."[231] In other
words, Hegel finds Kantianism to be "idealism," a "subjective dogmatism"
that can only be overcome or *grounded* when consciousness depends on an
Other for definition, a consciousness that will eventually find "difference"
and contradiction within itself, within the Other, and everywhere else.[232]

Readers with only a passing familiarity with Hegel's master/slave or lord/
bondsman dialectic will recognize its terms here: when consciousness becomes master of itself ("Meister zu werden") and is not subject to the Other, it
attains self-consciousness.[233] For Hegel, this very dialectic provides what Kant's
transcendental subject could not, "reality to this essence of self-consciousness."
My aim in the next chapter is to explain some of the specific features of this
"reality," the ways in which Hegel consistently grounds this dialectic of a very
material, yet strikingly contemporary sort in the Middle Ages. Hegel, that is,
inverts Kant's dialectic (to echo Marx's motif of "inversion") and formulates
his own dialectical insights about self-consciousness against the Kantian transcendental subject, which he finds to be overidealized and ungrounded.[234] The
medieval terms of both Kant's and Hegel's dialectics make the point. Whereas
Kant stages the dialectic as an abstract scholastic struggle in which "no com-
batant has ever gained the least bit of ground, nor has any been able to base
any lasting possession on his victory,"[235] Hegel in his lord/bondsman dialectic
proffers a struggle between two persons of different status, the lord and the
bondsman, competing for the material possessions upon which their lives depend—first and foremost, land.

PART TWO

History

HORKHEIMER: The idea that freedom consists in self-determination is really rather pathetic, if all it means is that the work my master formerly ordered me to do is the same as the work I now seek to carry out on my own free will; the master did not determine his own actions.

ADORNO: The concept of self-determination has nothing to do with freedom. According to Kant, autonomy means obeying oneself.

HORKHEIMER: A misunderstanding of feudalism.

ADORNO: A necessary false consciousness, ideology.

HORKHEIMER: German idealism, bourgeois ideology: the absolute positing of the semblance of self-determination in feudalism from the standpoint of the bourgeoisie.

3

The Lord and the Bondsman

It has not occurred to any one of these philosophers to inquire into the connection of German philosophy with German reality, the relation of their criticism to their own material surroundings.

MARX AND ENGELS

Germany will not be able to emancipate itself from the *Middle Ages* unless it emancipates itself at the same time from the *partial* victories over the Middle Ages.

MARX

Marx's views about Hegel and Hegelianism are well known. What is not well known is that Marx, in writing these remarks above with Engels, overlooked two important things about his predecessor: Hegel *did* in fact connect "German philosophy with German reality," and he deeply understood that "*partial* victories over the Middle Ages" were insufficient. Of course, it is clear what these words are about. Marx, here and elsewhere, needs to declare his difference from Hegel because he adopts more or less wholesale Hegel's dialectic. As he says: "I . . . openly avowed myself the pupil of that mighty thinker. The mystification which dialectic suffers in Hegel's hands by no means prevents him from being the first to present its general form of working in a comprehensive and conscious manner."[1] But had Marx permitted himself to realize that Hegel's dialectic is not simply a mystification but an exemplary instance of relating "criticism" to "material surroundings," we would be thinking very differently about Hegel today. We would understand how presciently Marxist he often is.

In this chapter, I wish to present this different Hegel—a Hegel whose famous dialectic of the master and the slave, above all, can be shown to be a materialist critique of feudalism so rigorous and perceptive, so illustrative of the dynamics of identity/difference, as to be the signal instance of what makes theory "critical" in the first place. We continue, then, to follow the history of identity/difference, pivoting from assessing the place of this logical, dialectical form in medieval philosophy, as outlined in the previous two chapters, to its exemplary operations within the most memorable section of the *Phenomenology of Spirit*, where Hegel places this special dialectic within history, showing in detail how identity/difference, of all logical terms, is an adequate depiction of the struggle for recognition and possession out of which emerges a universal form of self-consciousness at a particular moment in time. We move, therefore, from philosophy and theory to "history," as signaled by the title of Part II of this book, yet—in aspiring to be true to dialectical form—we will be looking closely at Hegel's insights into the connection between history and theory, between criticism and its material surroundings (to echo Marx), discerning what exactly gives Hegel his proto-Marxist edge, what makes him theoretical.

This decidedly critical Hegel comes into view when we recognize that, both by historical accident and ethical conviction, he stood in a privileged place from which to philosophize about feudalism and, in particular, the contemporary relations of lordship and domination—*Herrschaft* (lordship) or *Grundherrschaft* (landed lordship)—practiced in Germany, and only partially identified by Marx.[2] What James J. Sheehan documents in his *German History, 1770–1866*—that Hegel's was a feudal Germany—is corroborated by many other studies:[3] "After reviewing five centuries of agrarian history, Jerome Blum concluded that in the middle of the eighteenth century, 'the face of rural Europe looked much as it had in the Middle Ages. . . . The great mass of people . . . lived at the narrow margin of subsistence, as much at the mercy of the shortage of food as their forbears had been in the thirteenth century.' "[4] Even if after 1750 we may observe the beginnings of improvements in agricultural processes, organization, and education, Sheehan insists that we "should not overestimate the rate or extent of change in the German country side."[5] For our purposes here in historically situating Hegel, it can be noted that Germany, both western and eastern Germany (or Prussia), is a prime example of uneven and mixed economic development with feudal arrangements persisting within the newer capitalist ones long after Hegel's death.[6] This is not to say that Hegel should be read as a sociologist reporting the facts of the feudal matter. It is to say, very bluntly, that Hegel effectively lived in the Middle Ages (if the persistence of feudalism, and so many of the old institutions outlined in my preface, are any indication) and that, accordingly, his narrative of master and slave relations resonates with the feudal political conditions of agrarian Germany. He, in other words, came to a persuasive and lasting theoretical statement about feudalism itself in his master/slave dialectic, knowing full well that the struggle between possession and ownership of land ultimately characterizes the personal relations of domination in *Herrschaft*.

As if in pursuit of this thesis, Herbert Marcuse wrote, "Hegel's early philosophical concepts were formulated amid a decaying German Reich. . . . The remains of feudal despotism still held sway in Germany, the more oppressive because split into a multitude of petty despotisms. . . . Serfdom was still prevalent, the peasant was still a beast of burden."[7] And more specifically, Theodor Adorno remarks that this "chapter of the *Phenomenology* historically conjures up feudalism."[8] Our task is to improve upon these insights by following closely Hegel's dialectical scenario of the master and the slave, teasing out its feudal terms and images, describing its feudal dynamics and logics, and taking stock of the fact that Hegel adds feudal *content* to the already medieval dialectical *form* of identity/difference (chap. 2), resulting in an example that explains struggle, no matter the historical setting.[9] Here, I will assemble and review versions of the master/slave dialectic in Hegel's works where it has never been properly studied in one place—the *System of Ethical Life, Philosophy of Right, Philosophy of Mind*, the lectures on the philosophy of history—and then return to the most studied example in the *Phenomenology of Spirit*, where I hope to show that Hegel's presentation of the feudal struggle for possession, considered by most commentators to be abstract and idealistic, is fully embedded in materiality and history.[10]

The Feudalism of the Dialectic

Jean Hyppolite pithily summarizes the lesson of the master/slave dialectic in saying that it "consists essentially in showing that the truth of the master reveals that he is the slave, and that the slave is revealed to be the master of the master."[11] There are several other good summaries of Hegel's insights,[12] but I want to linger on one of the most influential explications of Hegel's dialectic—that by Alexandre Kojève, whose views have led to a consensus of critical opinion about this portion of the *Phenomenology*. Kojève had effectively kicked off the Hegelian renaissance in France with his lectures at L'École Pratique des Hautes Études beginning in the late 1930s. These lectures were heard and/or absorbed by the likes of Georges Bataille, André Breton, Alexandre Koyre, Jacques Lacan, Emmanuel Lévinas, Maurice Merleau-Ponty, Raymond Queneau, Jean-Paul Sartre, and Eric Weil.[13] Kojève also had an important colleague in the Hegelian Hyppolite, who translated Hegel's *Phenomenology* into French in the spirit of Kojève's reading, and whose students included Louis Althusser, Gilles Deleuze, Jacques Derrida, and Michel Foucault.[14] Hegel's theory of "Otherness," generated by the dialectic of desire and recognition involving the master and the slave, has been ubiquitous in critical writing,[15] thanks in large part to Kojève and his students.[16]

The strengths of Kojève's reading are very clear. Kojève renders the master/slave dialectic as itself a lucid narrative of the coming to self-consciousness, drawing out the Hegelian premise that this coming to self-consciousness involves not simply another's recognition of one's own desire and subjectivity; it also requires putting oneself at risk. As Kojève puts it, "to speak of the 'origin' of Self-Consciousness is necessarily to speak of the risk of life"; it is to speak of a "fight to the death for pure prestige," putting "the life of the other in danger—in order to be 'recognized' by the other."[17] Readers of the English edition of the *Phenomenology* will find these remarks especially illustrative of paragraphs 178 to 189. Kojève also characterizes the remainder of the narrative (paragraphs 190–96 of the English edition) by pointing out that this "fight to the death" must become a different kind of struggle. For, after all, how does a dead person recognize anyone?[18] The "fight to the death" is no option, as it forecloses the opportunities for self-consciousness. There has to be a struggle whereby each side seeks to "overcome" the other, and this is the important point, "dialectically."[19] This is the struggle between the master and the slave per se; both sides resolve the struggle not by eliminating the other but rather by remaining in a relationship of inequality and interdependency. It is the battle of wills and a struggle for recognition.

It is the nature of this inequality that concerns me and which compels me to dare part ways with Kojève and most other commentators, who at this point take an even sharper phenomenological turn than I believe is necessary, a turn toward those perceptual problems of recognition and intersubjectivity in which death becomes a determining factor at the expense of other factors.[20] The trouble is that this phenomenological turn is not, it may seem odd to say, very Hegelian, because this move abstracts and obscures the underlying material problems of possession evident in Hegel's master/slave dialectic. Possession is indeed the glaring missing term in many analyses of this portion of the *Phenomenology*, including Kojève's.[21] This critical omission is crucial because, for Hegel, possession, be it possession of self (as self-consciousness) or of things (as in the mastery of equipmental totalities), is achieved through labor and is expressed phenomenally or socially by one's relationship to labor.[22] Hegel would not want the questions of labor and possession to be kept apart (and neither would Marx, for that matter), nor would he want us to blanket over the specificity of this struggle for possession, overdetermined as it is by rank and status—the feudal particulars of "lord" qua "lord" and "bondsman" qua "bondsman," and their own relationship to labor and property.

I did mean *lord* and *bondsman* and not *master* and *slave*, nor *maître* and *esclave*. And so did Hegel. This is my first point: we have been continuously

THE LORD AND THE BONDSMAN   69

mistranslating Hegel. Kojève's, Hyppolite's, Lacan's, and Slavoj Žižek's (mis)translations are cases in point, and they are only the tip of the post-Hegelian iceberg.[23] It is indeed the lord/serf or lord/bondsman dialectic, and below we shall see that these feudal terms confirm Hegel's interest in feudal forms of possession in the *Phenomenology of Spirit.* Meanwhile, this is not only a problem of translation. Most English commentators, despite the fact that the most widely used English edition of the *Phenomenology* gets it right in rendering *der Herr* and *der Knecht* as "lord" and "bondsman," hold that Hegel meant nothing by these words other than a generality about masters and slaves. We cannot discount Kojève as an influence here, too, given the ubiquity of what's been called, rightly or wrongly, "French theory" in the academic humanities in the United Kingdom and North America.

Yet Hegel is relatively consistent in his use of terms. In texts such as the *System of Ethical Life, Philosophy of Right,* the lectures on the philosophy of history, the *Philosophy of Mind,* and the *Phenomenology of Spirit,* Hegel uses *Herr* and *Knecht* with purpose and distinction.[24] That he means these to be feudal terms is indicated by the fact that whenever he examines slavery in Greek and Roman society, he prefers a different term, *Sklave,* for "slave."[25] For instance, in *Philosophy of Right,* Hegel explains: "Thus in Roman law, for example, there could be no definition of 'man', since 'slave' [Sklave] could not be brought under it—that very status of slave indeed is an outrage on the conception of man."[26] In the same work, Hegel goes on to compare *Sklaverei* and *Herrschaft,* emphasizing how both slave-masters and feudal lords justify their domination over others:

> The alleged justification of slavery [Sklaverei] (by reference to all its proximate beginnings through physical force, capture in war, saving and preservation of life, upkeep, education, philanthropy, the slave's own acquiescence, and so forth), as well as the justification of a slave-ownership [Herrschaft] as simple lordship [Herrenschaft] in general, all historical views of the justice of slavery [Recht der Sklaverei] and lordship [Herrenschaft], depend on regarding man as a natural entity pure and simple, as an existent not in conformity with its concept (an existent to which arbitrariness is appropriation).[27]

It should be clear, with the insertion of the German terms in brackets, that the English rendering has not served its readers well, for the point of this passage is to say that "the justification of *Sklaverei* . . . *as well as* the justification of *Herrschaft* as *Herrenschaft*" rest on an idea of humanity as a "natural entity pure and simple" that can be appropriated and taken as property as can (supposedly) any other natural object. While Hegel observes, in other words, that two kinds of domination across history have something terrible in common, he is not claiming that *Sklaverei* and *Herrschaft* are therefore the same. If they were, he would not have used two different terms.[28]

Where these two forms of domination differ is in the distinction between *Sklave* and *Knecht*. Here is how Hegel unpacks the distinction, elaborating on his remarks above:

> The position of the free will, with which right and the science of right begin, is already in advance of the false position at which man, as a natural entity and only the concept implicit, is for that reason capable of being enslaved. This false, comparatively primitive, phenomenon of slavery is one which befalls mind when mind is only at the level of consciousness. The dialectic of the concept and of the purely immediate consciousness of freedom brings about at that point the fight for recognition and the relationship of lord *and bondsman*.[29]

Hegel's thought unfolds across passages—that is the point of his dialectical exposition or *Darstellung*—and this one is no exception. He begins by saying that the science of right (*Rechtswissenschaft*) is already ahead of "the primitive phenomenon of slavery [Sklaverei]," already far beyond any notion of *Recht der Sklaverei* (above) that would justify the enslavement of humans. Where things change is in the "dialectic" that brings about a new situation and a new way of thinking about human freedom—or one could say, the new situation that brings about that "dialectic" between the concept of freedom and the immediate or spontaneous sense of freedom (which is the primitive, non-universal form).[30] Either way, Hegel means to talk about a "dialectic" that wasn't previously available to the "sklave"—namely, "the fight for recognition [Anerkennens] and the relationship of lord and bondsman [das Verhältnis der Herrenschaft und der Knechtschaft]." But when that "dialectic" begins, so too does a new identity (*Knecht*) and a new relation, to self and to other (*Herr*). This distinction explains why Hegel changes terms here, shifting from a discussion of *Sklaverei* to that of *Knechtschaft*, and why—most importantly—he never uses *Sklave* or *Sklaverei* to refer to the *Knecht* and his new opportunities for self-consciousness in the *Phenomenology of Spirit*.[31] Hegel wants to keep these terms apart, and he is consistent about these distinctions in his early *First Philosophy of Spirit* (1803–4), in which he never uses the word *Knecht*, because there he is trying to explain how enslavement transpires;[32] and in his later *Philosophy of Mind*, especially sections §432,[33] §433,[34] and §435.[35] There, Hegel observes differences between *Knecht* and *Sklave* in ways consistent with his thinking in the *Philosophy of Right*.[36]

A word makes a world of difference. That Hegel omits *Sklaverei* in the relevant portion of the *Phenomenology* makes historical sense, in turn help-

ing us to discern the historical frame of reference in which he sets his lord/
bondsman dialectic (if it's not obvious already).[37] For instance, in the lectures on the philosophy of history, he states "that self-consciousness which
independence confers, [the Greeks] could not have"; of "the *Greek spirit*,"
he believes that the principle of freedom "is peculiar to the individual," that
freedom is not a universal whereby self-possession can be attained as a moral
imperative.[38] The idea of freedom here is not premised on, or motivated by,
an antagonism toward a powerful Other nor does it involve that element of
mediation that will be crucial to the struggle for possession, land: "Greek
freedom of thought is excited by an alien existence; but it is free because it
transforms and virtually reproduces the stimulus by its own operation."[39]
As such, there is no dialectic of desire or recognition of the kind Hegel lays
out in the relevant portions of the *Phenomenology of Spirit*, nor a struggle for
possession.[40] Indeed, Hegel says in numerous places that ancient slaves never
achieve universal self-consciousness. While anyone with a pulse should be
politically unsympathetic with that view, political wishes should not distort
Hegel's point (though this is by no means to exclude the best possibilities
of a Left Hegelianism, which distinguishes the Frankfurt School, especially
Adorno). We also cannot assume, as many commentators have, that Hegel's
Herr/Knecht dialectic is a commentary strictly about classical antiquity.[41]
That would be a philosophical mistake—at least in Hegelian terms—and it
would be missing Hegel's point about history.[42] For it is only in the Romantic
era, as Hegel understands it, only in the European or Christian Middle Ages,
in other words, that we begin to see modernity and freedom. In Christianity, "self-consciousness had reached the phases of development [Momente]";
and, "under Christianity Slavery is impossible [die Sklaverei ist im Christen-
tum unmöglich]."[43] Granted, serfdom, as many have noted before, including medieval commentators, is a form of slavery and is explicitly called that,
but not all slavery is precisely serfdom—*unless* Hegel is speaking in absolute
and undialectical terms, whereby opportunities for self-consciousness are
altogether unavailable for the slave who is himself constituted purely as an
object, a possession.[44]

　　Yet, for Hegel, feudalism—whether it is that exampled in the Middle Ages
or in practices in contemporary Germany—is the specific political structure
and social arrangement within which modernity and freedom are realized,
a point to be well taken if we are to give any credence to this important and
most widely cited passage:

> In the same way that serfdom [Leibeigenschaft], which made a man's body
> [der Leib] not his own, but the property of another, dragged humanity

through all the barbarism of serfdom [der Knechtschaft] and unbridled desire, and the latter was destroyed by its own violence. It was not so much *from*
serfdom [aus der Knechtschaft] as *through* serfdom [durch die Knechtschaft]
that humanity was emancipated.[45]

Hegel is writing here on the German Middle Ages, but this point is iterated
across his oeuvre. It would be unwise to ignore the consequences of the historical specificity of the lord/bondsman dialectic—and the largely feudal
frame in which he formulates it.[46] Likewise, it would be unsound to ignore
precisely what Hegel means by emancipation "through serfdom." It means
that history has to reach a point where *Knechtschaft*, not *Sklaverei*, is prevalent, so that through serfdom (*durch die Knechtschaft*) emancipation and
universal self-consciousness can be achieved. My point here is to grant that
this particular dialectic can mean many things, even the many things of the
French Hegelians, but no amount of idealizing Hegel can do away with the
precise terms of feudalism on display here.[47] If we insist on seeing this dialectical scenario as an allegory for all struggles across history, and if we find
that its particular set of contradictions and reversals are compelling enough
to apply across diverse bodies of thought, then we will want to know how
Hegel, in his usual fashion, can carry off phenomenology *as* history: feudalism affords him that opportunity—a first chance to adopt the medieval as a
perspective on modernity.

The Dialectic of Possession

Possession swallows its tail.

ED PAVLIC

In seeking to understand the meaning of Hegel's *Herr/Knecht* dialectic as a
struggle for possession, we must begin with the classic question of feudalism so well articulated by the historians J. A. F. Thomson and Marc Bloch:
"Whose land is this?"[48] Likewise, the historian J. J. Sheehan asks of the German situation, "Who controls the land?" explaining how "this turns out
to be an extremely difficult question to answer," owing to the ambiguities
of ownership in feudalism.[49] The question, in fact, goes to the crux of the
contradiction in feudalism: numerous persons within the feudal hierarchies,
from bottom to top, could answer, "This land is mine!" "It is mine because
I manage it," says the manorial lord. "It is mine because my family has been
working on this land for generations," says the peasant farmer. "No to both
of you, this is my land because I hold the deed that goes back centuries," says
the neighboring magnate. "No to all three of you, because your deed is false

because it was written by monks," says another. And so on. There begins the conflict or antagonism up and down feudal society. Historians are unanimous on the point that feudalism is characterized by this peculiar struggle for possession, a struggle between "ownership" and "effective possession" of land—the former a mode of possession via legal right and military force, the latter a mode of possession via labor. Marxist historians especially, such as Perry Anderson, Barry Hindess and Paul Q. Hirst, and Rodney Hilton, accept that this struggle generated the new forms of peasant self-consciousness exhibited throughout the late Middle Ages, whereby serfs broke their servile bonds and became themselves landholders.[50]

Hegel is working this angle so as to cast the struggle for possession and the contradictions between ownership and effective possession as the motor of his *Herr/Knecht* dialectic, and in so doing he writes in miniature a history of feudalism or, better, a dialectical scenario that pointedly emphasizes the central problem of any feudal formation. That much is clear in the *System of Ethical Life*, the *Philosophy of Right*, and the lectures on the philosophy of history. We shall treat these texts here, bearing in mind that *System of Ethical Life* is especially relevant for being either a draft of the *Philosophy of Right* or the *Phenomenology of Spirit*. In these three texts, we find the feudal problems of labor, possession, alienation, surplus, and extraction that will be relevant to our rereading of *Phenomenology of Spirit* and, ultimately, to a sense as to why Hegel is presciently Marxist.

In *System of Ethical Life*, Hegel, in true dialectical fashion, discusses these topics within a narrative frame about the transition from one form of labor to another. He speaks not about the transition from feudalism to capitalism, nor of these as modes of production in the Marxian sense. Rather, his interest is to speak of the ever-changing *relationship to labor* (as opposed to the Marxian interest in the shifting and ever-alienating relationships to the means of production). Hegel calls these two relationships "the living natural relation" and the "fixed relation." The natural relation or natural labor is a whole way of life that satisfies all need through labor.[51] The "fixed" or "universal" relation appears to involve the more historically familiar forms of labor ranging from feudalism to protocapitalism that generate dispossession and alienation. Hegel's chief interest is in the confrontation between these two forms of labor. While his wording on this point seems obscure—"The living natural relation becomes nevertheless a fixed relation which it was not previously; also universality must hover over this natural relation and overcome this fixed relation"[52]—some terminological clarification can help. By *universal*, Hegel does not mean the more colloquial "applicable to everyone or every case" nor the more philosophical sense of "a generality adequate to every particular under its class." Rather, he uses the terms *fixed* and *universal* to speak of an effect, of what happens when a universal *confronts* a particular, when a feudal or protocapitalist form of labor absorbs these specific and various organic labor processes through generalizing demands such as the parceling and specialization of labor tasks. When natural labor confronts for the first time a new, universalized mode of labor not emergent from the particulars of "life," much less the laborer's and family's own needs, when such a universal is imposed on natural labor, alienation begins. Natural labor becomes "partitioned" and "more mechanical, because variety is excluded from it, and so it becomes itself something more universal, more foreign to [the living] whole." Any natural labor that is not integrated into "universality" or the new laboring organization becomes a remainder, a surplus. This surplus becomes the subject of a struggle for possession, and a further cause of alienation.[53]

That the dialectical struggle concerns possession is quite clear, as the following passage indicates: "Thus this possession has lost its meaning for the practical feeling of the subject and is no longer a need of his, but a *surplus*. . . . The subject is [not] simply determined as a possessor, but is taken up into the form of universality; he is a single individual with a bearing on others and universally negative as a possessor recognized as such by others."[54] At one point, Hegel describes this "universal negative" that is now possession as a force, like a magnet, compelled toward unification—in other words, toward repossession.[55] At another point, he speaks of the "recognition of possession."[56] It is in this latter form that we come upon the struggle that would be (for twentieth- and twenty-first century readers) a centerpiece of the *Phenomenology of Spirit*, and which for Hegel in *System of Ethical Life* assumes the problematics of freedom, property, and possession:

> But because the individual as such is purely and simply one with (his) life, not simply related to life, it is impossible to say of life, as it could be said of other things with which he is purely in relation, that he possesses it. . . . In this recognition of life or in the thinking of the other as absolute concept, the other (person) exists as a free being, as the possibility of being the opposite of himself with respect to some specific characteristic. . . . At this (level) a living individual confronts a living individual, but their power (*Potenz*) of life is unequal. Thus one is might or power over the other. . . . This relation in which the indifferent and free has power over the different is the relationship of *lordship and bondage* (or master and servant).[57]

With regard to the last set of editorial insertions by the translators, Hegel writes: "Dieses Verhältniß, das indifferente und freye, das mächtige ist, ge-

gen das differente, is das Verhältniß *der Herrschafft und Knechtschafft*."[58] We proceed: "The master is in possession of a surplus, of what is physically necessary; the servant lacks it [der Herr ist im Besitz eines Überflusses des physischen Nothwendigen überhaupt, und der andere im Mangel desselben]".[59] The bondsman recognizes the lord's freedom, the lord as a "free being," but does he recognize his own freedom in this ineluctable power relation?[60] Does he achieve self-consciousness?

The answer to this question brings us to the center of the feudal arrangements, and ever deeper into the *System of Ethical Life*, where Hegel speaks of "the classes" of society. These he divides into three—the "absolute and free," the "honest" class, "and a class of unfree or natural ethical life," which are lords (the military, landed class), the bourgeoisie, and the peasantry.[61] Hegel explains that "the work [of the lordly class] can be nothing but the waging of war or training for this work," and its labor is the "indifferent labor of government and courage"; the military class sees to the "security of their property and possessions" of the other two classes, a view to which Hegel will return in his discussion of this dialectical scenario in the German Middle Ages in the lectures on the philosophy of history. The middle class, the "honest" class, does not, of course, figure anywhere in the lord/bondsman relation, though it does stand as a mediator or administrator between these two classes in the transfer and management of surpluses—looking already like Marx's bourgeoisie, which comes to own labor through exchange.[62] Finally, the third class is the "peasantry," whose labor is "more of a mean, affecting the soil or animal, something living."[63] Through labor, the peasantry expresses its social being, its "ethical life," and stands in a special relation with the first class—the military class, the lordly class, the absolute class: "The ethical life of this class is trust in the absolute class, in accord with the totality of the first class. . . . On account of its totality [as a class] it is also capable of courage and in this labor and in the danger of death can be associated with the first class."[64] It is here that we hear the echo of self-consciousness—a peasantry "capable of courage" at the risk of death, much like the first class, which itself exhibits courage. There is symmetry here, as well as opposition, in other words. There is not only the potential for a struggle between the first and third class but also an opportunity for peasant self-consciousness to emerge out of its dependency.[65]

As is evident to the translators of *System of Ethical Life*, Harris and Knox, Hegel is talking about late feudalism and "the possibility of serfdom."[66] While he seems here to be speaking about a new or transitional feudalism of the kind that creates and sustains a bureaucracy that is a class in itself—the bourgeoisie—he understands these landed, labor relations to be essentially feudal. No early nineteenth-century citation of "the peasantry," at any rate, can bracket the feudal situation of the said peasantry, as Hegel confirmed in his later *Philosophy of Spirit* (1805–6).[67] And any modern historian knows this fact, too. Otto Brunner writes in his authoritative history of Germany: "In Germany, despite revolution and reform, the old 'feudal society,' the old society of the Estates, continued to exist with only minor changes."[68] Walter Schlesinger expands this point:

> Thus, well into modern times, a form of lordship continued that was nothing but the private and public lordship over land and people descended unchanged from the early Middle Ages. The principalities of the Schwarzburgs and the Reuss were constructions of a similar sort, as was the principality of Waldeck whose nineteenth-century "sovereignty" should not deceive us; in reality, here was another undivided lordship from the Middle Ages that had not given way to a "modern" state. Such too was the lordship of Schonburg, swallowed up by the Electorate of Saxony in 1740 but retaining jurisdiction by right of its own authority until 1878—a medieval noble lordship that finally disappeared in the Bismarckian state.[69]

This is not a polemical point, nor one that is particularly theoretical: within such a history, Hegel can see that the fundamental structures of feudalism are present, surviving political changes, and in need of diagnosis. To him the questions of land and *Grundherrschaft* remain available for response, figuration, and philosophy—even given his early enthusiasm for the abolition of the French estates whereby one can celebrate the real-time destruction of feudalism as a slow, but ongoing, process.[70] It is here that we must not explain away, as so many readers of Hegel do, what *Knecht* means—how it is a major contemporary term for the forms of servitude most medieval and many modern Europeans experienced.[71]

We won't need to cite historians further, at least not in a way to make salient Hegel's feudal dialectics. For Hegel himself takes a markedly historical and historicist turn toward feudalism in the *Philosophy of Right*, a work that, again, appears to have been drafted as the *System of Ethical Life*. In the early portions of *Philosophy of Right*, especially in the section entitled "Property," Hegel explains possession, beginning with its literal sense to grasp and use an object and continuing to the more metaphorical forms of possession, which "extend the range of my power" to possess. These extensions are "mechanical forces, weapons, tools."[72] It so follows, Hegel explains, that labor is the work of possession, an act of the will to shape one's surroundings: "To impose a form on a thing is the mode of taking possession."[73] Hegel offers agricultural examples: "tilling of the soil, the cultivation of plants, the taming and feeding of animals, the preservation of game, as well as contrivances for utilizing raw materials or the forces of nature and processes for making one material produce effects on another, and so forth."[74] Eventually, one's desire for possessions transforms into another kind of possession—the possession of self. Here, we have to be clear: Hegel is talking about "self-consciousness" in terms consistent with those in the *Phenomenology of Spirit*—the work of identity formation itself, over and against not just plows and plants and nature, but rather other people, Other consciousnesses from which to distinguish the Self. Hegel says this of the farmer: "It is only through the development of his own body and mind, essentially through his self-consciousness's apprehension of itself as free, that he takes possession of himself and becomes his own property and no one else's."[75]

This is precisely the moment where Hegel speaks of "the relationship of master and slave," or "lord" and "serf" ("das Verhältnis der Herrenschaft und der Knechtschaft"),[76] and indeed it is here that he cites the relevant portion of the *Phenomenology of Spirit*, referencing and confirming the notion that the "fight for recognition" should be seen as a struggle for possession. Hegel's point is quite ambitious, actually, charting a social transformation over the course of history, the end point at which slaves recognize themselves and recognize their masters as being dependent on slaves. The beginning of that point, the end of an older model of identity, is the Middle Ages. His subsequent examples make this clear when he starts to qualify notions of possession, such as possession in "use," in which "the distinctive character of the property of a feudal tenant is that he is supposed to be the owner of the use only, not the value of the thing."[77] Other examples include "dominion," "the relations of *dominium directum* and *dominium utile*" that involve "estates in fee with the ground rents and other rents, dues, villeinage, &c."[78] It is here that Hegel makes a crucial revision to the *System of Ethical Life* in the *Philosophy of Right*—namely, that not every plurality of persons can be thought of as a lord/bondsman relation, but rather only those social relations emerging explicitly within feudalism.[79]

Hegel packs all of this analysis into a few pages in the *Philosophy of Right* yet elaborates on these ideas at substantial length in his lectures on the philosophy of history, our final example before returning to the *Phenomenology of Spirit*. In these lectures, he fleshes out the lord/bondsman dialectic with more concrete (and familiar) historical examples, exploring possession in the German Middle Ages. We can read the passages quoted below with Kojève's "risk" in mind, but also begin to acknowledge the historiographic principle at work in Hegel—the movement from violence to institutions, from the initial "fight for recognition" at the risk of death to the resolution of inequality between the two parties, whereby the latter yields his or her will and property to the former, and whereby the lord/bondsman relation appears as such. Hegel writes:

> The need for protection is sure to be felt in some degree in every well-organized state: each citizen knows his rights and also knows that for the security of possession the social state is absolutely necessary. . . . Men must first be placed in a defenceless condition, before they were sensible of the necessity of the organization of a State. . . . As observed above, the idea of duty was not present in the Spirit of the Germans; it had to be restored. In the first instance volition could only be arrested in its wayward career in reference to the merely external point of *possession*; and to make it feel the importance of the protection of the State, it had to be violently dislodged from its obtuseness and impelled by necessity to seek union and a social condition.[80]

That was the setup. Hegel goes on to trace the historical emergence of the lord/bondsman dialectic, and its attendant struggle for possession:

> Individuals were therefore obliged to consult for themselves by taking refuge with Individuals, and submitted to the authority of certain powerful persons, who constituted a private possession and personal sovereignty out of that authority which formerly belonged to the Commonwealth. As *officers of the State*, the counts did not meet with obedience from those committed to their charge, and they were as little desirous of it. . . . They assumed to themselves the power of State, and made the authority with which they had been intrusted [sic] as a *beneficium*, a heritable possession. As in earlier times the King or other magnates conferred fiefs on their vassals by way of rewards, now, conversely, the weaker and poorer surrendered their possessions to the strong, for the sake of gaining efficient protection. They committed their estates to a Lord, a Convent, an Abbot, a Bishop [*feudum oblatum*], and received them back, encumbered with feudal obligations to these superiors.[81]

Hegel here is explaining in more overt historical terms the conditions necessary for all of his lord/bondsman and, more broadly, feudal dialectics.[82] For Hegel, possession itself is what forms a feudal condition (or realm) in the first place, is what settled the nomads: "The ferocity and savage valor that characterized the predatory life of the barbarians—[is] pacified and brought to a settled state by possession."[83] Here again the narrative moves from Hobbesian natural violence to institutions. And this social transformation brings with it a transformation of desire—a redirection of what Hegel calls the "martial spirit" of the barbarians, now manifesting itself in the fierce protection of "private interests" and "private property."[84] The fight, or the desire for the fight, has been sublimated into political arrangements (bringing us half way to Marx's "relations of production").

Yet in the same way that possession is the very making of the feudalism, it is also its undoing—characteristic of those well-known "dialectical reversals" of Hegel.[85] As we learn in the lectures on the philosophy of history, the internal contradictions of feudalism transform into outright antagonisms—even revolution. Our first task is to think of the dialectical reversal as possession gone wild, the accumulation of so many goods that the entire system risks collapsing under its own weight and can prop itself up only by using ideological means. Enter the medieval church, which possesses the powers of the Holy in the sacraments, which possesses the Truth "in virtue of knowledge, teaching, and training," which possesses "enormous property," and, finally, by way of crusades, which possesses "all Holy places of note—Bethlehem, Gethsemane, Golgotha, and even the *Holy Sepulchre*."[86] The centripetal tendencies of possession in the church especially—and this is Hegel's Lutheranism talking—is what gives feudalism its critical mass, generating ever more the very contradictions that destroy the entire apparatus and make possible the Reformation, Luther, and the modern state.[87] By critiquing the church in this way, Hegel is talking about the worst in "private property" but a potential revolution against its alienating tendencies. We should not only remember these points as we look forward to Marx, who so inveighed against private property, but also bear in mind that we are now alighting upon one of the most clear and telling lessons of the lord/bondsman dialectic itself, as summarized by Hyppolite—a lesson of dependency in possessive lordship.[88] Indeed, for Hegel, this lesson has, in the lectures on the philosophy of history, a feudal twist:

> The principle of free possession however began to develop itself from the protective relation of feudal protection; i.e. freedom originated in its direct contrary. The feudal lords or great barons enjoyed, properly speaking, no free or absolute possession, any more than their dependents; they had unlimited power of the latter, but at the same time they also were vassals of princes higher and mightier than themselves, and to whom they were engagements—which, it must be confessed, they did not fulfil [sic] except under compulsion.[89]

Subinfeudination, the ever-ascending orders of domination characteristic of feudalism, brings a whole new character to the maxim, derived from the so-called master/slave dialectic in the *Phenomenology of Spirit*, that the master is really the slave, dependent upon the slave to recognize his or her mastery. The new lesson of this dialectic is that the lord is the serf, no more in possession of the land than the serf, because he stands below a greater lord. Yet, as Hegelian history has it, the serfs begin to repossess themselves (their selves) and form alliances irrespective of lords: "Individuals brought into closer relation by the soil which they cultivated, formed among themselves a kind of confederation or *conjuratio*. They agreed to be and to perform on their own herald that which they had previously been and performed in the service of the feudal lord alone."[90] This, in a very real sense, is a class consciousness that Hegel will call "self-consciousness" in the *Phenomenology of Spirit*, to which we turn, now that we have established the feudal frame of Hegel's lord/bondsman dialectic.[91]

Phenomenology of Spirit: "Jenes is der *Herr*, dies der *Knecht*"

Because we understand the terms and problems necessary to recognize the feudal frame within which Hegel situates his lord/bondsman dialectic, we can say something more specific than Adorno's throwaway remark cited above, something more than this tantalizing single sentence by Robert Solomon: "The imagery here is rather that of a feudal lord, growing fat and lazy on the sweat of his servant (probably servants, but let's leave it at one)."[92] To be clear, the section in question, entitled "Independence and Dependence of Self-Consciousness," does not start out with feudal references, nor does it declare its medievalism from the first, until the episode itself passes from the struggle to the death to the struggle for recognition and for possession. Yet as soon as it enters into the struggle for possession, Hegel appropriately names the chief players, once called only "two opposed shapes of consciousness": "The former is the lord, the other is the bondsman [jenes is der Herr, dies der Knecht]."[93] This naming is extremely significant, for it is only at this point that the feudal problems of possession, dispossession, and possession in dispossession are on full display, giving full meaning to the subtitle to this section, "Lordship and Bondage [Herrschaft und Knechtschaft]."[94]

Here, for example, is a segment of Hegel's lord/bondsman dialectic that emerges as entirely consistent—in theoretical and historical terms—with the other Hegelian works I discussed above:

> The lord [Herr] relates himself mediately to the bondsman [Knecht] through a being (a thing) that is independent, for it is just this which holds the bondsman in bondage; it is his chain [Kette] from which he could not break free in the struggle, thus proving himself to be dependent, to possess his independence in thinghood [seine Selbständigkeit in der Dingheit zu haben erwies].

> But the lord is the power over this thing, for he proved in the struggle that it
> is something merely negative; since he is the power over this thing [die Macht
> über dies Sein] and this again is the power over the other (the bondsman),
> it follows that he holds the other in subjection [so hat er in diesem Schlusse
> diesen Anderen unter sich]. Equally, the lord relates himself mediately to the
> thing through the bondsman: the bondsman, *qua* self-consciousness in gen-
> eral, also relates himself negatively to the thing, and takes away its indepen-
> dence [der Knecht bezieht sich als Selbstbewußtsein überhaupt auf das Ding
> auch negativ und hebt es auf]; but at the same time the thing is independent
> *vis-à-vis* the bondsman, whose negating of it, therefore, cannot go the length
> of being altogether done with it to the point of annihilation; in other words,
> he only *works* on [bearbeitet] it.[95]

We can now recognize more here than a vocabulary often considered difficult
to fathom; we can look for a hermeneutical and historical payoff. Take, for
instance, "The lord relates himself mediately to the bondsman through a being
(a thing) that is independent," or "The lord is the power over this thing." What
is this "being," this "thing"? It is not "life" as is usually glossed with reference
to the earlier portions of this episode, but rather "land"—the struggle over
which is a struggle for possession, the definition of identity in possession.[96] The
bondsman "relates himself negatively to the thing" because the thing is not his,
the land is not his. What is this "negation" by which the bondsman relates to
land? Negation is work, "cutting," cultivation, the activities of "plowing" cited
in the *Philosophy of Right*—all of which are exercises in effective possession
of land, a labor or "negating of it" that can never be done, for the bondsman
"cannot go the length of being altogether done with it," because no amount of
work will bring him into possession of it. *Negation* is, therefore, the appropriate term for this labor, because it is thoroughly alienating for the bondsman.[97]
The lord enjoys the fruits of the bondsman's negation or labor through his
extraction of this labor, his forcible dispossession and his powerful possession, by which he installs himself between the bondsman's labor and its yield:
"For the lord, on the other hand, the *immediate* relation becomes through this
mediation the sheer negation of the thing, or the enjoyment of it [Dem Herrn
dagegen *wird* durch diese Vermittlung die *unmittelbare* Beziehung als die reine
Negation desselben oder der *Genuß*]".[98] The lord gains an immediate relation
to the land through, paradoxically, mediation. Hegel clarifies:

> but the lord, who has interposed the bondsman between it and himself, takes
> to himself only the dependent aspect of the thing and has the pure enjoyment
> of it. The aspect of its independence he leaves to the bondsman, who works
> on it.

[der Herr aber, der den Knecht zwischen es und sich eingeschoben, schließt sich dadurch nur mit der Unselbeständigkeit des Dinges zusammen und genießt es rein; die Seite der Selbständigkeit aber überläßt er dem Knechte, der es bearbeitet.][99]

This is a social relationship: the one who enjoys is not the one who works. The one who enjoys is the one who consumes with a labor of expenditure, a negation of another sort. In short, if the "thing" that is land holds the bondsman "in subjection," it is on account of the feudal arrangement per se, and it is the contradiction inherent in feudalism that creates an opening for the bondsman to escape his servitude.[100]

Thus the lord/bondsman dialectic in the *Phenomenology* is not as ahistorical as it initially seems, nor is it pure idealism, some kind of phenomenological retreat from materiality. Nor is it "social" in the baggiest sense of the term. It is feudal. I shall insist on this reading in view of the suggestion that "it would be wrong . . . to try to build up Hegel's account of this (and other) historical episodes into an historicist reading of the *Phenomenology* as a whole."[101] I cannot claim to have supplied a reading of the "whole" of the *Phenomenology* (though in chap. 5 I will discuss other feudal examples in this work). But any notion that it is "wrong" to think about Hegel more historically and contextually is absurd and contrary to the premises of intellectual history.[102] Such exhortations to keep Hegel in the ideal, as Hyppolite particularly has recommended, have not prevented Hegel's readers, however, from hazarding a historical framework for the lord/bondsman dialectic. This dialectical scenario has been contextualized as having an essentially Platonic foundation,[103] or as referring to ancient Greek culture and reading "almost like a burlesque on Aristotle's account of slavery in the *Politics*,"[104] or as a reflection on the Haitian revolution.[105] To my mind, feudalism is the easier and most obvious answer to the question of historical context for Hegel's *Herr/Knecht* dialectic, since this is after all the historical frame in which, at least according to Hegel, self-consciousness becomes at all possible.

Marx and the Middle Ages

We now can understand more fully the Hegelian background of one of Marx's more classic accounts of ideology and fetishism and witness the establishment within Marxism of a long tradition of critique. I have in mind Marx's claim that in capital "[the] definite social relation between men themselves . . . assumes here, for them, the fantastic form of a relation between things."[106] This *locus classicus* comes out of Marx's effort to contrast capitalism with feudalism, to contrast capitalism with, I suggest, *Hegelian feudalism* so typified by the lord/bondsman dialectic. From the so-called early Marx to the so-called late Marx, there is no hiding the Hegelian background to Marx's analysis of capitalism's emergence from feudalism.[107] Take the following concession by Marx and Engels in the *German Ideology* to historical commonplaces:

> Nothing is more common than the notion that in history up till now it has only been a question of *taking*. . . . Everywhere there is very soon an end to tak-ing, and when there is nothing more to take, you have to set about producing. From this necessity of producing, which very soon asserts itself, it follows that the form of community adopted by the settling conquerors must correspond to the stage of development of productive forces they find in existence. . . . By this, too, is explained the fact, which people profess to have noticed every-where in the period following the migrations of the peoples, namely, that the servant was master [daß nämlich der Knecht der Herr war].[108]

From possession to production signals the move from Hegel to Marx. Here, Marx and Engels are transforming commonplaces into facts; what they mean by "the period following the migrations of peoples" is the Middle Ages, feu-dalism, which in Hegelian fashion supplies the basic lesson of the lord/bonds-man dialectic, "that the servant was master."

Indeed, Marx never ignores the explanatory potential of *Grundherrschaft* nor of the lord/bondsman dialectic. As he writes in the later *Grundrisse* (1857–58):

> The relation of personal servitude, or of the retainers to their lord, is es-sentially different. For it forms, at bottom, only a mode of existence of the land-proprietor himself [Grundeigentümers selbst], who no longer works, but whose property includes, among the other conditions of production, the workers themselves as bondsmen [die Arbeiter selbst als Leibeigne] etc. Here the *master-servant relation* (Herrschaftsverhältnis) as essential element of ap-propriation.[109]

Herrschaftsverhältnis: this is the feudal relation of domination within *Herr-schaft*, which Marx's translator inappropriately renders as "*master-servant relation.*" Marx then elaborates upon this relation in a way that evokes not only Hegel's feudal, lord/bondsman dialectic but which mimics the care with which Hegel handled the issues of what makes a *Knecht* and what makes a *Herr*:

> Basically the appropriation of animals, land etc. cannot take place in a master-servant relation [Herrschaftsverhältnisses], although the animal provides

service. The presupposition of the master-servant relation [Herrschafts- und Knechtschaftsverhältnis] is the appropriation of an alien *will*. Whatever has no will, e.g. the animal, may well provide a service, but does not thereby make its owner into a *master* [*Herren*]. This much can be seen, here, however, that the *master-servant relation* [Herrschafts- und Knechtschaftsverhältnis] likewise belongs in this formula of the appropriation of the instruments of production; and it forms a necessary ferment for the development and the decline and fall of all original relations of property and production, just as it also expresses their limited nature. Still, it is reproduced—in mediated form—in capital, and thus likewise forms a ferment of its dissolution and is an emblem of its limitation.[110]

Marx's terms are very clear, for they were Hegel's terms, to be sure, centered in the latter's various lord/bondsman dialectics.[111] In this passage and in so many other places in the *Grundrisse* Marx is referring to "Herrschafts- und Knechtschaftsverhältnis." As Marx knows, and as Hegel teaches, the "master-servant relation" requires two wills in dialectical relation, a struggle that, as Marx says (following Hegel), has an outcome—namely, the transformation of social and productive relations themselves, "a necessary ferment for the development and the decline and fall of all original relations of property and production." And with that Hegelian insight, Marx goes on to render this dialectic useful for historical materialism, in saying that this feudal dialectic "is reproduced—in mediated form—in capital." In other words, Marx conceives of the Middle Ages, as do many post-Hegelians, as always in decline, always a historical remainder, yet, paradoxically, always a determination even in the age of capital, in which the struggle for possession persists. The terms of feudal "dissolution" thus appear analogous to those same terms in capitalism. If feudalism comes to an end, we can be certain that a certain feudal contradiction survives well into the age of capital, and it is this contradiction that remains central to Marxist thought.

We are now in a position to understand what Marx is doing with the Hegelian Middle Ages in *Capital*. For starters, Hegel himself theorizes the relations of domination in feudalism as a personal relation between individuals: "Individuals were therefore obliged to consult for themselves by taking refuge with Individuals, and submitted to the authority of certain powerful persons, who constituted a private possession and a personal sovereignty out of that authority which formerly belonged to the Commonwealth."[112] Marx accepts this Hegelian view of *Grundherrschaft*. That much is evident when, in the *German Ideology*, he and Engels write that, in feudalism, "the social relations between individuals . . . appear at all events as their own personal relations, and are not disguised as social relations between things."[113] With the

Hegelian Middle Ages in mind, Marx can contrast the modern and the medieval, again and again, as when he writes in *Capital* his most famous words about fetishized social relations in capitalism: the "definite social relation between men themselves . . . assumes here, for them, the fantastic form of a relation between things."[114] It is only against the background of feudalism's relations "between individuals" that this alternative is even evident. It is only against *and with* Hegel that Marx can offer this formulation, in other words. (In the next chapter, we will explore this very idea in our analysis of Marxian commodity fetishism, which, I will show, draws from Hegel's analysis of eucharistic fetishism in the Middle Ages.)

Suffice it to say here that Marx clearly sees the juxtaposition of feudal and capitalist relations of domination as critically generative, a location from which to view social relations of production as plainly visible, "as they really are." Readers forget that both Marx and Engels in the *German Ideology* made hay of exactly this critical point of view in their reflections on feudalism: "The social structure and the State are continually evolving out of the life process of definite individuals, but of individuals, not as they may appear in their own or other people's imagination, but as they really are."[115] And Marx, for his part, resumes this critical stance in *Capital* when, for instance, we are invited to "leave this noisy sphere, where everything takes place on the surface and in full view" and enter "into the hidden abode of production" where "the secret of profit-making must at last be laid bare."[116] Herbert Marcuse knew to articulate this precise move of "going behind" appearances in Hegelian terms.[117] We know that the Marxian critique of ideology emerges out of the theoretical possibilities of the Hegelian Middle Ages—everywhere present in Marx, itself "reproduced . . . in mediated form." Let's now explore this idea more deeply in the next chapter, the idea that the Hegelian Middle Ages matter, in more ways than one, to Marx.

The Eucharist and the Commodity

The transubstantiation, the fetishism, is complete.

MARX

Marx knew it. He knew there is no better way to talk about commodities than to talk about the eucharist. It's an obvious point, insofar as Marx speaks frequently of the transubstantiation of raw materials into commodities and finally into money. But that he refers to a fundamentally medieval eucharist drawn from Hegel has not been appreciated.[1] Marx's analysis of the commodity fetish in that famous chapter in *Capital*, "The Fetishism of the Commodity and Its Secret," has its foundations not in Hegel's *Philosophy of Right*, where one can discover, as Herbert Marcuse once said, some Marxist thinking about commodities and labor, but rather, I suggest, in Hegel's differently energetic work on religion concerning specifically the sacramental feelings and fetishism of early and medieval Christianity.[2] The germane texts are Hegel's early theological writings and lectures on the philosophy of history, which, taken together, disclose the prominence of his explorations into fetishism as a cultural, religious, and institutional mandate to produce, praise, value, and consume that one Thing at the very center of medieval culture—the eucharist. Marx, I will suggest, translates the Hegelian eucharist into the commodity; more broadly, he accepts from his predecessor a sacramental theory of fetishism that explains, in ways never before recognized, Marx's most memorable insight about intersubjectivity and labor: "[The commodity-form] is nothing but the definite social relation between men themselves which assumes here, for them, the fantastic form of a relation between things."[3]

To discover Hegel right at the center of Marx's lasting contribution to the critique of capital, then, is to know the *other* secret behind the "Secret" of the commodity—not the fetishism per se but the Hegelianism of the fetishism, and how that, in turn, points us to the specifically Hegelian idea that fetishism emerges as a function of *relation* and *materiality* and is not, as most poststructuralist accounts have it, an abstraction from materiality.[4] But there is something else we discover pertaining to one of the stories told by this book, the life of identity/difference. Namely, if the lord/bondsman dialectic, as outlined by Hegel, is an object lesson in how identity/difference operates within history, with consequences for human self-consciousness, then for Hegel and Marx fetishism indicates the conceptual limits of this dialectical pair of terms. Both, in other words, realize that dialectics requires a figural supplement, i.e., fetishism, to explain what identity/difference cannot—the thingliness of belief and fantasy, and the insistent materiality of the objects we produce and consume. We are here witnessing a case where dialectics needs more than its own concepts. It needs figures, too—other narratives, other modes of thinking, other ways of seeing and believing—to complete dialectics as both a critical practice and a style, particularly a phenomenological style capable of narrating the intersubjective encounters not only between persons, or persons and things, but also, strangely enough, between concepts. Chapters 5 and 6, dealing with literature, critique, dialectics, and conceptual figuration, will resume this exposition all the way to the utopian end. Meanwhile, let's see what Marx borrows from Hegel.

The Thing

Some summary of the Marxian commodity would be helpful, so that it is clear *why* Marx would, in the first place, want to adopt ideas from Hegelian, medieval sacramentality: he does so, I suggest, as an alternative to the categories of identity and difference, which to him seem insufficient in explaining a certain fantastic social logic that is not reducible to philosophical logic. The logical problem begins almost immediately in *Capital*, when, according to Marx, commodities are exchanged once they are viewed as possessing the same value. Four mugs will get you one stool; or twenty dollars, which can buy you four mugs, will get you one cheap table. Through such measures, commodities can be viewed as equivalent to one another, possessing the same exchange value enabling you to exchange one for another. What you give out is returned to you – a thing for a thing. Of course, putting it that way, we can see that lurking behind all of this is a conceptual problem: for how can things be equivalent and in some respects, qualitatively identical, without violating the principle of the non-contradiction of identity, whereby two qualitatively different things cannot be both formally *and* substantially equivalent? Aristotle in his *Metaphysics* calls the non-contradiction of identity "the most certain of all" principles.[5] And Marx accepts this principle. He posits that the equivalence of two things is strictly a question of *quantitative* equivalence in the amount of exchange value (which is based on equivalent quantities of abstract labor in the production of commodities).

Yet the problem of quality lingers when the value between two things is expressed by a "third thing"—a certain quality of exchange value they obviously inevitably share: "both [things in exchange] are therefore equal to a third thing, which in itself is neither the one nor the other. Each of them, so far as it is exchange-value, must therefore be reducible to this third thing."[6] Yet what is this "third thing"? Does it exist only as an epistemological category (as some mediating element generated out of the dialectic of identity/ difference) or does it have a material basis as a thing in its own right hovering above other things? This "third thing," as it turns out, is not Marx's favorite metaphor, owing not only to the questions it raises, as above, but also to the fact that Marx wants the "third thing" to be real, never only a creature of relative being. And so he enfolds the "third thing" into the commodity itself, which he names consequently the "twofold thing":

> A commodity is a use-value or object of utility, and a 'value'. *It appears as the twofold thing it really is* as soon as its value possesses its own particular form of manifestation, which is distinct from its natural form. This form of manifestation is exchange-value, and the commodity never has this form when looked at in isolation, but only when it is in a value-relation or an exchange relation with a second commodity of a different kind. *Once we know this our manner of speaking does no harm, rather as abbreviation.*[7]

In the "value-relation or an exchange relation," one commodity stands as the "form of manifestation" of the value of the other. This is the basic interplay of identity/difference; in exchange, the identity of one commodity's value is expressed in its material difference from another. Yet because the "twofold thing" that is the commodity subsumes the "third thing," we are right to ask a very realist question. If all commodities are identical with respect to value, why can't a commodity express its *own* identity in its *own* difference, rather than always expressing the identity of another commodity? In other words, Can the commodity truly be a twofold thing, consubstantial, two things at once, two versions of itself in one place—both its identity in identity and its identity in difference? The categories of identity/difference begin to mutate here under the pressure of conceptual difficulties that are themselves heavy with historical problems.

It would sound as if we were approaching the postmodern Marx, *avant la lettre,* were it not for his own "manner of speaking," as he calls it above. Marx wishes to take some figurative liberties with his analysis so that he can narrate some very wondrous materializations seemingly at odds with classical logic.

Simply witness how Marx translates "determinate" and "congealed quantities of homogenous labour" into a quality—a quality left over when complex labor and use value are subtracted:[8] "If we leave aside . . . the useful character of the labour, what remains is its quality of being an expenditure of human labour-power." In the face of seemingly impossible materializations, Marx speaks marvelously about what is "hidden within the commodity," the "visible incarnation" of "all human labour," itself "materially different" from use value, but material or "objective" no less. When he says that exchange value is crystallized, "congealed," "materialized," "objectified," and embodied in the commodity, he is arguing for the existence of the mysterious twofold thing—literally consubstantial.[9]

Our problem now is to approach the mystery with Marx and visualize what the twofold thing might be, and how it might be equivalent to the other twofold things that are commodities, such as coats:

> In its value-relation with the linen, the coat counts . . . therefore as embodied value, as the body of value (Wertkörper). Despite its buttoned-up appearance the linen recognizes in it a splendid kindred soul, the soul of value. . . . As a use-value, the linen is palpably different from the coat; as value, it is identical with the coat, and therefore looks like the coat. Thus the linen acquires a value-form different from its natural form. Its existence as value is manifested in its equality with the coat, just as the sheep-like nature of the Christian is shown in his resemblance to the Lamb of God.[10]

Marx knows he is getting carried away here in personifying linen in this way, but whatever it takes to figure forth the meaning of the twofold thing, even if it means asking you to assume the point of view of the linen looking at the coat and accept that a devout Christian actually resembles "the Lamb of God."

Marx continues to validate this way of seeing and thinking: "In a certain sense, a man is in the same situation as a commodity. . . . Peter only relates to himself as a man through his relation to another man, Paul, in whom he recognizes his likeness. With this, however, Paul also becomes from head to toe, in his physical form as Paul, the form of appearance of the species man for Peter."[11] In several places in *Capital*, Marx asks us to identify with commodities within this intersubjective space—the fetishized space of capital:

> [The commodity-form] is nothing but the definite social relation between men themselves which assumes here, for them, the fantastic form of a relation between things. In order, therefore, to find an analogy we must take flight into the misty realm of religion. There the products of the human brain appear as autonomous figures endowed with a life of their own, which enter into

relations both with each other and the human race. So it is in the world of
commodities with the products of men's hands. I call this the fetishism which
attaches itself to the products of labour as soon as they are produced as commodities, and is therefore inseparable from the production of commodities.[12]

Everywhere you turn, these fantastic forms are reflected back at you. But to
see these forms, or to know quite how to imagine such crazy things as walking
tables ready to dance—another great example from *Capital*[13]—Marx wants
us to "take flight into the misty realm of religion," which I will now suggest
is another way of saying that we must take flight into the "misty realm of
Hegel"—starting with the early Hegel who himself speaks about Christianity
in strangely familiar ways.[14]

The Sacrament of the Fetish

In Berlin, in 1826, a group of Catholic priests complained about Hegel to
the Ministry of Religious and Educational Affairs "about allegedly offensive
comments on transubstantiation . . . in his lectures."[15] It must have been interesting, needless to say, hearing Hegel vent about the eucharist. But we have
to take his polemic in bits and in order of escalating vehemence. Hegel's early
work on this subject is not so vituperative, but it is conceptually and figuratively rich and is the philosophical underpinnings of his strident critique of
medieval Catholicism in the later lectures on the philosophy of history.

Let's begin with Hegel's view of sacramental intersubjectivity. In "The
Spirit of Christianity and Its Fate," Hegel deals with the Gospel accounts of
the Last Supper, among other things, and offers a version of sacramental communion or eucharist relation that will begin to look, retrospectively, familiar
to Marx's ideas about "the fantastic form of a relation between things." In
this text, Hegel explains that the bread and wine at the Last Supper symbol-
ize an aspiration, a hope to render visible the relations of love between Jesus
and his disciples: "since Jesus calls the bread and wine, which he distributes
to all, his body and blood given for them, the unification is no longer merely
felt but has become visible." How do things play a part in making these relations visible? Hegel's answer is that these relations are made visible by things
remaining ordinary, exactly what they are. These things are neither overly
meaningful as sacred symbols nor are they allegories, signs of something divine, and so forth. Above all, these things are approachable and enjoyable,
never alien or alienating: the bread, for instance, is simply "linked to a reality,
eaten and enjoyed in a reality."[16] Hegel elaborates on this idea in what will be
a crucial formulation:

Objectively considered, then, the bread is just bread, the wine just wine; yet both are something more. This "more" is not connected with the objects (like an explanation) by a mere "just as": . . . "just as you all share in this bread and wine, so you all share in my sacrifice"; or whatever other "just as" you like to find here. Yet the connection of objective and subjective, of the bread and the persons, is here not the connection of allegorized with allegory, with the parable in which the different things, the things compared, are set forth as severed, as separate, and all that is asked is a comparison, the thought of the likeness of dissimilars. On the contrary, in *this* link between bread and persons, difference disappears, and with it the possibility of comparison. Things heterogeneous are here most intimately connected.[17]

Note that Hegel here is (like Marx after him) not thinking with the logical categories of identity/difference by which, precisely, you have "the thought of the likeness of dissimilars." Such logics are not enough, nor is allegory, or for that matter dialectics, insofar as what visibly unifies the "Things heterogeneous" is a communion of "feeling."[18] Hegel, in other words, replaces logical form with sacramentality and expounds upon the sacramental relation per se, which erases the difference between persons and things: "difference disappears. . . . Things heterogeneous are here most intimately connected." All identity, and no difference. But here we're not blindly feeling our way around in the night in which all cows are black, because the sacramental relation remains visible, and that is an important point for what we're trying to learn about the relation between Hegel and Marx on this topic. Again, as Hegel explains this relation: "the unification [of persons] is no longer merely felt but has become visible."[19]

Before we can associate these ideas with Marx, we have to be clear that Hegel likes this subjective state. He does not name it "fetishism." Rather, he is here speaking of "feeling" as that "something more" whereby difference disappears: "The spirit of Jesus, in which his disciples are one, has become a present object, a reality for external feeling. Yet the love made objective, this subjective element becomes a *thing*, reverts once more to its nature, becomes subjective again in the eating."[20] It is important to remember, however, that Hegel does have fetishism in mind, insofar as he believes that in the history of Christianity these ideal sacramental relations within what he calls "folk religion" eventually go wrong and are institutionalized within the later forms of "private religion" that corrupt "feeling" and, in fact, produce "fetishism." For instance, in his essay "On the Prospects for a Folk Religion," Hegel says that the practices of "folk religion" (early Christianity, i.e.) have transformed over time into the rituals of "private religion," in which "feelings [are] artificial and forced," quite different from the situation presented by "folk religion," to which Hegel repeatedly turns by way of contrast: "The indispensable characteristics of ceremonies designed for a folk religion are . . . that they contain little or no inducement to fetishistic worship [Fetischdienste]—that they not consist of a mere mechanical operation devoid of spirit. . . . A folk religion must be a friend to all life's feelings."[21] The point here is that Hegel's pronouncements on feeling, the relations of feeling, and the eventual objectification or thingification of feeling, are all commentaries on a phenomenon that we now recognize as "fetishism," as Marx formulates it. Hegel's terms are Fetishglauben, Fetischdienste.

A case in point is Hegel's rather unusual theses about nineteenth-century sacramental practices in which "our most human feelings seem alien":

> But our religion would train people to be citizens of heaven, gazing ever upward, making our most human feelings seem alien. Indeed, at the greatest of our public feasts we proceed to the enjoyment of the holy eucharist dressed in the colors of mourning and with eyes downcast; even here, at what is supposed to be a celebration of human brotherhood, we fear we might contract venereal disease from the brother who drank out of the communal chalice before. And lest any of us remain attentive to the ceremony, filled with a sense of the sacred, we are nudged to fetch a donation from our pocket and plop it on a tray. How different were the Greeks![22]

It's easy to see how Hegel ticked off priests in Berlin! Since his earliest writings, he railed against modern religious fetishism and its attendant problems of sacramentality, while constructing a historical past before fetishism when "feeling" made the relations of love visible and the differences between things invisible. In other words, medieval Christianity and modern Catholicism typify, as we will now see, the age of fetishism and "private religion."

In his lectures on the philosophy of history, for example, Hegel offers a case study of medieval, sacramental feeling that differs little from his views of contemporary Catholicism. Medieval Christianity places one thing "at its very center," as Hegel says elsewhere, "the Host."[23] This central thing of unity, the eucharist, appears first as institutional mandate to *enjoy* and *adore* something arbitrary, sacramental bread and wine. He goes on to credit Luther (not surprisingly) for being the first to recognize the Host for what it was, valueless yet valued only by compulsion—"a mere external thing, possessed of no greater value [Wert] than any other thing." There is no "folk religion" here, only a "private religion" that sustains objectification, Thingification for the sake of it, without any subjective connection: "The most prominent feature in this sacrament," Hegel writes, "is, that the process by which Deity is manifested, is conditioned by the limitations of particularity—that the Host, this *Thing*, is set up to be adored as God." The need for this adoration, he says, is "infinite," if not automatic: "for the Host is adored even apart from its being partaken of by the faithful."[24] It is as if the thing requires a relation of expropriation precisely because the sacramental relations between persons are now invisible, whereby what's only visible are the relations to things that are valued for their own sake:

> The Holy as a mere thing has the character of externality; thus it is capable of being taken possession of by another to my exclusion: it may come into an alien hand, since the process of appropriating it is not one that takes place in Spirit, but is conditioned by its quality as an external object [Dingheit]. The highest of human blessings is in the hands of others.[25]

And so it is that medieval social relations are imagined as already alienating—"a separation between those who possess this blessing and those who have to receive it from others—between the Clergy and the Laity. The laity as such are alien to the Divine." Hegel describes a separation between persons that does not appear as such in the social relation, since the relation itself is mediated by the religion whose "essence" is mediation.[26] That "element of mediation" is, as Hegel says, the eucharist,[27] which we can now call the fetishized medieval commodity—the figure yet screen for uneven social relations and relations of expropriation and alienation.

This should be enough to allow us to turn back to Marx. The point is that in that first chapter in *Capital*, Marx communicates that there is something perversely religious about commodity relations in capital. Here is the passage again:

> [The] definite social relation between men themselves . . . assumes here, for them, the fantastic form of a relation between things. In order, therefore, to find an analogy we must take flight into the misty realm of religion. There the products of the human brain appear as autonomous figures endowed with a life of their own, which enter into relations both with each other and the human race.

For Marx, products live in a strange realm indeed, and it's a realm that runs by the rules of Hegel's sacramental ideal in early Christianity, within which "Things heterogeneous are here most intimately connected." Marx calls these so-called ideals, these rules, "fetishism." While Hegel would call them "feeling" and not "fetishism," he articulates fetishism as the reification of those very sacramental practices—any practice that translates feelings into things for the purposes of expropriation. If Marx speaks of commodities so frequently in terms of transubstantiation and other miracles and mysteries, and if he insists that the "misty realm of religion" is that in which we must properly understand commodity fetishism, then the reason for this emphasis is clear: his commodity is quite like Hegel's eucharist, and their ideas about fetishism are, likewise, rather close.

The Miracle of the Commodity

Contrasts and comparisons help. For instance, Marx has a different, and I would even say more theorized, understanding of fetishism than what was generally available at the time in the orientalist or colonialist fantasies about non-European religions.[28] His thinking about fetishism, moreover, does not seem to be inspired by Auguste Comte, whose own ideas about fetishism narrowly concerns the "primitive" belief in the animation of things (on this, critics have overemphasized Marx's debt to Comte). What draws the Hegelian and Marxian formulation together, and rather apart from Comte's model, is the notion that fetishism is not necessarily a question of belief so much as, more plainly, a question of *relation* and whole societies. So, on the one hand, Comte had foreclosed the explanatory possibility of a *systemic* model of fetishism, writing that "the only real fault of the Fetichist regime . . . is its unsuitability to the formation of vast societies"; "Fetichism afforded [feeling] no field for development except private life. . . . Here therefore we find Fetichism laying the necessary foundation of the social state, but not able to build it up."[29] On the other hand, Marx holds that a theory of fetishism involves necessarily the investigation of how things "*enter into relations* both with each other and the human race."[30] Or, again, as he sets up the problem of commodity fetishism: "The mysterious character of the commodity form . . . reflects the social relation of the producers to the sum total of labour as a social relation between objects, a relation which exists apart from and outside the producers."[31] So, it would seem clear that Marx is not drawing from Comte in devising a theory of commodity fetishism, or if he is, he isn't reading him very closely!

Marx's inspiration here is, rather, Hegel, insofar as both view fetishism as a matter of social relation. While Marxian fetishism will continue to be productively read in the Freudian and Lacanian vein, such an approach should not obscure the Hegelianism in Marx's own account of fetishistic social relations and should rather start by avowing it.[32] To be sure, Marx disagrees with Hegel on the *character* of those relations—and *how* they are "visible," how they "appear." But even here it is obvious that Marx is inverting Hegel in the way he's prone to do when he wishes to be Hegelian but suffer no losses for the gambit, because their views on commodity fetishism are symmetrically the opposite, two sides of the same coin. In other words, they are virtually saying the same thing but their focus on different historical periods puts their points at odds with one another. For Hegel, social relations are visible in the idealized sacramental space of early Christianity, in which "the unification [of persons] is no longer merely felt but has become visible"—only to become invisible in the Middle Ages. For Marx (and Engels), however, it is the inverse: in the Middle Ages, the social relations are visible, because "individuals . . . [do] not appear in their own or other people's imagination, but as they really are."[33] By lining up Marx's theory of commodity fetishism with Hegel's ideas about sacramental fetishism and feeling, and by juxtaposing what Hegel says about the Middle Ages with what Marx says about modernity, we can appreciate that, for Marx, the mystery of commodity culture is actually this: it is not that the relations between persons are *replaced* by relations between things, as those famous lines are typically read. It is rather the opposite: the relations between things now appear *as* relations between persons. Things are personified, in the same way that for Hegel things in the Middle Ages (falsely) embody a Real Presence and are God.

That is one miracle of the commodity. What's further miraculous about Hegelian sacramentality is how the sacraments take on value in consumption. Hegel could not have offered a better example of consumption as the production of value than when writing on the sacraments. Fetishism and feeling, for Hegel, arise in consumption, which in turn produces the signs of fetishism or, more simply, the fetish. As we saw above, in early Christianity the bread and wine are signs of communion—or of relations per se—not at consecration, when *Hoc est enim corpus meum* is spoken and the Real Presence is embodied, but upon the obliteration of the sign, the bread that is "eaten and enjoyed."[34] More fully, Hegel explains that sacramental objects do not replace the visible relations between persons as signs or allegories of those relations; rather, they are a part of them: "Unification is no longer merely felt but has become visible. It is not merely represented in an image, an allegorical figure, but linked to a reality, eaten and enjoyed in a reality, the bread." This sort of devotion must involve, as Hegel would put it in more phenomenological terms in his lectures on the philosophy of religion, negation.[35] Adoration requires, in other words, the destruction of the "external thing" via its incorporation with the believer, both bodily and subjectively. He makes this point clear in yet another work, the *Phenomenology of Mind*, in his remarks *cum* polemic against Catholicism (which he views as a religion of "externality," "bondage," and "superstition"): "And, first of all, God is in the

'host' presented to religious adoration as an *external thing*. (In the Lutheran
Church, on the contrary, the host as such is not at first consecrated, but in
the moment of enjoyment, i.e. in the annihilation of its externality, and in the
act of faith, i.e. in the free self-certain spirit: only then is it consecrated and
exalted to be present God.)"[36] Catholicism, for Hegel, forecloses the unify-
ing possibilities of sacramental practices whereby (he says parenthetically)
sacramental objects appear as sacred when consumed—in a moment when
Thingliness, subjectivity, and the communal relations between persons and
things combine, and flash up all at once, in a moment of value linking enjoyment, annihilation, acts of faith, and exaltation.

There seems to be something here in Hegel for Marx, for whom the value
of commodities "appears" similarly; value is expressed, in the last instance, in
consumption—as he explains in *Grundrisse*:

> Production, then, is also immediately consumption, consumption is also im-
> mediately production. Each is immediately its opposite. But at the same time
> a mediating movement takes place between the two. Production mediates
> consumption; it creates the latter's material; without it, consumption would
> lack an object. But consumption also mediates production, in that it alone
> creates for the products the subject for whom they are products. The product
> only obtains its "last finish" in consumption. A railway on which no train
> runs, hence which is not used up, not consumed, is a railway only δυνάμει
> [potentially], and not in reality.[37]

Marx's examples here are telling; what gives the railway its utility as an exchange value is its use, its destruction, its consumption—the moment at
which use value flashes up, reaches a kind of perfection or "last finish," and
then disappears: "Only by decomposing the product does consumption give
the product the finishing touch"; "a product becomes a real product only by
being consumed."[38] So if, with Fredric Jameson, we wonder why use values
seem to vanish from the opening pages of *Capital*, we might say that Marx
wants to show that they never truly existed in capital—consumed instantly at
the moment of their emergence in the circuit of production and consumption.[39] *This is, then, effectively appearance as a mode of disappearance.*[40] This
is also an effectively Hegelian point, a double explanation of the subjective
and the objective: "production thus produces not only the object but also the
manner of consumption, not only objectively but subjectively."[41] Place a bit
more emphasis on "subjectively," and we get fetishism in Hegelian terms—
a fetishism continuously generated out of the turns of production and
consumption.[42]

The Matter of Fetishism

It is at this point that we can begin to acknowledge that another "miracle of the commodity" is its persistent materiality, which is not the same as its use value, in keeping with the common formulation that use value equals matter and exchange value is an abstraction from matter or, better, the so-called "form of the commodity." Yes, in many ways it is—Marx will say as much— but there's more to it than that. To think further about the materiality of commodities—and especially the materiality of exchange values—we need to unthink the consensus about commodities.[43] For many readers, Marx speaks of fetishism so as to emphasize how all things are equalized by the disavowal of their use values and materialities; it behooves us, so the idea goes, to worry only about quantities, abstractions, and exchange value. This view betrays a poststructuralist, if not prescriptively postmodern, consensus about Marx that best characterizes Jean Baudrillard's "semiological reduction," by which exchange and use values are collapsed in postmodernity so as to render the commodity as an *in*substantial image.[44] Indeed, much of Marx's thinking on the commodity, and of what's possible and impossible with the traditional logical categories themselves, has been read through largely poststructuralist frameworks, which risk translating Marx's Hegelian semiotic into a play of differences of the kind generated by a stabilized, hyper-Saussurean version of identity/difference.[45] I am in agreement with Baudrillard, as well as Jean-François Lyotard,[46] on the *significance* and ambivalence of use values; as my previous section demonstrated, it is right to think of use values as also signs. But a problem with this notion emerges when we return to Marx's "manner of speaking" and to the question of the "twofold thing," in which it seems that Marx never stops thinking about the body of the thing, the form of the commodity.

Nor should we. For Marx says that our task is to understand that while all kinds of human labor (or "complex labor") produce diverse useful objects (use values), as commodities they all share that "substance," what he names "simple labor" or "homogenous" labor—the very "substance of their values" within the social field of exchange.[47] In this substantial insistence, Marx's choice of terms is revealing. For what would seem to be an Aristotelian substance afoot, in which the German, "gleicher Substanz" or "gemeinschaftliche Substanz" should always suffice, he prefers instead to modify "substance" as "body," *Warenkörper*, which roughly translates as "use body" but which is frequently rendered by translators as "use value."[48] He also speaks of *Wertkörper*, which roughly translates as "value-body" or "embodiment of value,"[49] but which, again, is usually rendered as "exchange value." We can see that, in the case of "use value," the translation already performs an abstraction Marx never meant, directing thought from "körper" to "value," from its thingliness to its abstraction as worth. Likewise, translation commits an abstraction upon "exchange value," eliding what is beautifully oxymoronic about "Wertkörper," as a semantic twofold thing in which value is compressed somehow into its body—to say nothing of the complication that "wert" can also mean "usefulness." Marx is thinking carefully at the level of the word. In demonstrating the linguistic existence of "the twofold thing"[50]—that this thing is something that you say, materializing it in words—he shows that the relation between "Waren*körper*" and "Wert*körper*," concrete and abstract labor, use and exchange value, involves a set of primary terms whereby bodies, "Körper," always remain. We must always have our minds on the matter, in other words, insofar as Marx posits that two bodies or "körper" can exist in one slice of space: "A commodity is a use-value or object of utility, and a 'value'." Perhaps the best way to understand a strange Marxian proposition about commodities now made even stranger, indeed a useful way to imagine the differences and identities that are indicated by use value and exchange value, is to recall the sacramental frame, in which it's always a question of the commodity's two *bodies*, a question of equalized yet preserved differences within a collective fantasy of *Körper,* in accordance with St. Paul's injunction in 1 Corinthians 11:17: "we who are many are one body."

The twofold thing, then, results from consubstantiation of the sort most often associated with Luther, who also holds that God's body and bread, blood and wine, are co-existents.[51] It characterizes even earlier sacramental theologies, such as that of John Wyclif in his *De eucharistia*.[52] No doubt, sacramentality itself, in the scholastic and Aristotelian traditions, had always pressed up against orthodox logic and belief so much that it'd be characterized as heresy from time to time—as in the case of Wyclif in the early 1380s in England. And it is sacramentality that allows Marx an unorthodoxy of his own in the discipline of logic, a way of distorting willfully identity/difference so as, ironically, to solve the problem of how "'unlike things can be commensurable' i.e. qualitatively equal," which, as Aristotle knew, "'is . . . in reality, impossible'"—in fact only possible in what Theodor Adorno calls the "utopia of the qualitative."[53]

Use Value as Fetish, Exchange Value as Matter

We can now take up an epistemological consideration. It is not that with the advent of modernity, "use value," once properly regarded in the Middle

Ages, becomes fetishized into abstraction in capitalism. Rather, it is that, oddly enough, with the appearance of capital come the conditions of *knowing* and *seeing* things as use values. To put it another way, capital offers a new perspective on things, and use value seems to designate precisely one such perspective. For statements like these express the idea that use value is only *recognizable within* commodities, rather than somehow appreciated outside of capital, outside of history and commodities: "The totality of heterogeneous use-values or physical commodities [Warenkörper] reflects a totality of similarly heterogeneous forms of useful labor"; "Commodities come into the world in the form of use-values or material goods [Gebrauchswerten oder Warenkörpern], such as iron, linen, corn, etc."[54] Commodities show up, as it were, within the subjective conditions that had been established by "the manner of consumption." Marx must mean that, on the one hand, *use value itself is a fetish rather than a placeholder for "the authentic" or the "useful"*—a shifting descriptor equally predicated upon the *relations* in which the thing is situated: "Hence we see that whether a use-value is to be regarded as raw material, as instrument of labour, or as product is determined entirely by its specific function in the labour process, by the position it occupies there: as its position changes, so do its determining characteristics."[55] On the other hand, as we saw in the previous section, *exchange value is no farther from matter, from the material, from the bodily, than is use value.*

Many years later, Adorno and, more recently, Slavoj Žižek, would show that use value and exchange value are subject to such dialectical exchanges, whereby one incorporates the substance of the other. It is interesting that for both thinkers, transubstantiation figures centrally. For his part, Adorno tellingly states that commodity fetishism is "the auto religion [that] makes all men brothers in the sacramental moment with the words: 'That is a Rolls Royce'."[56] He goes on to say: "The masochistic mass culture is the necessary manifestation of almighty production itself. When the feelings seize on exchange value it is no mystical transubstantiation."[57] In more plain terms, there is no "mystical transubstantiation" in view of what is, to Adorno, a social fact: all has already been transubstantiated, because all things have been commodified, feel what you wish about them. His larger point, however, is to return to Marx's important sacramental metaphors (without acknowledging their Hegelian origin) and revise them in such a way that use value itself becomes a creation of capital. For Adorno, it is not that exchange value destroys use value (as per the common reading) but rather that exchange value, by some odd, reversed transubstantiation, *becomes* use value: "If the commodity in general combines exchange value and use value, then pure use value, whose illusion the cultural goods must preserve in a completely capitalist

society, must be replaced by pure exchange value, which precisely in its capacity as exchange value deceptively takes over the function of use value."[58]
Adorno's point, therefore, is consistent with the Hegelian reading of Marx,
confirming the instability of the term "use value" yet verifying its status as an
epistemological category, if not an item of ideology itself.[59]

Žižek, like Adorno, revises the concept of use value and does so through,
among other things, an analysis of the soft drink Coke, which is said to exhibit the logics of postmodern commodification. Coke is not concocted, argues Žižek, to quench your thirst or "provide any particular satisfaction; it
is not directly pleasing and endearing." Unlike "water, beer or wine," it has
no purpose, and is thus a commodity that does not have, never did have, a
use value. It is a commodity in its purest form and only embodies the desire
itself to consume this or any commodity, the "pure surplus of enjoyment
over standard satisfactions."[60] There is, then, no longer a secret essence to the
modern commodity, no conversion of use value to exchange value, not even
a consubstantiation of use value and exchange value. Even so, there lingers
in Žižek's dazzling analysis the old Hegelian languages of transubstantiation
and fetishism that make, unbeknownst to the analyst, this fizzy new commodity seem rather old:

> The paradox . . . is that Coke is not an ordinary commodity whereby its
> use-value is transubstantiated into an expression of (or supplemented with)
> the auratic dimension of pure (exchange) Value, but a commodity whose
> very peculiar use-value is itself already a direct embodiment of the supra-
> sensible aura of the ineffable spiritual surplus, a commodity whose very mate-
> rial properties are already those of a commodity.[61]

The language of eucharistic fetishism works here because Žižek is explaining
a conversion that is *at once* a materialization and appearance, which is a very
old form of appearance from the Middle Ages—those outlandish transub-
stantiations whereby Christ's body underneath the appearance of bread mi-
raculously materializes into a bleeding, wobbly piece of flesh before the eyes
of unbelievers, proving to them the reality of sacrament. Essence becomes
appearance, subject becomes accident, and Christ's crucified flesh, once invisible, is now visible.[62] Likewise, Coke is that Real Thing, but it is also the
sacramental, Hegelian thing—to be consumed and fetishized in ways that are
ceremoniously medieval.

So how does Hegelian fetishism inform Žižek's view of the origins of the
Lacanian symptom? Not as one would hope, especially in view of my own
claim that fetishism is the symptom, or by-product, of a dialectic of identity/

difference gone wrong. Žižek, fully aware of the significance of the medieval/modern distinction in theorizing fetishism, writes the following:

> In societies in which commodity fetishism reigns, the "relations between men" are totally defetishized, while in societies in which there is fetishism in "relations between men"—in precapitalist societies—commodity fetishism is not yet developed, because it is "natural" production, not production for the market which predominates. This fetishism in relations between men has to be called by its proper name: what we have here are, as Marx points out, "relations of domination and servitude"—that is to say, precisely the relation of Lordship and Bondage in a Hegelian sense, and it is as if the retreat of the Master in capitalism was only a *displacement*: as if the de-fetishization in the "relations between men" was paid for by the emergence of fetishism in the "relations between things"—by commodity fetishism. The place of fetishism has just shifted from intersubjective relations to relations "between things": the crucial social relations, those of production, are no longer immediately transparent in the form of the interpersonal relations of domination and servitude (of the Lord and his serfs, and so on); they disguise themselves—to use Marx's accurate formula—"under the shape of social relations between things, between the products of labour."[63]

Žižek has Marx right. And he has Hegel right, for the most part, beginning with his (this time) correct use of terms referring to Hegel's dialectic of "lord" and "bondsman," not "master" and "slave"—a key issue in translation discussed in the previous chapter.[64] Yet it is clear why the medieval terminology matters: Žižek is talking about the Middle Ages, but in a way that unconsciously expresses the very insights of the Hegelian Middle Ages that Marx himself adopted. Here, Žižek accepts the Hegelian premise of natural labor, or what he calls "natural production." He also accepts that the Hegelian dialectic of lord/bondsman is a feudal one, which redounds through Marx. So *why*, given that all the pieces already fit, pointing to the Hegelian understructure, does Žižek then impute the invention of the symptom to Marx?: "One has to look for the discovery of the symptom in the way Marx conceived the passage from feudalism to capitalism."[65] Nay, if one must insist on inventions in this fashion, then why can it not be said that Hegel invented the symptom?

The Dialectic between Hegel and Marx

This occlusion of what is most presciently Marxist about Hegel is a technique perfected by Marx himself. Marx, after all, is famous for "inverting"

Hegel in order to ground his dialectic in material history but in so doing he mystifies what is theoretically inventive about his predecessor and, more to the point, what is already grounded about Hegel. This inversion results in a curious mirroring that generates a dialectic out of the dialectical inversion itself, whereby Marx's relation to Hegel now appears to be oppositional but symmetrical but in the end never really an easy matter of inversion, because it seems rather clear that Marx finds Hegel's critique of the Middle Ages to be so theoretically productive as to work as a critique of capital—such that the mysteries of the Middle Ages readily translate, in Marx's hands, into those of capital. The demystification of capital, in other words, demands an appraisal of the Middle Ages: there cannot be one critique without the other (a process we will study in detail in the next chapter). Marx, we might recall, first presents the Middle Ages, that "medieval Europe, shrouded in darkness," in that pertinent section in *Capital*, the part on fetishism.[66] He puts it there to set capitalism into relief but, just as polemically, to supply the anti–Middle Ages to Hegel's own. Yet this effort to be different from Hegel by means of a "dialectical inversion" has a result Marx might not have expected—a surprising synthesis of the Hegelian and Marxian dialectic motivated by the persistence of the Middle Ages, not only in the real time of history but in the working out of *theory*, here especially the theory of fetishism, in which it is quite hard to make a clean modern break and turn definitively from the medieval. So while we can offer the easy formulation that what the Middle Ages are to Hegel, modernity is to Marx, it is better to say that both stand on the *same side* of theory, dialectic, and critique, and they are only divided (or inverted) by history, by the force of time and self-willed periodization.

But if Marx's modernity in the first volume of *Capital* does often look like Hegel's Middle Ages,[67] then this resemblance cannot be explained by a historiographic perspective that seeks to fulfill the secularization thesis, however persuasive it is. To be sure, Benjamin's remark that "Christianity . . . transformed itself into capitalism"[68] makes sense on its own and can be used to describe how you get from Hegel to Marx, whereby eucharists become commodities; priests become political economists; and laborers take on the mantle of the new "priests" transubstantiating use values into exchange values, and so forth. Yet the secularization thesis—at times often quite straightforward seeming—is immediately complicated in its embroilment with *dialectics*, which is a veritable eddy of temporalities, histories, desires, and concepts. And Marx knows this, which is why, in the name of dialectics, he looks suspiciously upon a historiography that easily narrates the transition from medieval to modern and instead cares to recast the problem of the "medieval" and the "modern" within a different temporal logic and new point of view. In other words, Marx isn't concerned only to make empirical observations about the persistence of this or that medieval mode of production or institution in modernity (that *Capital* looks very different from the 1844 manuscripts, in their narrative arcs, is proof of this idea). Rather, he is after something more complex, something that identifies the medieval residing in a new domain that subsumes, evacuates, and rewrites history—the domain of capital—but which cannot entirely expunge the medieval from its own economic structures and social logics, because—to think this problem through dialectically—capital needs those structures in place, those logics in mind, and the medieval just happens to express this necessity within capitalism. And so we see capital for what it is: not entirely material or completely ideal or "mystical," capital is both. It is a social substance out of which the medieval rises, unbidden, to enter into appearances, flashing up to be recognized at moments when capital churns out new commodities, new fetishes, new fantasies, new territories. What enables Marx, us, or anyone to see these moments "as they are"—some parts fetishism, some parts ideology, some parts form and style—is dialectics, that great art of perception and knowing.

PART THREE

Literature

The philosopher must possess just as much aesthetic power as the poet. Men without aesthetic sense are our literal-minded philosophers.

HEGEL? HÖLDERIN? SCHELLING?

5

Fürstenspiegel, Political Economy, Critique

There is no such thing really as was because the past is.
WILLIAM FAULKNER

Literature, as I have called Part III of *The Birth of Theory*, is the final rubric under which falls my exposition of the dialectic. How did we get here? In parts I and II, under the rubrics of Theory and History, I presented the invention of dialectical thought in the Middle Ages and detailed its perfection in the hands of Hegel and Marx, who in strikingly similar ways activate dialectical habits of mind in the critique of contemporary circumstances. For Hegel, these circumstances involve largely feudal modes of production; for Marx, capitalism. We learned that what joins Hegel and Marx together is what sets them apart: history, or the different historical objects of their own critique. By bearing in mind the analogy that what feudalism is to Hegel, capitalism is to Marx, we can grasp precisely why Hegel is not the forlorn idealist or helpless mystic of so much critical theory but is rather quite presciently Marxist in his formulations. Likewise, Marx is more Hegelian than we have ever supposed, and that is not a bad thing either, because Hegel's dialectic gives him his theoretical (rather than only polemical) edge. By the end of that discussion, however, we saw that both Hegel and Marx sussed out the conceptual limits of the dialectic and, in turn, supplemented its explanatory capacities with a theory of fetishism, which opens up an alternative fund of figures and ideas to help them characterize and critique either belief or ideology. This chapter, and the next, deals with the issues of figuration more directly, by thinking about literature as a testing ground for dialectics for Hegel and later dialectical thinkers—literature (particularly novels) as a site where we practice and observe dialectics, exercising our critical and imaginative faculties.

Yet literature, to speak of it as an abstraction, has been the place where dialectics have often gone to die. Or, if one construes the history of critical theory to be a comedy of capers and hijinks, Literature personified has tried at all costs to get away from Dialectics in its most vulgar (i.e., reflectionist) guise—circling the table, head-faking first this way then that, before running up and over the sofa, and out the door. But I maintain that dialectical criticism can be revitalized in a return to the literary of a certain, already theoretical kind—to a premodern dialectical mode that links figure and concept, as I suggest at the end of the final chapter. Let's let that ponderous notion sit, however. My aim for this chapter is to disclose a certain intimacy between literature and dialectics, an undeniable affinity when it comes to reading and thinking about the past, the present, and the future. To say this mundanely: I claim that dialectical literary historicism starts with Hegel and does so with a predictably peculiar beginning in the literary Middle Ages, which Hegel and the best dialectical thinkers after him take as a repository of genres through which to rethink and critique the modern.

We can acquaint ourselves with this unusual generic problem by recalling Marx's famous statement that "Hegel remarks somewhere that all great world-historic facts and personages appear, so to speak, twice. He forgot to add: the first time as tragedy, the second time as farce." Marx made this up. No one has ever found that certain "somewhere," Hegel's *exact* quote where he claims that "all great world-historic facts and personages appear . . . twice."[1] Yet were the *Phenomenology of Spirit* to speak for Hegel's own generic take on such "world-historic facts and personages," then Marx could have more accurately said something like, "the first time as tragedy, the second time as romance, the third time as Fürstenspiegel." For these latter two genres—romance and Fürstenspiegel—are, as Hegel understood them, medieval genres, and they constitute two of the major (and unnoticed) structuring devices at the very center of the *Phenomenology of Spirit,* two genres Hegel adopts, above all, to critique the modern and theories of the modern. Here, I will take Fürstenspiegel as a case in point—that old political genre by which authors supply detailed counsel to princes and kings on how to govern a realm effectively. In many ways, Fürstenspiegel is the première genre for political observation, because authors who follow the form and offer political advice must weigh multiple interests at the same time, from those of the king as a person to the entire social whole, from those of the retainers surrounding the king to the important and relatively autonomous legal and economic institutions within the realm. As I show, Hegel adopts the political genre of Fürstenspiegel for more trenchant purposes—namely, to critique a discipline that, in modernity, had a special purchase on explaining economic and political realities: political economy. Specifically, Hegel takes on the greatest practitioner of the discipline, Adam Smith, by staging an encounter between political economy and its predecessor, Fürstenspiegel. This encounter makes perfect sense, because, as I demonstrate, the histories of Fürstenspiegel and political economy are intertwined over a large swath of time—from medieval Fürstenspiegel literature to nineteenth-century German idealism and historical materialism onward to twentieth-century Marxism and historicism. There are a lot of histories at play here, but the point in this discussion is straightforward: we cannot understand fully what political economy seeks to do, or how it functions as an ideology, without first understanding what it most wants to avoid and suppress in its modernizing aspirations—the archaic, the medieval. Likewise, we will never understand completely Smith's famous "invisible hand" without appreciating its antecedent and opposite, the "visible hand" of princely rule and economic governance.

My aim in this chapter, then, is twofold: it is to show that Hegel tests the explanatory capacity of political economy against its older complement, Fürstenspiegel writing; and it is to demonstrate that this very pairing of a medieval genre with political economy has become, after Hegel, a signature analytical move within Marxism. Such critical generic anachronism, as this recourse to archaic genres might be called, is not only central to the familiar "ideology critique" (*Ideologiekritik*) of appearances and conditions—be they economic, political, or ethical—but it marks, I propose, the inception of a critical practice that is then developed in the work of Mikhail Bakhtin and Fredric Jameson. Ideology critique, in other words, emerged out of an engagement with the Middle Ages—specifically, by thinkers reflecting on the persistence of the medieval within an unevenly developed modernity. And it all starts with Hegel, who teaches us that the medieval—*pace* political economy—can never be willfully forgotten because it never really goes away.

Hegel's Fürstenspiegel

There is a curious structure in the *Phenomenology of Spirit*. At its center is a historical narrative that takes us from ethics in the Greek state in a section called the "Ethical Order" (§444–83), with its famous references to Antigone and her tragic situation, to the major section on "Culture" (*Bildung*), which concludes with some gripping passages on the French Revolution and the Reign of Terror (§590–95). What falls in the middle of this narrative arc from the ancient world to the recent Reign of Terror is, literally, what's always in the middle in traditional historiography: the Middle Ages. Students of the *Phenomenology*, that is, suddenly find themselves reading about indelibly medieval, Fürstenspiegel themes in the section entitled "Culture and its realm of actuality" (§488–526). What draws our attention to this material, and perhaps what might keep us from recognizing this medieval moment in Hegel's text, is the odd fact that Hegel here discusses a distinctly modern author, Adam Smith, who famously sought to modernize the old discipline of political economy.[2] Our purpose here is to understand why Hegel found it necessary to set within a medieval frame—indeed, the medieval genre of Fürstenspiegel writing—the modern problem of political economy; why he felt it best to discuss Adam Smith in this anachronistic setting.[3]

Hegel's Fürstenspiegel story appears, again, in "Culture and its realm of actuality," and it matches the famed lord/bondsman dialectic in terms of what it tells us about Hegel's critical mind. And a story it is. When, according to Hegel, consciousness aligns itself with both a sovereign and his wealth, it becomes "noble," yet this noble consciousness soon understands that its courtly involvements require self-sacrifice, "the heroism of *service*, the *virtue* which sacrifices the single individual to the universal."[4] This noble labors "in the interest of ruling power," and by such "obedience" and "free sacrifice" the sovereign whom this noble serves gains "actual power," while the noble himself works as a counselor.[5] Yet—in a predictable dialectical reversal—the noble becomes ignoble by offering suspect if not bad advice to the sovereign: "His counsel about what is best for the general good [is] ambiguous and open to suspicion." The noble counselor begins to be silent in court and becomes a "*haughty* vassal": "He has in fact reserved his own opinion and his own particular will in the face of the power of the state. His conduct, therefore, conflicts with the interests of the state and is characteristic of the ignoble consciousness which is always on the point of revolt."[6] Hegel, as if it weren't apparent already, signals generic features of Fürstenspiegel narrative—that of the silent counselor, whose reticence makes him a *placebo* figure by default (after the Latin, "I shall please"), to boot, the arrogant counselor who is only self-interested. And not surprisingly, as Hegel says, "the heroism of silent service becomes the heroism of flattery," and by such flattery, things get out of hand, puffing up the monarch who now rules by "*unlimited monarchy*: *unlimited*, because the language of flattery raises this power into its purified universality."[7] The monarch is, in other words, a "pure individual, no longer only in his own consciousness, but in the consciousness of everyone."[8] His universality is generated by the recognition of those around him, but because such recognition is occasioned by flattery—rather than, say, as in the lord/bondsman dialectic, the material struggle for possession—there is no genuine relation between sovereign and vassals, no relation of identity in difference. And so the sovereign remains in absolute difference: "By his name, then, the monarch is absolutely separated off from everyone else, exclusive and solitary."[9] In this respect, he embodies the "sovereign exception," and indeed the germane theme of the "king's two bodies" is here the king's two consciousnesses, his own unto itself, and his subjectivity as recognized by flatterers.[10]

Things go from bad to worse. The nobles (now plural) crowd around the monarch, letting him know they "not only are ready and prepared for the service of the state power, but that they group themselves round the throne as an *ornamental setting*, and that they are continually *telling* him who sits on it what he *is*."[11] It comes as no surprise to learn that in this situation, the monarch ends up "relinquishing . . . power," on the realization that all of his authority comes from a mere language game of flattery and bad counsel. Fallen and without will, he is now "at the mercy of every more powerful will" at court.[12] And those nobles around him become ignoble and alienated, having rent in two the social fabric (or "substance") that once united these persons as a functioning court and, one assumes, kingdom. In these circumstances, finally, the monarch, who at the very beginning of this tale embodied "wealth," is now "the deposed universal,"[13] and wealth—and the problem of wealth altogether—takes on a life of its own, "develops an *intrinsic being of its own*."[14] One could even say that wealth here becomes *value*, emerges as a thing itself, an emergence coterminous with that of the state but also with the failure of a certain mode of governance about which medieval Fürstenspiegel texts themselves warn. We'll soon resume this tale with Diogenes.

For now, however, we can address the odd but interesting detail noted above: Hegel *begins* this whole Fürstenspiegel story with a reference to Adam Smith's *Wealth of Nations*. Why? Why commence a medieval narrative with an obvious paraphrase of Smith, who describes modern economy and production, among so many other things? Let's juxtapose passages. Hegel offers the following proposition seven paragraphs into "Culture and its realm of actuality":

> Wealth produces universal labour and enjoyment for all. . . . Each individual is quite sure that he is acting in his own interest when seeking this enjoyment. Yet . . . it is evident that each in his own enjoyment provides enjoyment for all, just as in working for himself he is at the same time working for all and all are working for him.[15]

Compare these words to what is obviously the most famous passage from Smith's *Wealth of Nations* on the "invisible hand" of the market:

> Every individual necessarily labours to render the annual revenue of the society as great as he can. He generally, indeed, neither intends to promote the public interest, nor knows how much he is promoting it. . . . He is in this, as in many other cases, led by an invisible hand to promote an end which was no part of his intention. . . . By pursuing his own interest he frequently

promotes that of the society more effectually than when he really intends to promote it.[16]

The straightforward answer to the question—why does Hegel begin his Fürstenspiegel story with a reference to Adam Smith's *Wealth of Nations*—is that Hegel cycles Smithian ideas of "wealth" and "labor" through his medievalized narrative about the "haughty vassal"—all to show that Smith's paradigm of self-interest and individual avariciousness, which purportedly add up to a collective or social good, for Hegel, doesn't add up and is anything but good. The ethic of Smith's invisible hand is to Hegel problematic, to say the least, and Hegel uses that old genre of ethical reflection, Fürstenspiegel, to reflect on the new ethic of wealth proffered by Smith.

Hegel, it now becomes clear, is interested in criticizing and rethinking the modern, in challenging what amounted at the time to best-selling theories of the modern, as no doubt Smith's *Wealth of Nations* was. In a moment, I will suggest why Hegel ingeniously uses medieval Fürstenspiegel to accomplish this task. Meanwhile, we can note that this sort of critical reflection about the modern, about the social whole, is encoded within Hegel's own Fürstenspiegel narrative. Near the end of this narrative, Hegel refers to "Diogenes in his tub," smack dab in the middle of the marketplace. He is the example of a man who can find no outside to this "whole world of perversion," no matter his intellectual and rhetorical strategies, because he sits at its very center; he is in the thick of it. Diogenes is also a stock Fürstenspiegel character. His story runs from medieval treatments of Diogenes and Aristippus within Fürstenspiegel narratives all the way up to Hegel's time—both in a play by Johann Elias Schlegel, *Die drei Philosophen*, which is "a sort of Fürstenspiegel" featuring Diogenes as a main character,[17] and in Christoph Martin Wieland's 1770 *Socrates Mainomenos (graece) oder die Dialogen des Diogenes von Sinope*. Wieland also published a Fürstenspiegel text in 1772, *Der goldene Spiegel oder die Könige von Scheschian*.[18] (This all reminds us that Fürstenspiegel writing was alive and well during Hegel's own lifetime, with a prominent instance of the genre offered by Johann Jakob Engel, who was tutor to Frederick William III of Prussia, former professor of moral philosophy at the Joachimsthalsche Gymnasium in Berlin [which was founded on the ideals of Christian neohumanism],[19] and author of the widely read work plainly called *Fürstenspiegel* [1798].[20])

And so what does Hegel do with this Fürstenspiegel character, Diogenes? He sets him in the role of the critic (which bolsters his fame as "the best known Cynic").[21] Diogenes is the "plain mind" who seeks to make an "example" of reality, "either in the form of a fictitious case or a true story"—all in the effort "to represent the existence of the good and noble as an isolated anecdote, whether fictitious or true." The goal, in other words, is to typify reality as an "*espèce*, a mere 'sort' of thing," so as to make the present visible, legible.[22] Diogenes, in other words, does what Fürstenspiegel narratives themselves do—make examples.[23] But examples are made not simply for the sake of it, nor is this sort of exemplarity easy to come by. On the transformative potential of this self-consciously exemplary practice, Hegel has this to say: "Finally, should the plain mind demand the dissolution of this whole world of perversion, it cannot demand of the *individual* that he remove himself from it, for even Diogenes in his tub is conditioned by it."[24] Hegel runs through a series of conclusions just like this one on the problem of whether a critic can gain a perspective on the social whole, or withdraw from it, or put into words its contradictions.[25] And in so doing he returns to a problem raised earlier in the *Phenomenology* about the futility of critiquing the social whole, which is "a perversion invented by fanatical, gluttonous despots and their minions, who compensate themselves for their own degradation by degrading and oppressing others, a perversion which has led to the nameless misery of deluded humanity."[26] It so happens that Hegel writes these words, too, within the medieval frame, adopting the genre of romance in an exploration of themes from, again, Smith's *Wealth of Nations*.[27] Whatever problems of ideology Hegel raises in this earlier romance section—and they are problems strikingly similar to Slavoj Žižek's formulations (after Sloterdijk) about an ideology in which, as the saying goes, "they know very well what they are doing, but still, they are doing it"[28]—they are answered here in the Fürstenspiegel material. For Hegel sees in Diogenes what Jean-Paul Sartre saw: the old cynic whose name alone evokes the strategies of ideology critique (*Ideologiekritik*) or, as Hegel puts it, the "unveiling of being," the discovery of things, conditions, beings as they are.[29] But Hegel, unlike Sartre seeking to reform Marxist "ideological" criticism in his *Critique of Dialectical Reason*, finds promise in Diogenes, because his critical strategies embody not the lessons or content of Fürstenspiegel literature; rather, his way of thinking, his point of view, now mimics the formal or formalizing work of the genre itself in his effort to typify and estrange conditions, to make an example of the present that one can apprehend in the now and act on. Remember, Diogenes is in the middle of the *marketplace*. All it takes to get outside of the market, its bustle and ideology, is to rise from the tub!

Hegel thus shows us that at the very end of this Fürstenspiegel episode, consciousness has been educated in how to be an active critical consciousness, in how to gain critical insight by dint of revolt against the accepted state of things: "a spiritual self . . . is of truly universal worth" because it "*is* the self-disruptive nature of all relationships and the conscious disruption of them; but only as self-consciousness in revolt is it aware of its own disrupted state, and in thus knowing it has immediately risen above it."[30] In revolt, and by acknowledging the contradiction within himself, this critic rises above . . . only, of course, to be presented with a new problem, in the next section on the relation between "insight" and "faith" (which is as far away from the problems of political economy as one can go). The point in all of this is obvious and reminds us that Hegel talks about Diogenes here not simply to signal a genre for the sake of sheer nostalgic fun, but to twist the knife already thrust into the pages of the *Wealth of Nations* and show, as I will now argue, that this book fails as an economic description of the modern.

Political Economy

We are now turning to the historical reasons why Hegel pairs Adam Smith and Fürstenspiegel. I propose that Hegel (as well as Smith) knew that Fürstenspiegel narratives were an earlier instantiation of what would later become political economy. To see what Hegel and Smith saw, we have to look at the overlap of political economy and Fürstenspiegel during the emergence of cameralist theories of state in German intellectual history that in their earliest forms, according to George Steinmetz, "reactivated an Aristotelian tradition in which the state's goal was to encourage work discipline, trade and economic growth (the 'common welfare')."[31] The Aristotelianism of this body of work is key here, because it signals the steady tradition of writing that runs from the Fürstenspiegel texts and wisdom of Aquinas and Aegidius to the models of Fürstenherrschaft written in the late Middle Ages and read in Hegel's time. For instance, a work by Conrad Heresbach, *De educandis erundisque Principum liberis*,[32] was read up into the eighteenth century in the German states,[33] and texts on Fürstenlehre were absorbed into the humanist forms of education that Hegel himself would see afoot in his home state, the kingdom of Württemberg.[34]

Heresbach's *De educandis* is representative—that it is intended for the instruction of child princes, even more so[35]—insofar as it contains all the expected Fürstenspiegel wisdom on the importance of advice and the pitfalls of receiving bad advice from flatterers ("adulatores"),[36] with citations of authorities ranging from Aristotle and Plato to Cicero, Plutarch, Aquinas, and countless others. There is also plenty on right rule as opposed to tyranny. But *De educandis* also contains sections called "De Commerciis," and across its pages one can find meditations on the *varia* of not only household but also state *oeconomia*, including matters of taxation, tribute, trade, and contracts.

Such passages signal an interest in "policy," a word that begins to take on a special meaning in early modernity.[37] Heresbach's, and texts like his, are not a manual on how to handle economic contingencies so much as a statement on the *interests* of the prince in economic life and the practices of liberality and moderation that flow from his supposed virtues, which are always emphasized in Fürstenspiegel writing. What we have in this text, then, is an early instance of political economy—indeed a *Polizeiwissenschaft* or *Marktpolizei*. For in policing the market, princes pursued policies to control commodity prices, trade, wages, and—over all—adopted a decidedly political approach to economy, as was practiced (especially close to Hegel's home and time) in Prussia, as Karl-Heinz Lindner's *Marktordnung und Marktpolizei unt. bes. Berücks. Preußens* showed long ago.[38] So influential was this approach to the state and "state-wealth" that Michel Foucault called it "an absolutely German specialty that spreads throughout Europe and exerts a crucial influence."[39]

Smith would deem all of this material to be blather. In his *Wealth of Nations*, he seeks, among other things, to modernize the discipline of political economy *away* from Fürstenspiegel literature, the German literature of administration and *Marktpolizei*—those "theories," quoting Smith, that "have had a considerable influence, not only upon the opinions of men of learning, but upon the public conduct of princes and sovereign states." Smith summarizes, in his introduction, the contents of his fourth chapter, entitled "Of Systems of Political Economy," which deals directly with the discipline of political economy in all its varieties with attention devoted to these princes, sovereign states, and especially the problems with a variety of royal statutes limiting exports and the transport of products out of the old feudal provinces. Surprisingly, however, this is the chapter in which Smith issues his most famous remark on the role of the avaricious individual in society and the invisible hand, cited above: "He generally, indeed, neither intends to promote the public interest, nor knows how much he is promoting it. . . . By pursuing his own interest he frequently promotes that of the society more effectually than when he really intends to promote it." And, again, this is the same quotation Hegel draws from to reflect on these matters of political economy within the Fürstenspiegel frame. Hegel's choice in this regard makes perfect sense, as does the link between the medieval and the modern exhibited in this portion of the *Phenomenology of Spirit*.

Musing on the genre of Fürstenspiegel and the problem of wealth, Hegel found his way to the chapter in the *Wealth of Nations* in which Smith deals directly with this older, but still contemporary, genre. There, Smith's "invisible hand" is the vanished hand of princes pursing policy, as advised by Fürstenspiegel, while at the level of the individual, self-interest in the *Wealth of Nations* is expressed as the conscientious disavowal of "ancient provincial laws," the old way of doing things.[40] We can appreciate precisely how Smith decides to exemplify such self-interest and its ethic. Of the corn merchant, for example, he writes: "If, while his own country labours under a dearth, a neighbouring country should be afflicted with a famine, it might be his interest to carry corn to the latter country in such quantities as might very much aggravate the calamities of the dearth" at home.[41] Damn everyone else. Dismantling past and present legislation royal statute by royal statute, Smith remonstrates against the "temporary laws" that seek to forestall this self-interest that is the "powerful . . . principle . . . of carrying on the society to wealth and prosperity,"[42] though (conversely) merchants can rightly "extort" from "the legislature" laws that advance their own self-interest by which, in turn, "the public would certainly be a gainer."[43] Everywhere Smith finds that princely and especially statutory interference with the market ("absurd regulations of commerce")[44] work against his central principle, to paraphrase, to pursue one's own interests. In fact, his most famous line about the "invisible hand" is also a prescription for statesmen and sovereigns to stop manipulating markets:

> The statesman who should attempt to direct private people in what manner they ought to employ their capitals would not only load himself with a most unnecessary attention, but assume an authority which could safely be trusted, not only to no single person, but to no council or senate whatever, and which would nowhere be so dangerous as in the hands of a man who had folly and presumption enough to fancy himself fit to exercise it.[45]

No doubt, this quotation bolsters all the clichés you can muster about so-called "free" markets, celebrated in the name of Smith, but in historical terms (which are also *theoretical* terms) we can know what Smith's "invisible hand" really means as a modernizing principle only when we account for its premodern and early modern background. Which is Hegel's point: set this modernizing principle within the contexts of its articulation or purported applicability, ground the principle within some other historical frame besides England—indeed, place the principle within a European frame in which, historically, there is a significant lag in economic development in contrast to Smith's England—and suddenly the limits and non-universality of Smith's descriptions in *Wealth of Nations* are quickly disclosed, here amounting to yet another theory of the modern among the many available in Hegel's time.

So, too, we see that Hegel stages this critique by dint of a medieval genre, Fürstenspiegel, that supplies readers attuned to it a concrete sense of his larger philosophical project in the *Phenomenology of Spirit*. For the fact of the matter is that Fürstenspiegel is the genre of Bildung like none other, and we hardly need to be reminded that Bildung or Bildungsroman is the very point and form of Hegel's *Phenomenology of Spirit* itself.[46] Indeed, it's not enough to note (as is always done) the kindred and influential attempts at Bildungsroman by Hölderlin (*Hyperion*) or Goethe (*Wilhelm Meister's Apprenticeship*).[47] It's better to say something specific: at this precise moment in the *Phenomenology of Spirit*—the moment of Fürstenspiegel—Hegel conforms to the tasks of Bildung he set for himself in writing this philosophical work. As he insists in his Preface (§4) and Introduction, we are to experience in his book "the long process of culture [Bildung] toward genuine philosophy," the "series of configurations which consciousness goes through along this road is, in reality, the detailed history of the *education* [Bildung] of consciousness itself."[48] Significantly, Hegel only turns back to these important issues of Bildung in the aforementioned passages, complete with their medieval forms, contents, and problems, to trace out just one of the steps toward "genuine philosophy," the emergence of critical perspective, which (as to be expected) lapses back into more problems of faith, Enlightenment, and other modern issues. Crucial to this Bildungsroman is not only tragedy then comedy, as Marx said, but Fürstenspiegel, as Hegel found the form persisting in his own historical present.[49]

Marx's Misreading of Fürstenspiegel

Had Marx acknowledged all that is in this section of the *Phenomenology of Spirit*, "Culture and its realm of actuality," things might have turned out differently in terms of how the critique of political economy was initially phrased and framed, with credit going to Hegel for his formulations, rather than blame for something he didn't do. We recall, for instance, that Marx says, in the "Economic and Philosophic Manuscripts of 1844," that "Hegel's stand-point is that of modern political economy."[50] Marx is here critiquing the *ethics* of political economy and aligning Hegel with the ethics presented in Smith. Marx goes on to refer explicitly to "the struggle of the 'Noble and Base Consciousness'"—the very passage we have been investigating here— and states that "wealth, state-power, etc., are understood by Hegel as entities estranged from the *human* being," but estranged only in "abstract, philosophical thinking."[51] So, let's get this right: Hegel critiques the central insight of Smith's *Wealth of Nations*, sets it within the Fürstenspiegel frame in order to test market principles within a different (likely German) historical context, offers us a *cautionary tale* about the estrangement of wealth and value from the human, shows that Smith's desire to break from the past is at most aspirational and at best problematic, and Marx ups and says "Hegel's standpoint is that of modern political economy"?[52] It is not clear which point is more inaccurate: that Hegel's standpoint is only "modern" or that it is "that of political economy."

At least one can be honest about why Hegel and Marx are *fundamentally* different even while both are *decidedly dialectical*. I've already alluded to the problem in referring to Europe's economic belatedness. Clearly, it would take Marx to write the proper critique of industrial capital when such a project was a real historical possibility; his critique of political economy, and all that he brilliantly discusses in his volumes of *Capital,* is lasting (and inspires every bit of this book). But that fact should not keep us from understanding that what Marx says of Aristotle and the labor theory of value—that Aristotle's was not yet the time, place, or mode of production for such a theory to emerge—can be said of Hegel and the critique of capital:[53] Hegel offers no critique of capital, in the mode of Marx, because Hegel's context was not Marx's. Hegel could only get so close to what Marx understood without traveling in a time machine or for that matter in a boat: he never visited England, and Marx lived in London for most of his life. Thus, Hegel's economic modernity remained, on the one hand, *theoretical* in his reading of the *Wealth of Nations* beginning back in his days as a *Hofmeister* (i.e., a servant) in the household of Carl Friedrich von Steiger—reading that book in the house library[54]—and, on the other hand, *experiential*. Hegel read what he read, but saw what he saw: everywhere around him the economic belatedness of Europe and its often painful steps towards modernization—governmental and legal reform above all—in a context where the *ancien régime* and the feudal estates were anything but *ancien* and still a determining factor in how law, policy, and government in Prussia and elsewhere were to be established.[55] *Hegel knew that the modern reckons ceaselessly with the medieval.*

Hegel's dialectic is, then, formally and logically that of identity/difference, as discussed in chapter 2, but its temporal mode is that of the archaic and the emergent, epitomizing, like no other theoretical form, uneven development, as it would come to be called within Marxist analysis to indicate the co-presence of times and histories, each on different tempos. Of course, the dialectic already discloses itself temporally according to its "moment / Moment" (in English and German). But these innocent descriptions of the dialectic can be misleading, because "moment" seems to connote a singular experience, something along the lines of an "instant," thus concealing the temporal plurality therein, and the temporal multitudes that expand out horizontally within this moment to constitute the present, and the temporal pluralities that radiate in every other direction to be recognized as the past and the future, then and now, yesterday and today, medieval and modern, Monday and Friday. The true *dialectical* sense of "moment" spells a moment crowded with other moments—in other words, a moment "whose determinateness is regarded as a concrete whole."[56] It is on account of this temporal plurality that a "moment" is knowable or historicizable only in relation to other moments, what's before, what's after, and most importantly, what's within. Hegel's dialectic expresses something he would never name but everywhere practiced—uneven development—and it makes perfect sense that the dialectic of the medieval/modern would be compelling to him, as it would be for both Bakhtin and Jameson, to whom I now turn.[57]

The Gargantuan Critique of Political Economy: Bakhtin

Marx loved literature. As his son-in-law Paul Lafargue (of "right to laziness" fame) tells it:

> [Marx] knew Heine and Goethe by heart and often quoted them in his conversations; he was an assiduous reader of poets in all European languages. Every year he read Aeschylus in the Greek original. He considered him and Shakespeare as the greatest dramatic geniuses humanity ever gave birth to. His respect for Shakespeare was boundless: he made a detailed study of his works and knew even the least important of his characters. His whole family had a real cult for the great English dramatist; his three daughters knew many of his works by heart. When after 1848 he wanted to perfect his knowledge of English, which he could already read, he sought out and classified all Shakespeare's original expressions. . . . Dante and Robert Burns ranked among his favourite poets.[58]

Still, it must be admitted after decades upon decades of debate about "base," "superstructure," "ideology," and "culture" that, on balance, Marx in his written work was uninterested in aesthetics or anything resembling literary historicism, apart from some letters to Engels and comments on Shakespeare in the "Economic and Philosophical Manuscripts of 1844," the *Grundrisse*, and *Capital*.[59] Had he wished to write a history of aesthetic on the scale of Hegel's voluminous set of lectures on the topic, he would have done so. His choice in this respect had consequences for those who equally loved literature but wished to philosophize about it in a dialectical manner: such readers turned to Hegel to formulate, however ironic it may seem, a proper Marxian literary historicism. And when one holds Hegel up as an example of literary historicism—precisely the kind of critical practice in which literature is said to estrange and demystify its own historical present—one is inevitably constrained to talking about the Middle Ages persisting in the present, by means of residual yet enduring genres, forms of social life, or indeed a combination of both.

Take the case of Mikhail Bakhtin, whose own literary historicist project includes reflections on the Middle Ages that are more extensive than any offered by his contemporary Georg Lukács, himself a contender for the title of writing an aesthetics approaching the ambition (but not completeness) of Hegel.[60] Bakhtin works well as an example, because his is not the first name to come to mind when talking about Hegel, owing to his refusal to say anything positive about dialectic.[61] But I would suggest that our attention to the medieval brings into special focus the otherwise hidden connection between Hegel and Bakhtin—a connection that goes to the essence of what it means to do dialectical interpretation and, in the case of Hegel and Bakhtin, stage a critique of political economy through the frame of medieval genre.[62]

We begin with what Bakhtin says about the novel in relation to other genres. In his essay "Epic and Novel," he asserts that novelistic discourse is best understood as a "zone of contact" in which all previous genres "become more free and flexible"; they become "dialogized, permeated with laughter, irony, humor, [and] elements of parody."[63] Take the epic, for example. There's no more exalted genre, according to Bakhtin, because it allows for no "individual or personal point of view"; "it is impossible to experience it, analyze it, take it apart, penetrate its core."[64] Over the course of literary history, however, epic enters into this zone of contact and "passes through the intermediate stages of familiarization and laughter."[65] Within this zone, the epic succumbs to an especially destructive laughter, a "laughter [that] destroys the epic."[66] As a consequence, the epic point of view (sealed off, distanced, and hierarchical) gives way to the jocund perspective, in which all is "brought close."[67] Bakhtin elaborates on what the new point of view entails:

> Laughter has the remarkable power of making an object come up close, of drawing it into a zone of crude contact where one can finger it with familiarity on all sides, turn it upside down, inside out, peer at it from above and below, *break open its external shell* [разбивать его внешнюю оболочку / razbivat' ego vneshiuiu obolochku], look into its center, doubt it, take it apart, dismember it, *lay it bare* [обнажать / obnazhat'] and expose it, examine it freely and experiment with it.[68]

Something has happened here. We've gone from the epic, whereby "it is impossible to experience it, analyze it, take it apart, penetrate its core," to laughter, which enables a unique kind of inquiry into the nature of things.

Evidently, Bakhtin packs more into his famed "dialogism" than the notion of an open-ended plurality of voices and perspectives, both past and future, comprising a concrete, social discourse in the present. He includes, that is, the language of critique, but not any language: it is language usually reserved for the critique of political economy and the procedures of "laying bare" the relations of commodity production and the dynamics of value therein. "Break open its external shell," as Bakhtin says. Indeed, in these words we hear not only Marx's aspiration to invert Hegel's dialectic and penetrate "the mystical shell" and, by dint of proper critique, "discover the rational kernel."[69] We also hear tones from Marx's quintessential passage on the critical procedures of "laying bare" conditions, as they are, and not as they appear:

> Let us therefore, in company with the owner of money and the owner of labour-power, leave this noisy sphere, where everything takes place on the surface and in full view of everyone, and follow them into the hidden abode of production, on whose threshold there hangs the notice 'No admittance except on business'. Here we shall see, not only how capital produces, but how capital is itself produced. The secret of profit-making must at last be laid bare.[70]

For Bakhtin, then, dialogism includes more than laughter. It includes yet another tongue: the critique of political economy.

If, for Hegel, the critique of political economy is voiced by a medieval genre persistent within modernity (Fürstenspiegel), for Bakhtin, that same critique, that same procedure of demystification, is expressed by the residual, but vital, medieval vocality within modern discourse. Granted, in his essay "Epic and Novel," Bakhtin does not claim any special medieval significance for laughter and the comic, but there is a reason for this silence: he assumes ahead of time the medieval significance of these modes. For in an earlier essay ("From the Prehistory of Novelistic Discourse"),[71] he already argued that medieval Latin parody "is exactly like the modern novel."[72] It may be a surprise to read Bakhtin writing about Latin in this fashion—the supposedly universal language of the equally hegemonic western church—and declaring that it is "exactly like" the polyvocal discourse of the novel. Yet so strongly does Bakhtin view parody to be a fundamental component of medieval literary critique and satire that he continues to surprise in his description of Latinate practices we would, at first blush, consider *monological*:

> Only here, in the Latin literature of the Middle Ages, the complex and contradictory process of accepting and then resisting the other's word, the process of reverently heeding it while at the same time ridiculing it, was accomplished on a grand scale throughout all the Western European world, and left

an irradicable [sic] mark on the literary and linguistic consciousnesses of its peoples.[73]

What happens in medieval Latin parody, in other words, is representative of those fundamental shifts in discourse "throughout all the Western European world." That's quite a claim. But it is characteristic of how Bakhtin prefers to discuss the dialectical features of language contact. Not only that, however: we find, as well, a critical perspective born of these "contradictory" (dialectical) processes: "The process of parodying forces us to experience those sides of the object that are not otherwise included in a given genre or a given style."[74] Parody, by supplying multiple points of view on objects, stands as a critique of a certain singular perspective on reality, characterized by "one-sidedness": "Parodic-travestying literature introduces the permanent corrective of laughter, of a critique on the *one-sided seriousness* [одностороннюю серьезность / odnostoronniuiu ser'eznost'] of the lofty direct word."[75] In such a formulation, there's no hiding Bakhtin's critico-dialectical language, insofar as "one-sided" is a phrase both Hegel and Marx use frequently to describe non-dialectical processes or analyses, terms or forms that require dialectic to make them properly two-sided or contradictory. (For his part, Marx himself finds "one-sidedness" to be the fundamental error of political economy, and of Hegel!)

So how does medieval Latin parody bear on modern literary form? Bakhtin's answer is compelling in its periodizing claims:

> At the waning of the Middle Ages and during the Renaissance the parodic-travestying word broke through all remaining boundaries. It broke through into all strict and closed straightforward genres. . . . And there arrived on the scene at least, the great Renaissance novel—the novels of Rabelais and Cervantes. It is precisely in these two works that the novelistic word . . . revealed its full potential.[76]

Not only does this medieval mode of critique suffuse other genres; rather, it is perfected within them and refined as a critique of a very specific sort, resonant (again) with the critique of political economy as a merely "one-sided" point of view on economic activity.

In citing Rabelais and talking of the breaking of "remaining boundaries," Bakhtin surely has one thing on his mind: the carnivalesque. Meet Gargantua from Bakhtin's study from the 1940s, what English speakers know now as *Rabelais and His World*. In a work that could easily pass as the product of a medievalist, Bakhtin had in mind the critique of political economy as—it seems odd to say—an explanation of Rabelais's greatest character. For Gargantua is the supreme demystifier, if ever there were one, whose aim (to put

it in dull terms) is to eradicate exchange value altogether and handle objects as so many use values, with multiple applications. For in every object
he finds a radically new use: "Objects are reborn in the light of the use made
of them."[77] In his manipulation of objects, he suspends "all alienation" to
"test every object, examine it from all sides, enter into it, turn it inside out,
compare it to every phenomenon, however exalted and holy, and analyze
weigh, measure, and try it on,"[78] and in the process he "liberates objects from
the snares of false seriousness, from illusions and sublimations inspired by
fear"[79]—even if it means repurposing everyday objects as toilet paper.[80] False
seriousness, the "sober forms of seriousness" of "official medieval culture"[81]
sounds like a species of false consciousness, which Gargantua dispels and de-
mystifies with his "free, experimental, and materialistic knowledge."[82] It's not
sufficient to describe this analytical language and carnivalesque procedure,
in the old New Historicist fashion, as "transgression" and the disruption of
social hierarchies.[83] For his part, Bakhtin states that Gargantua partakes of
the "new experimental science," but no science we know of in the late Middle
Ages adopts this distinct language whose vocabulary comes straight from the
pages of *Capital*. As Marx says in his analysis of the central object of capitalism itself, the commodity: "We may twist and turn a single commodity as we
wish; it remains impossible to grasp it as a thing possessing value. However,
let us remember that commodities possess an objective character as values
only in so far as they are expressions of an identical social substance, human
labour."[84] Bakhtin echoes this passage in his figuration of Gargantua as the
beholder, and demystificator, of objects, and he can behold them in ways no
traditional political economist can.

Gargantua, then, is the indelibly medieval character who is immune (or
oblivious to) alienation, who christens things according to their immediate
use value, and saves them from exchange, abstraction, ideology, and illusion.
But he is not the only one capable of critique, nor is the critique limited to his
overly analytical behaviors. Everything from farting, pissing, shitting, eating,
overgrown bodies, gaping mouths, terms of abuse, and, yes, cartwheels oppose sacrosanct attitudes and practices.[85] These practices (do we call them?)
constitute a "contradictory oneness,"[86] but such a phrase—and the many
others like it—describes not the superficial dialectical features of these Gar-
gantuan and otherwise grotesque behaviors, but something deeper about
the totality of these images. They remind us, more systemically, that Bakhtin
finds in the work of Rabelais *figures* for the dialectic, if not literary vignettes
that supplement, again and again, Marx's own ambitions to revolutionize
philosophy by what, retrospectively, looks to be a Bakhtinian move. For does
not Marx's famous insistence that Hegel's dialectic is "standing on its head"

and must be "inverted" or "turned right side up" express, fundamentally, the carnivalesque "revolution" from the abstract to the concrete, from the ideal to the material, from the official to the folk? Cartwheels, for Bakhtin, replace the head for ass, training our attention on materiality and bodies in what has to be a proper dialectical inversion.[87]

And here is where the modern novel comes in and where the distinctions between medieval and modern, both in generic and theoretical terms, continue to blur on account of the transhistorical critique Bakhtin seeks to fashion, even as he describes his own project as a historical account of laughter.[88] In the same way the grotesque body is always in a state of "becoming," the novel "is the only developing genre and therefore it reflects more deeply, more essentially, more sensitively and rapidly, reality itself in the process of its unfolding."[89] Just as the grotesque body swallows the whole world,[90] the novels swallow all genres, "draws them ineluctably into its orbit precisely because this orbit coincides with the basic direction of the development of literature as a whole."[91] The grotesque body blubs and slobbers joyfully outside of official culture while seeming to suck it all in. Likewise, "the novel has an unofficial existence, outside 'high literature'" and "gets on poorly with other genres," because it "parodies other genres" and is "permeated with laughter"; it is "associated with the eternally living element of unofficial language and unofficial thought (holiday forms, familiar speech, profanation)."[92] These parallels between medieval and modern can mean only one thing. Bakhtin demonstrates that if you must describe the ideological work of the modern novel, then it is fair to use the language of the critique of political economy first fashioned in the Middle Ages: you observe that within novels "one can disrespectfully walk around whole objects; therefore, the back and rear portion of an object (and also its innards, not normally accessible for viewing) assume a special importance. The object is broken apart, laid bare."[93] The parodic practices of the Middle Ages, redolent with the language of the critique of political economy, actualize themselves in modernity in the novel. So much for Flaubert thinking that Rabelais "struck down the Middle Ages."[94]

In fact, so close is the connection between medieval and modern that none of this estrangement and demystification was available *before* the Middle Ages in the world of the ancient epic. To put it more forcefully, there can be no dialectical phenomenology in the ancient world, according to both Hegel and Bakhtin—another point to reveal Bakhtin's obvious Hegelianism and an excuse for us to draw into this discussion, finally, Hegel's account of Antigone, Greek tragedy, and the epic world in the *Phenomenology of Spirit*. For this episode tells us something about the perceived, periodized differences between consciousness in the antique world and that in the Middle

Ages—a distinction already discussed in chapter 3 in relation to the identity of the ancient "Sklave" and medieval "Knecht." According to Hegel, Creon, who is King of Thebes, refuses burial to Polynices because he is an enemy of the state; Antigone seeks to bury him because he's her brother and divine law requires it. To Hegel, this tragic situation is the worst of unhappy dialectics and cannot even be dignified with the word *dialectical.* For both sides never come together. Each asserts itself against its absolute opposite.[95] And each, be it Creon or Antigone, has legitimate reasons for their actions based on divine or human law, as well as gender roles, "one sex to one law, the other to the other law."[96] As Hegel morosely puts it, "The ethical consciousness, however, knows what it has to do."[97] And therein lies the problem with the Greek ethical state. There is no out. There is only "one-sidedness," duty, and guilt.[98] In Hegelian terms, the problem is "universal individuality," and not "particular individuality."[99] In Marxian terms, it is ideology. However you parse it, never is there contradiction in an ethical life "without contradiction," nor is there the possibility for a critique of ideology, for "the testing of law has been given up."[100] The point here is that it's fine to speak of this episode (as readers often do) as an individual fruitlessly struggling against the state, exampling in turn the so-called tyranny of the universal, and so forth, but Hegel's larger point is a periodizing one, which we can state in the following way, taking full advantage of the parallels between Antigone's encounter with Creon and the bondsman's encounter with the lord much earlier in the *Phenomenology of Spirit*. Simply put: were Antigone living in the Middle Ages, she would contend with Creon in the same way the bondsman struggles against the lord to achieve independence and self-consciousness. Yet unfortunately for her that kind of struggle is not possible in the epic world, nor is the dialectical process toward universal self-consciousness available to help her.

Bakhtin accepts this rather insistent form of Hegelian periodization, which (if it weren't clear already) purports to describe the difference between ancient and medieval worlds, rather than the usual fare these days over the medieval and modern divide. In the "Epic and Novel," he shows that genres that emerged *before* the novel and the Middle Ages—such as epic—foreclose the possibility of dialectical phenomenology, because their contexts are "distanced" and "separated from contemporary reality"[101]—in other words, too self-referential and mesmerized by an Otherness that is simply self-originated, and therefore undialectical:[102]

[The phrase] "I myself," in an environment that is distanced, exists not *in* itself or for *itself* but for the self's descendants, for the memory such a self anticipates in its descendants. I acknowledge myself, an image that is my own,

but on this distanced plane of memory such a consciousness of self is alienated from "me." I see myself through the eyes of another. This coincidence
of forms—the view I have of myself as self, and the view I have of myself
as other—bears an integral, and therefore naive, character—there is no gap
between the two. We have as yet no confession, no exposing of self. The one
doing the depicting coincides with the one being depicted.[103]

Here we read Bakhtin in one of his more phenomenological moments, and it
would seem, too, that he is reflecting on the insights of Hegel's lord/bonds-
man dialectic by transposing its phenomenological terms into the antique
context, where the said dialectic fails, as to be expected. Like Hegel, Bakhtin
claims that self-consciousness, as fleetingly figured in classical epic, is not
fully realized and is instead "a consciousness of self [that] is alienated from
'me.'"[104] For him, only medieval dialogism produces the forms of novelistic discourse that make literary and linguistic self-consciousness a distinct
possibility as a way of seeing, "a powerful means of grasping reality."[105] In
short, it takes the medieval to make the modern. And it also takes Hegel for
Bakhtin to formulate his best dialectical ideas about language, pace the many
instances where the latter doth protest too much about the former.

The Dialectic of Medieval Hermeneutics: Jameson

What Bakhtin (and Lukács) asserted about the novel are, by the time Fredric
Jameson published his game-changing The Political Unconscious (1981), commonplaces within Marxist aesthetics and theories of the novel. For instance,
the claim that the novel, since Don Quixote, "demonstrates . . . that process-
ing operation variously called narrative mimesis or realistic representation"
whose task is the "systematic undermining and demystification" of traditional "paradigms," would come as no surprise to readers in 1981.[106] After all,
take away the Marxian talk about "demystification" and such an assessment
is just a shade away from the standard view about literary realism in early
novelists like Richardson, whose "words bring his object home to us in all its
concrete particularity."[107] Jameson plainly knows that dialectical theory is not
advanced by such an idea—however important it remains—and certainly
neither is a theory of genre, much less the Hegelian-Marxian project to put
literary and political history in meaningful conversation with one another.

    And so Jameson builds up a new hermeneutic on the clearing of the old,
while sweeping to the side countless alternatives to make the following audacious and refreshingly counter-intuitive remark about the history of interpretation:

> It is clear that the most influential and elaborate interpretive system of recent times is that of psychoanalysis, which may indeed lay claim to the distinction of being the only really new and original hermeneutic developed since the great patristic and medieval system of the four senses of scripture.[108]

This statement is compelling not for its veracity, for right off the bat anyone could nominate at least a half-dozen other interpretive systems between the "patristic and medieval system" and Freud as candidates for something "new and original." It is intriguing, rather, for being said at all.

My intention is to explore Jameson's meaning here in the context of my larger argument about the centrality of the literary Middle Ages to dialectical criticism and the critique of ideology: without the Middle Ages as a generic and hermeneutic resource, there is no dialectic, period, and Jameson everywhere in his work evinces this point without as much as stating it.[109] That this goes unsaid in his work makes sense, however, because Jameson's task is to develop contemporary critical theory in a poignant way, not to celebrate the medieval period. Indeed, what makes Jameson's claim that psychoanalysis is "the only really new and original hermeneutic developed since the great patristic and medieval system of the four senses of scripture" a head-turner is not the inclusion of the medieval theory but rather the exclusion of Marxist hermeneutics. Why is this "system of the four senses of scripture" more *original* than Marxist theory? This would seem like a scathing indictment; to suggest that a medieval idea is better than a modern one is seldom a benediction about the latter. But an indictment it is not, because Jameson aims to improve Marxist theory by combining it with this medieval model, all in the effort to offer an hermeneutic that was, it almost goes without saying, "new and original" in the year *The Political Unconscious* was published. But my history in this entire chapter is to suggest that Jameson's alignment of the medieval and the modern within dialectical criticism was inevitable . . . and begins in Hegel as a way to join the critique of political economy with literary historicism.

To begin with, Jameson, like Bakhtin when he set out to understand laughter, seeks to recuperate the fourfold model from its misinterpretation in the hands of Northrop Frye, whose *Anatomy of Criticism* "comes before us as a virtual contemporary reinvention of the four-fold hermeneutic associated with the theological tradition."[110] Yet Frye "stem[s] the possibilities of collective and social interpretation which the hermeneutic had seemed to open."[111] Jameson therefore aims to return to that hermeneutic its collective project, by building not on Frye but on the work of the medievalist Henri de Lubac and his magisterial *Exégèse médiévale*.[112] For Jameson, the convergence of medieval hermeneutics, research from the field of medieval studies, and modern genre theory yield just the right mélange for a new Marxist theory of literature, which (like the fourfold model itself) compels a reader to think historically and contextually, reflecting at once both on the past and the present, as well as on the reader's situation within society and history writ large.[113]

How is the model already sufficient for Marxist interpretation? In answering, we can acknowledge immediately that the fourfold model, as Lubac defines it, is much too rigid to be a useful way of understanding medieval biblical hermeneutics, much less medieval dialectics. But Jameson is only interested in such hermeneutics in their most systematic form. As he sees it, with Lubac, the first or literal level of the medieval model demands that the reader approach the text (in this case, the Old Testament) as a "historical fact" but in a way that preserves the "literality" of this and other "original texts."[114] Invariably, the reader soon appreciates that this "historical fact" involves a "particular collective history—that of the people of Israel, or in other words a history culturally alien to the Mediterranean and Germanic clientele of early Christianity," but when this collective, historical fact is viewed allegorically, in the second level, it is reduced to a "purely biographical narrative, the life of Christ."[115] The movement, in other words, is from the collective in plural terms to something like the collective individual of Christ, the ideal person who is "valorized" in biographical or Gospel accounts. There's no stopping here, however, lest the reader fall into the folly of "one-sidedness," because there are only versions of *one* thing, the collective—here, the collective consciousness of Israel or collective figure of Christ. We need the next two levels to balance things out. In the third level, the individual suddenly appears: here, in the moral level, the reader derives a lesson about the "individual soul" and views the collective condition of the people of Israel (in exile, alienated, wandering, and "in bondage") as relating to the individual sin, "a bondage from which personal conversion will release him or her."[116] While the insertion of the individual here is an answer to the first two levels, which could only offer individuality as a *collective* concept, there emerges, again, the risk of one-sidedness—the solipsism of a person thinking only of himself, bracketing thoughts of collectivity. And so comes the fourth level, the anagogical, which resolves the agon of the individual and the collective (now one, then the other) into universal history itself, which respects both instances at once. Here, the collective returns but not in terms of the singularly collective individual or Christ, but rather in terms of *all* individuals *as* individuals collected together, the body of believers, who stand for the "destiny of the humankind as a whole." The process is now complete, for

Jameson this "solution" bears great significance: "The historical or collective dimension is thus attained once again, by way of the detour of the sacrifice of Christ and the drama of the individual believer; but from the story of a particular earthly people it has been transformed into universal history and the destiny of humankind as a whole—precisely the functional and ideological transformation which the system of four levels was designed to achieve in the first place."[117]

My exposition of Jameson's fourfold model is, I realize, all trees and no forest.[118] So it's time to be blunt. None of Jameson's readings in *The Political Unconscious* scale the levels of the fourfold model (though, incidentally, Slavoj Žižek does precisely that with Jameson's medieval model).[119] Which should tell us something—namely, that Jameson's fourfold model is an exercise in its own right in thinking dialectically, training attention on the co-presence of temporal, economic, political, and generic orders. Those medieval relays between the individual in the now and the church at some point in the past or future stand for exactly this kind of temporal interchange. As any dialectical model should, Jameson's points to the contemporaneity of pasts, presents, and futures. The fourfold model is nothing if not a display of temporal mindfulness and a medieval dialectic of its own kind, a working through of "levels" that express the most discussed dialectical topics within Marxism: the individual and the collective. Indeed, these levels are the "problem" of Marxism—the stuff of the positive hermeneutic Jameson seeks to offer—and as such they are not the dialectic whose form or structure is straightforwardly that of identity/difference (see chap. 2), or if it is, it is extremely complex: the interpreter moves between the fourfold model's various levels and ruminates upon their *different* points of view in a *relational* way and experiences a transformation of consciousness that ends in a newly realized consciousness not only of the self but of what is total and *collective*. Phrased like that, it becomes clear that identity/difference can take on many shapes, many contents, which suit the utopian project underlying *The Political Unconscious*.

In his "Conclusion: The Dialectic of Utopia and Ideology," Jameson turns to the medieval model in order to give *new* meaning to the "demystifying procedures" attendant to the Marxist critique of false-consciousness.[120] The effort here, for Jameson, is to improve Marxist analysis, supplementing that critique of conditions, inevitably a "negative" project, with a more positive, and utopian, mode of analysis, or what he will call a "positive hermeneutic":

> The historically original form of the negative dialectic in Marxism—whether ideology is in it grasped as mere "false consciousness," or more comprehensively, as structural limitation—should not be allowed to overshadow the

presence in the Marxian tradition of a whole series of equivalents to . . . [a] positive hermeneutic.[121]

Jameson goes on to list some examples of such a "positive hermeneutic" in "Ernst Bloch's ideal of hope or of the Utopian impulse" or "Mikhail Bakhtin's notion of the dialogical as a rupture of the one-dimensional text of bourgeois narrative"—both of which, among others, "hint at a variety of options for articulating a properly Marxian version of meaning beyond the purely ideological."[122] But, again, Jameson offers not a Blochian or Bakhtinian "reading" of literature. Rather, and in his own way that nonetheless takes after Hegel, he prefers to pair medieval and Marxist hermeneutics in order to disclose the utopian impulses of modern literature:

> [The] varied options [of interpretation] can be measured against the stan-
> dard of the medieval system of four levels, which helped us to distinguish the
> resonance of the "moral" level—that of the individual soul, or of the libidinal
> Utopia of the individual body—from that ultimate and logically prior level
> traditionally termed the "anagogical," in which even such individual visions
> of Utopian transfiguration are rewritten in terms of the collective, of the des-
> tiny of the human race. Such a distinction allows us to spell out the priority,
> within the Marxist tradition, of a "positive hermeneutic" based on social class
> from those still limited anarchist categories of the individual subject and in-
> dividual experience.[123]

Jameson is obviously adjusting the model here, shifting its ground from me-dieval theology to Marxian orthopraxy of a profoundly new, nuanced, and culturally informed kind.[124] In short, the fourfold model is the "positive" so-lution to the problem of Marxian negative hermeneutics, a way of seeking "meaning beyond the purely ideological." Before, then, seeking an outside to literature and, more broadly, modernity, Jameson seeks the outside of mod-ern theory, aiming to lay bare its own limits and expose its ideological impo-sitions to be only "negative," as if all that dialectics require is negation.

But what does this medieval hermeneutic, which is, after all, a protocol for reading sacred and secular writing alike in the Middle Ages, tell us about modern writing? To think a "Marxian version of meaning beyond the purely ideological" is to attend to the utopian impulses within modern writing, which reveal themselves to be impulses expressive of "uneven development" not only in economic history but in literary form. As Jameson notes in his chapter on Conrad entitled, "Romance and Reification":

> Our business as readers and critics of culture is to "estrange" this theme [a
> tale of courage and cowardice] in a Brechtian way, and to ask ourselves why
> we should be expected to assume, in the midst of capitalism, that the aesthetic

rehearsal of the problematics of a social value from a quite different mode of production—that feudal ideology of honor—should need no justification and should be expected to be of interest to us. Such a theme must mean something else: and this even if we choose to interpret its survival as an "uneven development," a nonsynchronous overlap in Conrad's own values and experience (feudal Poland, capitalist England).[125]

Quite how a feudal "theme" can "mean *something else*" gets at the dialectical project of *The Political Unconscious* and the critical effort to imagine the co-presence of the medieval and the modern within fiction and history. Accordingly, at moments when Jameson names the "political unconscious" of a given text, as he does in chapter 3, "Realism and Desire," we find, in the case Balzac's *La Rabouilleuse*, a utopian project, "raising, in symbolic form, issues of social change and counterrevolution, and asking itself how the force necessary to bring about a return to the old order can be imagined as doing so without at the same time being so powerful and disruptive as to destroy that order itself in the process."[126] In the "political unconscious," just as in the medieval model, then, there are relays, within the imaginative and utopian frame, between past and present, and each dialectically refigures the other. The point is that there is more than just nostalgia at work in Balzac, just as there is more to Jameson's effort than just a negative dialectic. For one can always point to Balzac as a conservative or "a royalist and apologist for the essentially organic and decentered *ancien régime*" in the same way one can decry, as Marx did, "a whole catalogue of desolations that range from the destruction of older social forms to the degradation of values and activities of individuals and their transformation into sheer exchange value."[127] But the Jamesonian difference (which I believe is also the Hegelian difference within Jameson's work) is to elevate this kind of observation, this kind of co-temporal reflection, to the very task of dialectical thought itself: "To think dialectically is to invent a space from which to think these two identical yet antagonistic features together all at once"[128]—the medieval and the modern, the feudal and the capitalist—*always* in a relation of identity/ difference.

Jameson averred that *The Political Unconscious* has an "unavoidably Hegelian tone," and we hear now that tone as a chord of several Hegelian tones—dialectical, "retrospective," aesthetic, and now a new tone: this book is Hegelian because Hegel and Jameson make the same critical move.[129] One thinker turned to the medieval dialectic to innovate within modern philosophy, and the other turned to a medieval dialectical hermeneutic to innovate within critical and literary theory. This is more than a coincidence, but it is also just short of an acknowledgment of the *mediévalité* of the dialectic itself as it emerges in Hegel. As it stands, however, Jameson's use of the fourfold model is as close as any theorist has come until now to admitting that Marxist dialectics must not only come to terms with its predecessor—the dialectic from the Middle Ages—but also absorb its procedures.

6

On Dialectical Interpretation

I dwell in Possibility—
EMILY DICKINSON

Getting Hegel, Wilhelm von Humboldt, and Leopold von Ranke to agree on something would be a marvelous occasion. But in nineteenth-century Berlin there was never any such marvel—especially if you expect these fellows to agree on what the literary imagination is good for. Is the literary imagination only for poetry? How might it improve historiography? What about philosophy? Each took a stab at these questions. Wilhelm von Humboldt, for example, held that poetry matters not a whit to history; historians should not expect poetry to tell us about the past nor should they decide that poetry is as eventful as political history. For poetry, he thought, deals with human actions in such a way as to render the accidents of reality, the arbitrary unfolding of history, into a fiction of necessities and plotted motivations. Likewise, when it comes to historiography, so claimed von Humboldt, historians should eschew poetic flourish and write in lucid prose. Von Ranke, that great innovator of historical science, was a bit more accepting of poetry. He acknowledged that historiography is an art, somewhere between philosophy and poetry. Yet unlike these latter two disciplines and practices, history concerns itself with "the real," not "the ideal" of philosophy and art. Even so, von Ranke maintained that a historian might employ the "imagination," the poetic faculty, but only to assimilate into a whole the "documentary traces" of the archive. Never, however, should such an exercise produce poetry itself—only prosaic historical narrations.[1]

Then there was Hegel, with his own point of view. For him, poetry is historical *because* it is ideal. Von Ranke was wrong on that score, Hegel thought. And Hegel kept on thinking along these lines, seeking to use his brand of idealism to think through the problem we now recognize by the phrase "literature and history." He had a range of views on the historicity of poetry, all of them patently philosophical. He thought that because poetry is temporal, it mimics historical experience in its unfolding.[2] He also had a sense of genre, feeling that poetry, especially epic poetry, draws narrative history (events, persons) into itself, translating the prosaic details of life into the imagination and presenting events in "succession."[3] He also believed—and this gets at what it means to speak of his thought as a "system"—that because poetry's medium is language, poetry is "the property of spirit" and thus already resides in history as a particular instantiation of the "concept" of a given age.[4] No matter how he approaches the question of poetry's historicity, he seeks to avoid reducing poetry to historiography, which is why he emphasizes that poetry presents not "the content or meaning of an historical fact that has actually occurred, but some fundamental thought more or less closely akin to it, in short a collision of human experience."[5] Poetry, that is, expresses not historical trivia but rather the *concept* of a historical period that makes consciousness what it fundamentally is at that moment. It is no wonder, then, that Hegel conceives of poetic production as a kind of phenomenology whose mode must be historicized by juxtaposing genre and context, form and consciousness, figure and concept.[6] For Hegel, in other words, the dialectical interpretation of literature requires not that we meditate long and hard on the "literature/history" binary, as we wracked our brains doing in the 1970s to the 1990s with New Historicism holding sway as the last compromise solution, practically deconstructive in its collapse of the binary itself. Rather, Hegel demands that we *raise* this distinction to a higher one where there is no distinction at all: figure/concept. In Hegel's hands, then, some of the textbook topics in Romanticism—imagination, poetry, philosophy, genius—are refashioned as dialectical problems, test cases for how conceptualization can at once be construed as figuration.

   To the extent, then, that the historicization of poetry was a debate, it is fair to say that Hegel won.[7] For nearly every literary critical procedure that juxtaposes genre and history owes at least *some* debt to Hegel and, in particular, to his idea that genres are *like* concepts, adequate or inadequate (in the philosophical sense) to the contexts in which they emerge, grasping or failing to grasp the conditions of their own emergence. When, for instance, Georg Lukács maintained that certain genres such as the novel, romance, and epic exhibit a relative "distance" or "closeness" to the greater context of "life," we find Hegel as the template for this literary historicism.[8] When Mikhail Bakhtin suggested that one genre over another, the novel over the epic, expresses more completely the "social life of discourse" as a "stylistic unity" of opposed languages—likewise.[9] When Pierre Macherey established a hermeneutic whereby the history of forms and the history of ideology find their dual expression in literary works through *adequation gone wrong*—through "conflicts in meaning" within the "postulated unity" of the text—we discover Hegel once more.[10] And, lastly, when Fredric Jameson endeavored to reconcile genre and history—"romance" and "reification," to echo the title of one of his investigations—we find Hegel again, though here Jameson is not exactly keeping any secrets about the "unavoidably Hegelian tone . . . of *The Political Unconscious.*"[11] Even as this small sample suggests, whatever their differences and local variations, literary historicisms have Hegel to thank for conceiving literary history and social history as distinct but related to each other in the way concepts grasp, or fail to grasp, their referents: does literary discourse adequate itself to history? Is history too big for literature to grasp? What third referent does literature and social history, together as concepts, point to, or seek to grasp?[12]

Yet, for all that, Hegel's is only a partial victory, even if the likes of von Humboldt and von Ranke have recessed from view, more or less. For it still can be said that these modern literary historicisms do not appreciate the full extent of Hegelian conceptuality or the backgrounds and traditions that gave Hegel reason to develop *conceptual figuration* and its accompanying *phenomenological style.* I am, again, referring to the premodern dialectics that have concerned us in this entire book, and which supply a plethora of examples whereby figure is concept, and concept is figure. The story I have to tell here begins with a forgotten episode—indeed trend—in dialectical thinking in the nineteenth century, when (as I will show) there was a missed opportunity for a number of philosophers and literary critics to formulate an aesthetic theory that paid equal attention to figuration and conception. This failure to couple concept and figure in theoretical criticism is not some local problem from a hundred-plus years ago. It is, rather, indicative of dialectical thought more generally and is therefore the lens through which I reassess the larger history of dialectical literary historicism from Hegel, to that nineteenth-century moment, to the great literary historicisms of the twentieth century, to historical reflection in the present. My aim is to extract lessons from that larger history of dialectical thinking in the hopes of opening the door to a rapprochement between concepts and figures, which can open lines of communication between dialectical and anti-dialectical theorists inspired especially by Deleuze and Guattari (offering, as they do, the most influential criticism of dialectics). But this rapprochement in theory can happen only when premodernity stays within the theoretical frame and when, especially, premodern writing is regarded as a powerful example of utopian expression, where the figures of the past meet the concepts of the present, giving definition to dialectical habits of thought energized by their own historicity.

Green Hegelians

The histories of literary theory and dialectical thought, such as they are, do not tell of Hegelian literary historicism in the nineteenth century, even when its procedures are strikingly familiar. This section explores the literary historicism that emerged out of the larger Hegelian Revival in the United Kingdom and the United States, a movement that comprehends the work of many philosophers,[13] who published widely in ethics, politics, socialism, rhetoric, historiography, aesthetics, and literary criticism.[14] Some of them translated works by Hegel in editions that are still used today, such as the Penguin edition of Hegel's lectures on aesthetics.[15] My focus here, however, will be those literary critics who responded to the calls of Hegelianism and demonstrated an interest in the problem of literature and history in something like the formation we have recognized from the 1970s to the 1990s. Although today we can address certain "literature" and "history" problematics through a number of perspectives (formalist, post-structuralist, Marxist, New Historicist, none of the above) in the late nineteenth century, Hegelianism, I argue, was the only means by which this very problematic could be explicitly posed and redressed within Anglo-American literary criticism.[16] This Hegelianism was so new that it represents one of the initial trends in modernism that caricaturize and then reject Victorian critical methods in favor of continental models;[17] literary historians freely declaimed their differences from Ruskin, Arnold, and Pater while writing under the influence of Hegel.[18] But the success of this historicism is another thing altogether; again, it goes unmentioned in discussions of theory today. From the perspective of a history of dialectical thinking that understands, after the long premodern tradition, how crucial the linking of concept and figure is, we will discover this Hegelianism to be too literary and not conceptual enough—even though indeed this literary historicism had its beginnings in philosophy, starting with T. H. Green (1836–82).

A biographical word about Green is in order. He was a fellow at Balliol College, Oxford, and held the Whyte's professorship of moral philosophy. Engaging in social work throughout his life, he "believed strongly in extending access to higher education to poorer students and working men." He "also campaigned for the admission of women to Oxford University." His intellectual impact was quite enormous. His "philosophy . . . set a standard of academic rigour which helped change the character of British philosophy from the early twentieth century," and "every important philosopher in Britain between 1880 and 1914 responded in some way to his work."[19] For our immediate purposes, however, we can note that Green introduced German idealism to Oxford, making sure that exams, for the first time, contained questions on

Kant and Hegel. Other contemporary philosophers were, no doubt, turning to Hegel at the same time as Green, but he remains important for our purposes owing both to his work in literary criticism, in which his debt to Hegel is clear, and to his influence on literary criticism and aesthetics.

In 1862, Green published *Works of Fiction*, a modest attempt to propose how genre should be regarded historically. In retrospect, his work might appear as yet another study of genre in the Aristotelian mode, but the sheer fact that he arranges genres such as epic, tragedy, and the novel in a progression that is historical in its own right, irreducible to the history of governments as conceived by, say, Thomas Babington Macaulay,[20] Henry Hallam,[21] and Francis Palgrave,[22] discloses his Hegelianism and his sense that history can be brought to bear on literature without construing literary texts as only political documents, much less experiments in realism.[23] His Hegelianism here is best distinguished by what it isn't. Green's *Works of Fiction*, we must recognize, is the first attempt in the Anglo-American scene not only to return to Hegel but to recuperate Hegelian *literary* historicism from the public ridicule Hyppolyte Taine's now notorious version garnered from such commentators as Nietzsche, who thought Taine to be Hegel's avatar in a "coarse and stupid France."[24] Green, that is, would not dissolve genre, like Taine, by putting texts in the service of predetermined historical causes such as "race," "surroundings," and "epoch" in what appears to be essentially a Comtean, rather than Hegelian, analysis—the application of scientific principles (better, metaphors) to the study of history and its "causes" and, in this case, generic invention.[25] Rather, Green insists that generic invention itself is a historical act, as relevant to our sense of history as are laws and political systems.[26] That's the more properly Hegelian view of genre—the view that genre is among the many determinations within a social whole, each determining the other and each manifesting these multiple determinations as "collisions" and contradictions.

Green had not continued as a literary critic—he published instead in ethics and politics, though at many points he would include literary analyses within his philosophical tracts—but the importance of his literary work is known in the success of his students, such as Bernard Bosanquet (1848–1923), to whom Green "introduced . . . the works of Kant and Hegel," before he turned more intensely to "the writings of John Ruskin and Hegel," among his other interests in logic.[27]

Bosanquet was a fellow of University College, Oxford, before resigning that post in 1881 to move to London, where he pursued social work. Like his teacher, he sensed that the views of Ruskin, Pater, Morris, and Arnold needed refining, an opinion nowhere more evident than in his *History of*

Æsthetic (1892), which "became a standard text in a study rather neglected by British philosophers of his own time."[28] This book is a critical review of the aesthetic consciousness from the Greeks to the moderns inclusive of Ruskin, Morris, and Arnold. In it, Bosanquet essentially assesses the history of aesthetic by means of a Hegelian touchstone (to evoke the Arnoldian phrase). For instance, Ruskin is not Hegelian enough.[29] Indeed, Bosanquet implies that artistic consciousness (the aesthetic proper) from the Middle Ages on develops toward Hegel, and that from Hegel on, the aesthetic is articulated through concealed or partially disclosed versions of this German idealist's ideas. Evidently, given his emphasis on texts, Bosanquet narrows the aesthetic itself down such that Hegel's other aesthetic forms—architecture, sculpture, painting, music—disappear: *literature itself now falls into relief as the primary yet final aesthetic form.* Hegel, of course, sponsored that view, seeing poetry as the highest form, culminating in what is now one of his most controversial views, "The End of Art."[30] But quite how this idea played out is evident; part of the larger argument I will make below about this genealogy of literary historicism is that nineteenth-century critics mistook the Hegelian "End of Art" as the "end of the concept" in art, consequently resulting in an imbalance in the Hegelian dynamic of figure/concept. They err, in short, on the side of figure and in so doing fail to realize the advantages of a properly dialectical criticism.

Suffice it to say, however, that Bosanquet understood well that Hegelianism can sponsor a distinctly social criticism connecting the past to the present. Criticism can reflect back upon the history of the aesthetic itself as a means to reflect on present method. In his chapter "Questions on Æsthetic To-day," Bosanquet announces new strategies for writing aesthetic histories: "The divorce from history which is so marked in recent methodising æsthetic ought not to continue." But this does not mean you throw history at the problem: "It cannot be necessary to compile a complete history of civilization and place it by the side of a complete history of art." Here Bosanquet is following, again, Hegel, who in his lectures on aesthetics says that one cannot facilely reconcile political history ("the known historical data") with aesthetic history:

> [A] double difficulty appears: either the known historical data, when taken into the poem, may not be wholly compatible with that fundamental [poetic] thought, or, conversely, if the poet retains this familiar material but alters it in important points to suit his own ends, a contradiction arises between what is firmly fixed in our minds and what the poet has newly introduced. It is difficult but necessary to resolve this contradiction and division and produce the right undisturbed harmony; after all, reality has an indisputable right to respect its essential phenomena.[31]

Any effort in historicizing poetry, in other words, must involve a principle of mediation to reconcile the different but dialectically related domains of literature and history—domains in contradiction with one another. We now recognize this idea in the contemporary critical insistence against reflectionism, in which literary works are transparent to history, as witnessed in Macherey's valid claim that "history is not in a simple external relation to the work. . . . Thus, it is not a question of introducing a historical explanation which is stuck on to the work from the outside."[32] There needs to be, again, mediation to counter any assumptions about *immediacy* and presence, whereby history, always present in a work as a kind of content, can be illuminated by way of "explanation . . . from the outside" (Macherey) irrespective of genre; or, as Hegel puts it, the historical information that "is firmly fixed in our minds" when we set about to read poetry historically. Resolving the contradiction between literature and history, for Hegel, means that we first recognize the contradiction and acknowledge its presence *in* the literary work itself. (One can see how these ideas are shaped in the hands of Adorno, who, in his famous lecture "On Lyric Poetry and Society," would relocate the contradiction to the space *between* poetry and its context: "Social concepts should not be applied to the works from without," just as "the lyric reveals itself to be most deeply grounded in society when it does not chime in with society.")[33]

For his part, when it comes to situating literary works within history, Bosanquet urges that critical analysis of "epic and the drama . . . the novel, or bourgeois epic"—note that these are the three genres of Green's concern—needs a more active "allusion to the times of their greatness and the conditions of their genesis," lest the literary history become, as he puts it, "wearisome." Bosanquet, in other words, here is naming the principle of mediation "allusion," knowing that a more nuanced idea about historical causes and determination must be advanced, alongside an awareness that genre is itself determinative. "Allusion," that is, troubles any sense of easy historical causes and effects and posits indirection as a mode of literary referencing or pointing. It is a realization of Hegel's suggestion that poetry offers "some fundamental thought *more or less closely akin* to" history, which looks to be the nineteenth-century equivalent of the literary "symptom," as Macherey deploys it.

To draw out further his principle of mediation, Bosanquet claims to combine existing critical tendencies: the "historical system of Hegel" as inspired by the "spirit of Mr. Ruskin, Mr. Morris, and Mr. Pater."[34] By this assertion, Bosanquet intends to introduce Hegelian historicism into a literary formalism that seeks to acculturate persons through the reading and teaching of literature. It is easy, however, for him to incorporate, if not sublate, these three thinkers, especially Ruskin, whose gothic is, in its own peculiar way, as Hegelian as anything one can imagine (as David Carrier has argued),[35] and Pater, who does in fact draw on Hegel's aesthetics.[36] Yet what Bosanquet himself is calling for is a formalist-historicist dialectic that includes literature—a dialectic out of which emerges an aesthetic that renders visible a teleology of forms and their connection to epoch-specific modes of consciousness, to history as a Hegelian would have it.[37] It is not the burden of Hegelianism to name mediation per se, so much as to practice it. After all, in the contexts out of which Hegelianism continually re-emerges, Hegelianism is itself the philosophy of mediation. Any literary historicism inspired by it would follow suit, as we will now see.

Hegelian without Knowing It

Lacan once said that "everybody is Hegelian without knowing it."[38] To say this of mid-twentieth-century French theory and philosophy is one thing, because Lacan's point is obvious, uttered amidst the Hegel craze after Kojève. But can the same thing be said of philosophy in the mid- to late-nineteenth-century England and the United States? It can, as long as the reader understands that almost all of the relevant parties were not hard-core phenomenologists or Hegelian logicians, nor for that matter card-carrying Hegelians on all points—an issue I will address again in the final section of this chapter. It's a complicated picture, to begin with, but one that nonetheless identifies a shift in the way critics began talking about literary and social history. My idea that in the nineteenth century there are "Hegelians without knowing it" is intended only to say that there is a critical unconscious at work in this period resulting from the influence of German idealism—Kant certainly, but in these instances, most particularly Hegel, whose work was made increasingly available in English translation. One of those translators, Bosanquet, is, I believe, a great indicator of the newer critical tendencies afoot at the end of the century, when we witness a shift in literary historicisms away from the better-known versions of Margaret Oliphant or George Saintsbury, who wrote diachronic, generic histories conscientiously set apart from social history.[39] Rather, some critics engaged Hegel's work directly. Even more wrote a new kind of literary history that is ostensibly Hegelian and distinctly sociopolitical, authorizing itself on the premise now familiar to Green and Bosanquet—that literary history and social history have been kept apart within current interpretive models and are in need of a theoretical instrument to mediate these two histories and produce a "social text." Literary criticism, up to this point, had not yet seen this model, but critics like William John Courthope, Leslie Stephen, and Vida Dutton Scudder all took advantage of it.[40]

Courthope (1842–1917) was a poet, an editor of Pope, and a civil service commissioner before his election to the chair of poetry at Oxford in 1895.[41] In 1901, he published *Life in Poetry, Law in Taste,* which is a collection of lectures he delivered in this professorship. He clearly had philosophical interests and cared to grapple with the idealists at Oxford. For example, he discusses art and the "imitation of external things," or the artistic "methods of imitation" from Kant, Fichte, Schiller, and Goethe to Schlegel and Hegel, and he is not persuaded by the notion that each period (and this includes "the Symbolic, the Classic, and the Romantic" of Hegel's scheme) is characterized by a specific manner of imitation.[42] He goes on to engage with Bosanquet's critique of Aristotle, as well as his views on poetry and morality, but then alights on this point, which is hardly original to Courthope: "The purpose of all the Fine Arts is eminently social," or "in the late days of national life artistic creation is always accompanied by criticism," sometimes "after the great period of instinctive creation has exhausted itself"—reminding one of Hegel's famed "End of Art" thesis precisely as Bosanquet had understood it.[43] Courthope defines "Life in Art and Law in Taste" as "the opposite sides of the same proverbial shield": the former is "the recreation in organic form of the universal ideas or impressions which the mind derives from Nature" and the latter "the intuitive perception of the conditions of life."[44]

It does indeed seem dialectical to speak of opposites of the same thing, difference expressed in a unity. Even so, by no means programmatic, Courthope is a critic of his time, situated within the latest debates and evincing methods, readings, and dialectical turns of thought that were only possible in a post-Hegelian climate. That much is clear in his six-volume *A History of English Poetry,* which he wrote between 1895 and 1910. His aim in this work is to do something different but similar, fitting not only to the themes he lays out in *Life in Poetry, Law in Taste* but, ironically, to the great Hegelian identity/difference. In particular, he proposes a principle of literary history "on altogether new foundations" from Thomas Warton, Pater, and Taine.[45] He wishes to seek for "unity" in history, as would a "political historian," hoping "to use the facts of political and social history as keys to the poet's meanings."[46] Yet rather than placing literary and political history together, blurring the distinction between the two so that all genres become essentially historical novels, Courthope offers a "principle": poetry's "growth and movement" shadows the "movement of political history," with its institutions—commercial, military, legal. In the historical movement of poetry and "other arts of expression," we derive "new modes of thought, fresh types of composition, improved methods of harmony."[47] Literary developments in one "generation are carried forward," and improved, "in the next." "Mind works upon mind."[48]

By these motifs of development, movement, "mind," and "modes of thought," Courthope is soft-peddling the principle of historical determination, because he intends to show that literature, economy, politics, and culture are interdependent but offer differing points of view on the greater historical context and are diverse manifestations of a larger history, what he calls "life of the nation as a whole."[49] In this respect, Courthope closely approximates the Hegelian understanding of a social "whole," *Geist* or Spirit, which designates a historical period or totality whose idea is materialized in various cultural productions, including literature, art, and law. What particularly signals Courthope's idealist view of history is the ways in which he resists, in his socially inflected literary history no less, construing social and economic class as the *only* determinations on literature, as the only context or set of "facts" that informs writing. For instance, Courthope certainly sees a difference between Dante and Langland, the former of "noble birth," the latter "the descendent of perhaps small landowners." But for him, the distinction in social status and economic class does not explain the difference between their poems and their social significance. Rather, "the divergence between their ideas owes to a difference in the local circumstances to which the ideas had to be applied." Courthope, by assessing how literary works manifest a historical idea that transcends class or politics but which is equally immanent to literature, politics, and economy, is adopting a particular kind of Hegelianism here, and it's not that involving Hegel's own distinction between personal morals or *Moralität* and social ethics or *Sittlichkeit*.[50] Rather, Courthope is touching on the contemporary Hegelian glosses on these very ideas in Hegel—glosses that are inevitably post-socialist, indeed post-Marxist, in the way they ask how these terms are relevant to questions of economic and social class, as in Green's argument that ethical obligations in society are not governed by class or status obligations.[51] F. H. Bradley, likewise, understood that artistic production is a "duty . . . very hard to reduce . . . to a duty of any station," while Bosanquet critiqued Marx and philosophical materialism, questioning the idea that "economic facts alone . . . are real and causal; everything else is an appearance and an effect."[52] What we can take away from all of these statements, Courthope's included, is not a rejection of a socially committed criticism, or Marx for that matter, as much as what any thinker in his right mind would reject today as well, vulgar materialism. As Bosanquet puts it, economic facts alone are not "any prior determining framework of social existence, but simply certain important aspects of the operation of the human mind, rather narrowly regarded in their isolation from all others." There cannot be a false contrast, he continues to say, between "the mechanical pressures of economic facts and the influence of ideas"[53]—a notion that may be palatable to those who recall Lenin's remark that "an intelligent idealism is closer to an intelligent materialism than is a stupid materialism."[54] For the purposes of my historical illustration, the critical tendency here is to adopt a socially inflected form of literary history that includes idealism, that is attentive to a totality in which "mind works upon mind," but which doesn't reduce literature to historical facts. To be clear, it cannot be said that Courthope is a Hegelian by discipline, but he is following new trends that avowedly redefine the current habits of literary criticism and supply a new way of thinking about literature as social. He was keen to be *au courant* and involve himself in debates about idealism, the philosophical approaches to literature, and indeed the aesthetic precisely on these questions of the relation between literature and history.

What can be said of Courthope can also be said of Leslie Stephen (1832–1904), who was the father of Virginia Woolf and a man of many talents: athlete, mountaineer, electioneer, history writer (he chatted once with Abraham Lincoln), author, literary journalist, editor of the *Dictionary of National Biography*, lecturer at Trinity College, Cambridge, and president of the London Library (succeeding Tennyson). He knew just about everybody in the literary scene.[55] That he emerges as a relevant figure is surprising, for he was, after all, an intellectual adversary of a prominent Hegelian, none other than Green. But it is precisely in the contestations between this Cambridge Rationalist and the Hegelians at Oxford and elsewhere that we find their debate to be delimited by an argument about Hegelian idealism itself and the kinds of aesthetic necessary to draw form and history together in mutually expressive ways.[56] And as a member of the Ethical Society with Green, Bosanquet, and Bradley, he found further affiliation with them on questions having to do with political responsibility and class.[57] Stephen shows this agreement both in his literary historicism and in his reliance on, as we shall soon discover, Courthope, whose work appeared idealist enough to inform Stephen's own opinions about what makes literature historical.

At Oxford in 1903, Stephen delivered (by proxy) a series of lectures on literature, which occasioned his election to the Ford lectureship in English history at Oxford. Like Courthope and Bosanquet, he argued that the present state of literary historical criticism was wanting and that a new literary historicism, a new "method," can open historians' eyes to literature, and the formalists' minds to history. At present, he writes, historians "are too much overwhelmed by State papers to find space for any extended application of the method,"[58] restricting their researches to the ostensible "historical" texts. (The Oxford historian J. R. Green is, to him, one such historian.) And the formalists, for Stephen, are too formal, leaving out historical explanations for generic changes, changes that are, granted, as much "individual" or "idiosyncratic" as they are "due to [the author's] special modification by the existing stage of social and intellectual development."[59] Of formalists, he writes, it is as if "the true canons for dramatic or epic poetry . . . had been laid down once and for all by Aristotle or his commentators; and the duty of the critic was to consider whether the author had infringed or conformed to the established rules, and to pass sentence accordingly."[60]

While Stephen appears to be opposed to a strict Aristotelian formalism—what we might name here as "genre but no social history"—he does have his special and now-expected targets, those previous attempts to bring history and form together. For instance, he writes that "Ruskin . . . always assumed . . . that men ceased to paint good pictures simply because they ceased to be good men. He did not proceed to prove that the moral decline really took place, and still less to show why it took place. . . . I shall be content to say that I do not see that any such sweeping conclusions can be made as to the kind of changes in literary forms with which we shall be concerned."[61] So to perceive properly these "changes" in form, he insists "that criticism, as Professor Courthope has said, must become thoroughly inductive," realizing that "the same change takes place in regard to political or economical or religious, as well as in regard to literary investigations."[62] Here, again, then, is that same model of history in which different cultural productions reveal the same transformations in the historical whole.

Stephen talks through this methodological problem of reconciling the "mental atmosphere" with the "social structure":

> The material upon which he [the author] works is the whole complex of conceptions, religious, imaginative and ethical, which forms his mental atmosphere. That suggests problems for the historian of philosophy. He is also dependent upon what in the modern phrase we call his 'environment'—the social structure of which he forms a part, and which gives special direction to his passions and aspirations. That suggests problems for the historian of political and social institutions."[63]

Stephen seeks to bring two disciplines together: political history and philosophy. Naturally, he suggests that "the historian of political and social institutions" is alert to the "social structure" that supplies authors a "special

direction" for their "passions and aspirations," but that he designates philosophy as that field of investigation appertaining to "the whole complex of
conceptions," that "mental atmosphere," means that he is thinking about
idealism, in particular. It's an idealism, moreover, whose task is to tend to the
literary or "imaginative" side of the binary of literature/history, insofar as the
"historian of political and social institutions" already deals with the other.
While his methodological prescription is easy to guess—the critic must work
on both levels at once[64]—we can pause here to appreciate that for Stephen
formal questions are now in the domain of philosophy rather than, strictly
speaking, literary appreciation, signaling the philosophical influences on literary criticism at the time.

Having thus pled for a "method . . . [that] implies a necessary connection between the social and literary departments of history,"[65] Stephen demonstrates it, and it is here that his language touches upon Courthope's and
upon the then fashionable Hegelian motifs. His consistent thesis involves
an analysis of form and history: literary forms develop and stay in vogue
when they are "produced by the class which embodies the really vital and
powerful currents of thought which are moulding society."[66] We are back to
the idealist notion of thought as a social force, as evident in Courthope. But
Stephen, like Courthope, does not mean to move the question away from
class or "the social," nor does he valorize the "individual," setting aside, for
example, Thomas Carlyle's genius "hero" meriting special notice.[67] Rather,
Stephen suggests that authorship is constituted by an aesthetic that is both
politically engaged and formally innovative. Any focus on an individual author or "genius" should not necessitate a retreat from history, whereby the
author is construed to be an exception.[68] Rather, authors are brilliantly representative because their art is at once a critical insight into their age. Literary and social history must be brought to bear in interpretation because
authors themselves make penetrating assessments of their own age with their
art, and we simply need the right combination of disciplinary tools to understand their perceptions. This is a model of Literature and Society that Ruskin
and Arnold would not recognize, much less endorse, but it would ring true
to Vida Dutton Scudder, who amplifies the aesthetic exhibited by Stephen
and Courthope.[69]

Scudder (1861–1954) was one of the first two American women admitted
to the University of Oxford (1885), and she went on to teach at Wellesley
College from 1887 to 1927, after which she lectured weekly at the New School
for Social Research. She was an organizer for the Women's Trade Union
League, and she is now both a saint in the Episcopal church and an icon in
the history of lesbian intellectuals.[70] Like some of the Hegelians in the United

Kingdom, Scudder was a Christian socialist, keenly interested in the transitions of past and present state forms to more equitable versions. And like the Anglo-Hegelians, she of course saw the limits to the moral and political teachings of Carlyle, Arnold, and Ruskin—this despite the fact (or because of the fact?) that she attended lectures by Ruskin when at Oxford. By the 1890s, she notes, all "these men were silenced,"[71] including Morris, whose aesthetic vision was "narrow."[72] Scudder's way to improve the now obsolete criticism was, as to be expected, her book, *Social Ideals in English Letters* (1898), which is a critical literary history that begins with "Langland and the Middle Ages" and ends with Ruskin, Carlyle, Arnold, and Morris. Like Bosanquet, Scudder is ready to incorporate contemporary figures within her history, a critical move that itself is a trenchant critique, an expression of the idea that these figures are of the past and part of an aesthetic that can be traced from its medieval inception to its modern form.[73]

From one William to another, from Langland to Morris: that's the frame within which Scudder traces this aesthetic in which literary form meets and registers history: "Harmony of form," she writes, "subdues all discord of subject," that discord being "the expression of social life and its anomalies."[74] Literature shows forth "life under various phases" proceeding to a "higher yet unrealized truth, which the present ever suggests, toward which it ever moves."[75]

Construing literary invention in terms of motion, one phase after another, Scudder is keen to express that literary history is, in particular, the *generic* history of the "epic, the drama, and later the novel," and if the scholar attends to these genres, then she will discern "the gradual awakening of a social consciousness, bringing with it the perception of social problems and the creation of social ideals."[76] Like Stephen, Scudder finds that authors use their art, and choose their genres, to gain a perspective on their present (a move we discussed at length in chapter 5). What also makes her approach appear informed by contemporary Hegelianism—apart from her language about the harmony of discord—is not simply her charted teleology to absolute democracy (which rings familiar to Hegel's philosophy of history especially, as well as to Courthope's literary history) but rather her views about social class. Not ventriloquizing Ruskin's and Arnold's dicta about culture for the working classes, she asserts that "art knows no classes,"[77] heralding a methodology better suited in her mind to literary form "than the theories of the political economists."[78] By this imperative, Scudder argues for a "collective experience,"[79] one that (as with Courthope) enables a socially inflected criticism that is not reducible to class or economics but nonetheless regards the *social whole*. Such a collective experience is, for her, not only a synchronic one, however. It is also transhistorical—a collective that transcends literary periods and is only knowable by an aesthetic that can daringly draw together the medieval and the modern. Some of these collective connections are interesting. On the penultimate page of her study, for example, she links Langland to the cofounder of the Christian Social Union, who was himself influenced by T. H. Green and Charles Gore,[80] and whose Union collected not a few Hegelians.[81]

What I have argued about Courthope, Stephen, and Scudder, all writing in the context of the Hegelian revival, depends, in part, both on a supposition about Hegel's originality (what made him different from his contemporaries) and the need to estrange critical commonplaces today in order to refresh our sense of how Hegelianism operates within earlier literary criticism. Hegelianism in the nineteenth century afforded critics the opportunity to think historically about literary forms without the positivism à la Taine, without resorting to mechanistic causalities, and without subscribing to a realist historicism, in which the literary is altogether transparent to the historical;[82] Taine, for instance, had been hailed as "Balzac's son."[83] To put this another way, Bosanquet, Courthope, Stephen, and Scudder are not simply retooling the prevailing critiques of the plastic arts into a literary theory, but are, rather, deploying Hegelianism to calibrate literary form and history in particular, leaving the other arts behind.[84] Finding as inadequate the contemporary handling of form and history,[85] and preferring instead to put form and history on the same side, they appear to participate in a larger conversation conducted at Oxford, Cambridge, Edinburgh, and elsewhere about the relevance of morality to politics and the social to aesthetics. To be sure, they rejected Hegel's total ontology of Spirit—as did the British Hegelians, as Charles Taylor rightly suggests[86]—and replaced it with an ostensible political project, such as Scudder's notion of the author's "seeking soul" moving with history in a "line of progress"[87] toward the "social forms of the future";[88] or Courthope's and Stephen's idea of the mutually politically and formally engaged author.[89] These literary critics are not, therefore, Hegelians in a rigid and systematic sense, since even the contemporary Hegelians modified Hegel to the extent of moving beyond him.[90] Yet Courthope, Stephen, and Scudder, writing after Green and Bosanquet (among many others), all evince a unified result: for the first time literary criticism reads the "social text" of literature and does so by a commitment to a particular literary historical instrument, a *theory* that joins the telos of genre with the telos of political history.

The End of Historicism

Within the continental tradition, the Hegelian Revival, in which this new literary historicism was situated, has garnered only passing interest over the years. Benedetto Croce, for instance, ignored the neo-Hegelians so as to effect what he calls the "modernization of philosophy," shutting down idealisms at points remarkably similar to his own.[91] Similarly, the French Hegelians, Alexandre Kojève and Jean Hyppolite, whom we discussed in chapter 3, engaged in no substantial cross-channel dialogue with their British counterparts; Althusser, at a time when he was willing to think through, rather than against, Hegel, had made only cryptic and dismissive references to Anglo-American Hegelianism.[92] Herbert Marcuse, in *Reason and Revolution: Hegel and the Rise of Social Theory*, mentions this Hegelianism only long enough to distinguish it from "later Fascist ideology."[93] And Taylor gives it only two pages in his important study of Hegel.[94] Clearly, what goes for the Hegelian Revival goes for its nineteenth-century offshoot—Hegelian literary historicism, which has barely even made it to the printed page in the history of theory.

Yet the occlusion of Hegelian literary historicism need not only be placed at the doorstep of critical theory and philosophy. The problem is as much one of critical history and how critics have thought about their own histories and traditions: both Tony Bennett's *Outside Literature* and Paul Hamilton's *Historicism* fail to acknowledge that early Hegelianism mattered at all to the now familiar "literature"/"history" question.[95] This disavowal exposes what remains modernist about contemporary critical history itself, an in-built dehistoricizing impulse at odds with its very purpose to think historically. On this point, I refer to Raymond Williams's remarks on modernism as a commentary on the status of late nineteenth-century Hegelianism here: "The innovations of what is called Modernism have become the new but fixed forms of our present moment. If we are to break out of the non-historical fixity of post-modernism, then we must search out and counterpose an alternative tradition taken from the neglected works left in the wide margin of the century."[96] My critical history in the foregoing is intended to introduce "an alternative tradition" and to forestall such reductions of earlier, possible modernisms—reductions that would in turn yield a simplified if not incorrect picture of Anglo-American literary critical practice at the turn of the century where (Hegelian) historicism is supposedly absent and formalism is flourishing from the time of Arnold and Ruskin to that of the New Critics.[97] Indeed, these Hegelians, insofar as they rejected the old critical models of Ruskin and the rest, anticipate, if not make possible, the *coupure épistémologique* of High Modernism itself, with figures like T. E. Hulme and Ezra Pound proclaiming the end of Victorian humanism, naturalism, and romanticism. They are the break before the break.

Let me approach the issue of critical forgetting from another direction, turning once more to Lacan's exclamation that "everybody is Hegelian without knowing it" because "we have pushed to an extreme degree the identification of man with his knowledge, which is an accumulated knowledge."[98] Lacan's point, which he made to Hyppolite no less, can be reversed to emphasize a certain irony by which remembering is forgetting: "accumulated knowledge" about our critical pasts, that is, comes at the risk of forgetting what's Hegelian about them—"without knowing it." The farther contemporary historicisms go from Hegel, the deeper Hegel recedes into the critical unconscious as "accumulated knowledge," the more visible Hegelianism becomes in the structure of the historicist critique (as in Macherey).[99] And the farther historicisms go from Hegel, the more exhausted they become until they reach their own "End." We can test this claim by remaining hypothetically Hegelian and entertaining the greatest of dialectical fictions, that of a teleology leading us from thesis, to antithesis, to synthesis, to the Absolute. *Thesis*: Lukács the Hegelian effectively introduces to Marxism the "literature" and "history" question by disavowing forms of Soviet realism and by theorizing how other kinds of narrative divested of ostensible politics nonetheless betray (novel) or resolve (epic) the social and ideological contradictions of an age. *Antithesis*: Althusser negates Lukács's propositions on the grounds of their Hegelianism but offers no real alternative, save a scattering of essays on Brecht (in *For Marx*). *Synthesis*: Macherey unites these two opposites, continuing Lukács's "literature" and "history" inquiry by consolidating Althusser's patchy literary criticism into a total post-structuralist, Marxist hermeneutic, *A Theory of Literary Production*, which in its anti-realist, anti-reflectionist stance returns to the Hegelian emphasis on absence (i.e., non-topicality) and antagonism. *Absolute*: Jameson, just a few years later, tops Macherey with *The Political Unconscious*, a wide-ranging hermeneutic that "conceives of the political perspective not as some supplementary method, not as an optional auxiliary to other interpretive methods current today—the psychoanalytic or the myth-critical, the stylistic, the ethical, the structural—but rather as the *absolute horizon* of all reading and all interpretation."[100] This isn't to say that Jameson truly thinks of himself as the Absolute. Rather, it is to suggest that, with Jameson, Hegelianism outdoes itself by completing itself. It finds its telos. It ends.

How? Look again at the teleology. Each historicism attempts to subsume and then posit a better and better adequation of method to text than previous versions (of course such an attempt is itself the silent motor of this teleology).

Each builds on the previous with greater and greater theoretical complexity. *The Political Unconscious* is the Absolute in my Hegelian trajectory (Jameson's "absolute horizon") because it marks, I believe, the end of historicism vis-à-vis the "literature" and "history" problem as inherited from nineteenth-century Hegelianism. (Which is why Jameson has moved on to other kinds of historical writing, not with different commitments but certainly with a different sense as to the order of things in postmodernity, and this writing includes, of course, expositions of Hegel, such as *The Hegel Variations*.) This is not to say that literary-historical thinking has become vacuous, but rather the terms and traditions on which *this kind* of historicism is built have finally reached their limit: the question is whether historicism can be further conceptualized, whether it can go any farther in its pursuit of the concepts that make history legible in literature.

Meanwhile, historicism, and analytical forays into "culture" that distinguished the Frankfurt School, are no longer the prerogative of dialectical criticism, because (it seems to me) the "Marxist interpretation of literature" has reached a point, after a very long history, that I dare also call an "end," thanks to several related events: the widespread use of the term "dialectical" absent of any Hegelian or Marxist implications, a semantic drift similar to what happened with the term "deconstruction"; the growing distaste for the parochial "literary theory" and the schmorgasbord anthologies that present each flavor of theory for classroom consumption; the continuing importance of literature to other fields whose theoretical concerns are also at once political and economic concerns; the incorporation of literary theory into neo-speculative philosophies that are idealist at heart; the crisis in and repurposing of the humanities for increasingly corporatized public institutions. That you rarely hear about "literature/history" these days as a problematic binary speaks volumes about the waning of a dialectical approach to literature, even while books on important figures in the dialectical tradition continue to be published and questions about "historicism" continue to be asked in fields like classics and medieval studies.

Dialectics after Historicism

Yet there remains a place for dialectical criticism in the present and the future, but to see it, we have first to take dialectics back to the premodern. Early in *Archaeologies of the Future*, Jameson writes that

> it is important to understand the unique conceptual resources of medieval theology, which lie not so much in any particular piety as in its structure as

ON DIALECTICAL INTERPRETATION

a remarkably sophisticated form of what Lévi-Strauss called *pensée sauvage*, in its primitive forms a kind of purely perceptual knowledge developed in the absence of abstract or properly philosophical concepts and conceptualities. Medieval theology, like tribal thought, is figural rather than conceptual; but unlike myth it is an extraordinarily elaborated and articulated system of thought, developed after the emergence of classical philosophy as such and in full awareness of the latter's conceptual and linguistic subtleties and of the richness of its problematics. Theology thus constitutes a repository of figuration and figural speculation whose dynamics were not recovered until modern times, with psychoanalysis and *Ideologiekritik*. But it is important not to confuse this remarkable language experiment with religion as such, and better to focus on its fundamental mechanisms, rather than on any alleged subjective content such as faith or belief. Those mechanisms are summed up by the word *allegory*.[101]

This is a great paragraph, for the way it thinks and for the way it fashions a *version* of medieval theology for the history of the Marxist dialectic, in which a generality about "the medieval" or even "allegory" tells us something quite specific about the character of dialectical thought at a given time. Medieval theology here is said to exhibit "the absence of abstract or properly philosophical concepts and conceptualities," and at most Jameson says that it has particularly "unique conceptual resources." Yet as he proceeds with this point, he shifts from concept to figure and opposes the two terms—"Medieval theology, like tribal thought, is figural rather than conceptual"—only to shift back to concepts, recognizing that such theology absorbed "classical philosophy" and partook of its "conceptual and linguistic subtleties and of the richness of its problematics," only to shift back again to figure, in claiming that "theology thus constitutes a repository of figuration and figural speculation." It's hard to know whether medieval theology is figural or conceptual, whether Jameson finds figuration and conceptualization to be identical intellectual activities.

There is a bigger picture to behold now. Up to this point in this chapter we have set side-by-side nineteenth- and twentieth-century historicism within the dialectical tradition up to Jameson. Seeing these two bodies of thought in relation to each other we discover a pattern not unlike that in Jameson's passage, the equivocation over and splitting of figure and concept into something of an unhappy dialectic, an opposition not quite overcome. For example, the nineteenth-century Hegelians were notoriously incomplete in their Hegelianism, but incomplete in a certain way. As Herbert Marcuse said of them, "The more Hegelian in wording this idealism became, the further it removed itself from the true spirit of Hegel's thought."[102] Charles

Taylor agrees.[103] Even their contemporaries criticized this Hegelianism for its lack of Hegelianism: "Of Hegelian language repeated to us in place of Hegelian thought, we have had by this time a sickening surfeit," said Josiah Royce in 1885.[104] Hegelian "thought" is one thing, Hegelian "wording," Hegelian "language" quite another.[105] Whence comes the anti-Hegelian aspersion perfected by Richard Rorty:

> Hegel left Kant's idea of philosophy-as-science a shambles, but he did . . . create a new literary genre, a genre which exhibited the relativity of significance to choice of vocabulary, the bewildering variety of vocabularies from which we can choose, and the intrinsic instability of each. Hegel made unforgettably clear the deep self-certainty given by each achievement of a new vocabulary, each new genre, each new style, each new dialectical synthesis. . . . He also made unforgettably clear why such certainty lasts but a moment.[106]

It seems that the operative word here is "vocabulary." And so it goes: Kantian science and conceptual clarity is replaced by Hegelian style, genre, and verbiage, with the result being uncertainty and conceptual looseness and a longing for the days of Kant's fixed system, with each philosophical term (like "representation") defined in advance and each concept called a "category" and sequestered and stabilized in the a priori.

Yet from the perspective of a larger history of dialectic—that is, from a perspective that views Hegelian dialectics in their premodern context, adding a few of the thousand years' worth of examples to the mix—it can be said that the nineteenth-century Hegelians were not *dialectical* enough, because their preoccupation with "literature/history" meant that they were not following Hegel all the way or the premodern dialectical traditions in making one further abstraction that raises the opposition between "literature" and "history" to that between figure and concept, which for Hegel (as we saw at the outset and as is registered in Rorty's complaint) is no determinate difference. For Hegel's goal, as he declares in the preface to the *Phenomenology of Spirit*, is "to bring fixed thoughts into a fluid state [festen Gedanken in Flüssigkeit zu bringen],"[107] and this fluidity is accomplished, as Hegel later reveals, through exposition and the "dialectical form": "In keeping with our insight into the nature of speculation, the exposition [Darstellung or representation] should preserve the dialectical form [dialektische Form], and should admit nothing except in so far as it is conceived [es begriffen wird], and is the Notion [Begriff or concept]."[108]

Of course, you cannot talk about Darstellung in Hegel without mentioning Vorstellung—the former denoting fluid dialectical exposition in which

concepts are in motion, the latter a kind of static and religious picture thinking that has ancient and medieval significance. These terms are fundamentally taken by many theorists to be opposites.[109] But are they really? As those
who have read the *Phenomenology of Spirit* cover to cover know, Hegel returns to these issues of representation when he speaks of the passing away
of "figurative-" and "picture thinking," i.e., the dissolution of Vorstellung.
As Hegel explains it: "A representation or image [Die Vorstellung oder das
Bild] . . . has its actual existence in something other than itself"—"an 'other'
[einem andern] . . . whose coming into existence is the relationship, and is also
that in which the relationship itself gradually passes away."[110] Hegel would
seem to assert the necessity of Vorstellung to the dialectical process, because
Vorstellung is a mode of "thinking other" (like allegory) suitable to a dialectic of identity/difference, itself operating on the turns of familiarity and unfa-
miliarity, same and other.[111] What this "thinking other" involves, primarily,
is a thought that is at once a feeling; in Hegel's example here, it is the feelings
one has for family members: hence, his talk of feeling or *Empfindung,* emo-
tion or *Rührung.*[112] This link between Vorstellung and feeling is important,
because it reveals that Darstellung itself, which is supposed to be the opposite
of Vorstellung and therefore capable of handling any and all conceptual fixes,
also serves a figural purpose at the very moment it is intensely challenged in
its encounter with the unthinkable, such as the Absolute. Apparently, even
for Darstellung, it helps to think and feel something else, as Hegel says in his
preface: "What is required in the exposition of philosophy [Darstellung der
Philosophie] is, from this view point, rather the opposite of the form of the
Concept [Form des Begriffs]. For the Absolute is not supposed to be comprehended, it is to be felt [gefühlt] and intuited [angeschaut]; not the Concept
of the Absolute, but the feeling and intuition [Gefühl und Anschauung] of
it, must govern what is said, and must be expressed by it."[113] Under these
conditions, which are like those extreme test situations discussed in chapters
1 and 2 whereby the dialectic confronts what's impossible to conceive, like
nothingness, Darstellung is forced to become something else—an *intuiting*
of what's not yet fully graspable or materialized, a *feeling* for an object not
yet knowable; it is compelled to tarry at that preconceptual moment just as
Plotinus teaches us in his exposition of the "eye that has not yet seen," or
Nietzsche in his discussion of "image-less and concept-less reflection" (see
chap. 1). So, when Hegel says that what is required is "the opposite of the
form of the Concept," he is rendering Darstellung into a kind of Vorstellung,
a "thinking other" that is affective, non-conceptual, but completely necessary
to thinking the impossible.[114] In short, figurative and conceptual thinking are

always dialectically relevant to one another, and construing Darstellung and Vorstellung as antithetical terms does not, in the end, help literary criticism and critical theory.

That much is clear in my chosen examples. On the one hand, the nineteenth-century Hegelians erred on the side of figuration and *literary* history with no ear for concepts, or no curiosity about what makes Darstellung a kind of Vorstellung, and vice versa, or no eye for how Hegel may productively confuse these terms, especially in his lectures on aesthetics.[115] No wonder, then, they pondered the differences between philosophy and literature (as Bosanquet, Courthope, and Stephen do) only to decide in all cases that literature does it better, thinks more truly, laboring free of concepts and rigid, systematic thinking. On the other hand, taking Jameson's later work as an example, we find the mirror-opposite tendency: conceptualization is disconnected from figuration, with concepts given to modern thought and figuration to the characteristically premodern or "fantastic" mode.[116] What we find in Jameson, however, is characteristic of some of the problems in the traditions of dialectical theory that influenced his own thinking: equivocations about figure and concept, and questions about how much conceptual value can be imputed to figuration, or whether one should ascertain figuration—ascertain, in the older practice of protolinguistics—and clean it up so that figures can appear properly conceptual. For example, Althusser and Balibar's *Reading Capital* (their portion of this larger collaborative exercise) sought to draw out concepts from Marx's prose so that Marx, too, can emerge as the first proper Marxist *philosopher* whose dialectical writing should be qualified as "dialectical materialism," distinct from what smacks of Hegelian-derived "historical materialism."[117] Marx, in other words, is rendered fully anti-Hegelian by the application of concepts to his episodic prose. Then there is Adorno and Horkheimer, never fully Hegelian but always dialectical; they critiqued what they call philosophical positivism—the then analytic philosophy out of which Rorty comes—and pushed back against concepts *without* figuration. Adorno himself, in *Negative Dialectics*, is to be credited for singling out Darstellung as a topic, as that "nonconceptually mimetic moment of expression" essential to thinking and to philosophy.[118] To be avoided, Adorno says, is "conceptual fetishism" and Hegelian conceptuality.[119]

I readily admit that these thinkers, their best readers, would suggest that the right balance between figure/concept has already been struck and there's no need to go back to Hegel to revisit a settled issue. Yet I would contest even that opinion, in the name of a simple thought experiment for theorists to try. That is, we have long viewed conceptualization to require figuration and narrative—and debates within the philosophy of mind continue to inquire about the relation between concepts and (mental) language—but quite how we are to think this problem from the other side and construe figuration as a mode of conceptualizing is a bit more difficult absent Hegel. If anything, to propose that figures are concepts—or to exaggerate the issue and suggest boldly that literature is theory or philosophy—can lead to worries over the violence done to the "literary" or to the imagination, boundless in its abilities to think up new entities and strange worlds without the constraints of concepts. But from the side of dialectics, that's not been a worry. Martin Jay's brilliant history of the Frankfurt School—the *Dialectical Imagination*— proves the point in an unintended way by dint of what, ironically, it doesn't discuss: *imagination,* the soil out of which figures spring and the faculty Marx and Engels associated, with a grimace, with "the idealists."[120]

And so within dialectics there is the failure to be dialectical about figure/ concept. But the problem isn't only that of dialectics. It seems to me that this situation is also a consequence of the literature/history debate in its more recent version over the last few decades. I have focused on literary historicism in this chapter because dialectics has been most visible there, influenced as it is by important works like Jameson's *The Political Unconscious.* Yet it is also where schools of thought, which don't care to be aligned with Hegel or Marx, can be seen doing dialectics of a kind. New Historicism, for example, looks like a Hegelianism without Hegel,[121] a figurative method of reading without the hard concept of History but only "social energy," that anti-Geist Geist that gives literature both the capacity to be an anecdote—representative but not caused—and the power to be a monad, within which is expressed a total state of affairs. It is clear, in other words, that literary historicism contains within itself the opposition between figures and concepts, accepting that a historical period can be a concept (most would call it a "period") but that a literary work cannot be a concept without distortions done to its literariness.

My point here is not to say that a "return to Hegel" will cure all of what ails criticism. It is, rather, to continue this critical history a bit longer, this time including premodern examples and problems and seeing what comes of the exercise. I have already attempted such a history in chapters 1 and 2, with the inclusion of Plotinus, and I'd now like to return to his work because Plotinus understood what I think is a fundamental point for theory—namely, he knew that his dialectical expositions required a particular kind of prose that enables the very thought of figures as concepts, concepts as figures. In this respect, as we will see, Plotinus both anticipates Hegel's own phenomenological style and, more importantly, supplies us with a fresh perspective on what makes powerful anti-dialectical philosophies, such as we find in Deleuze and Guattari, dialectical in an elementary way.

Phenomenological Style

If Erich Auerbach in his famous essay "Figura" wanted to show how "a word [*figura*] grows into a historical situation and gives rise to structures that will be effective for centuries" on up to Dante,[122] my aim here is to suggest that in dialectics we bring forward from the past not only a word, *figura*, but the modes of thought and the styles of reflection that a solitary word cannot even begin to express. We are, in other words, looking at ways of thinking and writing, conceiving and figuring. In chapter 1, we saw Plotinus attempting to figure out how the repetition of identity, and the failure of such repetition to produce a copy, is the way to difference and multiplicity. We now return to that passage to observe the characteristic movement of his prose:

> Thus the Intellectual-Principle, in the act of knowing the Transcendent [One], is a manifold. It knows the Transcendent [One] in very essence [sic] but, with all its effort to grasp that prior as a pure unity, it goes forth amassing successive impressions, so that, to it, the object becomes multiple: thus in its outgoing to its object it is not (fully realized) Intellectual-Principle; it is an eye that has not yet seen; in its return it is an eye possessed of multiplicity which it has itself conferred: it sought something of which it found the vague presentment within itself; it returned with something else, the manifold quality with which it has of its own act invested the simplex. If it had not possessed a previous impression of the Transcendent [One] it could never have grasped it, but this impression, originally of unity, becomes an impression of multiplicity; and the Intellectual-Principle in taking cognizance of that multiplicity knows the Transcendent [One] and so is realized as an eye possessed of its vision.[123]

What's important for our purposes are not the ideas, but the way in which each term, each concept, is narrated, with attention to the intersubjective relations between the terms and concepts. The ins and outs of neoplatonism over the centuries cannot obscure the important fact that Plotinus adopts, popularizes, and most likely invents the phenomenological style in which philosophical exposition takes *the point of view of the concept*, just short of personifying concepts. Plotinus writes like this out of the necessity to rethink and reanimate cut-and-dried Aristotelian conceptuality. As he states, "Dialectic does not consist of bare theories and rules."[124]

By now a certain dialectical philosopher should come to mind. Hegel takes not mysticism from Plotinus, or mysticism from the entire mystical tradition that fascinated him,[125] but rather the phenomenological style of such mysticism where it intersects with conceptualism (and as a reading of any given mystic in the medieval European languages shows, be it Marguerite

Porete, Meister Eckhart, or Julian of Norwich, mysticism often confronts and absorbs scholastic conceptuality). Which is to say that the literary achievement of the *Phenomenology of Spirit* is this conceptual achievement, which would have been impossible without the fundamentally medieval invention of a phenomenological style capable of narrating from the point of view of the concept. Think what one will of the experience of reading Hegel, our encounter with his work is an encounter with phenomenological prose of an extraordinary kind, and the first to outdo Plotinus and his "figurative mode of expression [bildliche Weise des Aussprechens]," as Hegel calls it.[126] The *Phenomenology of Spirit* is a story of concepts, an art of *conceptual language, conceptual narrative,* and *conceptual figuration.* It teaches us how to talk about concepts, how to describe their becomings and dissolutions in real time. We now readily recognize this style in Husserl, Sartre, Lévinas, and Merleau-Ponty, who, for all of his revisions to phenomenology, knew the time of day in remarking that "no task is more urgent than in re-establishing the connection between, on the one hand, the thankless doctrines which try to forget their Hegelian origin and, on the other, that origin itself."[127] No theorist or philosopher will ever get beyond Hegel as long as he or she writes about concepts—questions about language, thinking, and concepts will always be asked—but to make this point is at once to assert the centrality of premodern dialectical style to modern theory, even of the anti- or non-dialectical cast.

Which brings me back to Deleuze, who fathered a new kind of anti-Hegelianism in his critique of the conceptual lexicon of dialectics, replacing Hegel's supposedly tired concepts with newer ones founded upon the work of Nietzsche. Yet, for all of his tirades about Hegel—and they are tirades—Deleuze is caught up in the larger narrative about dialectical thinking precisely for the way in which he approached the question of concept/figure in *Nietzsche and Philosophy,* drawing out concepts from Nietzsche's brilliantly lyrical effusions. See how his prose works:

Affirmation is posited for the first time as multiplicity, becoming and chance. For multiplicity is the difference of one thing from another, becoming is difference from self and chance is difference "between all" or distributive difference. Affirmation is then divided in two, difference is reflected in the affirmation of affirmation: the moment of reflection where a second affirmation takes the first as its object. But in this way, affirmation is redoubled: as object of the second affirmation it is affirmation itself affirmed, redoubled affirmation, difference raised to its highest power. Becoming is being, multiplicity is unity, chance is necessity. The affirmation of becoming is the affirmation of being etc.—but only insofar as it is the object of the second affirmation which raises

it to this new power. Being ought to belong to becoming, unity to multiplicity,
necessity to chance, but only insofar as becoming, multiplicity and chance are
reflected in the second affirmation which takes them as its object.[128]

Often it matters less what you say than how you say it. What we are after here
are not the concepts themselves, but their life within Deleuze's prose.[129] Deleuze here assumes a narrator's point of view, nigh omniscient in its inspection of concepts, tracking how concepts operate, what they do, how they in-
teract, split, rise, and so forth. This style appears not only in early Deleuze,[130]
and it is not strictly an example of this thinker failing to shake off Hegelianism—a case of which everyone in his academic environment had at the time.
Rather, it also runs through his work with Guattari. Both thinkers, in fact,
adopt a *phenomenological style* in order to ground ideas or (let's say) concepts
in the movement of prose and in the observational stance of the writer.

There's something to this stylistic project, too, which (as we'll soon see)
points up a real irony about the supposed agon between dialectics and Deleuze and Guattari. We are talking about figures again. That both philosophers insist upon the motility of concepts—the ways in which concepts live
and breathe in a lush, episodic prose—betrays their effort to think of concepts
as already figures, or figures for everything else in the "Deleuzian" worldview.
They speak of concepts as having their modalities, zones, planes, of concepts
as "concrete assemblages, like the configurations of a machine," of concepts
with "speed," with intensities and intensive features, "centers of vibration,"
and non-discursivity, and of course becomings.[131] (Most all of these qualities,
incidentally, are featured on the first two pages of Deleuze and Guattari's
introduction to *A Thousand Plateaus*, in which Kleist is the new Nietzsche
contra Hegel.)[132] Because no concept is ever a "general"—to echo a salient
critical point in *A Thousand Plateaus*—everything is a concept, and a concept is everything that is written. It is not unlike a figure, in fact. This point
is made explicit, and then some, in their *What Is Philosophy?* in which their
signal question is, "Must we conclude . . . that there is a radical opposition
between figures and concepts?" And their answer contains wisdom: "Most
attempts to fix their differences express only ill-tempered judgments that are
content to depreciate one or the other terms. . . . And yet disturbing affinities
appear on what seems to be a common plane of immanence. . . . All that can
be said is that figures tend toward concepts to the point of drawing infinitely
near to them."[133] *What Is Philosophy?* is nothing if not an extended argument
for figuration, just as Deleuzianism can begin to look quite amenable to dialectics once it is understood that the Deleuzian mode—what is supposedly
non-dialectical—resembles what dialectics itself once was in the Middle Ages

but is, in modernity, no longer. The irony, if it needs spelling out, is that those modern thinkers who don't "do" dialectics are in fact doing them in the older form.[134]

These tendencies in Deleuze and Guattari—let's admit that they are dialectical tendencies—should encourage one to look again at their work, sorting out what they say about Hegel from what they do with dialectics,[135] what they say about a given thinker from what they themselves hold (thinking here of Deleuze's own discussion of "reciprocal determination" in Leibniz).[136] It is not necessary, in other words, to oppose Deleuzianism and dialectics, despite Foucault's famous review in which it is claimed (tongue in cheek?) that "perhaps one day this century will be known as Deleuzian," with the clear idea that this can only happen if we "free ourselves from Hegel—from . . . all of dialectics."[137] But as long as Deleuzianism appropriates the phenomenological style of dialectics without the dialectics, it cannot offer a complete critique of or break from Hegel, seeing as—hysteron proteron—it already expresses a stylistic Hegelianism, which we have seen is a rather constant phenomenon in the history of philosophy after Hegel. Likewise, Deleuzianism without dialectics yields "post-Deleuzianism" of the worst kind, whereby Deleuzian theory and intellectual capaciousness is replaced by a hyperstylized discourse, a free-associative, metaphoric mode of criticism in which figure overtakes concept in ways even Deleuze and Guattari could not have imagined. For what prevails in such "theory," especially the neospeculative philosophies, is a kind of writing that relishes conceptual looseness and prosaic surfaces.[138]

There is a future for dialectics, too, in which figure and concept are brought back together in a way that activates the oldest but best modes of thought exampled in dialectics since Plotinus. Let's turn once more to Jameson, who writes a *Reading Capital* for our times, entitled *Representing Capital*. As wary as Jameson is of wandering off into "dialectical metaphysics" lacking conceptual grounding, early in *Representing Capital* he sticks his neck out: "I hazard the suggestion that figuration tends to emerge when the object of conceptuality is somehow unrepresentable in its structural ambiguity."[139] This is as close to linking figure/concept as I've seen in any contemporary dialectical writing. And some "hazard" it is! On many pages of *Representing Capital* Jameson stages, or finds staged in Marx, the necessary work figuration performs for dialectics. For example, he writes that

> [the] modulation into the figurative . . . is as always the sign that Marx's text has risen to a certain consciousness of itself, has reached a height from which for a moment it can look out across the totality of its object and of the system as a whole: the long-term memory of its argument as a whole, rather

than the short-term work of its decipherment of detail and of the dynamic of
capitalism's internal machinery. Here such figuration announces that we have
reached one of those moments in which the text prepares to solve one of its
riddles, decisively to answer one of its organizing questions.[140]

This passage gets at the heart of the matter, and the point isn't only about
Marx, as I'll soon suggest. To juxtapose figuration and conceptualization
works wonders, enabling thought to "look out across the totality of its object and of the system as a whole." Jameson never says it, probably because
he doesn't think it, but is there any other way to view this relation between
figure/concept but as a *necessary* one, none other than "dialectical metaphysics"? Where concepts fail, or when there is no concept to grasp a faintly
perceived or vaguely known or felt referent, then one makes the leap and ven-
tures forth with figures, which do their work long enough to enable a return
to the concept—a clearer view of and firmer grasp on the object in question,
as we saw in chapter 1. Figures get concepts unstuck; they also summon them,
and show us how concepts work. That the figure all along in this process
does conceptual work, and that the concept itself cannot be thought without
the figural leap, bespeaks the reciprocity between these two terms. What lies
at the center of the dialectical imagination, even Jameson's, is this dialectic
of figure/concept that is as old as Plotinus, who himself conceptualizes, in
the name of dialectic, the object of his inquiry through turns of figuration
and conceptualization—a process that we will encounter again in the next
section. Suffice it to say that one can tarry with the negative until the cows
come home from the night in which they were once all black, but without
the figure/concept dialectic to which one must turn after so much dawdling,
there can be no dialectical *movement* from moment to moment, concept to
concept. The figure/concept dialectic keeps the dialectic from *standing still*,
just as identity/difference, as I have argued throughout this book, are the
categories that make the dialectic the dialectic.[141]

   No set of conceptual terms have captivated the modern critical imagination as much as identity/difference, and—to turn the problem around—these
two have been given their figural frame, time and again across the history of
philosophy and theory. Hegel figures forth these concepts through the feudal
narrative of the bondsman and lord (chap. 3); and even if the medieval specificity of this narrative is only casually acknowledged by theorists and critics,
identity/difference enjoy other figurative lives, other modes of exemplification not even in the name of dialectics. These logical categories—they are
concepts, too—are today perhaps the preeminent dialectical *example*. And
when we take into account premodern dialectic, we realize that they always

have been—a realization that can open the dialectical imagination and dialectical interpretation to new possibilities that may be called "utopian."

Utopia—an Entire Universe, an Entire Ontology

The knowledge of future things is, in a word, identical with that of the present.
PLOTINUS

I would like to end this chapter on a speculative note, attempting a different kind of historicism attentive to the dialectic of figure/concept. The familiar text/context hermeneutic that characterizes historicism I don't think will go away, and there's no reason that it should, because it remains a strong interpretive model I myself practiced in a portion of chapter 3. What I am after here, rather, is a kind of dialectical interpretation that thinks in the historical terms the dialectic itself invites us to think—drawing our attention to the conceptual and figurative relays between past and present, in which retrospection is not a modernizing, or condescending, standpoint on the past as it presents itself to us in its telos, the present, but instead a way of acknowledging where the past figuratively exceeds its own time and place, its own concept, to make a future for itself in our own time—a past demanding recognition now. Such prospection or projection from the past is often a miss and goes unrecognized by us, and it is what makes the past the past and the new new, which disposes of all failed futures. But equally the past springs forth and catches our attention, asking us to recognize the parallels of expression and thought between then and now—a convergence that is a live dialectical "moment." Such correspondences produce not idealism but untimely history—not social history in the first instance but a history of thinking.

If what I am saying so far sounds inevitably Benjaminian, it is not. Benjamin does, of course, ask us to ponder an image, figure, or form (*Bild*), but he also enjoins us to be open to what he calls an "awakening" to "historical knowledge"—a procedure Susan Buck-Morss illustrates persuasively in her account of the "dialectical image," which from my point of view tempts the critic to perform an "image of" critique of the tried and true kind (image of the worker, image of this or that new social type or institution, and so forth).[142] For all its beauty and aura, Benjamin's dialectical image is the traditional historicist one, and thus not the one I have in mind, in light of the foregoing. I suggest instead that interpretation can begin with dialectical empathy and identification, acknowledging what figuration *makes authors say*, makes you say, when you commit to its own logic of exemplification. What does figuration *make you think*? Figurative *exposition* is the form of thought with its own momentum and determining force, taking you in directions you may not have expected before you commit to a given figure or form, narrowly or broadly conceived. But you go there anyway, ready for a dialectical surprise.

I end where I begin, then, with some reflections on Plotinus, telling a story not about dialectical inevitability, but rather dialectical wonder, the ways in which premodern dialectic can shake our confidence in the modernity of certain theoretical constructs now familiar to us and, reciprocally, open up a new past before us. Plotinus is relevant here, because he is a perfect example of how the conjoining of figure and concept reinvents the discipline of dialectic in late antiquity and thus stands as an advance, an expansion of the capabilities of *theoria* (from *theorein*, θεωρεῖν, "to speculate") in his time and our own. In his tract called "Problems of the Soul," Plotinus rejects the then contemporary tendency to confer human personalities onto planets and stars and derides the expectation that celestial beings attend to the beck and call (the prayers) of every individual on earth. Oddly, though, Plotinus still wants to say something about human and celestial behavior. Of the soul's capacity to perceive objects, he says the following:

> It is not essential that everything seen should be laid up in the mind; for when the object is of no importance, or of no personal concern, the sensitive faculty, stimulated by the differences in the objects present to vision, acts without accompaniment of the will. The soul does not take into its deeper recesses such differences as do not meet any of its needs, or serve any of its purposes.[143]

Leibniz once said that "we are automatons in three-quarters of what we do."[144] Perhaps Plotinus would suggest an even greater fraction when speaking about the behaviors of persons. That is, humans do not piece apart, or dissect then describe, their worlds in everyday life. Plotinus goes on to expand this new version of human intellection, the ways in which we negotiate space:

> Thus in local movement, if there is no particular importance to us in the fact that we pass through first this and then that portion of air, or that we proceed from some particular point, we do not take notice, or even know it as we walk. . . . In a process unfailingly repeated without variation, attention to the unvarying detail is idleness. So it is with the stars.[145]

So it is with the stars? Yes, as Plotinus says: "They pass from point to point, but they move on their own affairs and not for the sake of traversing the space they actually cover."[146] This link between persons and stars is strange, but interesting nonetheless, and enables Plotinus to say more, to say something different, about the agency of stars and of persons—basically, to argue that these agents aren't intertwined: stars are busy with their affairs, as we are with ours.

But in making that point, Plotinus alights upon some interesting ideas, as when he makes this claim about our perception of what's normal and what's exceptional:

> We do not habitually examine or in any way question the normal: we set to doubting and working out identifications when we are confronted by any display of power outside of everyday experience: we wonder at a novelty and we wonder at the customary when anyone brings forward some single object and explains to our ignorance the efficacy vested in it.[147]

This is an important and lovely passage not only because Plotinus's idea that "we wonder at the customary" is the opposite of Longinus's famous definition of the sublime, by which spectators marvel at what's extraordinary. Rather, Plotinus here exhibits a great capacity to think figurally and conceptually all at once. He broadens the ways in which one can conceptualize human ontology by first thinking about celestial beings—inevitably a figurative move for extremely obvious reasons—and then returning to the question of human habit. Without the resources of astrology, which supply the cache of images, themes, symbols by which to carry out a potentially daring thought, Plotinus would never have doubled back to reflect on human affairs in their most mundane sense: humans only investigate the norm when an exception presents itself to us, and then we study the exception, we assess the new, "the efficacy vested in it."

Recognize this idea? Plotinus's point is almost identical to Heidegger's classic conceptual distinction between "ready-to-hand" and "present-to-hand," between the everyday *Dasein* of comporting ourselves within equipmental totalities, the entirety of which we never investigate piece by piece when everything functions normally, and the exceptional states we often experience when things break down and demand that we *attend* to them, as an object qua object—say—a tool as a tool, which is constructed in a certain way, which must be mentally disassembled before any actual disassembly takes place for the repair.[148] Like Plotinus, who states that when "we pass through first this and then that portion of air, or that we proceed from some particular point, we do not take notice, or even know it as we walk," Heidegger makes a similar claim concerning place, which only discloses itself as a collection of things, so many points in three-dimensional space, when we adopt a theoretical attitude: "Places—and indeed the whole circumspectively oriented totality of places belong to equipment ready-to-hand—get reduced to a multiplicity of positions for random Things. The spatiality of what is ready-to-hand within-the-world loses its involvement character; and so does the ready-to-hand."[149] Plotinus, by means of such creative reflection about what lies in outer space rebuts his contemporaries, "our theorists of today,"[150] and in so doing generates ideas about being, intention, and everydayness that are far ahead of Augustine's temporal musings in such go-to works as *De Trinitate.*

Evidently, it doesn't take Heidegger to make a Heideggerean point, nor does premodern philosophy a Heidegger make, however interested he was in medieval thought. Plotinus figures, then conceives, his way to *Dasein,* and to appreciate that is to perform dialectical thinking just in the way Jameson proposes when he finds that sci-fi novels do exactly the kind of imaginative work necessary for dialectics: the "SF author is placed in a position of divine creation well beyond anything Agatha Christie or even Aristotle might have imagined; rather than inventing a crime of some sort, the SF writer is obliged to invent an entire universe, an entire ontology, another world altogether— very precisely the system of radical difference with which we associate the imagination of Utopia."[151] I do not mean to advance Plotinus as sci-fi, but rather I broaden the scope of utopian writing, which can include Plotinus, sci-fi, and so much else—to expand it beyond the question of whether Sir Thomas More was scooped by earlier authors in his thinking in his classic work, *Utopia.* For when Plotinus stretches his imagination to create a cosmos and reflect on unknowable celestial entities, he expands what can be said about human ontology and everyday comportment. He creates worlds and enlightens his own, perhaps even ours. And in the illustration, he performs the utopian thought experiment of indicating where the "radical difference" between worlds lies, as Jameson requires of utopian thinking: for Plotinus, humans live in a world of difference; the stars, a world of identity.[152] To draw the two together, the human and the cosmic, as Plotinus does in this tract, is to render figuratively his great conceptual contribution to the discipline of dialectic itself: the dialectic of identity and difference.

Plotinus's utopian moments are dialectical, plain and simple, precisely because dialectical thought has its utopian moments, even before the invention of the modern utopia or the Hegelian rediscovery of medieval dialectic. I therefore find Jameson's formulation useful as a springboard or motivation for thinking about premodern texts and ideas that can otherwise be easily dismissed as false, backward, or inexorably unscientific in the contemporary sense of the term. (Should we ever remember anything about premodern astrology if we can now observe an object 13.14 billion light years away, GRB 090429B, or know that at the center of the Perseus cluster of galaxies there is a black hole emitting a sound at "a frequency over a million billion times deeper than the limits of human hearing"?[153] Talk about "an entire universe"!) For as soon as we think of the premodern imagination as also a utopian one,[154] we get a clearer idea of why figuration is necessary for conceptualization, why dialectics is well suited for the interpretation of the past, and why dialectics keeps us honest about what it is we're doing and what we're seeing and saying, and where we're going. And what demands recognition are the ways in which figuration places authors in a thought-world and enables them to perform world making so granulated, creating worlds so rich in detail, that their own concepts spring up and, as with Plotinus, spring forward hundreds and hundreds of years. This is how dialectics takes up the task of figuring and conceptualizing the history of thought—drawing concepts out of abstraction and into history, placing figures by the side of concepts, and bringing both into contact with contemporary conceptual and figurative projects, so that parallels of articulation between ancient, medieval, and modern thought can be found and pondered. The conjunction of these forms of thought across time—that is also the making of history.

A utopian point of view can warrant the thought of the past as a possibility given to the present but born of historical difference, the sheer fact that because things were different then they can be different now and later—very different. There are other ways, other worlds, for this world. And dialectical interpretation, as a utopian form, opens up the relay between past and present to help us find these other ways, these other worlds, not as an escapist exercise or neoprimitivism, but as a new way of grounding critique in an identity that transverses historical difference but never erases it. What's more, dialectics do not necessarily admit historicism as it has been traditionally practiced nor do dialectics have to lead to or end in Hegel, or even begin in Hegel. As I argue: Hegel's role was, in part, to help us recognize the persistence of the premodern at almost every level of epistemological, political, social, and aesthetic articulation. My effort here, as it has been in this entire book, is also one of recognition, or even re-recognition, seeking to explain the signature moves of dialectics and dialectical interpretation in their premodern context and to show that a turn to this past opens up a future for dialectics in a present in which the resources of dialectical thinking and writing are needed now more than ever but remain scattered about among oppositions that in many respects seem to be false ones, such as those between formalism and historicism, Deleuzianism and dialectics, let alone Hegelianism and Marxism, and all the fields of theory that deploy identity/difference as a critical mode but are often at odds with one another. Such a rapprochement between theoretical fields (artificially) alien to one another is enabled by rethinking exactly what dialectics are, fundamentally. It's not for dialectical interpretation to write yet another history of philosophy or theory, nor is its goal that of devising new concepts in order to rush ahead hungering for fresh adequations to newly emergent realities or virtualities. My own aim at any rate is not to unify theory—that would be impossible—or to offer political lessons. It is only to point to the persistent dialectical mode that enables the thought of such a unity against the difference of the day.

Notes

Preface

1. Herman Melville, *Moby Dick* (New York: Signet, 1980), 319. All remaining quotations in this paragraph are on 320.

2. Melville, I might add, read Hegel; see Joshua and Sterling Stuckey, "The Death of Benito Cereno: A Reading of Herman Melville on Slavery," *Journal of Negro History* 67 (1882): 287–301.

3. Herbert Marcuse, *Reason and Revolution: Hegel and the Rise of Social Theory*, 100th Anniversary Edition (New York: Humanity Books, 1999), 311–12; Theodor W. Adorno, "The Schema of Mass Culture," *The Culture Industry: Selected Essays on Mass Culture*, ed. J. M. Bernstein (New York: Routledge, 2001), 87.

4. Theodor W. Adorno, *Negative Dialectics*, trans. E. B. Ashton (New York: Continuum, 1973), 11.

5. Ibid., 27.

6. Theodor W. Adorno, *Minima Moralia: Reflections from Damaged Life*, trans. E. F. N. Jephcott (London: New Left Books, 1974), 16.

7. G. W. F. Hegel, *Lectures on the History of Philosophy: The Lectures of 1825–1826*, ed. Robert F. Brown and trans. Brown and J. M. Stewart with the assistance of H. S. Harris, vol. 3 (Berkeley: University of California Press, 1990), 97.

8. Fredric Jameson, "Symptoms of Theory or Symptoms for Theory?" *Critical Inquiry* 30, no. 2 (2004): 403–8; here, 403. There is, to be sure, an analogous idea about the syntax and linguistic construction of thought (or "mental language") that is well established within the philosophy of mind, as Jerry Fodor's *The Language of Thought* (Cambridge, MA: Harvard University Press, 1975) clearly shows. Indeed, similar notions were posed in analytic philosophy in the early twentieth century, building on the work of Gottlob Frege and advancing the claim that ontological mistakes are at once linguistic mistakes, as argued by Alfred North Whitehead and Bertrand Russell (*Principia Mathematica*, 3 vols. [Cambridge: Cambridge University Press, 1910, 1912, 1913]). The philosopher can endeavor to construct a logical language adequate to the object world, as Rudolf Carnap proposed in his "Überwindung der Metaphysik durch logische Analyse der Sprache," *Erkenntnis* 2 (1932): 219–41. There are many more examples, but none of them are *dialectics*, and my interest in this book is to show how dialectics in their Hegelian and

premodern form have a claim not on these other areas of philosophy but on what is generally called "theory" in the humanities today.

9. See Jameson, "Symptoms of Theory," 403.

10. Ibid., 403, 405.

11. Studies that, likewise, tarry with the medieval in their treatment of contemporary theory are Amy Hollywood, *Sensible Ecstasy: Mysticism, Sexual Difference, and the Demands of History* (Chicago: University of Chicago Press, 2002); Bruce Holsinger, *The Premodern Condition: Medievalism and the Making of Theory* (Chicago: University of Chicago Press, 2005); Erin Felicia Labbie, *Lacan's Medievalism* (Minneapolis: University of Minnesota Press, 2006); *The Legitimacy of the Middle Ages: On the Unwritten History of Theory*, ed. Andrew Cole and D. Vance Smith, afterword by Fredric Jameson (Durham, NC: Duke University Press, 2010); and "The Medieval Turn in Theory," special cluster of essays ed. by Andrew Cole, *the minnesota review* 80 (2013): 80–158.

12. Suzanne Reynold's *Fiefs and Vassals: The Medieval Evidence Reinterpreted* (Oxford: Oxford University Press, 1994) is a cautionary reminder about where medieval economic realities end and social and political relations begin; about how to distinguish one from the other; and about how generalizable the medieval evidence really is. Indeed, one may prefer to focus not on modes of production and remnant medieval institutions and practices (as I do here) but on medieval *mentalités*. Whichever language or discipline one chooses to assess this past, however, there is no denying the large-scale continuities in German institutional, social, political, agrarian history, from medieval to modern.

13. J. J. Sheehan, *German History, 1770–1866* (Oxford: Clarendon Press, 1989), 97; 101–2. Other studies that confirm the persistence of feudal relations of production in Germany (or the German states) include David Warren Sabean, *Kinship in Neckarhausen, 1700–1870* (Cambridge: Cambridge University Press, 1998), *Power in the Blood: Popular Culture and Village Discourse in Early Modern Germany* (Cambridge: Cambridge University Press, 1984), and *Property, Production, and Family in Neckarhausen, 1700–1870* (Cambridge: Cambridge University Press, 1990); Mack Walker, *German Home Towns: Community, State, and General Estate, 1648–1871* (Ithaca, NY: Cornell University Press, 1971); Hans Kohn, *Prelude to Nation States: The French and German Experience, 1789–1815* (Princeton, NJ: Van Nostrand, 1967).

14. Arno J. Mayer, *The Persistence of the Old Regime: Europe to the Great War* (New York: Pantheon, 1981), 18–19; see also 22.

15. This entire paragraph quotes and paraphrases portions of Terry Pinkard's absolutely excellent *Hegel: A Biography* (Cambridge: Cambridge University Press, 2000), 1, 19 (see 88, 90), 53, 57, 278, 280, 330.

16. Raymond Williams, *Marxism and Literature* (Oxford: Oxford University Press, 1977), 121–27.

17. See "Proceedings of the Estates Assembly in the Kingdom of Württemberg, 1815–16," in *Hegel's Political Writings*, trans. T. M. Knox (Oxford: Clarendon, 1964), 246–94.

18. Pinkard, *Hegel*, 484.

19. *Hegel: Political Writings*, ed. Lawrence Dickey and H. B. Nisbet (Cambridge: Cambridge University Press, 1999), 248.

20. Ibid., 247; *Werke in zwanzig Bänden: Theorie-Werkausgabe* (Frankfurt: Suhrkamp, 1970), 11.99.

21. Karl Marx, "Wage Labour and Capital," in *The Marx-Engels Reader*, ed. Robert C. Tucker, 2nd ed. (New York: Norton, 1978), 205.

22. *The Collected Works of Karl Marx and Frederick Engels*, 50 vols. (New York: International Publishers, 1975–2005), 7:4; the editor states that "the leaflet published in Cologne has 'cause of the revolution' instead of 'Government' " (note a).

23. Things get complex, for Hegel, in his reflections on the history of philosophy, but even there, the medieval constitutes the modern, fundamentally; see chap, 1, n. 57.

Chapter One

1. Friedrich Nietzsche, *Untimely Meditations*, ed. Daniel Breazeale and trans. R. J. Hollingdale (Cambridge: Cambridge University Press, 1997), 186.

2. See James I. Porter, *Nietzsche and the Philology of the Future* (Stanford, CA: Stanford University Press, 2000).

3. Gilles Deleuze wrote: "If one looks at the *Birth of Tragedy* it is quite clear that Nietzsche wrote it not as a dialectician but as a disciple of Schopenhauer. We must also remember that Schopenhauer himself did not value the dialectic very highly. And yet, in his first book, the schema that Nietzsche offers us under Schopenhauer's influence is only distinguishable from the dialectic by the way in which contradiction and its resolution are conceived" (*Nietzsche and Philosophy*, trans. Hugh Tomlinson; fwd. by Michael Hardt [New York: Columbia University Press, 2006], 11). To which Nietzsche penned a response *en avance*: "Schopenhauer harshly accused Hegel and Schelling's epoch of lacking integrity—harshly but also unfairly: that old pessimistic counterfeiter—he did not have any more 'integrity' than his famous contemporaries did. Let us keep morality out of this: Hegel is a taste. . . . And not just a German taste but a European one!" ("The Case of Wagner: A Musician's Problem," in *The Anti-Christ, Ecce Homo, Twilight of the Idols, and Other Writings*, ed. Aaron Ridley and Judith Norman; trans. Norman [Cambridge: Cambridge University Press, 2005], 252). So much for discipleship.

4. Deleuze, *Nietzsche and Philosophy*, 157. See 197.

5. Friedrich Nietzsche, *Twilight of the Idols*, in *The Anti-Christ, Ecce Homo*, 228–29. In his "Attempt at Self-Criticism," written fourteen years after the initial publication of *The Birth of Tragedy* (1872), Nietzsche rails against his own dialectical mindset at the time, which affected his prose, what he calls "the ponderousness and dialectical disinclination of the Germans" (*The Birth of Tragedy and Other Writings*, ed. Raymond Geuss and Ronald Speirs; trans. Ronald Speirs [Cambridge: Cambridge University Press, 1999], 6)—a view Deleuze rejects in *Nietzsche and Philosophy* (see 11). I would suggest, however, that Nietzsche's proposal that *The Birth of Tragedy* is too dialectical and, as he says in *Ecce Homo*, "offensively Hegelian" (*The Anti-Christ, Ecce Homo*, 108) means that it was not *anti-Hegelian enough*. After all, nowhere does Nietzsche mention, much less critique, Hegel in *The Birth of Tragedy*. If anything, the older Nietzsche saw that his earlier revision of the dialectic is too much inside baseball and not enough cheering against the opposing team (retrospectively).

6. Raymond Williams was also tempted to read the clichéd dialectical form in *The Birth of Tragedy*, writing that "Tragedy, that is to say, in Nietzsche's view, dramatises a tension which it resolves in a higher unity. There is a structural reminiscence of Hegel in this, but the terms are entirely altered" (*Modern Tragedy*, ed. Pamela McCallum [Peterborough, ON: Broadview Press, 2006], 61; see 62).

7. Nietzsche, *The Birth of Tragedy*, 94. "Socrates' influence has spread out across all posterity to this very day" (ibid., 71). Nietzsche also states that "the teachers in our institutions of higher education have learned better than most how to reach a quick and comfortable accommodation

with the Greeks, even to the extent of abandoning sceptically the Hellenic ideal and completely perverting the true aim of classical studies" (96). Nietzsche more strongly words this idea in *Twilight of the Idols* in the section "The Problem of Socrates": "Perhaps wisdom appears on earth as a raven, inspired by a little scent of carrion?" (*Twilight of the Idols*, in *The Anti-Christ, Ecce Homo*, 162).

8. Nietzsche, *Untimely Meditations*, 60. Let's remember that in *Ecce Homo*, Nietzsche said: "Viewed impartially, the *Birth of Tragedy* looks very untimely" (*The Anti-Christ, Ecce Homo*, 108).

9. Nietzsche, *The Birth of Tragedy*, 28.

10. Ibid., 29.

11. Ibid. Nietzsche's reference to "disinterested contemplation" (ibid.) is, of course, a nod to Kant and Schopenhauer.

12. Ibid., 28, 30.

13. Ibid., 30/*Die Geburt der Tragödie*, in *Werke: Kritische Gesamtausgabe*, ed. Giorgio Colli and Mazzino Montinari (Berlin: W. de Gruyter, 1967–), III-1.39.

14. Ibid. 30/*Die Geburt der Tragödie*, III-1.39–40; on Socrates and concepts, see 74. We could quickly dismiss this as a non-dialectical passage, if our interest is solely in tracing the status of dialectical clichés like "contradiction," here on the side of the "primordial unity" where contradiction itself is contradicted by the very principle that issues it, unity: contradiction, that is, is just another term for "suffering," a term for the "hidden primal contradiction" that Prometheus experiences in his attempt to resolve the "irresolvable conflict between god and man" (49), and not a generative condition that breaks the unity apart, or makes distinctions whereby unities are discerned. Likewise, we could follow Nietzsche's conclusion about this passage and decide that the traditional dialectical matter of subjects and objects is moot because it's never broached, nullified from the first without ever the promise of subjectivity emerging among a world of objects or nondescript qualities: "Thus, the 'I' of the lyric poet sounds out from the deepest abyss of being; his 'subjectivity', as this concept is used by modern aestheticians, is imaginary" (*The Birth of Tragedy*, 30).

15. Nietzsche, *The Birth of Tragedy*, 30.

16. "Why I Am So Clever," *Ecce Homo*, in *The Anti-Christ, Ecce Homo*, 99. Too, we must not read "repetition with a difference," codified by Deleuze, into this passage because this notion neither proceeds from identity or unity, as posed in this excerpt, and instead begins in difference, if not sheer unmediated multiplicity. See Deleuze's formulation in *Difference and Repetition*, trans. Paul Patton (New York: Columbia University Press, 1994), the "anti-Platonism" of which is the fundamental point of contention; 29, 127–28.

17. Nietzsche here is elaborating on ideas contained in that long quotation from Schopenhauer; see *The Birth of Tragedy*, 78–79. But he proceeds in the opposite direction. For Schopenhauer the desideratum is not to differentiate but to unify, to move from personality to the "subject of pure knowing." Deleuze argues that Nietzsche's Hegelianism is an absorption of Schopenhauer's own *partial* break from Hegel, and Deleuze rationalizes this reading on account of the fact that Nietzsche nowhere refers to Hegel in this work (*Nietzsche and Philosophy*, 10, 162).

18. I intentionally reference Walter Benjamin here because his notion of the dialectical image seems to me to characterize a unique process of dialectical becoming, the "suddenly emergent" (*The Arcades Project*, trans. Howard Eiland and Kevin McLaughlin [Cambridge: Belknap Press of Harvard University Press, 2003], 462)—a "dialectics at a standstill" (ibid.) that is not the *end* of the dialectic (as Hegel usually means the similar idea of "picture thinking" everywhere in the *Phenomenology of Spirit*) but rather the *beginning*. For more, see chap. 6.

19. Plotinus, *The Enneads*, trans. Stephen MacKenna, abridged with an introduction and notes by John Dillon (New York: Penguin, 1991); cited by page number, followed by book and chapter number in brackets, here 377 [5.3]. This is from one of Plotinus's latest tracts (see Mac-Kenna, 364). *Ennead* 5.4 offers a different view of this process but is regarded as an early tract by Plotinus (see MacKenna, 387). Plotinus imputes "being" and intelligence to the One (see 389): "But if something arises from an entity which in no way looks outside itself, it must arise when that entity is in the fullness of its being: stable in its identity, it produces; but the product is that of an unchanged being: the producer is unchangeably the intellectual object, the product is pro-duced as the Intellectual Act" —"that is to say, becoming another intellectual being, resembling its source, a reproduction and image of that" (389 [5.4]). What makes this earlier position dif-ferent from the latter quoted in my main text is, quite simply, the clear borrowing of language from Plato's *Timaeus*, 42e5–6 (borrowings noted by MacKenna, 389nn69–70) that we do not find in the later tract. Here, simply, Plotinus is too Platonic. Plotinus himself acknowledges this weakness in Plato's thought, writing: "with all his affirmation of unity, his own writings lay him open to the reproach that his unity turns out to be a multiplicity" (*Enneads*, 357 [5.1]).

20. Plotinus, *Enneads*, 354 [5.1].

21. Ibid., 377 [5.3].

22. Ibid., 355 [5.1]. To complete the Benjaminian point: it is clear that here that movement happens by way of difference, not identity, and is a movement toward difference—a process that historical materialism could never accept insofar as what's gone before is never fully ab-sorbed to begin with. Indeed, what Plotinus outlines here is rather the opposite of sublation (delation?).

23. Nicholas of Cusa offers a similar demonstration in *De Li Non Aliud*; see chap. 2. In purely formal terms, at least, it would be useful to acknowledge that Plato in works evincing the powers of dialectic often restarts his discourse in the effort to approach problems from a differ-ent angle when matters get too difficult. One could call this a dialectical attempt in its own right, starting and stopping in the approach to difficulties. For an example, see *Parmenides*, 135a–e; *Sophist*, 236e–237c; 253d–257b, from *The Collected Dialogues of Plato*, ed. Edith Hamilton and Huntington Cairns (Princeton, NJ: Princeton University Press, 1989); I cite from this edition by page number and paragraph number.

24. *Hegel's Lectures on the History of Philosophy*, 3 vols., trans. E. S. Haldane and Francis H. Simson (London: Routledge & Kegan Paul, 1955), 2.416.

25. Ibid., 2.412.

26. G. W. F. Hegel, *The Science of Logic*, trans. and ed. George di Giovanni (Cambridge: Cambridge University Press, 2010), 360/§881; note that this edition does not delineate paragraph numbers, but I include them here, in brackets, for ease of reference and comparison; translation modified. All quotations in this paragraph are from this page.

27. For Hegel's most famous point, if you don't apprehend "abstract determination," then you cannot grasp the Absolute and will "palm [it] off" as "the night in which . . . all cows are black," a "cognition naively reduced to vacuity," to "the A=A" (*Phenomenology of Spirit*, 9/§16).

28. Hegel, *Science of Logic*, 360/§881.

29. Ibid.; see also §99, §108 on the kind of "abstract[ion]" at stake here. I have added ellipses to the phrase, "*A is*," in order to express something of the suspension inherent in the incomplete proposition Hegel is seeking eventually to complete in his analysis ending with the proposition, "*A is – A*."

30. To address two other important (but different) discussions of identity: Schelling takes

the proposition, A=A, to speak of form and content: if this proposition is the *form* or logical expression of the identity of A with itself, then so too is the *content* of "A" expressed in the formulation. Within identity one can think the *distinction* of form and content. See Friedrich Wilhelm Joseph Schelling, *System of Transcendental Idealism*, trans. Peter Heath (Charlottesville: University of Virginia Press, 1993), 20–21. Heidegger uses A=A to reflect on Parmenides' fragment: "for the same perceiving (thinking) as well as being" (*Identity and Difference*, trans. Joan Stambaugh [Chicago: University of Chicago Press, 2002], 27). Parmenides, says Heidegger, draws together "different things" (*Verschiedenes* [90]), which are thinking and being, and regards them as "the Same" (27). Note that neither of these is written from the point of view of the phenomenological observer.

31. Of course, this law of identity is at once the law of contradiction: "A is enunciated, and a not-A which is the pure other of A; but this not-A only shows itself in order to disappear. In this proposition, therefore, identity is expressed as a negation of negation. A and not-A are distinct; the two terms are distinguished with reference to one and the same A. Here identity is displayed, therefore, as *this differentiation of the terms in the one connection or as the simple difference in the terms themselves*" (Hegel, *Science of Logic*, 360/§882).

32. Citing Parmenides' assertion that "only being is, and nothing is not," Hegel claims that "this must be taken as the proper starting point of philosophy, because philosophy as such is cognition by means of thinking, and here pure thinking was firmly adhered to for the first time" (*The Encyclopaedia Logic, with the Zusätze: Part I of the Encyclopaedia of Philosophical Sciences with the Zusätze*, trans. T. F. Geraets, W. A. Suchting, and H. S. Harris [Indianapolis, IN: Hackett, 1991], 138/§86, addition 1).

33. Hegel, *Encyclopaedia Logic*, 140/§87, addition.

34. Ibid., 141/§88. Slavoj Žižek's *Less Than Nothing: Hegel and the Shadow of Dialectical Materialism* (New York: Verso, 2012) was published after I completed this book, and so I am unfortunately unable to account for it adequately here.

35. *Encyclopaedia Logic*, 140/§87, addition.

36. Ibid., 141/§88.

37. Hegel, *Science of Logic*, 84/§193.

38. Hegel, *Encyclopaedia Logic*, 140–41/§87, addition.

39. See Plato, *Parmenides*, 922–23/127e–129c. See M. Schofield, "Likeness and Likenesses in the *Parmenides*," in *Form and Argument in Late Plato*, ed. C. Gill and M. M. McCabe (Oxford: Clarendon, 1996), 49–77.

40. Plato, *Parmenides*, 923/129b.

41. Ibid., 930–31/135e–136c. Parmenides' main exhibit on this topic is, as famously known, the one and the many, beginning first with the topic of what the one is not. He arrives at the conclusion, "the one in no sense *is*" (141e), by arguing that there can be no likeness or unlikeness within the one, or no other kind of distinction. From here, Parmenides restarts the investigation to explore the consequences of the proposition "If a one *is*" (935/142b), which in thrusting being" into the inquiry simultaneously introduces difference, number, and motion into the very conception of the one. Here difference itself emerges as being in the formulation, "being *different* or *other*" (936/143b); unlike things are "like" in the sense that they both have the "character" of "difference" (940/148a). At points this approach to difference violates the law of noncontradiction of identity—"If they [two things] were like and unlike or had likeness and unlikeness in them, they would then have in them two characters contrary to one another" (950/159e); at other times, we witness demonstrations that make perfect sense until their conclusions result

in howlers like "the one both is, and is becoming, older and younger than itself and than the others" (946/155c; see also 943/151b, 944/152a).

42. I would suggest this claim also applies to *Sophist*, 1002–1003/256a–257b. There, Plato does not mention "relative being," but he does successfully demonstrate the reciprocity between the five primary forms. One, however, can quickly be reminded that what defines the identity in difference between the forms is, of course, a form. In chap. 2, I show how Plotinus and Proclus take this matter even further.

43. Plato, *Phaedo*, 58/75c–d; *Republic*, 715/476b, 720/480a. The following two papers derive "not-being" as a relative, but this too is a *form*—the form of difference: Stephen Ferg, "Plato on False Statement: Relative Being, a Part of Being, and Not-Being in the *Sophist*," *Journal of the History of Philosophy* 14, no. 3 (1976): 336–42; Cordero Nestor-Luis, "Du non-être à l'autre: La découverte de l'altérité dans le *Sophiste* de Platon," *Revue Philosophique de la France et de l'Étranger* 195 (2005): 175–89.

44. The same holds true for Plato's conclusions in the *Sophist* on the crucial question of the meaning of "not-being" and "is not." See G. E. L. Owen, "Plato on Not-Being," in *Plato: A Collection of Critical Essays*, 2 vols., ed. Gregory Vlastos (Garden City, NY: Anchor Books, Doubleday, 1970–71), 1: 223–67; John McDowell, "Falsehood and Not-being in Plato's *Sophist*," *Language and Logos: Studies in Ancient Greek Philosophy presented to G. E. L. Owen*, ed. Malcolm Schofield and Martha C. Nussbaum (Cambridge: Cambridge University Press, 1983), 115–34; David Bostock, "Plato on 'Is not,'" *Oxford Studies in Ancient Philosophy* 2 (1984): 89–119.

45. Plato, *Parmenides*, 156c–157a; trans. modified; see 157b, 161d, 165a. The terms of identity and difference helped Hegel move beyond Aristotle, who in writing from the perspective of the dialectician would not entertain writing narratives from the point of view of this or that concept, as we see in Hegel and Plotinus. Rather, it is enough for Aristotle to declare in the *Metaphysics* that "becoming is between being and not being" (*The Complete Works of Aristotle: The Revised Oxford Translation*, ed. Jonathan Barnes, 2 vols. (Princeton, NJ: Princeton University Press, 1984), 2/1571 [994a28–29]). Aristotle offers very brief examples of how "the man comes from the boy," "water comes from air" (ibid., 994a25,31). These are not narratives. For an extended discussion on becoming, see the fifth book of Aristotle's *Physics*, 378–407 [224a–41b]).

46. *Platonis Opera*, ed. John Burnet (Oxford: Oxford University Press, 1903), 156b.

47. Aristotle, *Metaphysics*, 1597 [1011b].

48. For Kant, "Between the two instants, there is always a time" (*Critique of Pure Reason*, trans. and ed. Paul Guyer and Allen W. Wood [Cambridge: Cambridge University Press, 1998], 315). For his explanation about time and the perception of transformation, which does away with the "instant," much less any micro-calculation about the degrees of difference, see 315–16. Arthur Schopenhauer reinstates the instant in his description of "the transition" from "the common knowledge of particular things to the knowledge of the Idea," which "takes place suddenly" (*The World as Will and Representation*, trans. E. F. J. Payne, vol. 1 [New York, Dover Publications, 1969], 178). In accounting for the "pure subject of knowing," he intends to erase even abstract determination in what has "passed out of all relation" (179). "Plurality and difference exist only . . . in the phenomenon" (180), only in the appearances one must move beyond in the identity of pure knowing.

49. As Leibniz holds, "any change from small to large, or vice versa, passes through something which is . . . in between; and that no motion ever springs immediately from a state of rest, or passes into one except through a lesser motion; just as one could never traverse a certain line or distances without first traversing a shorter one. . . . Noticeable perceptions arise by degrees

from ones which are too minute to be noticed. To think otherwise is to be ignorant of the im-
measurable fineness of things, which always and everywhere involves an actual infinity" (Gott-
fried Wilhelm Freiherr von Leibniz, *New Essays on Human Understanding*, ed. Peter Remnant
and Jonathan Bennett [Cambridge: Cambridge University Press, 1996], p. LIII/56; on "Principle
of the Identity of Indiscernibles," see section 230 on "time and place" enabling one to distinguish between things, but "things are nevertheless distinguishable in themselves").

50. One need only compare Plato's account of the master and the slave (*Parmenides*,
133d–134a) with Hegel's version to see that identity/difference is not available to Plato (more in
chap. 2).

51. Also absent in this "middle," strangely enough, is mediation, or any kind of mediating
Third between the two opposing pairs. For these, he has not theorized the notion that copies
of the same eventually produce difference (while also, of course, establishing and delineating
the categories of identity and difference). Plato does, however, offer a more successful account
of mediation in his demonstration that the five primary forms (being, motion, rest, sameness,
difference) relate to one another, partaking of other primary forms: "Motion, then, is both the
same and not the same" (*Sophist*, 1002/256a). What we have here is verification that dialectic,
as a process within language, can nonetheless limn the relations between the primary forms in
the intelligible, non-linguistic realm. This passage, in other words, is as much a proof of the
power of Platonic dialectic as an anti-Sophist rejection of "appearances" and "shadow play."
It is to show that "what is not" is "difference" itself (and not non-existence, non-being) (see
1003/257b).

52. Hegel, *Phenomenology of Spirit*, 19/§32.

53. Theodor Adorno, *Negative Dialectics*, trans. E. B. Ashton (New York: Continuum, 1973),
157, 158. For Adorno's take on the predialectical, see 159, 181, 202. This translation, which does
not always recognize the proper philosophical (or even Hegelian) terminology in the German,
should always be cross-checked with the translation by Dennis Redmond, available at http://
members.efn.org/~dredmond/ndtrans.html. In this book, I cite from the older print version (in
which, I admit, are all my reading notes).

54. Hegel, *Phenomenology of Spirit*, 100/§162.

55. Plotinus, *Enneads*, 353 [5.1].

56. For a different point of view, relevant to my inquiry, see Robert B. Pippin, "You Can't
Get There from Here: Transition Problems in Hegel's *Phenomenology of Spirit*," in *The Cambridge Companion to Hegel* (Cambridge: Cambridge University Press, 1993), 52–85; esp. 58. What
seems to be the impossible leap from "pure essence" to "difference"—from consciousness and
its object-obsessed inspection of "Forces" to self-consciousness and its subject-oriented reflections—is accomplished only through identity and difference or, better, a perspective on these
categories at work even within a given unity. We quickly realize that, for Hegel, an indelibly
"nineteenth-century" chapter on "Force and the Understanding" leads to problems that can be
resolved only by a turn to the most tried and true dialectical operations and theses prevalent
since Plotinus.

57. Hegel, in his lectures on the history of philosophy, discusses the relevance of medieval and postmedieval thought to the "questions of present philosophy" in his opening section
on "Modern Philosophy." Namely, medieval philosophy understood that "both sides must be
comprehended through thought as absolute unity; the *extremist opposition* is apprehended as
gathered into one unity" (*Hegel's Lectures on the History of Philosophy*, 3.164, my emphasis).
From there, according to Hegel, later in the history of philosophy, various forms of opposi-

tion follow and, I would say, descend; see 3.164–76. It is clear that for Hegel this thought of opposition and unity was not available in antiquity and that this medieval opposition (again, thought by dint of identity/difference) is fundamental to the founding of modern philosophy itself—and, as I will show more thoroughly in chap. 2—Hegel's own dialectic.

58. "Self-consciousness is possible if the rational being can—in one and the same undivided moment—ascribe an efficacy to itself and posit something in opposition to that efficacy" (Johann Gottlieb Fichte, *Foundations of Natural Right: According to the Principles of the* Wissenschaftslehre, ed. Frederick Neuhouser, trans. Michael Baur [Cambridge: Cambridge University Press, 2000]), 30; see 31).

59. Hegel, *Phenomenology of Spirit*, §2/2.

60. See also Hegel, *Encyclopaedia Logic*, 138/§86, addition 2.

61. The *Birth of Tragedy*, 14 and 76; 14, for the second quotation.

62. Ibid., 28; see also 76 and 110.

63. Ibid., 59, 110.

64. Ibid., 28, 30. See 14, 18, 43, 79, 102 (on concepts); on syllogisms, 70; on knowledge, 62, 66–67.

65. Ibid., 116.

66. Ibid., 103–4; for a related motif, see Nietzsche's comment on "the original phenomenon of drama—this experience of seeing oneself transformed before one's eyes and acting as if one had really entered another body, another character" (43).

67. Hegel, *Science of Logic*, 357/§871. And as we saw, Nietzsche speaks of these "two interwoven [gewobenen] artistic drives" that are Dionysios and Apollo (59/*Die Geburt der Tragödie*, III-1.78).

68. Deleuze caricaturizes the Hegelian dialectic everywhere in his reading of Nietzsche, citing the usual canard of thesis, antithesis, and synthesis: "It is not surprising that the dialectic proceeds by opposition, development of the opposition or contradiction and solution of the contradiction" (*Nietzsche and Philosophy*, 157). And consequent with his clichés about the dialectic, Deleuze entirely brackets *aufheben* in his discussion, forgetting that whatever is canceled or opposed remain "preserved" (see, for example, 196).

69. As Nietzsche states: "Even the most sublime moral deeds, the stirrings of pity, sacrifice, heroism and that elusive placidity of the soul . . . were derived by Socrates and his like-minded successors (down to the present) from the dialectic of knowledge" (*Birth of Tragedy*, 74). For a reading of Nietzsche in relation to Pyrrhonic skepticism, see Jessica Berry, *Nietzsche and the Ancient Skeptical Tradition* (Oxford: Oxford University Press, 2011).

70. See Karl Löwith, *From Hegel to Nietzsche: The Revolution in Nineteenth-Century Thought*, trans. David E. Green (New York: Holt, Rinehart & Winston, 1964).

71. Adorno, *Negative Dialectics*, 11; Herbert Marcuse, *Reason and Revolution: Hegel and the Rise of Social Theory*, 100th Anniversary Edition (New York: Humanity Books, 1999), 311–12; Fredric Jameson, *Valences of the Dialectic* (New York: Verso, 2009), 15.

72. Fredric Jameson, *The Political Unconscious: Narrative as a Socially Symbolic Act* (Ithaca, NY: Cornell University Press, 1981), 285.

73. Jameson, *Valences of the Dialectic*, 15–16.

74. Ibid., 16.

75. See Jameson's chapter "Utopia as Replication," in *Valences of the Dialectic*, 410–34.

76. Ibid., 434; see 423.

77. Slavoj Žižek is always credited for this remark, but Žižek himself credits Jameson:

"Today, as Fredric Jameson perspicaciously remarked, nobody seriously considers possible alternative to capitalism any longer, whereas popular imagination is persecuted by the visions of the forthcoming 'break down of nature', of the stoppage of all life on earth—it seems easier to imagine the 'end of the world' than a far more modest change in the mode of production, as if liberal capitalism is the 'real' that will somehow survive even under conditions of a global ecological catastrophe" ("Introduction: The Spectre of Ideology," in *Mapping Ideology*, ed. Slavoj Žižek [New York: Verso, 1994], 1). For his part, Jameson credits only a "someone" in "Future City," *New Left Review* 21 (2003): 65–79; here, 76.

78. Remember, while Foucault famously states that genealogy "opposes itself to the search for 'origins'," or *Ursprüngen*, he never denied beginnings and rather believed that this same Nietzschean science should "cultivate the details and accidents that accompany every beginning" (*Language, Counter-memory, Practice: Selected Essays and Interviews*, ed. Donald F. Bouchard; trans. Bouchard and Sherry Simon [Ithaca, NY: Cornell University Press, 1977], 140, 144).

79. Walter Benjamin, *Origins of German Tragic Drama*, trans. John Osborne (London: Verso, 1998), 45.

Chapter Two

1. See my Coda in this chapter.

2. See my discussion of these thinkers below.

3. M. J. Inwood, *A Hegel Dictionary* (Oxford: Blackwell, 1992), s.v.; Glenn Alexander Magee, *The Hegel Dictionary* (New York: Continuum, 2010), 72–75.

4. Dmitri Nikulin, in *Dialectic and Dialogue* (Stanford, CA: Stanford University Press, 2010), classifies some medieval philosophers and theologians as either *via antiqua* or *via moderna*, Proclus on the one hand and Nicholas of Cusa on the other; see 28, 31–33, 53–57, as if to say there can be no medieval influence.

5. G. W. F. Hegel, *The Science of Logic*, trans. and ed. George di Giovanni (Cambridge: Cambridge University Press, 2010), 381 [§955]; note that this edition does not delineate paragraph numbers, but I include them here, in brackets, for ease of reference and comparison; translation modified. The original is: "Wenn nun die ersten Reflexionsbestimmungen, die Identität, die Verschiedenheit und die Entgegensetzung, in einem Satze aufgestellt worden, so sollte noch vielmehr diejenige, in welche sie als in ihre Wahrheit übergehen, nämlich der Widerspruch, in einen Satz gefaßt und gesagt werden: Alle Dinge sind an sich selbst widersprechend" (*Wissenschaft der Logik. Bd.1, Die objektive Logik, Die Lehre vom Wese*, ed. Hans-Hürgen Gawoll and Walter Jaeschke [Hamburg: F. Meiner, 1999], 59).

6. Scholars have rightly (and recently) argued that identity and difference are Hegel's beloved categories and are perhaps the prevailing terms of the *Phenomenology of Spirit, Science of Logic, Philosophy of Mind* (i.e., the final portion of the *Encyclopedia*), and *Philosophy of Right*. See Philip T. Grier, ed., *Identity and Difference: Studies in Hegel's Logic, Philosophy of Spirit, and Politics* (Albany: State University of New York Press, 2007).

7. "Negative dialectics is . . . tied to the supreme categories of identitarian philosophy as its point of departure" (Theodor Adorno, *Negative Dialectics*, trans. E. B. Ashton [New York: Continuum, 1973], 147).

8. Martin Heidegger, *Identity and Difference*, trans. Joan Stambaugh (Chicago: University of Chicago Press, 2002).

9. "The detours, locutions, and syntax in which I will often have to take recourse will resemble those of negative theology, occasionally even to the point of being indistinguishable

from negative theology. . . . And yet those aspects of différance which are thereby delineated are not theological, not even in the order of the most negative of negative theologies" (Jacques Derrida, *Margins of Philosophy*, trans. Alan Bass [Chicago: University of Chicago Press, 1982], 6). The importance of *différance* to deconstruction goes without saying.

10. Jean-François Lyotard, *Le différend* (Paris: Editions de minuit, 1983); *The Differend: Phrases in Dispute*, trans. Georges Van Den Abbeele (Minneapolis: University of Minnesota Press, 1988), 65–66; 9–10.

11. *Inter alia*, see Gilles Deleuze and Félix Guattari, *A Thousand Plateaus: Capitalism and Schizophrenia*, trans. Brian Massumi (Minneapolis: University of Minnesota Press, 1987); and, of course, Deleuze, *Difference and Repetition*, trans. Paul Patton [New York: Columbia University Press, 1994], 80).

12. See Fredric Jameson, *Postmodernism, or, The Cultural Logic of Late Capitalism* (Durham, NC: Duke University Press, 1991), 345, 372, but esp. 31, with its memorable discussion of Nam June Paik, and *Valences of the Dialectic* (New York: Verso, 2009), 70, 498, 514, 532, 540.

13. For Niklas Luhman, the systems theorist of "dedifferentiation," ontology flows from prior distinction ("Identity—What or How?" in *Theories of Distinction: Redescribing the Descriptions of Modernity*, ed. William Rasch (Stanford, CA: Stanford University Press, 2002), 115, 118. Bruno Latour's "propositions," which in actor-network-theory help one overcome the Kantian gap between persons and things-in-themselves, "rely on the articulation of differences that make new phenomena visible in the cracks that distinguish them" (*Pandora's Hope: Essays on the Reality of Science Studies* [Cambridge, MA: Harvard University Press, 1999], 143).

14. See A. D. Conti, "Teoria degli universali e teoria della predicazione nel trattato *De universalibus* di William Penbygull: discussione e difesa della posizione di Wyclif," *Medioevo* 8 (1982): 137–203; here, 190.

15. Søren Kierkegaard, *The Sickness unto Death: A Christian Psychological Exposition for Upbuilding and Awakening*, ed. and trans. Howard V. Hong and Edna H. Hong (Princeton, NJ: Princeton University Press, 1980), 116n.

16. Boethius, *Porphyrii Isagoge translatio*, ed. L. Minio-Paluello (Bruges-Paris: Desclée de Brouwer, 1966). See the second tract on the Trinity in *Opuscula Sacra*.

17. I am thinking here of the Abelardian either/or, or *sic et non*, contained within a single identity, as described by Catherine Brown's third chapter, "Negation is Stronger," in her fascinating *Contrary Things: Exegesis, Dialectic, and the Poetics of Didacticism* (Stanford, CA: Stanford University Press, 1998).

18. Thomas Aquinas, *Opuscula theologica*, vol. 2 (Taurini: Marietti, 1954) (the *Super Boetium De Trinitate* is edited by Mannes M. Calcaterra).

19. See especially the first book of this work of five books: *Periphyseon*, ed. Édouard Jeauneau. Corpus Christianorum Continuatio Mediaevalis 161 (Turnhout: Brepols, 1996); and Dermot Moran's *The Philosophy of John Scottus Eriugena: A Study of Idealism in the Middle Ages* (1989; Cambridge: Cambridge University Press, 2004).

20. See especially Bruno's *De la causa, principio e uno*, in *Cause, Principle, Unity, and Essays on Magic*, trans. Richard J. Blackwell and Robert de Lucca (Cambridge: Cambridge University Press, 1998), esp. 99–100. For backgrounds, see Ingrid D. Rowland, "Giordano Bruno and Neapolitan Neoplatonism," in *Giordano Bruno: Philosopher of the Renaissance*, ed. Hilary Gatti (Aldershot: Ashgate, 2002), 97–120.

21. Likewise, something that looks like, or at least operates like, identity/difference can also be found within the tradition of speculative grammar that extends Aristotle's insights into "relative being," beginning with Priscian's *Institutiones grammaticae* 17.56, and including Petrus

Helias, Thomas Erfurt, Martin of Dacia, Aquinas, John Duns Scotus, and William of Ockham: these philosophers view as "empty" the kind of relation in which one term depends on an antecedent. Here I am both drawing from and projecting into D. Vance Smith's lucid discussion of speculative grammar and grammatical relation in his *The Book of the Incipit: Beginnings in the Fourteenth Century* (Minneapolis: University of Minnesota Press, 2001), esp. 159. Also see Rega Wood's fascinating discussion of Richard Rufus of Cornwall, particularly his idea that a point can be predicated of contrary qualities: "Indivisibles and Infinities: Rufus on Points," in *Atomism in Late Medieval Philosophy and Theology*, ed. Christophe Grellard and Aurélien Robert (Leiden: Brill, 2009), 39–64; here, 59.

22. Dialectic is also a cross-examination of an adversary's words, which the dialectician renders into a set of "inconsistencies" placed "side by side, show[ing] that they contradict one another about the same things, in relation to the same things, and in the same respect" (*Sophist*, in *The Collected Dialogues of Plato*, ed. Edith Hamilton and Huntington Cairns [Princeton, NJ: Princeton University Press, 1989]; I cite from this edition by page number and paragraph number; in this instance, 973/230b). This form of dialectic does not express dialectical thought or synthesis, as I'll delineate it below. Plato simply does not seek to show how the "inconsistencies" eventually line up in a kind of identity in difference, or dialectical resolution, however temporary.

23. Plato, *Republic*, 765/533b. See also 764/532.

24. Plato, *Sophist*, 999/253d.

25. Plato, *Phaedrus*, 511/265e; cf. *Republic*, 769/537c: "For he who can view things in their connection is a dialectician; he who cannot, is not."

26. Plato, *Phaedrus*, 522/277b; see Plato, *Sophist*, 969–70/227a–c. Persons fail at dialectic in the "inability to apply the proper divisions and distinctions to the subject under consideration," pursuing "purely verbal oppositions, practicing eristic, not dialectic" (*Republic*, 696/454a; see 771/539b).

27. Plato, *Sophist*, 963/220e–221c.

28. Plato, *Parmenides*, 954/164e. It stands to reason that Plato offers this explanation of dialectic in the *Statesman*: "Likenesses which the senses can grasp are available in nature to those real existents which are in themselves easy to understand, so that when someone asks for an account of these existents one has no trouble at all—one can simply indicate the sensible likeness" (*Statesman*, 1053/285e) while bearing in mind that "when there are no corresponding visible resemblances, no work of nature clear for all to look upon," the dialectician must work by "reason" alone in a description of unembodied "existents which are of highest value and chief importance" (1053–54/286a).

29. Plato, *Parmenides*, 923/129a–e.

30. Ibid., 940/148a.

31. The following passage, commonly taken to inspire Aristotle's later notion of "relative being," is (to my mind) an argument that sets up the conclusion—that difference is a Form: "among things that exist, some are always spoken of as being what they are just in themselves, others as being what they are with reference to other things" (*Sophist*, 1001/255c). If identity/ difference, as we know it now, seems to be intimated here, it is only done so in the service of propositions about intelligibles.

32. Plato, *Sophist*, 1006/259c.

33. See ibid., 983/240c.

34. Ibid., 999/253d.

35. Ibid., 1000–1003 /255a–57b.

36 Ibid., 1007/260b.

37. Ibid., 1002/256a–b.

38. The prose is as boggling as the point itself—a discursive feature that signals the lack of a properly dialectical, uniquely paired, category of identity/difference. Plato's sentences on the "instant," which we examined in the last chapter, result from the same deficiency—in that case, the abstract version of identity/difference. When things get boggling, when certain logical categories such as of identity/difference are nowhere to be found, words proliferate to a limit point and ideas curl in on themselves to become redundant in formulations like, say, difference is different from itself "because of its combination with difference." It is here when dialectic, which seeks to divide identities into their indivisibly constituent parts that, in turn, point upward to the Forms themselves, becomes a language game, an exercise in keeping up with the "emergence of fresh forms" (*Parmenides*, 927/133a), of newly discovered differences. More forms, more words; more words, more forms.

39. Plato, *Parmenides*, 928/133f–134a.

40. Aristotle, *Topics, The Complete Works of Aristotle: The Revised Oxford Translation*, ed. Jonathan Barnes, 2 vols. (Princeton, NJ: Princeton University Press, 1984); I cite from this edition by volume number and page number (even though the pagination between volumes is continuous), followed by the paragraph number; in this case, 1.168/101a–b.

41. Aristotle, *Rhetoric*, 2.2154/1355a.

42. For Boethius's discussion of Cicero's analysis of relatives or "contraries," "such as master and servant," see Boethius's *De topicis differentiis*, trans. Eleonore Stump (Ithaca, NY: Cornell University Press, 1978; 2004), 66–671197b–1198a. Both follow Aristotle. Boethius also consulted Themistius's paraphrases of Aristotle's organon (which contains the *Topics*, of course): see Stump, "Boethius's Work on the Topics," *Vivarium* 12 (1974): 77–93.

43. Philipp Melanchthon, *De dialecta libri* iv (Haganoe: Secerius, 1528).

44. Rudolf Agricola, *De inventione dialectica libri tres*, ed. Lothar Mundt (Tübingen: Niemeyer, 1992). On the transition from dialectic to rhetoric (sometimes accomplished in half measures), see Ann Moss, *Renaissance Truth and the Latin Language Turn* (Oxford: Oxford University Press, 2003); Jean Dietz Moss and William A. Wallace, *Rhetoric and Dialectic in the Time of Galileo* (Washington, DC: Catholic University of America Press, 2003).

45. See the magisterial book by William Kneale and Martha Kneale, *The Development of Logic* (Oxford: Clarendon, 1978; 1962), 23–378; see also Marta Spranzi, *Art of Dialectic between Dialogue and Rhetoric: The Aristotelian Tradition* (Amsterdam: John Benjamins Publishing, 2011), which focuses on the *Topics* and its long reception.

46. François Rabelais, *Gargantua and Pantagruel*, trans. M. A. Screech (New York: Penguin Books, 2006), 25. What's truly odd is that Bakhtin, author of the most widely translated and cited study of Rabelais and himself a thinker within the dialectical tradition (an argument I take up in chap. 5), does not discuss this passage.

47. Descartes, *Discourse on Method and Meditations on First Philosophy*, 4th edition, trans. Donald A. Cress (Cambridge, MA: Hackett, 1998), 5, 39.

48. In his *Outlines of Scepticism*, Sextus Empiricus perfected the dialectic of pondering both sides of a given problem (equipollence), but with the skeptic addendum that one withhold judgment along the way: "since the Dogmatists seem plausibly to have established that there is a standard of truth, we have set up plausible-seeming arguments in opposition to them, affirming neither that they are true nor that they are more plausible than those on the contrary

side, but concluding to suspension of judgement because of the apparently equal plausibility of these arguments and those produced by the Dogmatists" (*Outlines of Scepticism*, trans. Julia Annas and Jonathan Barnes [Cambridge: Cambridge University Press, 1994], 71 [2.7.79]). Hegel, not surprisingly, trashes Sextus Empiricus: "Scepticism proper . . . is the complete despair about everything that the understanding holds to be firm. . . . This is the high ancient scepticism, as we find it presented specifically in Sextus Empiricus. . . . This ancient high scepticism must not be confused with the modern one that was mentioned earlier (§39), which partly preceded Critical Philosophy and partly grew out of it. This consists simply in denying that anything true and certain can be said about the supersensible. . . . Philosophy does not stop at the merely negative result of the dialectic, as is the case with scepticism" (*Encyclopaedia Logic*, trans. T. F. Garaets, W. A. Suchting, and H. S. Harris [Cambridge, MA: Hackett, 1991], 131/§81). See also Hegel's essay, "Relationship of Skepticism to Philosophy, Exposition of Its Different Modifications and Comparison to the Latest Form with the Ancient One," in *Between Kant and Hegel: Texts in the Development of post-Kantian Idealism*, trans. George di Giovanni and H.S. Harris (Albany: State University of New York Press, 1985), 313–62; and Michael N. Forster, *Hegel and Skepticism* (Cambridge, MA: Harvard University Press, 1989).

49. As Chrétien says when Yvain and Gawain are set to fight in the romance *Yvain*: "And did they not love one another now? Yes, I answer you, and no. And I'll prove that each reply is correct" (Chrétien de Troyes, *Arthurian Romances*, trans. William W. Kibler [New York: Penguin Books, 1991], 370). Swift speaks of the Houyhnhnms, "Neither is reason among them a point problematical as with us, where men can argue with plausibility on both sides of the question" (Jonathan Swift, *Gulliver's Travels* [New York: New American Library (Signet Classic), 1983], 288).

50. For the locution, "drivelectic," see Erasmus's *Hyperaspites* (book 2), in *Collected Works of Erasmus: Controversies*, vol. 77, ed. Charles Trinkhaus and trans. Clarence H. Miller (Toronto: University of Toronto Press, 2000), 354. Erasmus wishes that students at Louvain and Paris "would all accept the commentaries of Lefèvre upon Aristotle's Dialectic" (*The Epistles of Erasmus from his earliest letters to his Fifty-first year*, vol. 2 [Longmans, Green, 1904], 224).

51. John Buridan, *Summulae de dialectica*, trans. Gyula Klima (New Haven, CT: Yale University Press, 2001).

52. See John David Gemmill Evans, *Aristotle's Concept of Dialectic* (Cambridge: Cambridge University Press, 1977), for a complete investigation of the *Topics*, above all, and a clear statement of Aristotle's departure from Plato.

53. Plato, *Sophist*, 973/230b–e.

54. Aristotle, *Metaphysics*, 2.1586/1004b.

55. Aristotle, *Prior Analytics*, 1.39/24a; see *De Interpretatione*, 1.32–33/20b. Likewise, dialectic criticism—or what Aristotle calls "examination"—involves, most frequently, questions that require only yes or no answers (*Topics*, 1.266/158a and *Sophistical Refutations*, 1.291/171b).

56. Respectively, Aristotle, *Sophistical Refutations*, 279/165b and *Topics*, 1.273/162a. Aristotle calls the general premises "primitive"—i.e., first premises: "A deduction is an argument in which, certain things being laid down, something other than these necessarily comes about through them. It is a demonstration, when the premises from which the deduction starts are true and primitive, or are such that our knowledge of them has originally come through primisses [sic] which are primitive and true; and it is a dialectical deduction, if it reasons from reputable opinions" (*Topics*, 1.167/100a).

57. Aristotle, *Topics*, 1.173/104a.

58. Ibid., 1.245/145b; see Aristotle's discussion of the different disciplinary perspectives on the nature of the soul, questioning whether these can be combined, in *On the Soul*, 1.643/403b.

59. Samuel Johnson, *Selected Writings*, ed. Peter Martin (Cambridge, MA: Harvard University Press, 2009), 398. In a similar vein, William Empson says that "part of the function of an allegory is to make you feel that two levels of being correspond to one another in detail, and indeed that there is some underlying reality, something in the nature of things, which makes this happen. Either level may illuminate the other." Empson calls this function "Mutual Comparison" (*The Structure of Complex Words* [Cambridge, MA: Harvard University Press, 1989], 346–47).

60. It can be recalled: for Aristotle, dialectical deduction (συλλογισμός) does the work of making difference, as stated in the *Prior Analytics*: "certain things being stated, something other than what is stated follows of necessity from their being so" (1.40 [24b]). This is a difference in language, chiefly syllogism. See also Aristotle, *Topics*, 1.167/100a–b, with the emphasis on reasoning from "reputable opinions."

61. Aristotle, *Topics*, 1.254/151a; see 256/152b. Of all entities, only the "soul" can bear these oppositions (*Topics*, 1.254/151a; see below).

62. Ibid., 1.229/136a.

63. Ibid., 1.169/102a.

64. Ibid., 1.180/108a–b.

65. Ibid., 1.188/112b.

66. Ibid., 1.207/123b.

67. "It is obvious that the same thing will never do or suffer opposites in the same respect in relation to the same thing and at the same time" (Plato, *The Republic*, 678 [436b]); "the same attribute cannot at the same time belong and not belong to the same subject and in the same respect" (Aristotle, *Metaphysics* 1588 [1005b]).

68. See Aristotle, *Topics*, 240/142a. In the following, Aristotle preempts the logical work of identity/difference: "the contrary named by the privation must of necessity be defined through the other; where as the other cannot then be defined through the other named by the privation; *for else we should find that each was being made known by the other*" (*Topics*, 248/147b; emphasis mine).

69. As I believe is his meaning. Real things, of course, are related to other real things. The point is that "relative being" does not materialize as actual being within any thing. Rather, relatives are a matter of perspective and comparison: Aristotle in chap. 7 of the *Categories* emphasizes what is "properly spoken of" relatives and their correlatives and concludes: "It is perhaps hard to make firm statements on such questions without having examined them many times" (14/8b). See Pamela Michelle Hood, *Aristotle on the Category of Relation* (Lanham, MD: University Press of America, 2004), for alternative interpretations.

70. Aristotle, *Categories*, 1.12/7a–b.

71. Ibid., 1.10/6a.

72. To follow Plato's thought process but apply it to a line of thinking he did not pursue: let's say that not-x is identical with itself but let's also establish, as the method requires, that not-x is not the Form known as Identity, in which not-x participates by virtue of being identical with itself. And so not-x is different from itself, participating in the form of Difference or not-x, which returns us immediately to not-x = not-x and to the strange assertion that not-x participates in itself. The point here is that the strictly logical operator of not-x already admits

identity/difference, but Plato did not conceptualize this because he rejected thinking strictly on the side of negation, on the side of not-x, out of which positivity emerges.

73. Aristotle, *Metaphysics*, 2.1017b27–1020b8.

74. For Hegel's statement on the "laws of thought," see Hegel, *Science of Logic*, 374–84 [§931–63].

75. Ibid., 382 [§957], 384 [§963].

76. Ibid., 384 [§963].

77. Ibid., 381 [§955]. Naturally, Hegel revisits the example of motion discussed by Plato (mentioned above), but unlike Plato is able to apply the categories of identity, difference, and contradiction in his explanation: "Something moves, not because now it is here and there at another now, but because in one and the same now it is here and not here; because in this here it is and is not at the same time. One must concede to the dialecticians of old the contradictions which they pointed to in motion; but what follows from them is not that motion is not but that it is rather contradiction as *existent*" (382 [§958]). He also discusses (though does not name) Aristotle's insights into relative being; see 383 [§960].

78. Hegel writes: "There is no proposition of Heraclitus which I have not adopted in my Logic [sic]" (*Hegel's Lectures on the History of Philosophy*, 3 vols., trans. E. S. Haldane and Francis H. Simson [London: Routledge and Kegan Paul, 1955], 1.279; the epigraph to this chapter is at 2.49). I use this translation, because the most recent translations omit this interesting material in the effort to provide chronological snapshots of Hegel's thinking late in life—extracting material thought to be delivered at an earlier date. See also Friedrich Engels, *Socialism: Utopian and Scientific* (Chippendale, AU: Resistance Books, 1999), 72.

79. *Hegel's Lectures on the History of Philosophy*, 3.37.

80. When scholars speak of dialectic with respect to Plotinus, they almost always pursue the non-Hegelian meaning of the term (consequently setting aside identity/difference), and when they refer to the Hegelian dialectic in relation to Plotinus—a very rare comparison—they typically omit the classical and medieval texts and practices that go by the same name. See Sarah Rappe, "Introspection in the Dialectic of the *Enneads*," in *Reading Neoplatonism: Non-discursive Thinking in the Texts of Plotinus* (Cambridge: Cambridge University Press, 2000), 67–90; Bernard Collette, *Dialectique et Hénologie chez Plotin*, Cahier de Philosophie ancienne, n. 18 (Brussels: Ousia, 2002); Annamaria Schiaparelli, "Plotinus on Dialectic," *Archiv für Geschichte der Philosophie* 91, no. 3 (2009): 253–87. John Shannon Hendrix's task is not to define dialectic or dialectical method apart from the expected description of the interplay between particulars and universals: "The Intellectual Principle is the realization of the dialectic of reason, in that it contains both the particular and the universal, in that it participates in both Reason Principle and the One" (*Aesthetics and the Philosophy of Spirit: From Plotinus to Schelling and Hegel* [New York: Peter Lang, 2005], 128; see also 123, 124, 128, 140). The long-forgotten twenty-nine-page tract by H. A. Overstreet, *The Dialectic of Plotinus*, University of California Publication in Philosophy (Berkeley: The University Press, 1909), offers a laudable start in comparing Hegel and Plotinus.

81. Gadamer argues that there is "absolutely nothing of this [Hegelian dialectic] in the dialectic of the Ancients" (Hans-Georg Gadamer, *Hegel's Dialectic: Five Hermeneutical Studies*, trans. P. Christopher Smith [New Haven, CT: Yale University Press, 1976], 16), yet Hegel, somehow, was able "to conjure up the speculative content hidden in the logical instinct of language," concealed in ancient philosophy like Plato's and Aristotle's (31). Hegel simply misread classical philosophy but nonetheless "worked out his own dialectical method by extending the dialectic of the Ancients and transforming it" (31; on Hegelian misreadings, see 23, 28, 30). Yet amidst such claims are tantalizing sentences about neoplatonism, which Gadamer passes over,

not mentioning even one philosopher by name: "Hegel relies above all on Plato's *Parmenides*, his understanding of it being shaped in large part by Neoplatonism's theological-ontological interpretation" (21; cf. 16); "The Neoplatonic origin of these concepts is not accidental" (32; see 32–33). None of these connections Gadamer pursues.

82. Gadamer, "Hegel and the Dialectic of the Ancient Philosophers," in *Hegel's Dialectic*, 32–33; see also Gadamer's *Truth and Method*, 362–79.

83. See Derrida's influential essay, with its meditations on *dénégation*: "How to Avoid Speaking: Denials," trans. by Ken Frieden, in *Languages of the Unsayable: The Play of Negativity in Literature and Literary Theory*, ed. Sanford Budick and Wolfgang Iser (New York: Columbia University Press, 1989), 3–70. For a contextualizing and suggestive study, see Stephen Gersh, *Neoplatonism after Derrida: Parallelograms* (Leiden: Brill, 2006).

84. Hannah Arendt writes that "in his time speculations Hegel has a strange predecessor. . . . That is Plotinus" (*Life of the Mind* [New York: Houghton Mifflin Harcourt, 1981], 44). See also Werner Beierwaltes, "Hegel und Plotin," *Revue internationale de philosophie* 24 (1968): 247–51; Markus Gabriel, "Hegel und Plotin," in *Hegel und die Geschichte der Philosophie*, ed. Dietmar H. Heidemann and Christian Krijnen (Darmstadt: Wissenschaftliche Buchgesellschaft, 2007), 70–83; Gabriel Chindea, "Le problème de la déduction des catégories chez Plotin et Hegel," *Revistă de studii etnologice și istorico-religioase* 9 (2008): 13–22; Oliver Davies, "Thinking Difference: A Comparative Study of Gilles Deleuze, Plotinus and Meister Eckhart," in *Deleuze and Religion*, ed. Mary Bryden (New York: Routledge, 2001), 76–86.

85. Plotinus, *The Enneads*, trans. Stephen MacKenna, abridged with an introduction and notes by John Dillon (New York: Penguin, 1991); cited by page number, followed by book- and chapter number in brackets, here 27 [1.3]. As Dillon notes, Plotinus "puts Aristotelian and Stoic logic in its place" (27n34).

86. For a general discussion of this tract, see Annamaria Schiaparelli, "Plotinus on Dialectic," *Archiv für Geschichte der Philosophie* 91, no. 3 (2009): 253–87.

87. Plotinus, *Enneads*, 26 [1.3].

88. Plotinus offers a much simpler definition of dialectic that is more strongly ontological than either Plato's or Aristotle's version, because while in the *Categories* (not a work on dialectic, we can remember, but absorbed into late medieval treatises on dialectic), Aristotle discusses the ten categories of reality, Plotinus states that the entire created order is already dialectical, that the soul operates dialectically just as the forms do. While Plotinus is sparing in his use of the word dialectic, it is proper for us to apply the adjective to his thought, since indeed his meaning is precisely that.

89. *Platonis Opera*, ed. John Burnet (Oxford: Oxford University Press, 1903), 156b. See chap. 1.

90. Alain Badiou sifts through the "general ruin of thought as such by the entire dialectic of the one" (*Being and Event*, trans. Oliver Feltham [London: Continuum, 2007], 31) and seeks to dismiss "negative theologies" (26) and, by implication neoplatonism, by going straight to their source—namely, Plato. Above all, he challenges the Platonic notion of the "non being of the one" to show that, in Plato's *Parmenides*, non-being is itself a form of being by "participation in the being-ness of to-be-non-being" (32). Because the "one" falls on the side of being, Badiou concludes that there is never "one" and only ever multiplicity or, better, multiples of multiples (29). And in a fashion that may seem Lacanian, the "one" exists only as a discourse-effect, an "operation," or indeed symptom that expresses itself from "behind" representation (24–25; 36). In this way, Badiou allegorizes premodern thought as a species of the apophatic modern.

91. Plotinus, *Enneads*, 353 [5.1]; see 355.

92. Aristotle solves this question in his God, the "unmoved mover" (*Physics* 8.5–6/258b–60) who sets its own inherent potentiality into motion, thus producing the actuality of all beings; the question of what "causes," "produces," or "changes" things concerns, in the "first science" that is theology, "motion" (*Metaphysics* 12.2/1269b 8–18), the movement from one state of being to another.

93. Plotinus, *Enneads*, 353–54 [5.1].

94. Ibid., 377 [5.3]. As Plotinus puts it, "Aristotle . . . begins by making the First transcendent and intellective but cancels that primacy by supposing it to have self-intellection" (358 [5.1]; see 380 [5.3]).

95. Ibid., 381 [5.3].

96. Ibid., 355, 359 [5.1]; see 402 [5.5].

97. Ibid., 355 [5.1], 361 [5.2].

98. Cf. Plotinus, *Enneads*, 387–90 [5.4], which Dillon (387) determines to be an earlier tract more careless about the distinction between the One and being and intellection; see for example 389. What makes this earlier position different from the latter quoted in my main text is, quite simply, the clear borrowing of language from Plato's *Timaeus*, 42e (borrowings noted by MacKenna, 389nn69–70) that we do not find in the later tract. Here, simply, Plotinus is too Platonic. Plotinus himself acknowledges this weakness in Plato's thought, writing: "With all his affirmation of unity, his own writings lay him open to the reproach that his unity turns out to be a multiplicity" (*Enneads*, 357 [5.1]).

99. St. Anselm, *Basic Writings: Proslogium, Monologium, Cur Deus homo, Gaunilon's on Behalf of the Fool*, trans. S. N. Deane, 2nd ed. (La Salle, IL: Open Court Publishing, 1962). Cited here: *Proslogium*, 8 [chap. 2], *Monologium*, 71 [chap. 19]. See, generally, *Monologium*, 52–56 [chaps. 8–9], 70–72 [chaps. 19–20]. To be clear, Anselm does deal with identity and difference, but only after having established God as Being—a move that deprives these logical categories of their greatest explanatory capacity in dealing with the impossible dialectical transition from nothing to being; see *Monologium*, 101–07 [chaps. 38–44]. Likewise, his discussion of "the terms *master* and *servant*" (ibid., 42 [chap 3]) reveals limits in his capacity to conceptualize identity in difference in a manner like . . . Hegel.

100. Plotinus's difficulties are compounded by the fact that he does not *consistently* follow the tradition of *tolma*—the Hellenic idea that the One became so intensely self-knowing as to become audacious in the wish to leap out toward multiplicity and Otherness. See A. H. Armstrong, "Gnosis and Greek Philosophy," in *Gnosis: Festschrift für Hans Jonas* (Göttingen: Vandenhoeck & Ruprecht, 1978), 87–124, see esp., 116; N. J. Torchia, *Plotinus, Tolma, and the Descent of Being* (New York: Peter Lang, 1993), 18, 31, 43. Cf. *Enneads*, 347 [5.1], 362 [5.2], where it seems to me that Plotinus, as is his wont, refers to established ideas (most often, the gods of Greek mythology) to reference familiar points of knowledge but re-orient them toward his own system.

101. In the twelfth century, the dialectic question of non-being, non-existence appears in ways more complex (and humorous) than Augustine could have predicted when he made his original association between evil and non-being. In Vitalis of Blois's *Geta*, dialectic leads the title character "not out of *aporia* but further and deeper into it: 'Therefore I am, therefore I am nothing. Damn this dialectic that completely undoes me'" (quoted in Brown's *Contrary Things*, 53).

102. Plotinus, *Enneads*, 382 [5.3].

103. Ibid.

104. Ibid., 354 [5.1].

105. Ibid., 383 [5.3].

106. Ibid., 352 [5.1]

107. See ibid., 351 [5.1]; 357 [5.1]. Plotinus fuses the Intellectual-Principle with being: "everything, in that entire content, is Intellectual-Principle and Authentic-Existence; and the total of all is Intellectual-Principle entire and Being entire" (351).

108. Ibid., 352 [5.1].

109. Plotinus, *The Enneads*, trans. Stephen Mackenna (Burdett, New York: Larson Publications, 1992), 549 [6.2], which is not available in the abridged version cited above; cf. Badiou, *Being and Event*, 37.

110. Raymond Klibansky, "Plato's *Parmenides* in the Middle Ages and the Renaissance: A Chapter in the History of Platonic Studies," *Medieval and Renaissance Studies* 1 (1941–43): 281–335.

111. *Proclus' Commentary on Plato's Parmenides*, trans. Glenn R. Morrow and John M. Dillon (Princeton, NJ: Princeton University Press, 1987), 109.

112. Ibid., 124.

113. Ibid., 125.

114. This crucial point, which anticipates Hegel's treatment of the universal and individual as a relation of identity/difference, requires an explanation. In Book II, Proclus goes on a detour to discuss this long-standing problem of the One and the Many, criticizing Plato for failing to include these two terms among the five primals: "Plato in the *Sophist* failed to list the One and the Many among the greatest kinds" (ibid., 132). He boldly states "that [the] One and Many are the most general of the kinds, the source of each Form's being both one and many" (131–32). Next, he immediately declares the One and the Many to be like another set of terms; they are "analogous to the primary Limit and the primary Unlimited" (132). Yet by suggesting that the One and the Many are analogous to Limit and Unlimited, Proclus enfolds this older Platonic binary right back into questions of likeness and unlikeness, insofar as he states, not many pages earlier in his commentary, that Limit and Unlimited are analogous to likeness and unlikeness, which are features of the Demiurge's intellect: "There is then a demiurgic Likeness and Unlikeness, the former analogous to the cause of the Limit, the other correlative with the Unlimited. The former brings things together (which is why he [Plato] says . . . "The like is like to the like"); the latter is separative, delighting in procession and variety and movement" (110). Try as he might, then, Proclus cannot get away from these terms of likeness and unlikeness, even if he attempts (unsuccessfully) to place the One and the Many above them—to say nothing of the fact that analogy—itself a mode of comparing likenesses among *differentiae*—is at stake here.

115. Ibid., 118. See also this elaboration: "And we must remember also that monads of all things whatever that are said to exist produce some of them as if from the entirety of their natures but diminished for particular instances, their specific character being preserved but becoming more partial in them. . . . For all images will naturally deviate in their essence from their paradigms—not to have the same formula, but one similar to that from which they came" (ibid.).

116. The henads are, in fact, connected to this order by means of yet another mode of likeness, *analogy*: each henad is "analogous . . . to the One" (ibid., 404). And henads relate to the monads by means of their "principle . . . in the monads which hold together multiplicity" (ibid.). See Proclus's example of the principle of light; 404–5.

117. Ibid., 346.

118. Ibid., 347.

119. Ibid., 347–48.

120. Plato, *Republic*, 746 [511b–c].

121. Aristotle, *Topics*, 245 [151a–b].

122. "That which cognizes must be its objects potentially, and they must be in it. But if there is anything that has no contrary, then it knows itself and is actually and possesses independent existence" (Aristotle, *On the Soul*, 685 [430b]).

123. Ibid., 646 [405b] and 650 [407b]. See also Book II, chaps. 11–12, on the contraries of the *sensoria* (672–75 [422b–24b]).

124. For even Plotinus and Proclus, try as they might, do not surpass Aristotle in thinking of the soul in this fashion. Plotinus states that "Dialectic . . . has no knowledge of propositions—collections of words—but it knows . . . what the schools call their propositions: it knows above all the operations of the Soul [and] what is affirmed and what is denied" (*Enneads*, 28 [1.3]). Proclus, for his part, takes this notion in a different direction, stating that in the soul, contradictions exist: "in souls the contraries . . . are unextended, yet they are multiple and separate and exhibit excursions and gyrations in performing their functions. But the contraries in Intellect, being unified to the highest degrees, partless and immaterial, and constituted by a single form are in created company with one another. . . . The contraries in souls exist with one another as such" (*Proclus' Commentary on Plato's Parmenides*, 114).

125. "The Divine Names," in *Pseudo-Dionysius: The Complete Works*, trans. Colm Luibheid (New York: Paulist Press, 1987), 65.

126. Ibid., 78. For the Greek and Latin text, see J.-P. Migne, *Patrologiae cursus completus: Series Graeca*, 161 vols. (Paris: Geuthner, 1857–89), 3.767–68.

127. *Pseudo-Dionysius: The Complete Works*, 115.

128. Ibid., 116, 117, 67.

129. Ibid., 61.

130. Ibid., 63.

131. Ibid., 115.

132. "The Celestial Hierarchy," in *Pseudo-Dionysius: The Complete Works*, 151.

133. Ibid., 147; see 149.

134. Ibid., 152–53. On modern paradoxical thought experiments, see Graham Priest, *Beyond the Limits of Thought* (Oxford: Clarendon Press, 2002).

135. See "Mystical Theology," in *Pseudo-Dionysius: The Complete Works*, 136.

136. Ibid., 138, 139.

137. "The Celestial Hierarchy," in *Pseudo-Dionysius: The Complete Works*, 152.

138. See Martin Heidegger, "Conversation On a Country Path about Thinking," in *Discourse on Thinking* (New York: Harper & Row, 1966); originally published as *Gelassenheit*, 1959. On the connection to Eckhart, John D. Caputo, *The Mystical Element in Heidegger's Thought* (New York: Fordham University Press, 1990), 171. See also Reiner Schürmann's helpful collection of Heidegger's assessments of Eckhart in his "Heidegger and Meister Eckhart on Releasement," in *Heidegger Reexamined: Art, Poetry, and Technology*, vol. 3, ed. Hubert Dreyfus and Mark A. Wrathall (New York: Routledge, 2003), 295–319.

139. *Martin Heidegger: Philosophical and Political Writings*, ed. Manfred Stassen (New York: Continuum, 2003), 93.

140. Slavoj Žižek, *The Parallax View* (Cambridge, MA: MIT Press, 2006), 4. Žižek turns to the non-dialectical traditions of dialectic as a remedy for Marxism: "To theorize this parallax gap properly is the first necessary step in the rehabilitation of the philosophy of *dialectical materialism*" (ibid.). Gayatri Chakravorty Spivak has argued for the necessity of "double binds" in modern life, the inhabiting of (at least) two identities and "learning to live with contradictory instructions" in the age of globalization; see *An Aesthetic Education in the Era of Globalization* (Cambridge: Harvard University Press, 2012), 1.

141. "The Celestial Hierarchy," in *Pseudo-Dionysius: The Complete Works*, 153.

142. Yet we should be clear that Pseudo-Dionysius preserves the "dissimilar similarities" (ibid., 151) from emerging into total identity—"one must be careful to use the similarities as dissimilarities . . . to avoid one-to-one correspondence" (152)—which I take to be a truly neoplatonic point, consistent with the kinds of critical questioning Parmenides put to Socrates when it seemed that the former was exhibiting his lack of training in dialectic (Plato, *Parmenides*, 935 [135d]) and proposing there to be a correspondence between Forms and things (927–28 [133c–d]). Indeed, as Pseudo-Dionysius states in the *Celestial Hierarchy*, "Everything, then, can be a help to contemplation" ("The Celestial Hierarchy," *Pseudo-Dionysius: The Complete Works*, 151)—if, granted, one is an initiate (see 152).

143. After all, any medieval philosopher who speaks of the "negation of the negation" obviously is relevant to a discussion of Hegel! See, for instance, his (now incomplete) tract known as "Existence Is God," in Meister Eckhart, *Parisian Questions and Prologues*, trans. Armand A. Maurer (Toronto: Pontifical Institute of Mediaeval Studies, 1981), 95, 100. The most widely available selection of Eckhart's writing, however necessarily limited that selection is, exhibits relevance to these considerations. Eckhart shows that contemplative "detachment" or *abegescheidenheit*—Heidegger's other favorite medieval term along with *Gelassenheit*—is, among other things, the method by which a person moves from difference and Otherness to identity and equality with the ground that is the One, the essence without distinction out of which the hypostases come: that "simple ground . . . into which distinction never gazed, not the Father, nor the Son, nor the Holy Spirit" (*Meister Eckhart: the Essential Sermons, Commentaries, Treatises, and Defense*, trans. Edmund Colledge and Bernard McGinn [New York: Paulist Press, 1981], 198 [Sermon 48]; see 181 [Sermon 2]). Eckhart proposes that negation is required to move from difference to identity insofar as detachment is, properly, this negation: "Now detachment approaches so closely to nothingness that there can be nothing between perfect detachment and nothingness" (286 ["On Detachment"]). Powerfully, he emphasizes that "detachment wants to be nothing at all" (ibid., 287). But this negation is in the service of likeness: "As far as it can, every agent makes something like itself, and its makes the other itself, that is, makes the other from other into itself. It begins from the other, withdraws from it, and draws it to itself" (146). Building on, yet refocusing, Aristotelian ideas in the *Metaphysics*, Eckhart proposes: "What is in the One is one" (146 ["Selections from the Commentary on John"]). Yet as we have seen, any discussion of the one and the many, must now be framed in the terms of likeness and unlikeness, and on this score, he elaborates later in his commentary: "As long as anything is becoming something else, it always has the grief of unlikeness and restlessness. . . . This is the case in what we are discussing: As long as we are not like God . . . we are restless and troubled about many things" (ibid., 172–73). On Heidegger's use of these terms from Eckhart, see S. J. McGrath, *The Early Heidegger and Medieval Philosophy: Phenomenology for the Godforsaken*, 134–50. For the aforementioned references to Aristotle, see Eckhart, *Essential Sermons, Commentaries*, 331, nn.108, 110; note 109, however, attributes Eckhart's words to Aristotle's *On the Soul*, but nowhere does there seem to be a match. Finally, on the potential link between Eckhart and Plotinus, see Eduardo Briancesco, "Memoria e identidad en la experienci de Eckhart," *Escritos de Filosofía* 19.37–38 (2001): 121–40.

144. See Jasper Hopkins, *Nicholas of Cusa on God as Not-Other: A Translation and an Appraisal of De li non aliud* (Minneapolis: University of Minnesota Press, 1979), 29 [1]; 117 [90]; 127 [100]; 133 [106]; and 29 [1]; 33 [5]; 83–109 [54–82].

145. Ibid., 29 [1]; 117 [89]. Cf., 141–51 [114–25], where the list of propositions begins to read like Aristotle's *Topics* in its forensic approach.

146. Ibid., 33 [5]. Nicholas of Cusa, as Blumenberg shows, brings contemplation to its highest point of observation, negating not only the self ("the mystic's ardent desire") but transcending creation in its entirety, "observing the world 'from outside' and 'from within'—between the standpoints of God and man" (Hans Blumenberg, *The Legitimacy of the Modern Age*, trans. Robert M. Wallace [Cambridge, MA: MIT Press, 1983], 515). By thinking that "divinity and nothingness have become interchangeable" (514), Nicholas "for the first time" deals with the "traditional antinomies of metaphysics" (514). Blumenberg is right that Nicholas overcomes antinomies but does not account for precisely how he comes to this achievement through identity and difference.

147. *Nicholas of Cusa on God as Not-Other*, 35 [7]; 33 [5]. As Nicholas says of his invention of this term out of Anselm's so-called ontological argument: "It is that which for many years I sought by way of the coincidence of opposites—as the many books which I have written about this speculative matter bear witness" (*Nicholas of Cusa on God as Not-Other*, 41 [12]).

148. Ibid., 31 [4]. For more on the Cusan and dialectic, see C. L. Miller, *Reading Cusanus: Metaphor and Dialectic in a Conjectural Universe* (Washington, DC: Catholic University of America Press, 2003).

149. Picking up on the limits of Plato's theorizing of otherness and the neoplatonic insight into this quality, Nicholas writes: "Dionysius the Areopagite said that even God is called Other—something which is denied in the *Parmenides*" (*Nicholas of Cusa on God as Not-Other*, 129 [100]). To be sure, the expected relations of identity and difference can be found in Nicholas's work, too: all things, issuing from God, bear a relation of identity in difference in the more traditional philosophic sense; Nicholas's discussion of "Trajan's column" confirms this reading (see 63–65 [34–35]); and all things bear a relation of identity and difference to one another, as his discussion on the "carbuncles" confirms (see 75 [45]).

150. See ibid., 69–71 [41]; see 53 [23]; 59 [31]; 67–69 [38]; on participation, see 65–67 [36], 73 [43].

151. Ibid., 51 [21]. Jasper Hopkins, in *Nicholas of Cusa's Metaphysic of Contraction* (Minneapolis: A. J. Banning Press, 1983), states: "Nicholas's discovery of the twofoldness of the ontological dimensions, and therefore of the duality of the ontologies (i.e., the ontology of identity and the ontology of difference), is the nucleus of the entire Cusan philosophy" (36). This is a very important point, though I would add (by now, obviously) that the discovery is not only Nicholas's. See also Nancy J. Hudson, *Becoming God: The Doctrine of Theosis in Nicholas of Cusa*, which argues that the procession-return model, which maps onto difference/identity and potentially robs creatures of their individuality (174), is not accepted by Nicholas, since he rejects "theosis as return" (173) on the grounds that if there is "participation" then there is never difference to begin with, and so no return is necessary.

152. *Nicholas of Cusa on God as Not-Other*, 41 [12]. Summarizing Hegel's reading of Giordano Bruno, Hans Blumenberg states: "The *coincidentia oppositorum* . . . is not the dialectic" (*The Genesis of the Copernican World*, trans. Robert M. Wallace [Cambridge: MIT Press, 1987]), 384. Elsewhere, he finds the *coincidentia oppositorum* to posit a "world-bound language" that can nonetheless "lead upward beyond world-boundness precisely by negating . . . perceptual contents." He suggests that this "method" reflects Nicholas's "negative theology," in which transcendence is praxis, the activity of thinking to the "limit of theoretical accomplishment" (*Legitimacy of the Modern Age*, 491). Blumenberg, aware of Nicholas's reading of Plotinus and interest in neoplatonism (496–87; 501, 517, 523; cf. 515) and the translatability of his method across theology, anthropology, and cosmology (492; 507), omits a crucial point, however: *this*

is obviously dialectic. His reasons for this omission are straightforward and consistent with his attack on the secularization thesis: in the same way the modern is not a secularized Middle Ages, modernity cannot brook having its inventions, such as the dialectic, back projected into the Middle Ages and called "method" (495; see 496–97). Blumenberg's view is widely shared, for what we come to know now as "the dialectic," with the definite article, is discussed with seldom reference to the strong premodern antecedents that go by the same name.

153. For a kindred study, see Werner Beierwaltes, *Identität und Differenz: Zum Prinzip cusanischen Denkens*, Rheinisch- Westfälische Akademie der Wissenschaften (Opladen: Westdeutscher, 1977).

154. *Nicholas of Cusa on God as Not-Other*, 45 [16].

155. Ibid., 49 [19].

156. Ibid., 47 [18].

157. Ibid., 27 [27].

158. Ibid., 57 [29].

159. Ibid.

160. Ibid., 59 [30].

161. Hegel, *Science of Logic*, 84 [§193].

162 Ernst Cassirer, *Individuum und Kosmos in der Philosophie der Renaissance: Die platonische Renaissance in England und die Schule von Cambridge* (Leipzig: Teubner, 1927), 11.

163. Edmond Vansteenberghe, *Le Cardinal Nicolas de Cues (1401–1464)* (Paris, 1920; reprinted in Frankfurt am Main: Minerva, 1963), 282.

164. Erwin Metzke, "Nicolaus von Cues und Hegel: Ein Beitrag zum Problem der philosophischen Theologie," *Kant-Studien* 48 (1956–57): 216–36; here, 216.

165. Mine is not, to be clear, a historiographic demonstration that medieval philosophy "worked its way" to identity/difference, which is then purportedly perfected and made appropriately critical in modern dialectal and post-dialectical thought. Rather, philosophers used it for centuries after Plotinus and Proclus, rather consistently. There are, as I noted at the outset, a variety of philosophical investigations different from those I discuss here, but even these specialized inquiries uniquely involve the same kind of thought, the thought of identity in difference, that was the invention of the Middle Ages.

166. Hegel, *Phenomenology of Spirit*, 47/§74.

167. Here I use the translation entitled (confusingly) *The Phenomenology of Mind*, trans. J. B. Baillie, 2nd ed. (Courier Dover Publications, 2003), 22, which better translates this passage than Miller (23/§39): "Man kann wohl falsch wissen. Es wird etwas falsch gewußt, heißt, das Wissen ist in Ungleichheit mit seiner Substanz. Allein eben diese Ungleichheit ist das Unterscheiden überhaupt, das wesentliches Moment ist. Es wird aus dieser Unterscheidung wohl ihre Gleichheit, und diese gewordene Gleichheit ist die Wahrheit. Aber sie ist nicht so Wahrheit, als ob die Ungleichheit weggeworfen worden wäre, wie die Schlacke vom reinen Metall, auch nicht einmal so, wie das Werkzeug von dem fertigen Gefäße wegbleibt, sondern die Ungleichheit ist als das Negative, als das Selbst im Wahren als solchem selbst noch unmittelbar vorhanden."

168. See Hegel, *Phenomenology of Spirit*, 38/§61.

169. Ibid., 52/§82; 55/§86. In these paragraphs I intentionally focus on Hegel's most widely known work, the *Phenomenology of Spirit*. But this text is not, clearly, his earliest effort to reflect on identity/difference. Rather, the following work is: *Jenaer Systemwürfe II: Logik, Metaphysik, Naturphilosophie*, ed. Rolf-Peter Horstmann (Hamburg: Felix Meiner Verlag, 1982), which was unpublished in Hegel's lifetime but written in 1804–5. See especially the *Logik*.

170. Theodor W. Adorno, "Skoteinos, or How to Read Hegel," *Hegel: Three Studies*, trans. Shierry Weber Nicholsen (Cambridge, MA: MIT Press, 1993), 89.

171. This is not to exclude "for another" (115/§189), or "für ein anderes" (Hegel, *Werke in zwanzig Bänden: Theorie-Werkausgabe* [Frankfurt: Suhrkamp, 1970], 3.150), as detailed in that chapter on the lord/bondsman dialectic.

172. Hegel, *Phenomenology of Spirit*, 14/§25.

173. It's here that we can recognize that, likewise, Spirit itself is not a phantom but a form—the sum total of all these relations of difference, but a sum that is itself in a relation of identity/difference to its parts: it is and is not its parts, thereby reminding us that whatever counts as a historical whole is never complete or without contradiction, real or abstract. As such, then, it is right to think that Spirit stands as the figure (not Hegel's term) for identity/difference itself.

174. Hegel, *Phenomenology of Spirit*, 58/§91.

175. Ibid., 59/§92.

176. Ibid., 59/§94.

177. See ibid., §96.

178. Ibid., 60/§96.

179. See ibid., 62/§103, 63/§105.

180. Ibid., 64/§109.

181. Ibid., 64–65/§109. I second H. S. Harris that Hegel here is speaking against skepticism: see his *Hegel's Ladder*, 2 vols. (Indianapolis: Hackett, 1997), 1.211, 215–16; on the significance of ancient skepticism (as opposed to modern), see 1.225, 228.

182. Hegel, *Phenomenology of Spirit*, 61/§101.

183. Hegel, *Werke in zwanzig Bänden*, 3.86.

184. J. N. Findlay's note indicates that Hegel's target here is "the perpetual phenomenalism of Kantianism" (*Phenomenology of Spirit*, 528n238–39).

185. Hegel, *Phenomenology of Spirit*, 115/§189.

186. Ibid., 111/§178.

187. Hegel, *Werke in zwanzig Bänden*, 3.145.

188. Ibid.

189. Hegel, *Phenomenology of Spirit*, 112/§184.

190. Ibid., 113/§186.

191. Ibid., 114/§188.

192. Here Hegel uses the adverb *gleichgültig* (*Werke in zwanzig Bänden*, 3.150).

193. Hegel, *Phenomenology of Spirit*, 120/§197.

194. Ibid., 121/§199; 123/§202.

195. Hegel writes: "Consciousness itself is the *absolute dialectical unrest* [die absolute dialektische Unruhe] this medley of sensuous and intellectual representations whose differences coincide, and whose identity is equally again dissolved, for it is itself determinateness as contrasted with the non-identical. But it is just in this process that this consciousness, instead of being self-identical, is in fact nothing but a purely casual, confused medley, the dizziness of a perpetually self-engendered disorder" (*Phenomenology of Spirit*, 124–25/§205; *Werke in zwanzig Bänden*, 3.161).

196. Ibid., 125–26/205; *Werke in zwanzig Bänden*, 3.162; see also Preface, 16/§28.

197. Failure itself is, as Hegel, says in his Introduction to the *Phenomenology of Spirit*, central to the dialectical mode: "Since consciousness thus finds that its knowledge does not correspond to its object, the object itself does not stand the test; in other words, the criterion for testing is

NOTES TO PAGES 55-59

altered when that for which it was to have been the criterion fails to pass the test; and the testing is not only a testing of what we know, but also a testing of the criterion of what knowing is. *Inasmuch as the new true object issues from it*, this *dialectical* movement . . . is precisely what is called *experience* [*Erfahrung*]" (*Phenomenology of Spirit*, 54–55/§85–86; see also 62/§102).

198. Ibid., 219/§363; 220/§364.

199. Ibid., 147/§245; see 70/§116. Note how Hegel speaks of "mere *universals*, though each has its own essence against the other" (22/§39); of "this universal . . . *afflicted with an opposition*" (76/§128); of the "self-contradictory moments of individuality and universality" (259/§431); and "the contradiction of giving to what is particular an actuality which is immediately universal" (298/§489).

200. Hegel, *Phenomenology of Spirit*, 60/§96.

201. Ibid., 480/§789.

202. Ibid., 491/§805, trans. modified; *Werke in zwanzig Bänden*, 3.589–90. See generally, *Phenomenology of Spirit*, 489–91/§803–6. From these passages to the very end, Hegel speaks of becoming, withdrawal, inwardization, negativity, and history.

203. Hegel, *Science of Logic*, 140/§357.

204. Hegel, *Phenomenology of Spirit*, 40/§66; 39/§65.

205. See also ibid., 55–56/§86–87.

206. Ibid., 39–40/§65.

207. Charles L. Griswold refers to (but does not elaborate upon) "Hegel's neoplatonist interpretation of the *Parmenides*" in the lectures on the history of philosophy (see "Reflections on 'Dialectic' in Plato and Hegel," *International Philosophical Quarterly* 22, no. 3 (1982): 115–30; here, 117; referring to the Haldane edition, *Hegel's Lectures on the History of Philosophy*, 2.60–61).

208. Here I paraphrase the "transcendental idea" of the first antinomy; see Immanuel Kant, *Critique of Pure Reason*, trans. and ed. Paul Guyer and Allen W. Wood (Cambridge: Cambridge University Press, 1998), 470–71. Note that this first one is a version of Aristotle's dialectic topic in *Topics*, 101b28–33.

209. Kant rejects as "merely dialectical" (*Critique of Pure Reason*, 519) the opposing viewpoints, "two judgements dialectically opposed to one another" that are false "because one does not merely contradict the other, but says something more than is required for contradiction" (518), and that something more is itself erroneous and helplessly regressive (see 502, 508–9).

210. See Kant, *Critique of Pure Reason*, 518, on the distinction between dialectical opposition and analytic opposition, which is true opposition.

211. "The above proofs of the fourfold antinomy are not semblances but well grounded, that is, at least on the presupposition that appearances, or a world of sense comprehending all of them within itself, are things in themselves" (ibid., 519). In other words, Kant offers a dialectical solution of his own. Stating that the "two dialectically opposed judgments . . . may be false" (518), Kant "can point to the dialectic as an example of the great utility of letting the arguments of reason confront one another" (519) because the truth of "appearances" has been established: they are "nothing outside our representations" (ibid.) but in this we discover that appearances have a "transcendental ideality" and "are things in themselves." Behold, the "transcendental dialectic" (ibid.), in which the two vastly different positions produce, in this dialectic, the same thing—a thesis about appearances as "objects of sense" (ibid.).

212. See Kant, *Critique of Pure Reason*, 590.

213. Ibid., 497; I have retained Kemp Smith's translation of "a mere mock fight" (*Immanuel Kant's Critique of Pure Reason*, trans. Norman Kemp Smith [New York: St. Martin's Press, 1965],

423) for Guyer and Wood's "mere shadow boxing," because it is clear throughout that Kant means to depict vapid chivalric contests and traditional warfare, not pugilistic face-offs. More generally, see Guyer and Wood, eds., 497–98, and the following colorful passage: "Thus instead of charging in with a sword, you should instead watch this conflict peaceably from the safe seat of critique, a conflict which must be exhausting for the combatants but entertaining for you, with an outcome that will certainly be bloodless" (647).

214. Ibid., 645.

215. Ibid., 652. A technical contextual matter should be addressed. When Kant was finishing both the first and second editions of his *Critique* (1781, 1787), he was living in the age of "modern warfare," in which conflict by cavalry and sword was replaced by dragoon units, musket battalions, and new ballistic weapons, "machine[s] that could wreak as much havoc as one hundred men" (Geoffrey Wawro, *Warfare and Society in Europe, 1792–1914* [New York: Routledge, 2000], 1). See also Gunther E. Rothenburg, "Armies and Warfare during the Last Years of the Ancien Régime," in *The Art of Warfare in the Age of Napoleon* (Bloomington: Indiana University Press, 1980), 11–30, esp. 13, 14, 18. Bearing in mind that Kant was from Königsberg, Prussia, we can note Rothenburg's discussion of the considerable and influential military advances in ballistic weaponry and tactics under the Prussian monarch Frederick the Great (16–19). My point is that Kant, in his *Critique*, clearly and purposely describes scholastic, dialectical debate as an *antiquated* model of warfare between noble, sword-wielding contestants with otiose chivalric ambitions. For his thoughts on contemporary war, however, see his essay "Perpetual Peace," in *Perpetual Peace, and Other Essays on Politics, History, and Morals*, trans. Ted Humphrey (Indianapolis: Hackett, 1983).

216. *Critique of Pure Reason*, 100 ("Preface to First Edition," original emphasis).

217. See Christian Wolff, *Philosophia prima, sive Ontologia* (1730), *Cosmologia generalis* (1731), *Psychologia rationalis* (1734), and *Theologia naturalis* (1736–37). Kant's critique did not stop Hegel from carrying some of the same burdens of proof (cosmological, ontological). See Hegel, *Lectures on the Proofs of the Existence of God*, ed. and trans. Peter C. Hodgson (Oxford: Clarendon, 2007).

218. See John Edwin Gurr, *The Principle of Sufficient Reason in Some Scholastic Systems, 1750–1900* (Milwaukee: Marquette University Press, 1959).

219. *Critique of Pure Reason*, 100 ("Preface to First Edition," original emphasis).

220. Ibid., 109.

221. Ibid.

222. Ibid., 119, 120. Kemp Smith renders this second passage as: "the philosophers of his time, and of all previous times, have no right to reproach one another" (33).

223. Hegel did not deem Wolff to be a medieval throwback and would insist, instead, that this philosopher did not absorb enough medieval philosophy, rejecting the traditions as embodied by Boehme: "The philosophy of Wolff is hence no doubt built on foundations laid by Leibnitz, but yet in such a manner that the speculative interest is quite eliminated from it. The spiritual philosophy, substantial in a higher sense, which we found emerging first in Boehme, though still in a peculiar and barbarous form, has been quite lost sight of, and has disappeared without leaving any traces or effects in Germany; his very language was forgotten. . . . In theoretic philosophy Wolff first treats of Logic purified from scholastic interpretations or deductions" (*Hegel's Lectures on the History of Philosophy*, 3.350).

224. "Just as the Sophists of Greece wandered about amongst abstract conceptions on behalf of actuality, so did the scholastics on behalf of their intellectual world" (ibid., 3.44). Likewise,

for Hegel, Platonic and neoplatonic texts exhibit a dialectic concerned exclusively with opposition or union with the One.

225. Hegel, *Science of Logic*, vol. 1, trans. A. V. Miller (1969; Atlantic Highlands, NJ: Humanities Press International, 1989), 197; see also 192, 234, 236.

226. Kant, *Critique of Pure Reason*, 663; see 645 and 664.

227. *Hegel's Lectures on the History of Philosophy*, 426.

228. Ibid., 437.

229. Ibid., 447.

230. Ibid., 427.

231. Ibid., 426.

232. Ibid. Hegel writes of Kant's transcendental subject, "It apprehends simple thought as having difference in itself, but does not yet apprehend that all reality rests on this difference" (426). In discussing Kant's antinomies, Hegel writes: "But the Kantian philosophy does not go on to grapple with the fact that it is not things that are contradictory but self-consciousness itself. Experience teaches us that the ego does not melt away by reason of these contradictions" (451).

233. More fully: "sie weiss uber die Einzelnheit dies Selbstbewußtseins nicht Meister zu werden, beschreibt die Vernunft sehr gut, thut diess aber auf eine gedankenlose, empirische weise, die sich ihre warheit selbst wieder raubt" (Hegel, *Werke: Vollständige Ausgabe durch einen Verein von Freunden des verewigten*, ed. Philipp Marheineke et al., vol. 15 [Berlin: Duncker & Humblot, 1844], 502).

234. For a related argument, see Jürgen Habermas, "From Kant to Hegel and Back Again—The Move towards Detranscendentalization," *European Journal of Philosophy* 7 (1999): 129–57.

235. Kant, *Critique of Pure Reason*, 109–10; see also 663: "There is nothing in this to fear, though much to hope, namely that you will come into a possession that can never be attacked in the future." Conversely, in the "Transcendental Dialectic," Kant speaks of "possession" in a different sense, saying that a philosophical inquiry based on a properly non-dialectical understanding of "principles"—and the distinction between a priori and a posteriori knowledge and forms—can "incite us to tear down all those boundary posts and to lay claim to a wholly new territory that recognizes no demarcations anywhere" (385–86). This passage is tricky, but Kant here is distinguishing between the "transcendent," which involves, for instance, valid claims about a priori categories, and the "transcendental," which is an "illusion" (385).

Chapter Three

1. Karl Marx, *Capital: A Critique of Political Economy*, vol. 1, trans. Ben Fowkes (New York: Vintage, 1977), 103 (postface to the Second Edition).

2. Max Weber has defined these terms most memorably; see his *Economy and Society: An Outline of Interpretive Sociology*, ed. Guenther Roth and Claus Wittich, trans. Ephraim Fischoff et al., 2 vols. (Berkeley: University of California Press, 1978), esp. "Types of Legitimate Domination," 212–16, at 214; and on feudalism, see 255–65; also see "Power and Domination" and "Political and Hierocratic Organizations," 53–56.

3. Other studies that discuss feudal Germany (or the German states) include David Warren Sabean, *Kinship in Neckarhausen, 1700–1870* (Cambridge: Cambridge University Press, 1998), *Power in the Blood: Popular Culture and Village Discourse in Early Modern Germany* (Cambridge:

Cambridge University Press, 1984), and *Property, Production, and Family in Neckarhausen, 1700–1870* (Cambridge: Cambridge University Press, 1990); Mack Walker, *German Home Towns: Community, State, and General Estate, 1648–1871* (Ithaca, NY: Cornell University Press, 1971); and Hans Kohn, *Prelude to Nation States: The French and German Experience, 1789–1815* (Princeton, NJ: Van Nostrand, 1967).

4. J. J. Sheehan, *German History, 1770–1866* (Oxford: Clarendon, 1989), 97, 101–2 (Sheehan's ellipses).

5. Ibid., 102, 105.

6. See Perry Anderson's comments on Engels's letter to Bloch, in *Lineages of the Absolutist State* (London: NLB, 1974), 236–37; and Robert Brenner, "Agrarian Class Structure and Economic Development in Pre-Industrial Europe," in *The Brenner Debate: Agrarian Class Structure and Economic Development in Pre-Industrial Europe*, ed. T. H. Aston and C. H. E. Philpin (Cambridge: Cambridge University Press, 1985), 45. Scholars of medieval Germany and of late feudalism have similarly noted Germany's uneven economic development. See, for example, in addition to Anderson, Otto Hintze, "The Nature of Feudalism," in Fredric Cheyette, ed., *Lordship and Community in Medieval Europe: Selected Readings* (New York: Holt, Rinehart, & Winston, 1968), 22–31; Otto Brunner, "Feudalism: The History of a Concept," in Cheyette, *Lordship and Community*, 32–61, at 46, and, *Land and Lordship: Structures of Governance in Medieval Austria*, 4th ed., trans. Howard Kaminsky and James Van Horn Melton (Philadelphia: University of Pennsylvania Press, 1992); Walter Schlesinger, "Lord and Follower in Germanic Institutional History," in *Lordship and Community*, ed. Cheyette, 64–99.

7. Herbert Marcuse, *Reason and Revolution: Hegel and the Rise of Social Theory*, 100th anniversary ed. (New York: Humanity Books, 1999), 12–13; see also 3–4.

8. Theodor W. Adorno, *Aesthetic Theory*, ed. and trans. Robert Hullot-Kentor (Minneapolis: University of Minnesota Press, 1997), 345.

9. In describing his historical present as feudal, Hegel is positing a national or state unity that is otherwise absent before the unification of the German states under Bismarck. He is, in short, making a singularly polemical statement about the present and excluding (as we will see below in his *System of Ethical Life*) the small-merchant economy of the time. When one restores the emergent mercantile middle class to the historical and polemical scenario, one gets Marx. The point here is that Hegel deliberately chooses the medieval frame of reference to the exclusion of others.

10. For a recent attempt to read Hegel's master/slave dialectic in context of discourses of freedom in the age of colonial slavery, see Susan Buck-Morss, *Hegel, Haiti, and Universal History* (Pittsburgh, PA: University of Pittsburgh Press, 2009), who argues that Hegel "knew about real slaves revolting successfully against real masters, and he elaborated his dialectic of lordship and bondage deliberately within this contemporary context" (50). I grant the first assertion—and wouldn't exclude the Haitian Revolution from any consideration—but the second does not necessarily follow, for reasons that will become clear when I discuss a different "contemporary context," a persistently medieval or feudal one. See note 71.

11. Jean Hyppolite, *Genesis and Structure of Hegel's "Phenomenology of Spirit,"* trans. Samuel Cherniak and John Heckman (Evanston, IL: Northwestern University Press, 1974), 172.

12. See J. N. Findlay's commentary to the English translation of the *Phenomenology of Spirit* by A. V. Miller (see n. 93 below); Charles Taylor, *Hegel* (Cambridge: Cambridge University Press, 1975); and John O'Neill, ed., *Hegel's Dialectic of Desire and Recognition: Texts and Commentary* (New York: State University of New York Press, 1996), 7. O'Neill's edition contains an abundance of typos and should therefore be checked against the original versions.

13. It is not certain that Sartre attended Kojève's lectures, but it is clear that he held a great interest in the master/slave dialectic, following something of the then current philosophical fashion in France.

14. See Jean Hyppolite, *Préface de la "Phénoménologie de l'esprit"* (Paris: Aubier-Montaigne, 1966).

15. Robert B. Pippin, in *Hegel on Self-Consciousness: Desire and Death in the Phenomenology of Spirit* (Princeton, NJ: Princeton University Press, 2011), persuasively argues that this dialectical episode has divided philosophical disciplines, the practical from the speculative, and that the two can be brought back together via a renewed understanding of Kant.

16. For more on the French background, see Mark Poster, *Existential Marxism in Postwar France: From Sartre to Althusser* (Princeton, NJ: Princeton University Press, 1975); Michael S. Roth, *Knowing and History: Appropriations of Hegel in Twentieth-Century France* (Ithaca, NY: Cornell University Press, 1988); Judith Butler, *Subjects of Desire: Hegelian Reflections in Twentieth-Century France* (New York: Columbia University Press, 1987); Shadia B. Drury, *Alexandre Kojève: The Roots of Postmodern Politics* (Basingstoke, Hampshire: Macmillan, 1994). Primary texts are conveniently collected in *Hegel's Phenomenology of Self-Consciousness: Text and Commentary*, trans. Leo Rauch and David Sherman (New York: State University of New York Press, 1999). René Girard wrote on this dialectic, too; see his *Mensonge romantique, vérité romanesque* (Paris: Grasset, 1961), 101–17, though this clearly needs to be studied more.

17. Alexandre Kojève, *Introduction to the Reading of Hegel: Lectures on the "Phenomenology of Spirit,"* ed. Allan Bloom and trans. James H. Nichols (New York: Basic Books, 1969), 7.

18. See ibid., 8, 14–15.

19. Ibid., 15.

20. See ibid., 10–29. Peter Osbourne, *The Politics of Time: Modernity and Avant-Garde* (Verso: New York, 1995), 71, 76, notes that Kojève, after Heidegger, renders this dialectical narrative into a "philosophy of death," which "makes it extremely unreliable as an interpretation of Hegel."

21. References to "Being-for-itself" do not begin to appreciate the issues of possession as self-possession.

22. Kojève obscures this link, citing the dynamics of labor (*Introduction to the Reading of Hegel*, 24–25) but neglecting possession, save for this fleeting point: "The man who desires a thing humanly acts not so much to possess the *thing* as to make another *recognize* his *right*—as will be said later—to that thing, to make the other recognize him as the *owner* of that thing" (40).

23. Without pointing to the consequences of mistranslation, Žižek writes in a note: "'Lordship' and 'Bondage' are the terms used in the translation we refer to (Hegel, 1977); following Kojève, Lacan uses 'maître' and 'esclave', which are then translated as 'master' and 'slave'" (*The Sublime Object of Ideology* [New York: Verso, 1989], 26). For more on this matter, see chap. 4, n. 64.

24. This linguistic point has been appreciated only recently, and very briefly at that; see Gadamer in O'Neill, *Hegel's Dialectic of Desire*, 167; Chris Arthur, "Hegel's Master-Slave Dialectic and a Myth of Marxology," *New Left Review* 142 (1983): 67–75, at 69; and Osborne, *Politics of Time*, 71–72. Buck-Morss points to but does not pursue the meaning of the German terms *Knecht* and *Herrschaft* (*Hegel, Haiti, and Universal History*, 52n90, 53n91, 62n119).

25. In the following instances where Hegel analyzes forms of domination and work, he makes important distinctions between classical slavery and medieval serfdom: G. W. F. Hegel, *Hegel's Philosophy of Right*, trans. T. M. Knox (New York: Oxford University Press, 1967), 15, 18, 20, 30, 32, 39, 48, 53, 68, 162, 221, 241, 261 (*Werke*, 7:31, 39, 41, 72, 78, 99, 123–24, 142, 145, 183,

305, 409, 510); Hegel, *The Philosophy of History*, trans. J. Sibree (New York: Dover Publications, 1956), 229–30, 254–55, 256, 262, 287, 300, 301, 309, 312, 315–16, 334, 339 (*Werke*, 12:282–83, 311, 313, 320, 349, 364, 366, 375, 379, 382–83, 403–4, 410).

26. "So z. B. wäre für das römische Recht keine Definition vom *Menschen* möglich, denn der Sklave ließe sich darunter nicht subsumieren, in seinem Stand ist jener Begriff vielmehr verletzt" (Hegel, *Werke*, 7:31; *Philosophy of Right*, 15). Here and elsewhere, German terms inserted into English translations come from *Werke*.

27. Hegel, *Philosophy of Right*, 48; *Werke*, 7:123. Nick Nesbitt energetically tries to explain away the *Herrschaft* or feudalism (medieval and modern) I have identified in this passage (48/§57) in a version of this chapter I published in 2004. He suggests, instead, that Hegel here is critiquing "Atlantic slave labor" (*Universal Emancipation: The Haitian Revolution and the Radical Enlightenment* [Charlottesville: University of Virginia Press, 2008], 121). Nesbitt claims that in the *Philosophy of Right* Hegel "no longer speaks of *Knechten* and *Knechtschaft*," thus abandoning his interests in feudalism once displayed in the *Phenomenology of Spirit* (120). Nesbitt celebrates his claim, averring that "no commentators seem to have noticed" this shift from the earlier to the later text (ibid.)—the supposed shift from feudalism to modern slavery. Well, commentators haven't noticed because it didn't happen. Look at the German text. There in the *Philosophy of Right*, Hegel *does* in fact refer to *Knechtschaft* in the very passage Nesbitt discusses at length using only the English translation: "die Dialektik des Begriffs und des nur erst unmittelbaren Bewußtseins der Freiheit bewirkt daselbst den Kampf des Anerkennens und das Verhältnis der Herrenschaft und der Knechtschaft [The dialectic of the concept and of the purely immediate consciousness of freedom brings about at that point the fight for recognition and the relationship of lord *and bondsman*]" (*Werke*, 7:123; *Philosophy of Right*, 48, trans. modified). Again, as the passage plainly shows, Hegel discusses *two* systems of domination in his assessment of "historical views" (ibid.): *Sklaverei, Herrschaft, Herrenschaft; Recht der Sklaverei, Herrenschaft.* I am obviously sympathetic with any attempt to radicalize Hegel as Nesbitt tries hard to do, but facts are sometimes stubborn things, and Nesbitt's reading of Hegel here is confused. See also note 47.

28. The latter forms of slavery upon which *Herrschaft* depend cannot be thought of as different in *moral* terms from ancient forms of domination, which is why Hegel is comfortable in tracing continuities between forms of domination or *Herrschaft* from the so-called Oriental cultures to Roman societies to those in the German Middle Ages: "The transition to Greece . . . shows itself also externally, as a transmission of sovereignty [Übergang der Herrschaft]—an occurrence which from this time forward is ever and anon repeated. For the Greeks surrender the sceptre of dominion [Herrscherstab] and of civilization to the Romans, and the Romans are subdued by the Germans" (*Philosophy of History*, 221; *Werke*, 12:273). See also Hegel's consideration of *Herrschaft* in Rome in *Philosophy of History*, 306–12; *Werke*, 12:371–79.

29. Hegel, *Philosophy of Right*, 48; Knox's translation modified, and emphasis added. The whole passage in German is:

> Der Standpunkt des freien Willens, womit das Recht und die Rechtswissenschaft ist über den unwahren Standpunkt, auf welchem der Mensch als Naturwesen und nur als an sich seiender Begriff, der Sklaverei daher fähig ist, schon hinaus. Diese frühere unwahre Erscheinung betrifft den Geist, welcher nur erst auf dem Standpunkte seines Bewußtseins ist; die Dialektik des Begriffs und des nur erst unmittelbaren Bewußtseins der Freiheit bewirkt daselbst den Kampf des Anerkennens und das Verhältnis der Herrenschaft und der Knechtschaft. (*Werke*, 7:123-24).

30. On "primitive" self-consciousness, see below.

31. Hegel in other places maintains this distinction between the unself-conscious slave of antiquity and the feudal serf who may achieve self-consciousness. See Hegel, *Philosophical Propaedeutic,* trans. A. V. Miller, ed. Michael George and Andrew Vincent (Oxford: Basil Blackwell, 1986), 62; *Werke,* 4:80–81; and *Philosophy of History,* 259.

32. "If in his own case he stops short of death, he only proves to the other that he will accept the loss of a part or the whole of his possessions, that he will risk a wound but not life itself; then for the other he is immediately not a totality, he is not absolutely for himself, he becomes the slave of the other" (G. W. F. Hegel, *"System of Ethical Life" [1802/3] and "First Philosophy of Spirit" [Part III of the System of Speculative Philosophy 1803/4],* ed. and trans. H. S. Harris and T. M. Knox [Albany: State University of New York Press, 1979]), 240; see also 238: "Wenn er an sich selbst innerhalb des Todes stehen bleibt, sich dem anderen nur erweist als Verlust eines Teils oder des ganzen Besitzes daran setzend, als Wunden, nicht das Leben selbst, so ist er für den anderen unmittelbar eine Nicht-Totalität, er ist nicht absolut für sich, er wird der Sklav des anderen" (*Jenaer Systementwürfe: Das System der spekulativen Philisophie: Fragmente aus Vorlesungsmanuskripten zur Philosophie der Natur und des Geistes,* ed. Klaus Düsing and Heinz Kimmerle, vol. 1 [Hamburg: F. Meiner, 1986], 221, 11–16). As this passage makes clear, Hegel appropriately names this individual a slave because this *Sklav* has surrendered his possessions and his self in order to save his own life. Accordingly, there is no "cognizance of the other as such" (Hegel, *First Philosophy of Spirit,* 240), and therefore no dialectic or struggle. Hegel would never describe a *Knecht* in such a situation, because that identity always assumes an Other in the technical sense—which is why, incidentally, he names the *Knecht* as such in the lord/bondsman dialectic of the *Phenomenology of Spirit* (115/§189) only after the struggle to the death has been resolved, with neither party dying but with the subordinate not taken as a *sklave,* nor ever named that.

33. In §432 (and its *zusatz*) of the *Philosophy of Mind,* Hegel begins with the problem: "The fight of recognition is a life and death struggle [Der Kampf des Anerkennens geht also auf Leben und Tod]" (*Hegel's Philosophy of Mind,* trans. William Wallace, together with the *Zusätze* in Boumann's text [1845], trans. A. V. Miller [Oxford: Clarendon, 1971], 172/*Werke,* 10.221). He does not name the two sides in the struggle—no *Sklave,* no *Knecht*—apart from saying that each is a "natural being." If one "natural being" kills the other, then there is no struggle for recognition. Likewise, "if only one of two combatants fighting for mutual recognition succumbs, no recognition is achieved, for the survivor receives just as little recognition as the dead" (172). Hegel clarifies: "We must here remark that the fight for recognition pushed to the extreme here indicated can only occur in the natural state, where men exist only as single, separate individuals" (ibid.). In other words, in this "natural state," there is no "civil society"; hence, the fight to the death. For in civil society, already, "man is recognized and treated as a *rational* being, as free, as a person" (ibid.). The earlier "natural state of . . . self-consciousness" must therefore be overcome or sublated within civil society by a universal form of self-consciousness, which compels persons to recognize others as they wish themselves to be recognized. The point is that in §432 (and its *zusatz*) there is no proper lord/bondsman dialectic. Hegel then adds a curious rant against "duelling" (173), a "barbarism of the Middle Ages [in die Roheit des Mittelalters]" and a cultural holdover from feudalism (*Feudalsystem*) still practiced in modern society. Interestingly, however, he acknowledges that even in the medieval period, "civil society" is "more or less developed" (ibid.) And so his critique of the Middle Ages contains with it the kind of contrast we're examining, wherein the universal form of self-consciousness is possible in the Middle Ages (and later) but not in a scenario comprised of "natural beings"—that is, not in an earlier historical moment.

34. In §433 (and its *zusatz*) of the *Philosophy of Mind*, Hegel turns to the next moment by naming the new identities and struggle: "Thus arises the relation of lord and bondsman [das Verhältnis der Herrschaft und Knechtschaft]" (173, trans. modified/*Werke*, 10.223). So, too, arises "man's social life and the commencement of political union [das Zusammenleben der Menschen, als ein Beginnen der Staaten]" (ibid./ibid.). Where the unevenness of the relation emerges is in the preservation of aspects of the previous moment, the earlier "natural state of life [Natürlichkeit des Lebens]." Hegel knows to elaborate on this idea by drawing another historical contrast, lest this reference to the "natural state of life" confuse. And so he turns to the Greeks and Romans, not to discuss *Herrschaft und Knechtschaft* but rather "Sklaverei" (*Werke*, 10.224), in which—whenever freedom was obtained by revolts and so forth—that very "freedom still had the character of a natural state [die Bestimmung der Natürlichkeit]" (174/*Werke*, 10.224). But not so for the freedom the *Knecht* pursues, as described a few paragraphs later in §435: the "passage to universal self-consciousness [den Übergang zum allgemeinen Selbstbewußtsein]," the "beginning of true human freedom [den Beginn der wahrhaften Freiheit des Menschen]" (175/*Werke*, 10.225). Hegel, again, is making contrasts between the ancient and the medieval.

35. In §435 (and its *zusatz*) of the *Philosophy of Mind*, Hegel makes another historical contrast to talk about the necessity of going through a phase of unfreedom in order to attain freedom—a "necessary moment in the formation of every human [ein notwendiges Moment in der Bildung jedes Menschen]" (ibid., trans. modified/ibid.). He speaks of Athens and Rome (again) as examples of the prehistory of domination, especially by the Athenian tyrant Peisistratos ("Herrschaft der Peisistratiden"). As I have already shown (see n. 28, e.g.), Hegel will from time to time use the term "Herrschaft" to refer to forms of domination across history, and this is no exception. Yet note how he immediately makes a distinction as he concludes this digression: he refers to "serfdom and tyranny"—that is, to *Knechtschaft*, which he had been discussing all along, and *Tyrannei*, as embodied by Peisistratos. Finally, he offers this sobering sentence that absorbs the very point of his historical contrast: "Those who remain serfs [die Knechte bleiben] suffer no absolute injustice; for he who has not the courage to risk his life to win freedom, that man deserves to be a slave [Sklave]" (ibid./ibid.). The *Knecht* who doesn't seek his freedom and realize his universal form of self-consciousness will indeed be a *slave*. I interpret this passage to be saying that, yes, the fight to the death is necessary, it is after all an early step in the relevant section of the *Phenomenology of Spirit*, but there are other steps beyond this one, taking us into the lord/bondsman dialectic. You could say, then, that if Hegel's section on self-consciousness in the *Phenomenology of Spirit* follows a historical trajectory, then it clearly shows that a struggle to the death (the earlier natural mode of attaining freedom) precedes the struggle for possession (the later, medieval/modern mode of attaining freedom).

36. Here's another example of Hegel's distinction making in the *Philosophy of Right*: "Examples of alienation of personality are slavery [Sklaverei], serfdom [Leibeigenschaft], disqualification from holding property, encumbrances on property, and so forth" (*Philosophy of Right*, 53 [§66z]; *Werke*, 7.142).

37. Zdravko Kobe cautions me that Luther's Bible translation "doesn't use Sklave at all" (pers. comm.) and instead uses *Knecht* to render passages like Galatians 3.28: "There is neither Jew nor Greek, there is neither bond nor free [Knecht noch Freier], there is neither male nor female." I would note, however, that this was a very common translation and term, as witnessed in contemporary hymns such as "Ihr Knecht' des Herren allegleich" from the sixteenth century—*Knecht* here meaning "servant of the lord," not "person sold into slavery, bound in chains, and forced to work on plantations in the Colonies." The point, simply, is that Luther

and other reformers are using the contemporary language of servitude in their vernacular theology—i.e., the very terms that have meaning for 98 percent of the population who were at the time feudal serfs.

38. Hegel, *Philosophy of History*, 275, 238; *Philosophy of Right*, 220–22.

39. Hegel, *Philosophy of History*, 238.

40. Further, Hegel writes: "Of the Greeks in the first and genuine form of their Freedom, we may assert, that they had no conscience" (*Philosophy of History*, 253).

41. Steven B. Smith, "Hegel on Slavery and Domination," *Review of Metaphysics* 46 (1992): 97–124, agrees with this point (see 100, 107–10), but still maintains that Hegel's lord/bondsman dialectic is a commentary on ancient slavery.

42. Hegel writes that slavery was "a necessary condition of an æsthetic democracy, where it was the right and duty of every citizen to deliver or listen to orations respecting the management of the State in the place of public assembly, to take part in the exercise of the Gymnasia, and to join in the celebration of festivals. It was a necessary condition of such occupations that citizens should be freed from handicraft occupations; consequently, that what among us is performed by free citizens—the work of daily life—should be done by slaves. Slavery does not cease until the Will has been infinitely self-reflected—until Right is conceived as appertaining to every freeman, and the term freeman is regarded as a synonym for man in his generic nature as endowed with Reason. (*Philosophy of History*, 254–55; *Werke*, 12:311).

43. Hegel, *Philosophy of History*, 319 and 334; *Werke*, 12:403. See also *Philosophy of History*, 328 and 333. What Hegel means by "Slavery is impossible" is that slavery is "ontologically" impossible. On the "absolute Unfreedom" of late medieval sacramental practices, see "absolute slavery" (*Philosophy of History*, 378), which imprecisely translates "die absolute Unfreiheit" (*Werke*, 12:455). Likewise, "die Obedienz der unfreiheit" (*Werke*, 12.458) is translated as "the obedience of Slavery" (*Philosophy of History*, 380).

44. One passage appears to go against my case about Hegel's distinctions between the medieval *Knecht* and the ancient *Sklave*: in Imperial Rome, "[i]ndividual subjectivity. . . . finds so little limitation in the will of others, that the relation of will to will may be called that of absolute sovereignty [Herrschaft] to absolute slavery [Knechtschaft]" (*Philosophy of History*, 315–16; *Werke*, 12:383). These are, however, not Hegel's words but rather the ideas of one of his students that made it into Karl Hegel's or Georg Lasson's inclusive editions. This statement is not in the lectures of 1822–23 (*Vorlesungen über die Philosophie der Weltgeschichte* [1822/1823], ed. Karl Heinz Ilting, Karl Brehmer, Hoo Nam Seelman [Hamburg: F. Meiner, 1996], 417–18), nor is it in the first edition of the lectures of 1830–31 edited by Eduard Gans, *Vorlesungen über die Philosophie der Geschichte* (Berlin: Duncker and Humblot, 1837), which here only (and appropriately) tells of "der Sklaven" (325; see 325–26). Furthermore, the passage is absent from Heimann's notes from 1830/31 (*Philosophie der Geschichte: Vorlesungsmitschrift Heimann [Winter 1830/1831]*, ed. Klaus Vieweg [Munich: Fink, 2005], 156–57). Gans himself correctly writes: "Im Altertum waren es Sklaven, im Mittelalter Lehnsherr und Vasall, heute ist es der Herr und der Knecht. . . . Zwischen der Sklaverei und der Lohndienerei ist kein grosser Unterschied" (*Naturrecht und Universalrechtsgeschichte: Vorlesungen nach G. W. F. Hegel*, ed. Johann Braun [Tübingen: Mohr Siebeck, 2005], 63).

45. Hegel, *Philosophy of History*, 407, trans. modified; *Werke*, 12:487.

46. The most articulate opposition to the idea that Hegel uses feudal terms here is Malcolm Bull, "Slavery and the Multiple Self," *New Left Review* 231 (1998): 94–131, at 103–4.

47. Nesbitt, for example, misreads Hegel's pertinent section in the *Phenomenology of Spirit* (misidentified by Nesbitt as §57), describing its "overall focus on *Sklaverei*" and instead follows

Buck-Morss in viewing it as a commentary on the Haitian Revolution (*Universal Emancipation*, 227n69). Nesbitt's claim is misleading, because Hegel is precise in his terms and, again, never once mentions the word *Sklaverei* in these germane passages, so there is nothing "overall" about it apart from the projections of the interpreter.

48. See J. A. F. Thompson, *The Transformation of Medieval England, 1370–1529* (New York: Longman, 1983), 144. See also Marc Bloch's formulation: "The word ownership, as applied to landed property, would have been almost meaningless. . . . The tenant who from father to son, as a rule, ploughs the land and gathers in the crop; his immediate lord, to whom he pays dues, and who, in certain circumstances, can resume possession of the land; the lord of the lord, and so on, right up the feudal scale how many persons are there who can say, each with as much justification as the other, That is my field! Even this is an understatement. For the ramifications extended horizontally as well as vertically and account should be taken of the village community, which normally recovered the use of the whole of its agricultural land as soon as it was cleared of crops; of the tenant's family, without whose consent the property could not be alienated; and of the families of the successive lords" (Bloch, *Land and Work in Mediaeval Europe: Selected Papers*, trans. J. E. Anderson [Berkeley: University of California Press, 1967], 115–16).

49. Sheehan, *Germany History*, 93. *Herrschaft*, as Sheehan defines it, is essentially a struggle for possession—namely, control over land (see 25–26).

50. See Barry Hindess and Paul Q. Hirst, *Pre-Capitalist Modes of Production* (London: Routledge, 1975), 261; Perry Anderson, *Passages from Antiquity to Feudalism* (London: NLB, 1974); Rodney Hilton, *Class Conflict and the Crisis of Feudalism: Essays in Medieval Social History* (London: Verso, 1990).

51. Hegel, *System of Ethical Life*, 117: "Love, the child, culture, the tool, speech are objective and universal, and also are bearings and relations, but relations that are natural, not overcome, casual, unregulated, not themselves taken up into universality." The German *System der Sittlichkeit* is in *Schriften und Entwürfe (1799–1808)*, vol. 5 of *Gesammelte Werke*, ed. Manfred Baum and Kurt Rainer Meist (Hamburg: Felix Meiner, 1998); citations are given in the notes, where relevant, following page references to Harris and Knox's translation.

52. Hegel, *System of Ethical Life*, 117. Indeed, it seems that here Hegel is exploring the process of "sublation."

53. Life and labor part ways, and need is reoriented: "This sort of laboring, thus divided, presupposes at the same time that the remaining needs are provided for in another way, for this way too has to be labored on, i.e., by the labor of other men." And because my labors are a means to satisfy another's needs, rather than a means for possession, satisfying my own needs and wants, labor is alien to me: "But this deadening [characteristic] of mechanical labor directly implies the possibility of cutting oneself off from it altogether; for the labor here is wholly quantitative without variety" (*System of Ethical Life*, 117).

54. Hegel, *System of Ethical Life*, 118. The editors, Harris and Knox, comment: "At the earlier level enjoyment followed on the satisfaction of a need. Machinery makes possible the accumulation of capital, a surplus going beyond the satisfaction of a particular individual's need" (118n19).

55. "Owing to the new difference, the relation of the subject to his labor is superseded, but because infinity, i.e., legal right as such, must remain, there appears instead of that ideal connection with the surplus [possession] its conceptual opposite, the real connection with use and need. The separation is starker, but for that very reason the urge for unification [is stronger too], just as the magnet holds its poles apart, without any urge of their own to unity, but, when the

NOTES TO PAGES 74–76

magnet is severed, their identity being cancelled, [we have] electricity, a starker separation, real antithesis, and an urge for unification" (Hegel, *System of Ethical Life*, 120).

56. Ibid., 123.

57. Ibid., 124–25.

58. Hegel, *System der Sittlichkeit*, 305, my emphasis.

59. Hegel, *System of Ethical Life*, 126; 306.

60. "Might, or rather might individualized as strength, decides who dominates; and here, where the entire real personality is the subject, the relation of lordship and bondage must enter immediately" (*System of Ethical Life*, 138).

61. Ibid., 152.

62. Ibid., 153–56.

63. Ibid., 156; 338.

64. Ibid., 156.

65. We also bear in mind that for Hegel the peasantry is indeed a *class* in his sense of the term, which distinguishes it from "the class of slaves," which "is not a class." "So ist also z. B. der Sklavenstand kein Stand; denn er ist nur ein formell allgemeines; der Sklave verhält sich als einzelnes zum Herrn" (*System der Sittlichkeit*, 334). More fully: "According to the true concept of a class, the concept is not a universality which lies outside it and is an *ens rationis*; on the contrary universality is real in the class. The class knows itself in its equality and constitutes itself as a universal against a universal, and the relation between the different classes is [not] a relation between single individuals. On the contrary (by) belonging to a class the single individual is something universal and so a true individual, and a person. Consequently the class of slaves, for example, is not a class, for it is only formally a universal. The slave is related as a single individual to his master" (Hegel, *System of Ethical Life*, 152).

66. Hegel, *System of Ethical Life*, 156n39.

67. See *Hegel and the Human Spirit: A Translation of the Jena Lectures on the Philosophy of Spirit (1805–6)*, trans. Leo Rauch (Detroit: Wayne State University Press, 1983), 162–63.

68. Otto Brunner, "Feudalism: The History of a Concept," in Cheyette, ed., *Lordship and Community*, 46; see also Brunner, *Land and Lordship*. One cannot avoid seeing the adage about the "revolution happening in France as politics, in Germany as philosophy" lurking here.

69. Walter Schlesinger, "Lord and Follower," in Cheyette, ed., *Lordship and Community*, 92. See also Perry Anderson, *Lineages of the Absolutist State*, 272, 274, 276, 278. Schlesinger's article must be appreciated in its fuller, original form for its compelling analysis and citation of medieval literary materials such as the Anglo-Saxon poem *Genesis A*, which illustrates antecedent forms of *Herrschaft* that we might construe as informing Hegel on some level, and which might be relevant to a larger project to historicize Anglo-Saxon poetry in a materialist and transchannel fashion. See "Herrschaft und Gefolgschaft in der Germanisch-Deutschen Verfassungsgeschichte," *Historische Zeitschrift* 176 (Munich, 1953), 225–75; the German text of my block quotation is on 273.

70. See Joachim Ritter, *Hegel and the French Revolution: Essays on the Philosophy of Right*, trans. Richard Dien Winfield (Cambridge, MA: MIT Press, 1982); and Robert Wokler, "Contextualizing Hegel's Phenomenology of the French Revolution and the Terror," *Political Theory* 26 (1998): 33–55.

71. It is appropriate to remark here, perhaps polemically, that there are two predominant ways of reading the "radical Hegel" on the question of the Haitian Revolution and, more broadly, the modern forms of racialized slavery I've been suggesting were not Hegel's concern at

this point in the *Phenomenology of Spirit*. One way is represented by Buck-Morss's *Hegel, Haiti, and Universal History*, which pursues what Hegel "must have known" about Haiti but never says. There are many titles of this sort. The other way is exemplified by C. L. R. James, author of an influential study of the Haitian Revolution, *The Black Jacobins: Toussaint L'Ouverture and the San Domingo Revolution*, 2nd ed., rev. (New York: Vintage, 1963), which apprehends precisely the feudal problems I am illustrating throughout this chapter—particularly in the construal of slaves as "peasants." And of course James writes in the Marxist tradition, offering such works as *Notes on Dialectics: Hegel, Marx, Lenin* (Westport, CT: Lawrence Hill, 1980). I would also include Cedric J. Robinson here. His *Black Marxism: The Making of the Black Radical Tradition* (London: Zed Press, 1983) is a foundational text, in which chaps. 1 and 4 deal with racialization at the end of feudalism. Lastly, Frantz Fanon's *Black Skin, White Masks*, trans. Charles Lam Markmann (New York: Grove Press, 1967; 1952), argues, in part, for the limits of reading the lord/bondsman dialectic in the colonial context.

72. Hegel, *Philosophy of Right*, 46. One can of course multiply the relevant contrivances here.

73. Ibid., 47.

74. Ibid. Given references such as this, we should not always generalize about "Nature" in our readings of Hegel, but rather attend to forms of working on "nature"—agriculture.

75. Ibid.

76. Ibid., 48; *Werke*, 7:123.

77. Hegel, *Philosophy of Right*, 52.

78. Ibid., 51 and 53; *Werke*, 7:136. Hegel refers here to the "*contractus emphyteuticus*" (51) or, more commonly, "emphyteusis," a land use agreement, in which possession of land is granted under certain conditions of use such as the paying of taxes, rents, etc. This isn't necessarily a feudal practice, but Hegel here is suggesting that it is.

79. See Hegel, *System of Ethical Life*, 125.

80. Hegel, *Philosophy of History*, 369–70.

81. Ibid., 370.

82. On how lord-vassal relations took on an idiosyncratic character within the general feudal system, see the sources collected in *Das Lehnswesen in Deutschland im hohen und späten Mittelalter*, ed. Karl-Heinz Spieß and Thomas Willich (Idstein: Schulz-Kirchner, 2002).

83. Hegel, *Philosophy of History*, 396.

84. See ibid., 370 and 371, respectively.

85. Here we may contrast the gravity of possession in the Middle Ages with its relative and rather unmitigating significance in earlier historical moments; see Hegel, *Philosophy of History*, 229–30, 231, 256, 295, 303, 309, 311.

86. Ibid., 377–78, 381, 393, 416.

87. See ibid., 371, 383.

88. Hyppolite, *Genesis and Structure*, 172.

89. Hegel, *Philosophy of History*, 384.

90. Ibid., 384.

91. It is no wonder, then, that at the center of many readings of Hegel's lord/bondsman dialectic is a sense of revolution; indeed, this dialectic provides, and explains, those opportunities for the raising of consciousness. See Jean-Paul Sartre, *Being and Nothingness: A Phenomenological Essay on Ontology*, trans. Hazel E. Barnes (New York: Pocket Books, 1956); Alexandre Kojève, "Desire and Work in the Master and Slave," in O'Neill, ed., *Hegel's Dialectic of Desire*, 49–65, at 60; and Buck-Morss, *Hegel, Haiti, and Universal History*.

92. Robert C. Solomon, *In the Spirit of Hegel: A Study of G. W. F. Hegel's "Phenomenology of Spirit"* (New York: Oxford University Press, 1983), 451.

93. G. W. F. Hegel, *Phenomenology of Spirit*, trans. A. V. Miller (Oxford: Oxford University Press, 1977), 115; *Werke*, 3:151.

94. Hegel, *Phenomenology of Spirit*, 111; *Werke*, 3.146.

95. Hegel, *Phenomenology of Spirit*, 115–16; *Werke*, 3:150–51. The ideas expressed here first appear in Hegel, *System of Ethical Life*, 122–23.

96. Kojève's gloss on Hegel's "thing" is too abstract. Kojève doesn't specify the *thing* as *land*, because he ignores the feudal context of the *Phenomenology* (see *Introduction to the Reading of Hegel*, 17). An example of this abstracted analysis is the way in which Kojève posits that "food" is a thing: "For example, [the lord] eats food that is completely prepared" (18). But, we ought to ask, where does this food come from? Who prepares it, and how? It comes from land prepared by the bondsman. Kojève's designations, "natural existence" (22), "Nature" (23), or "raw material" (24) are not specific enough, nor Hegelian enough (granting that the last phrase is Hegel's), in the *material* ways that Hegel intends.

97. Here I follow Kojève's insight that "all action is negating" (*Introduction to the Reading of Hegel*, 4; see also 5 and 17).

98. Hegel, *Phenomenology of Spirit*, 116; *Werke*, 3:151.

99. Hegel, *Phenomenology of Spirit*, 116; *Werke*, 3:151.

100. Hegel, *Phenomenology of Spirit*, 115.

101. Robert Stern, *Hegel and the "Phenomenology of Spirit"* (London: Routledge, 2002), 86, who follows Hyppolite, *Genesis and Structure*, 27–50. See also Pinkard, *Hegel's "Phenomenology,"* 54–55; and Osborne, *Politics of Time*, 72.

102. My positing a feudal frame here should not be misunderstood as an attempt to literalize Hegel's dialectical scenario or to forget that this is a phenomenology, always already susceptible to allegory and transposition.

103. See George Armstrong Kelly, "Notes on Hegel's 'Lordship and Bondage,'" *Review of Metaphysics* 19 (1966): 780–802, who writes, "The problem of lordship and bondage is essentially Platonic in foundation, because the primal cleavage in both the history of society and the history of the ego is at stake" (788).

104. See Smith, "Hegel on Slavery," 104, 102, respectively.

105. See Buck-Morss, *Hegel, Haiti, and Universal History*.

106. Marx, *Capital*, 165. Marx and Engels also memorably comment on feudalism in the *German Ideology*: "The social structure and the State are continually evolving out of the life process of definite individuals, but of individuals, not as they may appear in their own or other people's imagination, but as they really are" (*Marx-Engels Reader*, 154). For further consideration of the Hegelian background for Marx's critique of ideology and fetishism, see chap. 4.

107. The Hegelian Marx was once a lingering question within Marxism—with the parameters of that debate established by Lukács, who read Marx as a Hegelian, and Louis Althusser, who against Lukács sought to winnow the younger Hegelian Marx from the later, supposedly un-Hegelian Marx of dialectical materialism; see Althusser's "On the Young Marx," in *For Marx*, trans. Ben Brewster (New York: Vintage, 1970), 49–86. This is not the place to settle questions about Marx's Hegelianism. Marx, of course, would develop some very critical things to say about Hegel's ideas about labor, possession, and private property, but Marx's objections are not always substantial, correct, or even consistent with his own premises about history; see *Capital: A Critique of Political Economy*, 3 vols. (Chicago: C. H. Kerr, 1906–9), 3:722n188.

108. *Marx-Engels Reader*, 196; Karl Marx and Friedrich Engels, *Werke*, vol. 5 (Berlin: Dietz Verlag, 1969), 64.

109. Marx, *Grundrisse*, ed. and trans. Martin Nickolaus (New York: Penguin, 1993), 500; *Marx-Engels-Werkausgabe*, vol. 42 (Dietz: Berlin, 1983), 423.

110. Ibid., 500–501/ibid., 423.

111. Chris Arthur is incorrect to suggest otherwise, when arguing that Kojève concocted the notion that Marx referred to Hegel's lord/bondsman dialectic: "The only difficulty with these presuppositions of the secondary literature is that Marx *never refers* to this section of the *Phenomenology*—never mind giving it any importance!—when, in his 1844 manuscripts, he embarks on a 'critique of Hegel's dialectic'. He discusses the *Phenomenology* as a *whole* and draws attention to its last chapter especially; he singles out three other sections for praise; but not one of them is on the master-servant dialectic. This should make us suspicious, therefore, of the claims made for the 'master-slave'" ("Hegel's Master-Slave Dialectic and a Myth of Marxology," 69). One need only refer to the *Grundrisse*, consult the fuller German version (not the English excerpts), and approach the passage with some flexibility and imagination about what Hegelianism means and could mean to Marx.

112. Hegel, *Philosophy of History*, 370. Hegel held the view of "this relation of bondage or of person to person" from early on; see *System of Ethical Life*, 126; *System der Sittlichkeit*, 306.

113. *Marx-Engels Reader*, 170; see also 168–69, and cf. 165–70 with 173.

114. Marx, *Capital*, 165.

115. *Marx-Engels Reader*, 154.

116. Marx, *Capital*, 279–80.

117. "Under the repressive conditions in which men think and live, thought—any mode of thinking which is not confined to pragmatic orientation within the status quo—can recognize the facts and respond to the facts only by 'going behind' them. Experience takes place before a curtain which conceals and, if the world is the appearance of something behind the curtain of immediate experience, then, in Hegel's terms, it is we ourselves who are behind the curtain" (Herbert Marcuse, *One-Dimensional Man: Studies in the Ideology of Advanced Industrial Society* [Boston: Beacon, 1991], 185).

Chapter Four

1. William Pietz ("Fetishism and Materialism: The Limits of Theory in Marx," in *Fetishism as Cultural Discourse*, ed. Emily Apter and Pietz [Ithaca, NY: Cornell University Press, 1993], 119–51) comes the closest in noticing these Hegelian sources (see 137, 140), but Pietz doesn't finally draw the connection between Hegelian sacramentality and the Marxian version, which he glosses so well: "They (we) are members of the body of Capital, whose value-essence transcends and yet incarnates itself in these material beings like the divine salvational power of Christ in the faithful members and sacramental objects of His church. Indeed, just as the mystery of the Catholic church as the body of Christ is concentrated and expressed in the sacrament of the Eucharist, so the whole mystery of capitalist society appears at its most visible and, at the same time, most mysterious in the form of interest-bearing money-capital" (149). Most other readers refer tangentially to the Real Presence metaphoric in Marx's discussion of the commodity and of money. See Catherine Gallagher and Stephen Greenblatt, eds., *Practicing New Historicism* (Chicago: University of Chicago Press, 2000), 165–66; and John Parker's great essay "What a Piece of Work Is Man: Shakespearean Drama as Marxian Fetish, the Fetish as Sacramental Sublime," *Journal of Medieval and Early Modern Studies* 34, no. 3 (2004): 643–72,

esp. 649, 655–56. My epigraph is from Marx's analysis of money (*Theories of Surplus Value*, pt. 3, trans. Jack Cohen and S. W. Ryazanskaya [Moscow: Progress, 1971], 498), but here I limit my inquiry to Marx's discussion of commodity fetishism—particularly, the commodity's sacramental materialities.

2. Karl Marx, *Capital: A Critique of Political Economy*, vol. 1, trans. Ben Fowkes (New York: Vintage, 1977), 163–77. Marcuse's analysis of Hegel's views of labor is revealing, of which "the tone and pathos of the descriptions [in the *Philosophy of Right*] point strikingly to Marx's *Capital*" (Herbert Marcuse, *Reason and Revolution: Hegel and the Rise of Social Theory* 100th Anniversary Edition [Amherst, NY: Humanity Books, 1999], 79).

3. Marx, *Capital*, 165. An earlier version of this formulation appears in the "Economic and Philosophical Manuscripts of 1844": "With the *increasing value* of the world of things proceeds in direct proportion the *devaluation* of the world of men. Labour produces not only commodities; it produces itself and the worker as a *commodity*" (*The Marx-Engels Reader*, ed. Robert C. Tucker, 2nd ed. [New York: Norton, 1978], 71).

4. W. J. T. Mitchell and William Pietz have written foundational papers on the sources and problems of Marx's theory of fetishism—even though of course this chapter is about different sources and problems. Mitchell identifies Charles de Brosse's *Du Culte des Dieux fétiches* as informing Marx's theory of fetishism; see *Iconology: Image, Text, Ideology* (Chicago: University of Chicago Press, 1986), 186, 190–91. In addition to the sources mentioned in note 28, Pietz nominates Hegel's *Philosophy of Right* as the text most analogous to Marx's thinking on the commodity; see "Fetishism and Materialism," 140–43.

5. More fully, Aristotle says: "Evidently then such a principle is the most certain of all; which principle this is, we proceed to say. It is, that the same attribute cannot at the same time belong and not belong to the same subject in the same respect. . . . This, then, is the most certain of all principles. . . . For it is impossible for any one to believe the same thing to be and not to be" (*Metaphysics*, *The Complete Works of Aristotle: The Revised Oxford Translation*, ed. Jonathan Barnes, 2 vols. [Princeton, NJ: Princeton University Press, 1984], 2.1588; 1005b).

6. Marx, *Capital*, 127. Of course, that "third thing" points us to the entire relationship of production in which surplus capital is generated and in which labor itself becomes a commodity.

7. Ibid., 152; my emphasis.

8. Ibid., 135–36.

9. Ibid., 153, 159, 142, 128, 135, 150, 129, 147.

10. Ibid., 143.

11. Ibid., 144n19.

12. Ibid., 165.

13. Ibid., 163–64.

14. Though Marx's talk of "magic and necromancy" (ibid., 169) resonates, historically, as aspersions against Catholicism.

15. *Hegel: The Letters*, trans. Clark Butler and Christiane Seiler, with commentary by Clark Butler (Bloomington: Indiana University Press, 1984), 531. Hegel stubbornly answers to the charges in a letter dated April 3, 1826.

16. G. W. F. Hegel, "The Spirit of Christianity," *Early Theological Writings*, trans. T. M. Knox (Chicago: University of Chicago Press, 1948), 249.

17. Ibid., 249.

18. A word on "allegory" is in order as a point of clarification. Hegel, in several places in his lectures on aesthetics associates "allegory" with "symbol" (see esp. *Hegel's Aesthetics: Lectures on Fine Art*, 2 vols., trans. T. M. Knox [Oxford: Clarendon, 1975], 2.303–14)—a view that also runs

through Benjamin's reflections on allegory (vis-à-vis collecting and Baudelaire). Both Hegel and Benjamin find allegory to be extractive or decontextualizing; Hegel, in saying that things "are set forth as severed, as separate" (as quoted in the main text); and Benjamin in writing that the allegorist "dislodges things from their context" (Walter Benjamin, *The Arcades Project*, trans. Howard Eiland and Kevin McLaughlin [Cambridge, MA: Belknap Press of Harvard University Press, 1999], 211; see also 21–22, 204–5, and 206 [on Baudelaire and symbol versus allegory]). Yet both offer alternatives to allegory: Hegel posits sacramental fetishism as a way of drawing dissimilars together through subjectivity and feeling, whereas Benjamin offers up the "collector" who "brings things together . . . keeping in mind their affinities and their succession in time." Obviously, the question of allegory, symbol, and temporality will be picked up by Paul de Man in "The Rhetoric of Temporality," *Blindness and Insight: Essays in the Rhetoric of Contemporary Criticism*, 2nd ed., rev. (Minneapolis: University of Minnesota Press, 1983), 187–228.

19. Hegel, *Early Theological Writings*, 249.

20. Ibid., 250–51.

21. G. W. F. Hegel, *Three Essays, 1793–1795: The Tübingen Essay, Berne Fragments, The Life of Jesus* (Notre Dame, IN: University of Notre Dame Press, 1984), 54, 55. The German is taken from "Fragmente über Volksreligion und Christendum," *Werke: Auf der Grundlage der Werke von 1832–1845*, vol. 1., ed. Eva Moldenhauer and Karl Markus Michel (Suhrkamp: Frankfurt/Main, 1969), 40.

22. Hegel, *Three Essays*, 56.

23. *Hegel: The Letters*, 531.

24. G. W. F. Hegel, *The Philosophy of History*, trans. J. Sibree (New York: Dover Publications, 1956), 390, 377–78; *Werke*, 12:454. Mitchell's notion of iconoclasm necessarily assumes the Protestant (iconoclastic) polemic against Catholic, fetishistic image worship (see *Iconology*, 196–97).

25. Hegel, *Philosophy of History*, 377–78.

26. Ibid., 377.

27. Ibid., 378.

28. Pietz ("Fetishism and Materialism," 134 and n. 44) cites these works as also relevant to Marx: Karl August Böttiger, *Ideen zur Kunst-Mythologie* (1826), Benjamin Constant, *De la religion* (1824). For Marx's particular reading of these and other texts, see *The Ethnological Notebooks of Karl Marx*, ed. Lawrence Krader (Assen, Neth.: Van Gorcum, 1972). On the colonial encounters with the condescendingly deemed fetish religions of West Africa and South America, and how these generated a relevant discourse on fetishism that applies to Marx, see Mitchell, *Iconology*, 205; Pietz, "Fetishism and Materialism," 130; 143; Anne McClintock, *Imperial Leather: Race, Gender, and Sexuality in the Colonial Conquest* (New York: Routledge, 1995), 181. Mitchell also points to how some contemporaries viewed Catholic and "Negroe" fetishism as analogous (197).

29. Auguste Comte, *System of Positive Polity*, vol. 3 (New York: Burt Franklin, 1868), 117, 123. "Fetichistic adoration," writes Comte, "always proceeds from personal motives" (90; see 85).

30. Comte's theory of fetishism concerns primarily the animation of things and is not an investigation into subject-object relations as I am describing them here. Hegel and Marx, in other words, are not *only* concerned with the idea that, as Comte puts it, "the Fetichist spirit . . . looks on all objects in nature as animate" (*System of Positive Polity*, 68). Comte had also partitioned "Fetichism" from theology, viewing the former as "spontaneous," the latter, "systematic" (67). Hegel would draw these together, and of course Marx would speak of "theological niceties" (*Capital*, 163) in discussing commodity fetishism. For more on Comte, see below.

31. Marx, *Capital*, 165.

32. One may ask whether Freud's definition of fetishism, even if it explains a *relation* of love, is meant to account for the material organization of social wholes, rather than their psychological organization. For example, one of the mysteries of Freud's famous take on fetishism is not that rather familiar final sentence about the "inferior organs" of women so much as the penultimate sentence on "social psychology," a moment where Freud could have theorized social fetishism further, but doesn't. He says: "Another variant, which is also a parallel to fetishism in social psychology, might be seen in the Chinese custom of mutilating the female foot and then revering it like a fetish after it has been mutilated. It seems as though the Chinese male wants to thank the woman for having submitted to being castrated" ("On Fetishism," *The Standard Edition of the Complete Psychological works of Sigmund Freud*, trans. James Strachey [London: Hogarth Press, 1953–74], 21, 157). And that's all he said, leaving the pieces for readers to pick up and reassemble with other fleeting references to social fetishism, such as the odd social displays of "thrashing of the fetish" in *Civilization and Its Discontents* (trans. and ed. James Strachey [New York: Norton, 1962], 74). My main point, in this digression, is to ask about the significance of Freud's remark that "the meaning of the fetish is not known to other people, so the fetish is not withheld from him: it is easily accessible and he can readily obtain the sexual satisfaction attached to it. What other men have to woo and make exertions for can be had by the fetishist with no trouble at all" ("On Fetishism," 21.154). In the earlier version of this chapter, I had suggested that what distinguishes the Hegelian-Marxian theory of fetishism from the Freudian explanation is that the former takes fetishism to be a function of social relations (plural) and the latter, private or personal relations. Michael Uebel, obviously the real reader of Freud, has persuaded me to reconsider that view and perhaps instead ponder whether Marx construes fetishism to be pathological, in the way Freud does in contemplating the degrees of fetishism, from the normal—"I love those boots, I love you"—to the pathological when the boots become the sole sexual object; on this, see Paul Gebhard, "Fetishism and Sado-masochsim," *Science and Psychoanalysis* 25 (1969): 71–80. For other pertinent titles on this vast topic, see Freud, *Three Essays on the Theory of Sexuality* (1905), *Standard Edition*, 7.125–243 (153–55 esp.), and "On the Genesis of Fetishism," *Vienna Psychoanalytic Society* (1909), which is discussed in Louis Rose, "Freud and Fetishism: Previously Unpublished Minutes of the Vienna Psychoanalytic Society," *Psychoanalytic Quarterly* 57 (1988): 147–66. See also William Pietz, "The Problem of the Fetish, I," *res* 9 (1985): 5–17; "The Problem of the Fetish, II," *res* 13 (1987): 23–45; "The Problem of the Fetish, IIIa," *res* 16 (1988): 105–23; E. L. McCallum, *Object Lessons: How to Do Things with Fetishism* (Albany: State University of New York Press, 1999).

33. *German Ideology, Marx-Engels Reader*, 154. Also, Marx writes: "The social relations between individuals [in feudalism] . . . appear at all events as their own personal relations, and are not disguised as social relations between things, between the products of labour" (*Capital*, 170).

34. On these sacramental words, see Lee Palmer Wandel, *The Eucharist in the Reformation: Incarnation and Liturgy* (Cambridge: Cambridge University Press, 2006).

35. Speaking of devotion and the sacraments, Hegel writes in the lectures on the philosophy of religion: "Negation exists within devotion and even maintains an outward configuration by means of sacrifice. The subject renounces something or negates something in relation to itself. It has possessions and divests itself of them in order to demonstrate that it is earnest. . . . Thus from this negation or from the sacrifice one advances to enjoyment, to consciousness of having posited oneself in unity with God by means of it. Sensible enjoyment is linked directly with what is higher, with consciousness of the linkage with God" (*Lectures on the Philosophy of Religion*, vol. 1, ed. Peter C. Hodgson, trans. R. F. Brown, Hodgson, and J. M. Stewart [Berkeley:

University of California Press, 1984], 446). In these lectures, Hegel's aim is to discuss religion as philosophy (rather than as theology).

36. G. W. F. Hegel, *Phenomenology of Mind: Being Part Three of the Encyclopaedia of the Philosophical Sciences*, trans. William Wallace (Oxford: Clarendon Press, 1971), 284–85.

37. Karl Marx, *Grundrisse*, ed. and trans. Martin Nickolaus (New York: Penguin, 1993), 91.

38. Ibid.

39. Fredric Jameson, *Postmodernism; or, The Cultural Logic of Late Capitalism* (Durham, NC: Duke University Press, 1991), 231. On the question of value, see Jameson's *The Political Unconscious* (Ithaca, NY: Cornell University Press, 1981), 250–51.

40. See also "Simple Reproduction," in Marx, *Capital*, 711–24, and 199.

41. Marx, *Grundrisse*, 92. One other telling formulation is this: "Once a commodity has arrived at a situation in which it can serve as a use-value, it falls out of the sphere of exchange into that of consumption" (*Capital*, 198). Of course, despite Marx's chiastic approach to production and consumption, we have to bear in mind their conceptual differences, at Marx's own urging: "Thereupon, nothing simpler for a Hegelian than to posit production and consumption as identical" (*Grundrisse*, 93).

42. Stuart Barnett writes that "Hegel thus defines the sign in a very modern way. It is defined as a relation between a signifier and a signified. Community, in turn, is defined as the establishment of this relation, as the harnessing of the potentially arbitrary nature of the sign. In as much as a sign cannot by definition be private, the sign comprises the space of community. . . . This is why bread is for Hegel the consummate sign. It is consumed and destroyed in the very act of signification" ("Eating My God," *Hegel After Derrida*, ed. Stuart Barnett [New York: Routledge, 1998], 138, 139).

43. Pietz implores us to rethink these issues in his "Fetishism and Materialism," *Fetishism as Cultural Discourse*, 119–51.

44. See Jean Baudrillard, "Fetishism and Ideology: The Semiological Reduction" (1970) in *For a Critique of Political Economy of the Sign*, trans. Charles Levin (St. Louis: Telos Press, 1981). For penetrating analysis, see Pietz, "Fetishism and Materialism," 122–23.

45. This criticism holds true for Giorgio Agamben's formulation in *Stanzas: Word and Phantasm in Western Culture*, trans. Ronald L. Martinez (Minneapolis: University of Minnesota Press, 1993); see 37 and 42 esp.

46. Jean-François Lyotard, *Libidinal Economy*, trans. Iain Hamilton Grant (Bloomington: Indiana University Press, 1993), in which the discussion of Marxian fetishism is also a discussion of Baudrillard (see 91, 105, 110, 129, 153).

47. Marx, *Capital*, 136; 135–36. Marx goes on to speak of the ubiquity of this substance, by way of various other examples: butyric acid and propyl formate, while different chemicals, are constituted by the same "substances," carbon, hydrogen, and oxygen (see 141).

48. For "gleicher Substanz," see Karl Marx, *Das Kapital: Kritik der politischen Ökonomie*, vol. 1 (Berlin: J. H. W. Dietz, 1926), 11/*Capital*, 134. For "gemeinschaftliche Substanz," see 25/151 and 31/151). For "Warenkörper," see 4/126; 5/128; 9/132; 10/133, 14/138; 23/148.

49. For "Wertkörper," see *Das Kapital*, 18/*Capital*, 143; 19/144; 22/147; 23/149; see also 24/150.

50. Yet fetishism was, and some respects still is (especially in the Kleinian line of psychoanalysis), a discussion of bodies and body parts; see Rose, "Freud and Fetishism."

51. *Luther's Small Catechism* (Mankato, MN: Luther Synod Book Co., 1966), 214; *The Adoration of the Sacrament*, trans. Abdel Ross Wentz, *Luther's Works*, vol. 36, *Word & Sacrament II* (Philadelphia: Fortress, 1959), 275–305.

52. John Wyclif, *De Eucharistia*, ed. John Loserth (London: Wyclif Society, 1892).

53. Marx, *Capital*, 151. "The utopia of the qualitative—the things which through their differences and uniqueness cannot be absorbed into the prevalent exchange relationships—take refuge under capitalism in the traits of fetishism" (Theodor W. Adorno, *Minima Moralia: Reflections from Damaged Life*, trans. E. F. N. Jephcott [New York: Schocken, 1978]).

54. Marx, *Das Kapital*, 9 / *Capital*, 132; 14/138. Cf.: "It is only by being exchanged that the products of labour acquire a socially uniform objectivity as values, which is distinct from their sensuously varied objectivity as articles of utility" (*Capital*, 166, 163, 177).

55. Marx, *Capital*, 289.

56. Theodor W. Adorno, "On the Fetish Character in Music and the Regression of Listening," in *The Culture Industry: Selected Essays on Mass Culture*, ed. J. M. Bernstein (New York: Routledge, 1991), 39.

57. Ibid., 40.

58. Ibid., 39.

59. See also: "What might be called use value in the reception of cultural assets is being replaced by exchange-value. . . . The use-value of art, its essence, is a fetish, and the fetish—the social valuation which they mistake for the merit of works of art—becomes its only use value, the only quality they enjoy" (Max Horkheimer and Theodor W. Adorno, "The Culture Industry: Enlightenment as Mass Deception," in *Dialectic of Enlightenment: Philosophical Fragments*, ed. Gunzelin Schmid Noerr and trans. Edmund Jephcott [Stanford, CA: Stanford University Press, 2002], 128).

60. Slavoj Žižek, *Fragile Absolute, or, Why Is the Christian Legacy Worth Fighting For?* (New York: Verso, 2000), 22.

61. Ibid., 22–23.

62. For examples, see Miri Rubin, *Corpus Christi: The Eucharist in Late Medieval Culture* (Cambridge: Cambridge University Press, 1991).

63. Slavoj Žižek, *The Sublime Object of Ideology* (New York: Verso, 1989), 25–26.

64. Žižek writes in a note at this point in his discussion: "'Lordship' and 'Bondage' are the terms used in the translation we refer to (Hegel, 1977); following Kojève, Lacan uses 'maître' and 'esclave', which are then translated as 'master' and 'slave'" (*Sublime Object of Ideology*, 26). Throughout his body of work, Žižek adopt the terms that suit his discussion, especially when talking about the Lacanian discourse of the master. In *Lacan: The Silent Partners* (New York: Verso, 2006), he refers only to master and slave (74–76); likewise in *The Parallax View* (Cambridge: MIT Press, 2006.), 185, *The Ticklish Subject: The Absent Centre of Political Ontology* (New York: Verso, 1999), 343–45, and *Metastases of Enjoyment: Six Essays On Women And Causality* (New York: Verso, 2005), 109. In *Tarrying with the Negative: Kant, Hegel, and the Critique of Ideology* (Durham, NC: Duke University Press, 1993), he begins talking about the lord/bondsman dialectic, then speaks of the lord-master and bondsman-slave, and then refers to the master/slave dialectic (33–34). By these various usages, one wouldn't precisely discover Hegel's feudal terms or frame, as discussed in chap. 3.

65. Žižek, *Sublime Object of Ideology*, 26.

66. Marx, *Capital*, 170.

67. For more on this idea, see chap. 3.

68. Walter Benjamin, "Capitalism as Religion," in *Selected Writings*, vol. 1, ed. Marcus Bullock and Michael W. Jennings (Cambridge, MA: Belknap Press of Harvard University Press, 1996), 290.

Chapter Five

1. The best try is Bruce Mazlish, "The Tragic Farce of Marx, Hegel, and Engels: A Note," *History and Theory* 11, no. 3 (1972): 335–37, citing Hegel's lectures on the philosophy of history, specifically the discussion of the double defeat of the Romans and Napoleon. Likewise, David Farrell Krell offers a great discussion of the mysterious quotation featured in the opening of Part III of this book; see his *The Tragic Absolute: German Idealism and the Languishing of God* (Bloomington: Indiana University Press, 2005), 16–18.

2. Georg Lukács discusses Hegel's other, earlier encounters with the work of Adam Smith in *The Young Hegel: Studies in the Relations between Dialectics and Economics*, trans. Rodney Livingstone (Cambridge, MA: MIT Press, 1976); see section 2.5.

3. This is by no means the only medieval material in the *Phenomenology of Spirit*, the most relevant to my discussion here being the earlier section called, "Virtue and the way of the world" (p. 228), with its romance themes of combat and an adventuring "virtuous knight" (232/§387). See my discussion below, n. 27.

4. Hegel, *Phenomenology of Spirit*, 306/§503. In §501, Hegel refers to "the sovereign power" as the "state power" (used in the previous paragraph; see 305), and so I likewise personify the state as a sovereign, acquiring ideal then actual power.

5. Ibid., 306/§503, §504. But this sovereign is "not yet in truth an actual *state* power" (307/§506, my emphasis). For he has yet to attain a "will" and, more particularly, "lacks a will with which to oppose counsel, and the power to decide which of the different opinions is best for the general good" (307/§506).

6. Ibid., 307/§506.

7. Ibid., 310/§511. Hegel underscores these language practices and says that both the sovereign and the noble are "two extremes" (309/§510), both "moments of language" (310/§510) that have "language" as their "*middle term*" (310/§510).

8. Ibid., 311/§511.

9. Ibid.

10. On the "sovereign exception" as it relates to writing a history of feudalism, see Kathleen Davis, *Periodization and Sovereignty: How Ideas of Feudalism and Secularization Govern the Politics of Time* (Philadelphia: University of Pennsylvania Press, 2008). See also, of course, Ernst Hartwig Kantorowicz, *The King's Two Bodies: A Study in Mediaeval Political Theology* (1957; Princeton, NJ: Princeton University Press, 1997).

11. Jean Hyppolite, in his otherwise riveting analysis of Hegel, reads the French Revolution too early into these sections, insofar as he takes Hegel here to be discussing "the reign of Louis XIV" and his famous phrase "L'Etat c'est moi" (*Genesis and Structure of Hegel's "Phenomenology of Spirit*," trans. Samuel Cherniak and John Heckman [Evanston, IL: Northwestern University Press, 1974], 405; see 400)—an *ancien régime* (410) ripe for overthrow. See also Terry Pinkard, *Hegel: A Biography* (Cambridge: Cambridge University Press, 2000), 211.

12. Hegel, *Phenomenology of Spirit*, 311–12/§512.

13. Ibid., 312/§514.

14. Ibid., 313/§515.

15. Ibid., 301/§494.

16. Adam Smith, *An Inquiry into the Nature and Causes of the Wealth of Nations*, vol. 1 (New York: E. P. Dutton, 1924), 339.

17. Herbert Rowland, "Imitation, Pleasure, and Aesthetic Education in the Poetics and Comedies of Johann Elias Schlegel," *Goethe Yearbook* 17 (2010): 303–25; here, 311. On the me-

dieval versions of Diogenes within Fürstenspiegel narrative, one can begin with Judith Ferster, *Fictions of Advice: The Literature and Politics of Counsel in Late Medieval England* (Philadelphia: University of Pennsylvania Press, 1996), 108–36.

18. Christoph Martin Wieland, *Socrates Mainomenos (graece) oder die Dialogen des Diogenes von Sinope* (Leipzig: Weidmann, 1770), and *Der goldene Spiegel oder die Könige von Scheschian* (Leipzig: Wiedmann & Reutlingen, 1772). On the relatively unknown Wieland, see John A. Mc-Carthy, *C. M. Wieland: The Man and His Work* (Boston: Twayne, 1979).

19. Heinz Wegener, *Das Joachimsthalsche Gymnasium, Die Landesschule Templin: Ein Berlin-Brandenburgisches Gymnasium im Mahlstrom der Deutschen Geschichte 1607–2007* (Berlin: Berlin Story Verlag, 2007). On the genre in question within the humanist reform, see Bruno Singer, *Die Fürstenspiegel in Deutschland im Zeitalter das Humanismus und der Reformation* (Munich: W. Fink, 1981).

20. See Johann Jakob Engel, *Fürstenspiegel* (Gotha: Bibliographischen Institut, 1828).

21. *Hegel's Lectures on the History of Philosophy*, 3 vols., trans. E. S. Haldane and Francis H. Simson (London: Routledge & Kegan Paul, 1955), 1.484. Cicero credits Diogenes for "distinguishing truth from error, which he called by the Greek name of dialectic" (*De oratore*, 2 vols., trans. E.W. Sutton [Cambridge, MA: Harvard University Press, 1948–], II.157).

22. Hegel, *Phenomenology of Spirit*, 319/§524.

23. On these medieval narratives, see the old but still relevant study by Wilhelm Berges, *Die Fürstenspiegel des hohen und späten Mittelalters* (Leipzig: K. W. Hiersemann, 1938).

24. Hegel, *Phenomenology of Spirit*, 319/§524.

25. Hegel, in other words, muses on what it means to give "witty expression to the *contradiction* that is present in . . . the actual world" (*Phenomenology of Spirit*, 320/§526), and what can be done with a world in which "everything [seems] to be self-alienated" (320/§526).

26. Hegel, *Phenomenology of Spirit*, 226/§377.

27. This romance section is the last of three in the chapter entitled "B. The Actualization of Rational Self-Consciousness through Its Own Activity," which itself paraphrases Smith's *Wealth of Nations* near the beginning:

> What [the individual] does *is* the skill and customary practice of all. This content, in so far as it is completely particularized, is, in its actual existence, confined within the framework of the activity of all. The *labour* of the individual for his own needs is just as much the satisfaction of the needs of others as of his own, and the satisfaction of his own needs he obtains only through the labour of others. As the individual in his *individual* work already *unconsciously* performs a *universal* work, so again he also performs the universal work as his *conscious* object; the whole becomes, as *a* whole, his own work, for which he sacrifices himself and precisely in so doing receives it back from it his own self. There is nothing here which would not be reciprocal. (213/§351)

28. Hegel writes: "Even when they complain about this ordinance as if it went against their own inner law, and maintain against it the opinions of the heart, they cling to it with their hearts, as being their essential being; and, if this ordinance is taken from them, or they place themselves outside it, they lose everything" (227/§378). The ideological problem, as Hegel explains it, is precisely that which presents a situation in which people act against their own interests, "their own inner law." And in a way that would surely be amenable to Slavoj Žižek's suggestion of the necessity of the big, fantastic Other ("extimated" or otherwise), lest your reality appear traumatically incoherent, Hegel proposes that if you dissolve the big Other that is the

"ordinance" imposed on persons, you "lose everything." See Žižek, *The Sublime Object of Ideology* (London: Verso, 1989), 29.

29. Jean-Paul Sartre, *Critique of Dialectical Reason*, vol. 1, trans. Alan Sheridan-Smith, ed. Jonathan Rée (London: Verso, 1991), 19.

30. Hegel, *Phenomenology of Spirit*, 321/§526.

31. George Steinmetz, *Regulating the Social: The Welfare State and Local Politics in Imperial Germany*, 21–22, with reference to Hegel as well, including the observation that he "stands at the threshold of the modern understanding of the state" (20). And entangled within this history is, no doubt, the Bavarian Illuminati whose Enlightenment agenda included secularization within government institutions and a rejection of feudal privileges; see Klaus Epstein, *The Genesis of German Conservatism* (Princeton, NJ: Princeton University Press, 1966); for reflections on a possible connection between this group (which fascinated Goethe and Herder) and Hegel, see Glenn Alexander Magee, *Hegel and the Hermetic Tradition* (Ithaca, NY: Cornell University Press, 2001), 56–57 (which cites Epstein).

32. See Conrad Heresbach, *De educandis erudiendisque principum liberis, reipublicae gubernandae destinatis, deque republica Christianè administranda epitome* (Frankfurt: Iohannem Feyerabend, 1592).

33. On Heresbach, see Meinhard Pohl, ed., *Der Niederrhein im Zeitalter des Humanismus: Konrad Heresbach und sein Kreis*, Schriften der Heresbach-Stiftung Kalkar, 5 (Bielefeld: Verlag für Regionalgeschichte, 1997). What I aim to show here is a different trajectory than what is evident in the reception of Mandeville's *Fable of the Bees*, which is often retrospectively brought into the discussion of political economy—particularly, on the question of individual vice adding up to a greater or collective good. I would, however, say that this poem and its prose moralization are relevant for the way they partake of Fürstenspiegel forms of advice. See Bernard Mandeville, *The Fable of the Bees: or, Private Vices, Publick Benefits*, 3rd ed. (London: J. Tonson, 1724).

34. Paul Joachimsohn, "Frühhumanismus in Schwaben," *Württembergische Vierteljahrshefte fur Landesgeschichte*, NF, 5 (1896): 63–126, 257–88. More generally, see Singer, *Die Fürstenspiegel in Deutschland*; Jutta Prieur, *Humanismus als Reform am Niederrhein: Konrad Heresbach 1496–1579* (Bielefeld: Verlag für Regionalgeschichte, 1996); Martin Szameitat, *Konrad Heresbach: Ein niederrheinischer Humanist zwischen Politik und Gelehrsamkeit* (Bonn: R. Hablet, 2010).

35. It relates to a work known in Europe as Pseudo-Plutarch's *The De Liberis Educandis*.

36. Heresbach, *De educandis*, 198.

37. Ibid., 282–97.

38. See Karl-Heinz Lindner, *Marktordnung und Marktpolizei unt. bes. Berücks. Preußens* (Breslau, 1929).

39. Michel Foucault, *Security, Territory, Population: Lectures at the Collège de France, 1977–78*, ed. Michel Senellart and trans. Graham Burchell (London: Palgrave Macmillan, 2007), 413. I am here also referring to Foucault's thoughts on the "development of the state of (military-economic) competition, and development of the *Wohlfahrt* state (of wealth-tranquility-happiness): these are the two principles that 'police' as a rational art of government must be able to coordinate. At this time 'police' was conceived of as a sort 'technology of state forces'" (474). See 413–14, where Foucault examines the link between early political economy (by Montchrétien) and *Polizeiwissenschaft*. Needless to say, Foucault's emphasis is on (as one would expect) "policing" and not so much "policy."

40. Smith, *Wealth of Nations*, 504; see 516.

41. Ibid., 404.

42. Ibid., 405. See also: "The natural effort of every individual to better his own condition, when suffered to exert itself with freedom and security is so powerful a principle that it is alone, and without any assistance, not only capable of carrying on the society to wealth and prosperity, but of surmounting a hundred impertinent obstructions with which the folly of human laws too often incumbers its operations; though the effect of these obstructions is always more or less either to encroach upon its freedom, or to diminish its security" (406).

43. "The private interest of our merchants and manufacturers may, perhaps, have extorted from the legislature these exemptions as well as the greater part of our other commercial regulations. They are, however, perfectly just and reasonable, and if, consistently with the necessities of the state, they could be extended to all the other materials of manufacture, the public would certainly be a gainer" (Smith, *Wealth of Nations*, 487).

44. Ibid., 496.

45. Ibid., 340.

46. Much scholarship in German medieval and reformation studies links Fürstenspiegel with Bildung, to the point that my assertion here is screamingly obvious. Suffice it to point to Beate Baier's study, among others: *Die Bildung der Helden: Erziehung und Ausbildung in mittelhochdeutschen Antikenromanen und ihren Vorlagen* (Trier: WVT Wissenschaftlicher Verlag, 2006): "Die Überzeugung, daß der ideale Herrscher nicht nur politische Macht, sondern auch Bildung besitzen soll, findet sich besonders in Fürstenspiegeln" (118).

47. John Russon comes closest to expressing this point: "To speak in the terms of historical analogue to the world of *Bildung*, we can call the first form the medieval form," which "parallels the unhappy consciousness" (*The Self and Its Body in Hegel's Phenomenology of Spirit* [Toronto: University of Toronto Press, 2001], 91–92). See also his remark that "*Bildung* is the world of those people who are purely revolutionary and who deny their present world any propriety of form" (91).

48. Hegel, *Phenomenology of Spirit*, 41/§68; 50/§78.

49. Speculatively, one wonders whether this succession of genres, romance then Fürstenspiegel, stages, in miniature, what Hegel had promised to examine in his Preface—"the diversity of philosophical systems as the progressive unfolding of truth" (2/§2)—only here, that history is a history of genre as a valid philosophical form. One can see that, from Descartes to Kant, romance is expunged from philosophical inquiry and sustained instead in the history of literature and music, only to return to philosophy with German idealism and of course Nietzsche. But Fürstenspiegel survives (exceptions such as Machiavelli notwithstanding) to Hegel's own day as a form of legitimate philosophical expression.

50. *Marx-Engels Reader*, 112. Though let's not forget that Marx said, in the same work, that "we have proceeded from the premises of political economy. We have accepted its language and its laws" (70).

51. Ibid., 111, 110.

52. Marx himself, by the bye, assumes this "standpoint" insofar as he overlays his critique onto Smith's own principle about collective avarice and social good: "The only force bringing them ["free persons"] together, and putting them into relation with each other, is the selfishness, the gain and the private interest of each. Each pays heed to himself only, and no one worries about the others. And precisely for that reason . . . they all work together to their mutual advantage, for the common weal, and in the common interest" (*Capital: A Critique of Political Economy*, vol. 1, trans. Ben Fowkes [New York: Vintage, 1977], 280).

53. See Marx, *Capital*, 151–52. Also worth remembering is: "Let us take England. Its classical political economy belongs to a period in which the class struggle was as yet undeveloped. . . . At the very moment when a bourgeois science of political economy at last seemed possible in Germany, it had in reality again become impossible" ("Postface to the Second Edition," *Capital*, 96, 98).

54. See Norbert Waszek, "Auf dem Weg zur Reformbill-Schrift: Die Ursprünge von Hegels Großbritannienrezeption," in *Politik und Geschichte: Zu den Intentionen von G.W.F. Hegels Reformbill-Schrift*, ed. Christoph Jamme and Elisabeth Weisser-Lohmann, Hegel-Studien, Beiheft 35 (Bonn: Bouvier, 1995).

55. Pinkard makes the point perfectly: "Precisely because of the pressures of the market on the members of civil society, the demands to pursue their own interests and to conform, Hegel argued forcefully, as he had been doing since his arrival in Jena, for the continued legal recognition of the estates and some of the corporate structure of the *ancien régime*, since, so he argued, only they could serve as the mediating bodies for the structures of mutual and equal recognition in the newly emerging market societies" (*Hegel*, 484).

56. Hegel, *Phenomenology of Spirit*, 17/§29.

57. One must also put in for "combined development," as Trotsky theorized it: "Unevenness, the most general law of the historical process, reveals itself most sharply and complexly in the destiny of the backward countries. Under the whip of external necessity their backward culture is compelled to make leaps. From the universal law of unevenness thus derives another law which, for the lack of a better name, we may call the law of *combined development*—by which we mean a drawing together of the different stages of the journey, a combining of the separate steps, an amalgam of archaic with more contemporary forms" (Leon Trotsky, *History of the Russian Revolution*, trans. Max Eastman [Chicago: Haymarket Books, 2008], 5).

58. Erich Fromm, *Marx's Concept of Man* (London: Continuum, 2004), 173–74. For a general discussion, see S. S. Prawer, *Karl Marx and World Literature* (Oxford: Clarendon, 1976).

59. *Marx-Engels Reader*, 102–4, 245–46; Marx, *Capital*, 138. More generally, see *Marx [and] Engels on Literature and Art: A Selection of Writings*, ed. Lee Baxandall and Stefan Morawski (St. Louis: Telos Press, 1973).

60. Comparing the two thinkers is Paul J. Contino, *The Master and the Slave: Lukács, Bakhtin, and the Ideas of Their Time* (Oxford: Oxford University Press, 2000).

61. In his *Problems of Dostoevsky's Poetics*, for example, Bakhtin criticized dialectic as a monological abstraction of the authentic intersubjective discourse, "dialogism." See *Problems of Dostoevsky's Poetics*, ed. and trans. Caryl Emerson (Minneapolis: University of Minnesota Press, 1984), 9–10, 24–26, 30–31, 167, 183, 279, 293.

62. There are few studies linking Bakhtin to Hegel. For the best effort, see Jean-François Côté, "Bakhtin's Dialogism Reconsidered through Hegel's 'Monologism'," in *Materializing Bakhtin: The Bakhtin Circle and Social Theory*, ed. Craig Brandist and Galin Tihanov (New York: St. Martin's Press, 2000), 20–42. See also Peter V. Zima, "Bakhtin's Young Hegelian Aesthetics," in *The Bakhtin Circle Today*, ed. Myriam Díaz-Diocaretz (Atlanta: Rodopi, 1989), 77–95. Craig Brandist and David Shepherd discuss the need to study Bakhtin more thoroughly in relation to Hegel and remark that the former's "thought remains profoundly Hegelian in its structure" ("From Saransk to Cyberspace: Towards an Electronic Edition of Bakhtin," *Dialogues on Bakhtin: Interdisciplinary Readings*, ed. Mika Lähteenmäki and Hannele Dufva [University of Jyväskylä Centre for Applied Language Studies, 1998], 7–22; here, 13; see also 14, 20). On Bakhtin's rejection of dialectics, as presented by Marx and Hegel, see Gary Saul Morson and

Caryl Emerson, *Mikhail Bakhtin: Creation of a Prosaics* (Stanford, CA: Stanford University Press, 1990), 236.

63. Mikhail Bakhtin, "Epic and Novel," *The Dialogic Imagination: Four Essays*, ed. Michael Holquist and trans. Caryl Emerson (Austin: University of Texas Press, 1981), 7.

64. Ibid., 16.

65. Ibid., 15.

66. Ibid., 23.

67. Ibid.

68. Ibid.

69. Marx, *Capital*, 103. One may also hear here, of course, Viktor Shklovsky's "lay bare the device" обнажать прием/*obnazhat' priem*), especially since Bakhtin uses the same verb, обнажать. Given that Bakhtin couples this process of "laying bare" with that of "breaking open the shell," I believe him to be referencing Marx. See Viktor Shklovsky, *Theory of Prose*, trans. Benjamin Sher (Elmwood Park, IL: Dalkey Archive Press, 1990), 147, 170. I thank David Hock, a graduate student in the Department of Slavic Languages and Literatures at Princeton, for these insights into Bakhtin's Russian. Peter Brooks identifies a related realist trope of "removing housetops in order to see the private lives played out beneath them" (*Realist Vision* [New Haven, CT: Yale University Press, 2005], 3).

70. Marx, *Capital*, 279–80.

71. See page 11, where Bakhtin refers to the earlier essay "From the Prehistory of Novelistic Discourse."

72. Mikhail Bakhtin, "From the Prehistory of Novelistic Discourse," *Dialogic Imagination* 77.

73. Ibid., 77–78. For Georg Lukács, Dante "represents a historico-philosophical transition from the pure epic to the novel," and, like Bakhtin, he finds parody to perform a necessary critique "of the chivalrous novels" (*The Theory of the Novel: A Historico-philosophical Essay on the Forms of Great Epic Literature*, trans. Anna Bostock [Cambridge, MA: MIT Press, 1971], 68). Above all, Cervantes showed that "the purest heroism is bound to become grotesque, the strongest faith is bound to become madness" (104), and so forth. But, unlike Bakhtin, Lukács concludes that these medieval parodic tendencies and inversions die along with the Middle Ages, because they were "so strongly bound up with the historical moment" (*Theory of the Novel*).

74. "From the Prehistory of Novelistic Discourse," *Dialogic Imagination*, 55.

75. Ibid., emphasis mine. David Hock, again, supplied the Russian here.

76. Ibid., 80.

77. Mikhail Bakhtin, *Rabelais and His World*, trans. Hélène Iswolsky (Bloomington: Indiana University Press, 1984), 374.

78. Ibid., 381.

79. Ibid., 376.

80. Ibid., 380.

81. Ibid., 380.

82. Ibid., 381.

83. The central study here is Peter Stallybrass and Allon White, *The Politics and Poetics of Transgression* (London: Methuen, 1986).

84. Marx, *Capital*, 138.

85. Bakhtin, *Rabelais and His World*, 223–24, 317, 325, 382, 353.

86. Ibid., 217.

87. Marx, *Capital*, 103; *Marx-Engels Reader*, 302. "Their simplest expression is the primeval phenomenon of popular humor, the cartwheel, which by the continual rotation of the upper and lower parts suggests the rotation of earth and sky. This is manifested in other movements of the clown: the buttocks persistently trying to take the place of the head and the head that of the buttocks" (Bakhtin, *Rabelais and His World*, 353).

88. See Bakhtin, *Rabelais and His World*, 37–51, 55–56.

89. Bakhtin, "Epic and Novel," *Dialogic Imagination*, 7.

90. Bakhtin, *Rabelais and His World*, 317.

91. Bakhtin, "Epic and Novel," *Dialogic Imagination*, 7.

92. Ibid., 4, 5, 7, 20.

93. Ibid., 23–24.

94. Jean-Paul Sartre, *The Family Idiot: Gustave Flaubert, 1821–1857*, vol. 3, trans. Carol Cosman (Chicago: University of Chicago Press, 1989), 105.

95. Hegel, *Phenomenology of Spirit*, 280/§466.

96. Ibid., 280/§465.

97. Ibid.

98. Hegel, *Phenomenology of Spirit*, 281/§467, 282/§468; see 280/§466.

99. Ibid., 430/§710, 444/§733; 279/§464. Hegel, of course, returns to *Antigone* in 431/§712.

100. Ibid., 279/§465. I am aware of readings of Hegel's tragedy that view Antigone as the individual struggling against the universal, the state: see Raymond Pietercil, "Antigone and Hegel," *International Philosophical Quarterly* 18 (1978): 289–310.

101. Bakhtin, "Epic and Novel," *Dialogic Imagination*, 13; see 15.

102. In "From the Prehistory of Novelistic Discourse," Bakhtin makes a similar point that during the peak of Roman civilization (i.e., "ancient times"), "the novel could not *at that time* gather unto itself and make use of all the material that language images had made available. . . . From the point of view of polyglossia, Rome was merely the concluding phase of Hellenism, a phase whose final gesture was to carry over into the barbarian world of Europe a radical polyglossia, and thus make possible the creation of a new type of medieval polyglossia" (*Dialogic Imagination*, 60, 63; see 67).

103. Bakhtin, "Epic and Novel," *Dialogic Imagination*, 34, which can be contrasted with Bakhtin's remarks in "From the Prehistory of Novelistic Discourse," ibid., 69, 71, 78.

104. Epic refuses "truly free investigation of the world" (Bakhtin, "Epic and Novel," *Dialogic Imagination*, 25; see 16). In the "destruction of epic distance," Bakhtin notes that "folklore and popular-comic sources for the novel played a huge role" (35). Furthermore, "in ancient times the novel could not really develop all its potential; this potential only came to light in the modern world" (ibid., 40). In modernity, beginning in the Middle Ages, the novel dominates by inclusion, not exclusion, and the medieval Rabelais marks this beginning, this new sense of novelty that indeed presages the future: "His book is a 'survey,' reflecting the actual events of the day. But at the same time the problems posed by the Rabelaisian images are broader and deeper by far than the usual survey, reaching beyond the contemporary picture" (Bakhtin, *Rabelais and His World*, 452); "He had an extraordinary sense of the new, not of the newfangled fashions but of that which was born from the death of the old and to which the future belonged" (ibid., 453).

105. *Rabelais and His World*, 211. This literary self-consciousness is also, of course, a feature of novelistic language: "The image of another's language and outlook on the world . . . , simultaneously represented *and* representing, is extremely typical of the novel" ("From the Prehistory

of Novelistic Discourse," *Dialogic Imagination*, 45). And this self-consciousness evinces what Bakhtin calls "linguistic consciousness": "The creating artist began to look at the language from the outside, with another's eyes, from the point of view of a potentially different language and style" (60).

106. Fredric Jameson, *The Political Unconscious: Narrative as a Socially Symbolic Act* (Ithaca, NY: Cornell University Press, 1981), 152.

107. Ian Watt, *The Rise of the Novel* (1957; Berkeley: University of California Press, 1967), 29.

108. Jameson, *Political Unconscious*, 61.

109. See, too, Jameson's reflections in a piece entitled, "On the Medieval," in *The Legitimacy of the Middle Ages: On the Unwritten History of Theory*, ed. Andrew Cole and D. Vance Smith (Durham, NC: Duke University Press, 2010), 243–46.

110. Jameson, *Political Unconscious*, 69.

111. Ibid., 71.

112. A translation has been available after the time of Jameson's writing; see Henri de Lubac, *Medieval Exegesis*, 4 vols., trans. Mark Sebanc (Edinburgh: T&T Clark, 1998).

113. For Jameson, in order to conceptualize a "dialectical use of genre criticism" (the subtitle to his chap. 2), one must incorporate other theories of genre—Frye, Propp, or Greimas—as well as proffer a theory of genre in its own right. Chap. 2 offers such a theory, taking as its example the medieval genre of romance (*Political Unconscious*, 118), which grows out of uneven development and the co-existence of mixed temporal modes (148) in the Middle Ages but which persists in the present day as a contradiction, to be harmonized within the novel form, romance being the precursor to the novel. For work in medieval studies on romance and contradiction, see Susan Crane, *Insular Romance: Politics, Faith, and Culture in Anglo-Norman and Middle English Literature* (Berkeley: University of California Press, 1986), 11, and, more generally, Sarah Kay, *Courtly Contradictions: The Emergence of the Literary Object in the Twelfth Century* (Stanford, CA: Stanford University Press, 2001).

114. Jameson, *Political Unconscious*, 29.

115. Ibid., 30.

116. Ibid.

117. Ibid., 31.

118. My exposition could as well have been replaced with the simple acknowledgment that the fourfold model works along the lines of the Greimas square, of which the four terms, for Jameson, dialectically generate "the ideal synthesis which would 'resolve' the initial binary opposition by subsuming it under a single unity" (*Political Unconscious*, 168; more fully, see ibid., 166–68; see also 48).

119. See Slavoj Žižek, *Enjoy Your Symptom! Jacques Lacan in Hollywood and Out* (New York: Routledge, 1992), 187n2.

120. Jameson, for example, corrects Lukács (whose method is too "reflectionist," as the familiar accusation goes; see *Political Unconscious*, 162) by situating the latter's insights about literary reification and typification within the broader Weberian narrative about rationalization and the transitions from feudalism to capitalism—with the idea being that these two processes, reification and rationalization, are interrelated and relevant to literary as much as social history.

121. Ibid., 285.

122. Ibid.

123. Ibid., 286.

124. Indeed, if one thing can be said about the history of the fourfold model, it is that the model is always fine-tuned or altered, with thinkers from Nicholas of Lyra to John Wyclif emphasizing one aspect over another, as we see here.

125. Jameson, *Political Unconscious*, 217; see 238, 240.

126. Ibid., 173; Jameson names this project as "Utopian wish-fulfillment" on p. 157.

127. Ibid., 166, 235. To be sure, condemning (rightly) a conservative or reflecting on those "desolations," even in 1981, would be nothing new (see Marx on the modes of subsumption [formal or real], Weber on rationalization, Lukács on reification, even Althusser on overdetermination).

128. Ibid., 235.

129. Ibid., 12.

Chapter Six

1. See Leopold von Ranke, *The Theory and Practice of History*, ed. Georg G. Iggers and Konrad von Moltke and trans. Wilma A. Iggers and von Moltke (New York: Bobbs-Merrill, 1973): my account of von Humboldt derives from pages 6–7, von Ranke, 41, 44; but see also 161, 157–58. For a fuller commentary, see Hayden White, *Metahistory: The Historical Imagination in Nineteenth-Century Europe* (Baltimore: Johns Hopkins University Press, 1973), 163–90.

2. *Hegel's Aesthetics: Lectures on Fine Art*, trans. T. M. Knox, 2 vols. (Oxford: Clarendon, 1975), 2.962.

3. Ibid., 2.982 and 2.965.

4. Ibid., 2.972.

5. Ibid., 2.994 and 2.997.

6. Ibid., 2.961, 990, 1002, 1128.

7. Hegel and von Ranke debated in Berlin over historical practice more largely; see John Higham, *History: Professional Scholarship in America* (1965; Baltimore: Johns Hopkins University Press, 1989), 91, 96–100.

8. Take, for instance, Lukács's words about the epic: "Utopian stylisation of the epic inevitably creates distance, but such distance lies between two instances of the empirical, so that the sorrow and majesty created by this distance can only make for a rhetorical tone. This distance may produce marvellous elegiac lyricism, but it can never, in itself, put real life into a content that transcends being, or turns such content into self-sufficient reality. Whether this distance leads forward or backwards, upwards or downwards from life, it is never the creation of a new reality but always only a subjective mirroring of what already exists" (Georg Lukács, *The Theory of the Novel: A Historico-philosophical Essay on the Forms of Great Epic Literature*, trans. Anna Bostock [Cambridge, MA: MIT Press, 1973], preface). One can postulate that Lukács, always the Hegelian, effectively introduces to Marxism the "literature" and "history" question by silently disavowing forms of Soviet Realism (which sees no distinction). It's no secret, however, that Lukács studied Hegel seriously, and that the misfortunes of his reputation owe to his Hegelianism, even when he had challenged Hegel: see *The Young Hegel: Studies in the Relations between Dialectics and Economics*, trans. Rodney Livingstone (Cambridge, MA: MIT Press, 1976); *Hegel's False and his Genuine Ontology*, trans. David Fernbach (London: Merlin Press, 1978).

9. Bakhtin, "Discourse in the Novel," *Dialogic Imagination*, 259, 262; see 284.

10. Macherey, it must be emphasized, is anti-Hegelian only in his rejection of those versions of Hegel in mid-twentieth-century France so popularized by Alexandre Kojève and Jean Hyp-

NOTES TO PAGES 135-36

polite. See Pierre Macherey, *A Theory of Literary Production*, trans. Geoffrey Wall (New York: Routledge, 1978).

11. Fredric Jameson, *The Political Unconscious* (Ithaca, NY: Cornell University Press, 1981), 12.

12. Of course, "contradiction" is the name for what happens when a concept fails to take, but here I would like to focus squarely on what it means to think, dialectically, about figures as concepts, literature as a conceptual production, and history as a concept.

13. To name several of the most prominent ones: Bernard Bosanquet, F. H. Bradley, Edward Caird, J. G. Hibben, Henry Jones, John Muirhead, Richard Nettleship, D. G. Ritchie, Josiah Royce, William Wallace. See Melvin Richter, *The Politics of Conscience: T. H. Green and His Age* (Cambridge, MA: Harvard University Press, 1964), 377; Geoffrey Thomas, *The Moral Philosophy of T. H. Green* (Oxford: Clarendon, 1987), 62–68.

14. In the United States, especially after the 1880s, there was a boom in Hegel in America, with a number of amenable expositions of Hegel's lectures on aesthetics, his Logics, and his lectures on the philosophy of history; see John Steinfort Kedney, *Hegel's Æsthetics: A Critical Exposition* (Chicago: S. C. Griggs and Co., 1885); William T. Harris, *Hegel's Logic* (Chicago: S. C. Griggs and Co., 1890). See also the essays by Henry Sussman and Gregory S. Jay in *Theorizing American Literature: Hegel, the Sign, and History*, ed. Bainard Cowan and Joseph G. Kronick (Baton Rouge: Louisiana State University Press, 1991); David Loyd Easton, *Hegel's First American Followers* (Athens: Ohio University Press, 1966); William H. Goetzmann, ed., *The American Hegelians: An Intellectual Episode in the History of Western America* (New York: Knopf, 1973); Henry Pochmann, *New England Transcendentalism and St. Louis Hegelianism: Phases in the History of American Idealism* (Philadelphia: Carl Schurz Memorial Foundation, 1948).

15. G. W. F. Hegel, *Introductory Lectures on Aesthetics*, trans. Bernard Bosanquet, ed. Michael Inwood (London: Penguin, 2004). For more on the introduction of Hegel to England and America, see these aptly entitled articles by J. H. Muirhead, "How Hegel Came to England," *Mind* n.s. 36, no.144 (1927): 423–47, and "How Hegel Came to America," *The Philosophical Review* 37, no. 3 (1928): 226–40.

16. By this claim, I present a kind of historical thinking different from that sketched by James Chandler, who assesses the historicity of historical novels and other literary forms (*England in 1819: The Politics of Literary Culture and the Case of Romantic Historicism* [Chicago: University of Chicago Press, 1998]). Rather, I look at literary historicism as it appears as a pre-given principle or theory in ways strikingly analogous to those methods in the 1980s. Kant, no doubt, was equally important to nineteenth-century English idealism, but it was Hegel, not Kant, who allowed for some important changes in literary critical style, ways of talking about history specifically; see Richter, *Politics of Conscience*, 36. See also Benedetto Croce's smart remark, "Kant did not feel or understand history" (*History, Its Theory and Practice*, trans. Douglas Ainslie [New York: Russell & Russell, 1960], 73).

17. On the turn to continental philosophy, see Sanford Schwartz, *The Matrix of Modernism: Pound, Eliot, & Early Twentieth-Century Thought* (Princeton, NJ: Princeton University Press, 1988).

18. Let me be clear. This chapter does not follow any kind of "philosophy and literature" methodology, and as such it risks satisfying neither literary critics who view Hegel as a discarded kernel in more advanced critical procedures nor philosophers, who usually view literary critics as depraved for dabbling in philosophy. In fact, this project is premised on the surprising agreement between three very different thinkers, Lacan, Habermas, de Man, all of whom insist that we have not accounted for many Hegelian genealogies and that indeed these are rather

disappearing things in a generally post- or even anti-Hegelian academic climate. See Jacques Lacan (*The Seminar of Jacques Lacan: Book II, The Ego in Freud's Theory and in the Technique of Psychoanalysis, 1954–1955*, ed. Jacques-Alain Miller and trans. Sylvana Tomaselli [New York: Norton, 1988], 73 and below); Jürgen Habermas (*The Philosophical Discourse of Modernity: Twelve Lectures*, trans. Frederick G. Lawrence [Cambridge, MA: MIT Press, 1987], 53; Paul de Man ("Sign and Symbol in Hegel's *Aesthetics*," *Critical Inquiry* 8 [1982]: 763). Furthermore, this chapter is not an exposition of Hegel's entire reception history through the twentieth century (through such thinkers as Alexandre Kojève, Jean Hyppolite, Michel Foucault, Jean-Luc Nancy, Martin Heidegger, Georges Bataille, Judith Butler, Ernesto Laclau, or Slavoj Žižek [Judith Butler et al., eds., *Contingency, Hegemony, Universality: Contemporary Dialogues on the Left* [New York: Verso, 2000]). I will, however, raise some obvious connections between the versions of Hegel that emerged in the late nineteenth century and those later versions in the Marxist tradition.

19. *Oxford Dictionary of National Biography*, 60 vols., ed. H. C. G. Matthew and Brian Harrison (Oxford: Oxford University Press, 2004), s.v. Green, Thomas Hill (entry written by Andrew Vincent).

20. See Thomas Macaulay's *The History of England from the Accession of James II* (Boston: Phillips, Sampson, 1849–61).

21. See, for instance, Henry Hallam's *Introduction to the Literature of Europe in the Fifteenth, Sixteenth, and Seventeenth Centuries* (Paris: Baudry's European Library, 1839).

22. Francis Palgrave, *History of the Anglo-Saxons* (London: John Murray, 1831).

23. They are the same as Hegel's three major genres of poetry, with the addition of the novel: epic, drama, lyric. Green throughout his philosophical writings combines Kant and Hegel, with no clear priority given to one over the other, but his Hegelianism in this example of literary criticism seems to outdo his Kantianism right in the middle of a sentence: "Our ultimate analysis can find no element in knowledge which is not supplied by ourselves in conformity to a ruling law, or which exists independently of the action of human thought. But though the world of nature is, in this sense, a world of man's own creation, it is so in a different way from the world of art and of philosophy. Thought is indeed its parent, but thought in its primary stage fails to recognize it as its own, fails to transfer to it its own attributes of universality, and identity in difference. It sees outward objects merely in their diversity and isolation" (T. H. Green, *Works of Fiction* [Ann Arbor, MI: Ann Arbor Press, 1911], 23).

24. Friedrich Nietzsche, *Beyond Good and Evil*, trans. R. J. Hollingdale (New York: Penguin, 1990), 186; see Gerald Graff, *Professing Literature: An Institutional History* (Chicago: University of Chicago Press, 1987), 74–76. René Wellek understands Taine to be a Hegelian, not a positivist; see his *A History of Modern Criticism: 1750–1960*, 5 vols. (New Haven, CT: Yale University Press, 1965), 4.36–38. See also Taine's comments on Hegel and his very Hegelian summing up of literature and philosophy (1.132–33 and 2:455).

25. Hyppolyte Taine, *History of English Literature*, 2 vols., trans. H. Van Laun (New York: Holt & Williams, 1872), 4, 13, 19.

26. Green, *Works of Fiction*, 30–31, 34–36, 39, 44.

27. *Oxford Dictionary of National Biography*, s.v. Bosanquet, Bernard (entry by A. M. McBriar).

28. Ibid.

29. Bernard Bosanquet, *A History of Æsthetic* (London: George Allen & Unwin, 1949; 1892), 451.

30. See Hegel, *Aesthetics*, 2.968–69. Curtis L. Carter sums up the debate about the "End of Art" in his "A Re-examination of the 'Death of Art' Interpretation of Hegel's *Aesthetics*," in *Art*

and Logic in Hegel's Philosophy, ed. Warren E. Steinkraus and Kenneth I. Schmitz (New Jersey: Humanities Press, 1980), 83–84. For a commentary, see Fredric Jameson, "'End of Art' or 'End of History'?" in *The Cultural Turn: Selected Writings on the Postmodern, 1983–1998* (London: Verso, 1998), 73–92.

31. Hegel, *Aesthetics*, 2.994.

32. Macherey, *Theory of Literary Production*, 93, 94.

33. Theodor W. Adorno, "On Lyric Poetry and Society," *Notes to Literature*, vol. 1, ed. Rolf Tiedemann and trans. Shierry Weber Nicholsen (New York: Columbia University Press, 1991), 37–54; here, 39, 43. On contradiction and dissonance in particular, see 49, 52.

34. See Bosanquet, *History of Æsthetic*, 463; 464–65.

35. See *England and Its Aesthetes: Biography and Taste; Essays by John Ruskin, Walter Pater, Adrian Stokes*, with commentary by David Carrier (Amsterdam: G+B Arts International, 1997), 21–22.

36. That is, Pater, at points in his *The Renaissance*, draws from Hegel's aesthetics, as the notes in Donald Hill's edition make abundantly clear; see Walter Pater, *The Renaissance: Studies in Art and Poetry*, ed. Donald L. Hill (Berkeley: University of California Press, 1980). Yet Pater himself was not interested in making direct theoretical links between literature and society, and he admitted, in his essay of 1893, "Plato and Platonism," that making such links is an open field (ibid., 9–10).

37. The "spirit" of Ruskin and Morris is, as Raymond Williams points out, the spirit of *form* (*Culture and Society: 1780–1950* [New York: Columbia University Press, 1958; 1983], 137–38).

38. Lacan, *Seminar of Jacques Lacan: Book II*, 73.

39. In her *The Literary History of England*, Oliphant writes: "The literary history of every country . . . is independent to a great measure of the political existence of the race in which it is developed, and except in so far as a period of remarkable intellectual activity in other ways is generally distinguished also by one of the great outbursts of literary genius which recur from time to time, it cannot be said to follow any of the rule of historical progress known to us" (Margaret Oliphant, *The Literary History of England*, 3 vols. [1882; New York: AMS, 1970], 1).

40. One could also focus on Edward Caird (*Essays on Literature*) and A. C. Bradley (his work on Shakespeare and Wordsworth). I do not, here, because neither espouses a historicism.

41. *Oxford Dictionary of National Biography*, s.v. Courthope, William John (entry by A. O. Prickard, revised by Katherine Mullin).

42. William John Courthope, *Life in Poetry, Law in Taste: Two Series of Lectures Delivered in Oxford, 1895–1900* (New York: MacMillan, 1901), 173, 174, 175.

43. Ibid., 178, 180, 183, 186, 187.

44. Ibid., 188.

45 Here we might recognize Thomas Warton as the purported "first historian of English literature in the full sense of the term" (René Wellek, *The Rise of English Literary History* [Chapel Hill, NC: University of North Carolina Press, 1941], 201). In his *History of English Poetry* (1774), he attended, in a rather ad hoc fashion, to the customs, manners, and tastes of a given period; see *History of English Poetry in Four Volumes* (1774; New York: Johnson Reprint Corporation, 1968).

46. William John Courthope, *A History of English Poetry* (New York: Macmillan, 1895), xv; see also 5.444–60.

47. Ibid., xv.

48. Ibid., xiv, xv.

49. Ibid., xv.

50. See G. W. F. Hegel, *Philosophy of History*, trans. J. Sibree (New York: Dover, 1956), 29, 43, 44; *Philosophy of Right*, trans. T. M. Knox (London: Oxford University Press, 1967), 156, 161. For Hegel, proper social conduct is not a personal morality (*Moralität*) but an ethics (*Sittlichkeit*), wherein the entire social body benefits from each individual acting responsibly within the state (*Philosophy of History*, 39). For Hegel, a state that operates for the interests of a particular class is ineffective and destructive.

51. See T. H. Green, *Lectures on the Principles of Political Obligation and Other Writings*, ed. Paul Harris and John Morrow (Cambridge: Cambridge University Press, 1986), 96.

52. F. H. Bradley, *Ethical Studies* (1876; Oxford: Clarendon, 1927), 205, and 173. See Bosanquet's exceptions to Marx in *The Philosophical Theory of the State* (1889; London: Macmillan, 1958), 28.

53. Bosanquet, *Philosophical Theory of the State*, 30.

54. Vladimir Lenin, *Collected Works*, 45 vols. (Moscow: Progress Publishers, 1972), 38.276.

55. *Oxford Dictionary of National Biography*, s.v. Stephen, Sir Leslie (entry by Alan Bell).

56. I am supplementing views about Stephen's utilitarianism; see S. P. Rosenbaum, "The Philosophical Realism of Virginia Woolf," *English Literature and British Philosophy*, ed. Rosenbaum (Chicago: University of Chicago Press, 1971), 316–56. More recently, see Anne Banfield, "Tragic Time: The Problem of the Future in Cambridge Philosophy and *To the Lighthouse*," *Modernism/Modernity* 7, no. 1 (2001): 43–75.

57. Richter, *Politics of Conscience*, 120–21.

58. Leslie Stephen, *English Literature and Society in the Eighteenth Century: Ford Lectures, 1903* (New York: G. P. Putnam's Sons, 1904), 1–2.

59. Ibid., 8.

60. Ibid., 3.

61. Ibid., 19–20.

62. Ibid., 5.

63. Ibid., 8.

64. Ibid., 9.

65. Ibid., 5.

66. Ibid., 218.

67. Ibid., 13.

68. Stephen engages a Hegelian idealist view of the state, which approaches politics not through a Marxian notion of class but by the dialectic between individual obligation and social morals and customs.

69. See Katherine C. Hill, "Virginia Woolf and Leslie Stephen: History and Literary Revolution," *PMLA* 96 (1981): 351–62. For a solid statement on Ruskin and Arnold, see Bruce Robbins, *Secular Vocations: Intellectuals, Professionalism, Culture* (Verso: New York: 1993), 14. On Arnoldian humanism, see Graff, *Professing Literature*, 3–7.

70. *Dictionary of American Biography: Complete Index Guide, volumes I–X, supplements 1–7* (New York: American Council of Learned Societies, 1981); supplement 5, s.v. Scudder. See Lillian Faderman, *Odd Girls and Twilight Lovers: A History of Lesbian Life in Twentieth-Century America* (London: Penguin, 1991), 23–24.

71. Vida Dutton Scudder, *Social Ideals in English Letters* (Boston: Houghton Mifflin, 1898), 124, 218.

72. Charles Well Moulton, ed., *The Library of Literary Criticism of English and American Authors* (Buffalo, NY: Moulton, 1901–5), 8.337. For more of her views on Ruskin, see Scudder,

Social Ideals, 248, 262, 271; on Arnold, 252; on Carlyle, 248–49, 262, 266, 274. A brief biography of
Scudder can be found in Gerald Graff and Michael Warner, eds., *The Origins of Literary Studies
in America: A Documentary Anthology* (New York: Routledge, 1989), 171.

73. As she says elsewhere: "True, the Latinists of the Middle Ages have a power and value
hardly yet appreciated; it has been rightly pointed out that Carlyle, Ruskin, and Bergson would
have written in Latin had they lived in the thirteenth century, and the medieval philosophers
and theologians are as great men as their modern successors" (Vida Dutton Scudder, *The Morte
Darthur of Sir Thomas Malory: A Study of the Book and Its Sources* [New York: Haskell House,
1965; 1917], vi).

74. Scudder, *Social Ideals*, 2. This may very well sound like the Adorno of "Lyric Poetry and
Society." It does, owing to Hegelianism, as I detail below.

75. Ibid., 4.

76. Ibid., 5.

77. Ibid., 24.

78. Ibid., 6.

79. Ibid., 3.

80. Ibid., 317.

81. Richter, *Politics of Conscience*, 122–27; 377. Another interesting intersection between
Hegelianism and medieval studies is witnessed in the following edition alone: *The Life and Letters of Leslie Stephen*, ed. Frederic William Maitland (London, Duckworth, 1910). Maitland was
the great historian of medieval law and much else.

82. See White, *Metahistory*, 133–264; Patrick Brantlinger, *Crusoe's Footprints: Cultural Studies in Britain and America* (New York: Routledge, 1990), 69, 74.

83. Wolf Lepenies, *Between Literature and Science: The Rise of Sociology*, trans. R. J. Hollin-
dale (Cambridge: Cambridge University Press, 1988), 5; *Balzac: A Critical Study*, trans. Lorenzo
O' Rourke (New York: Haskell House, 1973), 37.

84. Bosanquet states that "the weakness of the best English æsthetic of the last half-cen-
tury—the work principally of Mr. Ruskin and Mr. William Morris—lies in its restriction to
formative art." Take the case of Morris, whose criticism Scudder calls "narrow." What with
his obsessions with socialism, he was indeed engaging a social criticism stemming from Hegelian traditions, but when he committed to Marxism in the early 1880s, he was ignored by his
contemporaries—this already during a virtual reticence at the time in England about Marxism
within literary studies and within socialism, with groups like the Fabians employing instead Mill
as their model (see *Marxism and Art: Essays Classic and Contemporary*, ed. Maynard Solomon
[Detroit: Wayne State University Press, 1973], 303). Moreover, Morris was not a literary critic
per se, for he typically criticized art "addressed to the eyesight" (ibid., 84).

85. On these authors, see Chris Baldick, *The Social Mission of English Criticism, 1848–1932*
(Oxford: Clarendon, 1983).

86. Charles Taylor, *Hegel* (Cambridge: Cambridge University Press, 1975), 537–38.

87. Scudder, *Social Ideals*, 4.

88. Ibid.; see Green, *Lectures on the Principles of Political Obligation*, 233.

89. Also, Green renames Hegel's Spirit "common human consciousness" (*Lectures on the
Principles of Political Obligation*, 102, 109).

90. Though I would say that this Hegelianism is all the more conspicuous in view of the
emergent and increasingly popular literary pragmatism, whose principles are no principles. See
Louis Menand, *The Metaphysical Club* (New York: Farrar, Straus & Giroux, 2001).

91. Benedetto Croce, *Proemio alla "Critica" nel suo XLII anno* (Bari, Laterza & Figli, 1945), 7.

92. Says Althusser: "Until the end of the nineteenth century, bourgeois philosophy showed no serious interest in Hegel. By its nature, indeed, Hegelian philosophy could not have satisfied the rising bourgeoisie of mid-century" (Louis Althusser, "The Return to Hegel," in *The Spectre of Hegel: Early Writings*, ed. François Matheron and trans. G. M. Goshgarian [London: Verso, 1997], 178; see 174).

93. See Herbert Marcuse, *Reason and Revolution: Hegel and the Rise of Social Theory.* 100th Anniversary Edition (New York: Humanity Books, 1999; originally published in 1941), 393; see, more generally, 389–98.

94. Taylor, *Hegel,* 537–38.

95. Paul Hamilton suggests that Eliot "tries a more accessible Hegelian formulation on the readers of *The Athenaeum*" but actually "writes in apparent ignorance of the details of Hegel's philosophy of history and its hermeneutical development" (*Historicism* [New York: Routledge, 2003], 49, 50). I believe Hamilton perceives no way of linking Hegelian literary history to Eliot or his context, when clearly there were multiple ways. Letting alone the contexts I describe here, which lay the grounds for an opposition between form and history, Eliot in fact wrote his dissertation on one of the neo-Hegelians, F. H. Bradley.

96. He continues: "a tradition which may address itself not to this by now exploitable because quite inhuman rewriting of the past but, for all our sakes, to a modern *future* in which community may be imagined again" (Raymond Williams, "When Was Modernism?" in *The Politics of Modernism: Against the New Conformists* [New York: Verso, 1989], 35). Lyotard, similarly but less ethically, writes that "a work can only become modern if it is FIRST postmodern. Postmodernism thus understood is not modernism at its end but in the nascent state, and this state is constant" (*The Postmodern Condition,* 79).

97. My critical history is also meant to emphasize that Anglo-American traditions were not totally distinct from Continental ones—certainly not when it comes to the Hegelians, many of whom were grappling with Nietzsche, Bergson, Husserl, and Croce (*Bernard Bosanquet and His Friends: Letters Illustrating the Sources and the Development of his Philosophical Opinions,* ed. J. H. Muirhead [London: George Allen & Unwin, 1935], 257–59), during the time Bertrand Russell and G. E. Moore were devising an anti-Hegelian, anti-idealist language philosophy which would nicely supplement the later New Criticism.

98. Lacan, *Seminar of Jacques Lacan: Book II,* 73; de Man made a similar point in "Sign and Symbol in Hegel's *Aesthetics,*" 763.

99. Replace Hegel's Spirit with Macherey's Ideology and see the degree to which Hegel is the structure of Macherey: texts are never adequate to Spirit/Ideology (Macherey, *Theory of Literary Production,* 64) and, consequently, suffer from degrees of disjointedness from it at the cost of the work's unity. We get "conflicts in meaning" (ibid., 84).

100. Jameson, *The Political Unconscious,* 17, my emphasis.

101. Jameson, *Archaeologies of the Future: The Desire called Utopia and Other Science Fictions* (New York: Verso, 2005), 61.

102. Marcuse, *Reason and Revolution,* 393.

103. Taylor, *Hegel,* 537–38.

104. Josiah Royce, *The Religious Aspect of Philosophy: A Critique of the Bases of Conduct and of Faith* (1885; Gloucester: Peter Smith, 1965), xv. See also Richter, *Politics of Conscience,* 136.

105. We can remember, too, Marx's complaints in the 1844 manuscripts about Hegelian "*catch-phrases*" and the need to repeat "the Hegelian approach . . . word for word" (*Marx-Engels Reader,* 69, 106).

106. *The Rorty Reader*, ed. Christopher J. Voparil and Richard J. Bernstein (Malden, MA: Wiley-Blackwell, 2010), 129.

107. Hegel, *Phenomenology of Spirit*, 20/§33; *Werke in zwanzig Bänden: Theorie-Werkausgabe* (Frankfurt: Suhrkamp, 1970), 3.37.

108. Ibid., 41/§66, translation modified; *Werke in zwanzig Bänden*, 3.62.

109. Paul Ricoeur assesses Vorstellung as figuration (as opposed to conceptualization) in his "The Status of 'Vorstellung' in Hegel's Philosophy of Religion," in *Meaning, Truth, and God*, ed. Leroy S. Rouner (Notre Dame, IN: University of Notre Dame Press, 1982), 70–88.

110. Hegel, *Phenomenology of Spirit*, 273/§456.

111. As Hegel says in his preface, "Existence has thus merely passed over into *figurative representation* [Vorstellung]. At the same time it is thus something *familiar*, something which the existent Spirit is finished and done with" (ibid., 18/§30; see 6/§10).

112. Hegel, *Werke in zwanzig Bänden*, 3.336.

113. Hegel, *Phenomenology of Spirit*, 4/§6; trans. modified. See Michael Inwood's precise discussion of Empfindung and Gefühl in *A Hegel Dictionary* (Oxford: Blackwell, 1992); s.v. "feeling and sensation."

114. Catherine Malabou discusses Vorstellung as "the birth of representation" and suggests that it "temporalizes the conceptual content" of religion (*The Future of Hegel: Plasticity, Temporality, and Dialectic*, trans. Lisabeth During [New York: Routledge, 2005], 86)—which again, sounds like the work of Darstellung.

115. See, for instance, Hegel's discussion of a certain mystic, here linking Darstellung (not Vorstellung) to "feeling": "As an example, I will only cite Angelus Silesius, who, with the greatest audacity and depth of intuition and feeling, has expressed in a wonderfully mystical power of representation the substantial existence of God in things and the unification of the self with God and of God with human subjectivity" (*Aesthetics*, 1.371). The passage in German is: "Als Beispiel will ich nur Angelus Silesius anführen, der mit der größten Kühnheit und Tiefe der Anschauung und Empfindung das substantielle Dasein Gottes in den Dingen und die Vereinigung des Selbsts mit Gott und Gottes mit der menschlichen Subjektivität in wunderbar mystischer Kraft der Darstellung ausgesprochen hat" (*Werke in zwanzig Bänden*, 13.478).

116. I add the qualification of "later work," because Jameson's treatment of allegory or, more precisely, its hermeneutic, the fourfold model of biblical interpretation in the *Political Unconscious*, can be seen as an effort to link Darstellung and Vorstellung. See chap. 5.

117. That they even needed to perform this conceptual task speaks to the pressures that kept Marx from writing an aesthetics in the first place: in Germany, there was no taste for such "an unavoidably Hegelian" endeavor *in deserto*, given the ubiquity of the anti-Hegelian "scientific" historical school at the time of his later writings. On that school, see Hans Reill, *The German Enlightenment and the Rise of Historicism* (Berkeley: University of California Press, 1975). Marx and Engels did write about literature, mostly in their letters. See *Marx [and] Engels on Literature and Art: A Selection of Writings*, ed. Lee Baxandall and Stefan Morawski (St. Louis: Telos Press, 1973).

118. Theodor W. Adorno, *Negative Dialectics*, trans. E. B. Ashton (New York: Continuum, 1973), 18.

119. Ibid., 49; see 23, 25, 27, 28, 39, 45–46.

120. *German Ideology, Marx-Engels Reader*, 155.

121. Some of the Hegelian procedures of New Historicism have been identified, albeit polemically, by Frank Lentricchia, "Foucault's Legacy—A New Historicism?" *The New Historicism*, ed. H. Aram Veeser (New York: Routledge, 1989), 231–42; see esp. 231 and 237.

122. Erich Auerbach, "Figura," *Scenes from the Drama of European Literature* (Minneapolis: University of Minnesota Press, 1984), 11–76; here, 76.

123. Plotinus, *The Enneads*, trans. Stephen MacKenna, abridged with an introduction and notes by John Dillon (New York: Penguin, 1991); cited by page number, followed by book and chapter numbers in brackets, here 377 [5.3].

124. Ibid., 27 [1.3]. As the editor of this text notes, "This [statement] puts Aristotelian and Stoic logic in its place" (27n34).

125. See Glenn Alexander Magee's intriguing *Hegel and the Hermetic Tradition* (Ithaca, NY: Cornell University Press, 2001).

126. Hegel finds that Plotinus's "figurative mode of expression separates itself still more from the, in great measure, confused mythical ideas. The Idea of philosophy of Plotinus is thus an intellectualism or a higher idealism, which indeed from the side of the Notion [Concept] is not yet a perfect idealism" (*Hegel's Lectures on the History of Philosophy*, 3 vols., trans. E. S. Haldane and Francis H. Simson [London: Routledge & Kegan Paul, 1955], 2.412; *Werke*, 19:445). Of course, such a perfect idealism Hegel thinks is his own version; but as it stands, this is high praise for Plotinus in terms of acknowledging the intellectual and conceptual work his "figurative mode of expression" enables.

127. Maurice Merleau-Ponty, "Hegel's Existentialism," in *Sense and Nonsense*, trans. Hubert L. Dreyfus and Patricia Allen Dreyfus (Evanston, IL: Northwestern University Press, 1964), 63–64. This is a ubiquitous quote.

128. Deleuze, *Nietzsche and Philosophy*, 189.

129. Hegelian completists would leap at the opportunity to point out that Deleuze's terms, like "negativity of the positive" (*Nietzsche and Philosophy*, 180) have Hegelian analogues in the *Science of Logic* ("negation is equally positive" [33/§62]) and the *Encyclopaedia Logic* ("the negative is also positive within itself" [185/§119]).

130. In *Difference and Repetition*, for example, Deleuze writes in the characteristic phenomenological mode: "Difference is explicated, but in systems in which it tends to be cancelled; this means only that difference is essentially implicated, that its being is implication. For difference, to be explicated is to be cancelled or to dispel the inequality which constitutes it" (*Difference and Repetition*, trans. Paul Patton [New York: Columbia University Press, 1994], 228).

131. Gilles Deleuze and Félix Guattari, *What Is Philosophy?*, trans. Hugh Tomlinson and Graham Burchell (New York: Columbia University Press, 1994), 19, 36, 39, 23, 22, 18.

132. Gilles Deleuze and Félix Guattari, *A Thousand Plateaus: Capitalism and Schizophrenia*, trans. Brian Massumi (Minneapolis: University of Minnesota Press, 1987), 268–69, 356, 377–78.

133. Deleuze and Guattari, *What Is Philosophy?* 91–92; see 125, 193, 214, and the translator's preface, p. ix.

134. A dialectician, of course, would point to the consequences of omitting the dialectic right where the Deleuzian deploys its most long-standing enterprise to conflate figure and concept, as medieval dialectic so deftly does. Concepts are no longer hardwired to fail. Absent the disjunction between concept and realia, concept and experience, concept and concept, there is no contradiction, and without contradiction, there is no possibility for the classic critique of conditions and appearances—to cite Jameson, the kind of medieval "figural speculation whose dynamics were not recovered until modern times, with psychoanalysis and *Ideologiekritik*." And the garden variety Deleuzian could care less.

135. That, for example, Deleuze and Guattari link "conceptual personae" with "the powers of concepts" and "aesthetic figures" with "the powers of affects and percepts" (*What Is Phi-*

losophy? 65) evokes Hegel's own sense that "feeling" splits the difference between concepts and figures, the work of Darstellung and Vorstellung—as I discussed earlier.

136. Deleuze writes: "The collection of unconscious perceptions surely has no unity (dizziness), but nonetheless it receives a mental unity from the differential relations that are being exerted, and from a degree of reciprocal determination of these relations" (*The Fold: Leibniz and the Baroque*, trans. Tom Conley [Minneapolis: University of Minnesota Press, 1993], 108). Identity and difference? Dialectic? Jameson, in "Dualism and Deleuze" intriguingly reads the various conceptual pairings in *A Thousand Plateaus* but resists associating these with dialectics, until the very last sentence of his essay on the "the inner energy of the binary as sheer conflict"—"strife, the Eris of the ancients, which has triumphantly absorbed its contrary into the unity of opposites" (*Valences of the Dialectic* [New York: Verso, 2009], 181–200; here, 200). Eleanor Kaufman makes the persuasive (and different) point that Deleuze is captivated by that classic kind of Platonic dialectic, which is that process of division and definition (which I discuss in chap. 2); *Deleuze, the Dark Precursor: Dialectic, Structure, Being* (Baltimore: Johns Hopkins University Press, 2012).

137. Michel Foucault, *"Theatrum Philosophicum,"* in *Language, Counter-memory, Practice: Selected Essays and Interviews*, ed. Donald F. Bouchard; trans. Bouchard and Sherry Simon (Ithaca, NY: Cornell University Press, 1977), 165–96; here, 165 and 186.

138. See my "The Call of Things: A Critique of Object-Oriented Ontologies," *the minnesota review* 80 (2013): 106–18.

139. Fredric Jameson, *Representing Capital: A Commentary of Volume One* (New York: Verso, 2011), 56, 33–34.

140. Ibid., 68. Jameson also describes the "outbursts of figuration as Marx begins to touch the outer limit of what he has over and over again drafted" (39); he deems figuration to enable "a new moment of dialectical awareness" (135), and states that the "various points of figurations have also proved to function, not decoratively, but rather as moments in which something of the larger system comes into view" (127).

141. Walter Benjamin's "dialectical image" is, oddly, one that *does* stand still but is brimming with temporality, as if it is ready to move. No doubt, Benjamin is intrigued by the "figural [bildlich]" capacities of this image, rather than the purely conceptual, and for this reason, "one encounters" such images only in "language" (*The Arcades Project*, trans. Howard Eiland and Kevin McLaughlin [Cambridge, MA: Belknap Press of Harvard University Press, 2003], 463, 462). He is indeed attempting to construe the dialectic in figural *and* conceptual terms, and he is onto something by evoking the contemplative process necessary to ponder the dialectical image (as we discussed in chap. 1); in that respect, his remarks on "awakening" are especially relevant; *Arcades*, 463–64, even if the image, as Susan Buck-Morss shows, is some parts surrealist, some parts German baroque. But to my mind he does not develop this line of thinking—requiring later expositors to ponder his meaning; above all, again, Buck-Morss, *The Dialectics of Seeing: Walter Benjamin and the Arcades Project* (Cambridge, MA: MIT Press, 1989), 219–29, 241, 261.

142. Ibid., 261.

143. Plotinus, *Enneads*, 292 [4.4]; this tract is titled, in the edition, "Problems of the Soul [II]."

144. G. W. Leibniz, *Monadology*, in *Philosophical Texts*, trans. Richard Franks and R. S. Woolhouse (Oxford: Oxford University Press, 1998), 271–72.

145. Plotinus, *Enneads*, 292 [4.4].

146. Ibid., 293 [4.4].

147. Ibid., 325 [4.4].

148. Martin Heidegger, *Being and Time*, ed. and trans. John Macquarrie and Edward Robinson, 7th ed. (Oxford: Blackwell, 1967), 185 [sec. 145], 189–91 [secs. 148–50].

149. Ibid., 147 [sec. 112]. Reflecting on theoria/θεωρία, Heidegger writes: "By looking at the world theoretically, we have already dimmed it down to the uniformity of what is purely present-at-hand, though admittedly this uniformity comprises a new abundance of things which can be discovered by simply characterizing them" (177 [sec. 138]).

150. Plotinus, *Enneads*, 325 [4.4].

151. Jameson, *Archaeologies of the Future*, 101.

152. See Plotinus, *Enneads*, 299 [4.4], 78 [2.3], 89 [2.3].

153. On the Perseus black hole, see http://science.nasa.gov/science-news/science-at-nasa/2003/09sep_blackholesounds [accessed June 18, 2013].

154. See Michael Uebel, "Medieval Desert Utopia," *Exemplaria* 14 (2002): 1–45, and *Ecstatic Transformation: On the Uses of Alterity in the Middle Ages* (New York: Palgrave Macmillan, 2005).

Index

Torchia, N. J., 184n100
Trinity, 48, 177n16
Trotsky, Leon, 119

Uebel, Michael, 207n32, 228n154
uneven development, 109, 118–19, 130–31, 217n113
utopia, xvii, 21–22, 129–31, 161, 164–65, 218n126, 218n8

Vansteenberghe, Edmond, 49
Vincent, Andrew, 220n19
Vitalis of Blois, 184n101
Vorstellung, 152–54, 225n109, 225n115, 226n116, 226–27n135

Walker, Mack, 168n13, 194n3
Wallace, William A., 179n44, 219n13
Wandel, Lee Palmer, 207n34
Warner, Michael, 222–23n72
Warton, Thomas, 141
Waszek, Norbert, 214n54
Watt, Ian, 217n107

Wawro, Geoffrey, 192n215
Weber, Max, 193n2, 217n120, 218n127
Wegener, Heinz, 211n19
Weil, Eric, 67
Wellek, René, 220n24, 222n45
White, Allon, 215n83
White, Hayden, 218n1, 223n82
Whitehead, Alfred North, 167n8
Wieland, Christoph Martin, 112
William of Ockham, 178n21
Williams, Raymond, xv, 148, 169n6, 221n37, 224n96
Wokler, Robert, 201n70
Wolff, Christian, 59–60
Wood, Rega, 178n21
Woolf, Virginia, 143
Württemberg Debate, xv
Wyclif, John, 98, 218n124

Zima, Peter V., 214n62
Žižek, Slavoj, 22, 45–46, 69, 100–101, 113, 129, 172n34, 175n77, 186n140, 195n23, 209n64, 212n28, 219–20n18